Hers & His

A Problem
Solving Approach
to Marriage

June Helm
Ramona Kotz

The Dryden Press
Hinsdale, Illinois

To our husbands—
Tom, Richard, and Irv

Preface

The study of courtship, marriage, and family living focuses upon the facts derived from empirical research to provide an understanding of how people behave in these systems of interrelationships. The basic assumption underlying the application of research findings is that using this knowledge will improve the quality of human life.

This book is designed as a functional text for use in a study of courtship and marital relationships in a North American (United States and Canadian) context.[1]

By *functional* we mean that the content of the book should be applicable to situations experienced by students today. We do not intend to propose a formula for achieving a successful marriage. Instead, our approach is designed to help individuals develop an active problem-solving method to aid them in reaching their personal goals. In this applied approach to the study of courtship and marriage we present relevant empirical data, drawn primarily from the behavioral sciences, to improve the understanding of selected topics in this area. It is our contention that if one is able to read and interpret research literature, he[2] will be in a much better position to cope with his daily life and, specifically, with those decisions related to courtship and marriage.

The Common Sense Error

Critics of social science often suggest that the results of empirical research really could be deduced from common sense. The interest in human behavior exhibited by most people and their speculations concerning its nature sometimes lend credence to this statement. However, there is ample research evidence to soundly refute this claim. Many common beliefs held by large numbers of people are simply inaccurate.

Human behavior throughout the world is extremely variable. Appropriate behavior in one society may be totally unacceptable in another. Consequently, it is difficult to report on systematic human behavior without someone responding that such regularities are natural and obvious. For example, a common belief is that if one follows his instincts, satisfactory sexual relationships in marriage come naturally. However, the evidence from the growing body of knowledge about sexual functioning leaves one with no recourse but to answer that "doing what comes naturally" is learned. Clearly, the "commonsense" notion about sexual functioning is fallacious. Social scientists seek to discover what kinds of behavior occur systematically and under what conditions.[3] Only in this way can a more sophisticated body of knowledge be built.

The Study of Marriage and the Family

Interest in the study of marriage and the family is multidisciplinary. Home economics, sociology, psychology, anthropology, and economics are just a few of the disciplines which focus on the family through research and teaching. Many tools are used by persons operating in these disciplines to describe people and their relationships. *Concepts* are one of the most important of these tools, because they constitute the language of a content area. They are the distinctive verbal symbols assigned to generalized ideas abstracted from society. Concepts are basically descriptive, telling us about the nature of phenomena and their interrelationships and interactions. Marriage, for example, is a concept which connotes a system of relationships of many other concepts. To fully describe marriage it is necessary to identify the assumptions underlying the relationships of all these concepts. This organized structure of concepts and their relationships is called a *conceptual framework*.

A number of conceptual frameworks are used by students and scholars of marriage and the family to help them interpret the behavior of family members. Several noted sociologists, including Harold T. Christiansen[4] and F. Ivan Nye and Felix Berardo,[5] have provided sources of detailed descriptions of these frameworks. The main reason for identifying the conceptual framework used by a writer or speaker is to direct the attention of the reader or listener to certain concepts and their relationships. Thus a conceptual framework could be compared to a lens in a camera. By defining the concepts and assumptions one is able to focus more clearly on some phenomena and screen out others. In short, a conceptual framework defines the important concepts and specifies the underlying assumptions and how they are related.

Since the purpose of a conceptual framework is to focus upon the relevant phenomena and their interrelationships, it is important that the reader understand the framework used in this book. We are presenting the problem-solving framework as a unique and useful way to view marriage and family interaction.

Over the years students have criticised marriage and family courses for their tendency to dwell on negative rather than positive aspects of marriage. One of the reasons for this tendency was the desire to help families with serious problems. Of course, this produced more data about the negative than about the positive side of marriage.

The Problem-Solving Approach

It is our belief that a problem avoidance or awareness approach to the study of marriage may be beneficial; however, in the past too much emphasis has been placed on the *problems* and too little on the *process* of problem solving. The object of this book is to focus on problem solving as a positive process in courtship and marital interaction.

Problem solving is an ordinary, everyday activity; people are continually faced with new situations which they may interpret as problems. It is our contention that if students learn the basic fundamentals of problem solving, they can use them to solve their own specific problem. We cannot anticipate all the problems that will be generated in the rapidly changing world of the twentieth century. We propose, however, that the process of solving any single interpersonal problem has similarities to all other such problems and that learning this process is where the critical task begins.

In this book, marriage is defined in what is sometimes called *systems terminology*. The systems definition of marriage is particularly relevant to our problem-solving approach. It takes into account the dynamic and ongoing nature of marriage, allows for the assessment of all information which is input to the system, recognizes the possibility of viewing each member of the marital system as a separate subsystem, and takes into account the dynamic interplay between the marital system and others (such as occupational or kinship systems).

The problem-solving approach is explained in detail in the first chapter. The remainder of the book is devoted to what we hope is an objective presentation of a variety of problematic courtship and marital situations. For each problem, we discuss alternative courses of action and the consequences of each. It is up to the student to evaluate the usefulness and appropriateness of these solutions in terms of his particular values, goals, and resources. The student must make the final choice himself; no one else can do it. We have not exhausted all problems or alternative courses of action in the areas we have selected to cover. What we have attempted to do is present a realistic view of courtship and marriage set in a problem-solving perspective. We believe that a person who develops problem-solving skills will be better prepared to deal successfully with problem situations. It is with this challenge that we present our book to you.

Notes

1. Because of significant cultural differences, we have used statistics from the 1970 United States census, the 1971 Canadian census, and relevant studies in both countries.

2. Throughout the text the masculine pronoun *he* is used to refer to either a man or a woman—only because this is the generally accepted grammatical procedure.

3. The recent work done by sexologists W. H. Masters and V. E. Johnson, reported in *Human Sexual Response* (Boston: Little, Brown, 1966) and in *Human Sexual Inadequacy* (Boston: Little, Brown, 1970). complements earlier work by Alfred Kinsey and Albert Ellis in the area of sexual functioning.

4. Harold T. Christiansen, ed., *Handbook of Marriage and the Family* (Chicago: Rand McNally, 1964).

5. F. Ivan Nye and Felix Berardo, *Emerging Conceptual Frameworks in Family Analysis* (New York: Macmillan, 1966).

Contents

Part One
Introduction to Problem Solving

1

A Problem-solving Approach to Courtship and Marriage

As students begin a course in courtship and marriage they bring with them a variety of expectations about what marriage is and what it can do for them. These expectations run the gamut of possibilities from terrible to fantastic, dull to exciting. Some call marriage constricting, while others see it as a liberating experience; to some it implies a traditional life-style, while to others it is a relationship open to experimentation. The obvious conclusion is that people view marriage differently and choose to marry or not to marry for a variety of reasons. Given this diversity of viewpoints and multiplicity of goals, we have asked ourselves an important question: "How can we help people relate to the critical issues in courtship and marriage?" We have taken the approach of helping people think through their goals in the light of the alternatives available to them, so that they can make the best decisions for themselves. We cannot presume to know what is right or wrong for people with different values and orientations. Instead we attempt to raise critical questions which should be considered in this crucial area of human relations.

We view marriage as a problem-solving relationship. By this we mean that marriage is a means to certain long-range goals such as happiness, security, companionship, and the formation of a family. Each of these goals is problematic in the sense that its attainment is far from certain. Marriage commonly has been used by North Americans attempting to overcome barriers in achieving these long-range goals. One of the peculiar characteristics of marriage is that it involves problem solving within a system. *A marital system is composed of two individuals, their personal attributes, and the constantly changing relationship between them.*

Marriage as a System

A basic tenet of social systems analysis is that whatever a person does affects at least one other person. That is, person A's behavior is contingent upon what person B does, person B's behavior is contingent upon how person A reacts to person B's actions, and so on. In viewing marriage as a system, each spouse should consider not only what he wants but what his partner wants and how his partner will react to what he does.

Couples usually have some specific expectations of what they want in marriage, and their behavior with their partners is intended to realize these expectations. Expectations and the ways in which people achieve them determine the parameters (or, in systems terminology, the *boundaries*) of their marriage. For example, some people believe that marriage is the means for obtaining love and support, and they behave in ways which they hope will elicit these responses. Others believe marriage represents an exclusive sexual relationship between partners, and they behave in ways which they hope will ensure sexual exclusivity. Some are concerned with financial support and some with protecting and raising children. Any or all of these conditions—love, sexual exclusiveness, financial care, parenthood—may be considered as boundaries in the marriage system.

Marital boundaries are not rigid physical barriers; rather, they are the organization of the marriage (that is, the nature of the relationship of the couple and their attributes). Perhaps an example or two will help clarify this concept. The types of marriages described by sociologists John Cuber and Peggy Harroff in their book *Sex and the Significant Americans*[1] exemplify essential aspects of marital system boundaries. They view the marriages of their eastern U.S. middle and upper-middle class respondents as falling on a continuum from low interaction, low involvement with spouse to high interaction, high involvement. The authors' description of the types of marriages reflects where each type falls on this continuum as well as their value judgment of the qualitative aspects of each—conflict habituated, devitalized, passive-congenial, vital, and total. For our purposes these names reflect something of the nature of the couple's relationship to each other and hence tell us something about the boundaries of their marriage.

For instance, Cuber and Harroff describe *conflict-habituated* marriages as containing considerable, but generally controlled, conflict and tension. Both husband and wife privately acknowledge their ever present potential for conflict, their pervasive incompatibility, and the atmosphere of tension which permeates their togetherness. The hostile exchanges in these relationships are often so subtle that the casual observer usually misses them. In fact, much of the couple's interaction is devoted to channeling their conflict and bridling their hostility. According to Cuber and Harroff:

Some psychiatrists have gone so far as to suggest that it is precisely the deep need to do psychological battle with one another which constitutes the cohesive factor insuring a continuity of the marriage. Possibly so. But even from a surface point of view, the overt and manifest fact of habituated attention to handling tension, keeping it chained, and concealing it, is clearly seen as a dominant life force. And it can, and does for some, last for a whole lifetime.[2]

The *vital* couple, on the other hand, relate to each other quite differently. While the outside observer may report that they behave much the same as any other married couple—they love their children, gripe about their jobs, are proud of their career accomplishments—a closer, more intimate look reveals that such couples are intensely bound to each other psychologically in important ways. Their togetherness and sharing is genuine, and it provides their life essence. As Cuber and Harroff phrase it:

The presence of the mate is indispensable to the feelings of satisfaction which the activity provides. The activities shared by the vital pairs may involve almost anything: hobbies, careers, community service. Anything—so long as it is closely shared.

It is hard to escape the word *vitality*—exciting mutuality of feelings and participation together in important life segments. The clue that the relationship is vital (rather than merely expressing the joint activity) derives from the feeling that it is important. An activity is flat and uninteresting if the spouse is not a part of it.[3]

Contrary to the Hollywood image of marriage, most people cannot live on love alone. Neither can many couples in our society live as though they were the only two people in the world. Marriage is only one of many systems in our society, and it interacts to some degree with a number of others. If marital systems were really closed off from all outside systems, an intrusion of external events would lead to a loss of organization or the beginning of a breakup of the system, because there would be no way of dealing with anything from outside the system itself. However, interchange with other systems is an essential feature underlying the vitality of the marital system, its continuity, and its ability to change. What usually happens when an external event intrudes upon the marital system is a reorganization of its components, often at a higher or more complex level.

For example, suppose a wife is elected to the city council. The marital system will have to change, since some of the time and energy required in holding office will probably be taken from that which was previously devoted to the marriage. Either the husband will have to pick up some of the tasks and responsibilities of his wife (as well as forego other kinds of interaction with her) or else the couple will have to find some other person to do them. In the process, the nature of their marital system will adapt to meet the demands placed upon it by the political system. Of course, it would be difficult for marital systems to respond to all external demands. What usually happens is that they respond selectively to the endless variety of environmental stimuli, either by choice or by force.

For a marital system to exist, the individuals involved must share at least some of the same goals. The process of working toward these goals is called problem solving.

The Problem-Solving Process

Modern North American culture can be characterized as problem conscious in its attitudes toward marriage. For several decades research and practical applications have focused on identifying, studying, and attempting to solve critical marital "problems" such as dissimilar role expectations, sexual incompatibility, and poor money management. Within this context the very word *problem* and the process of *problem solving* have taken on negative connotations. Problem solving in this book is viewed as a positive, goal directed activity which, when successful, enriches the lives of those involved. Successful problem solving not only results in attainment of one's goals, it also gives one the exuberance of accomplishment—good feelings about oneself and a closeness with those who have shared in the struggle.

Problem solving activity can be performed by both individuals and groups. In brief, the problem-solving process begins when a situation is defined as problematic—when people realize that it may not be possible to accomplish something they desire. If the persons involved are committed to attempting to attain the goal, they begin to think of all possible ways this can be accomplished. Once all possible alternatives have been generated, they select those which are acceptable and possible on the basis of their abilities and restraints. Then, weighing what is involved in carrying out each particular course of action against its probability of success, they compare the most acceptable alternatives with each other until they have eliminated all but one—the best alternative for them. Once the best one has been selected, they embark upon the course of action it prescribes until either the goal is reached or it becomes clear that some other course of action is required. In the latter case, usually the next best alternative is tried, and so on until the goal is attained. When the desired end has been reached, the people usually evaluate how well the goal has been fulfilled.

The problem-solving process is graphically depicted in Figure 1-1 to 1-6. The remainder of this chapter will be devoted to a more detailed description of that process. In order to present the sequence of events in logical order, we have divided the process into seven parts—recognition, involvement, generation of alternatives, assessment of alternatives, selection of best alternative, action, and evaluation. Some people will find that the process works best for them if they overlap some of the steps, perform several simultaneously, or even use a different order.

Recognition

The problem-solving process begins when a situation is recognized or defined as problematic. Thus the first crucial question is whether or not a particular situation presents a problem.

A problem, from our perspective, is "any situation which involves a desired but unachieved end."[4] Implicit in every situation of this type is a goal whose outcome is not assured; that is, barriers or obstacles in the way must be overcome if the goal is to be reached. Situations in which the outcomes are never in doubt or in which goals are attained by habitual responses are not considered problems.

Cleaning up the apartment after a party (situation depicted in Figure 1-1 flow-chart as a parallelogram) is not seen as a problem by our definition because the outcome is not in doubt. No matter how messy the place is, it will eventually be cleaned up. (Follow the decision diamonds through to the process rectangle and out to the oblong—situation satisfied.) Getting rid of the cigarette burns on the furniture (situation), however, is another story; that is problematic!

Getting out of bed every morning when the clock rings (situation parallelogram in Figure 1-1) is not a problem if, in fact, the person actually gets up within a reasonable time after the alarm goes off, no matter how resentful or sleepy he may feel. In this case, habitual behavior is sufficient to attain the goal. (Follow the first two diamonds to the habit diamond and on out through the appropriate response rectangle to situation satisfied.)

Natural disasters, such as tornados, are not included in our definition of a problem because there is no way of controlling them; however, the rebuilding of a home or city in their aftermath is a problem. In the same vein, the problematic situation which must be faced when a spouse dies is not the death but how to successfully reorganize one's life without the loved one.

Whether a situation is seen as problematic for the individual or for the couple is important in our framework. A single person can usually live more for his own personal gratification than can someone who is married. Also, in marriage, what is important or annoying to one spouse may not be to the other. Take the case of a woman who usually leaves her clothes lying about. Assume that the messy house does not bother her but that it drives her husband up the wall. Since his expectation that she hang up her clothes is not shared by her, it is his problem, not hers. It will become her problem too only if her behavior annoys him so much that it begins to alter their relationship and create an obstacle in reaching one of her (or their) goals.

Other situations may be perceived as problems for the marital system itself. Setting up a budget is often such a situation. Assume that both partners agree that balancing the budget is very important (for unless both agree that they must live within their income, failure to do so will not be perceived as a marital problem). *Goal consensus* (in this case, agreeing that it is important to live within a budget) is the first step in the problem-solving process; put another way, goal consensus is the initial problem most couples must solve. Goal consensus assures that the major focus of future problem-solving activity will be an assessment of the best means of achieving

Figure 1-1 *Definition of the Situation as Problematic*

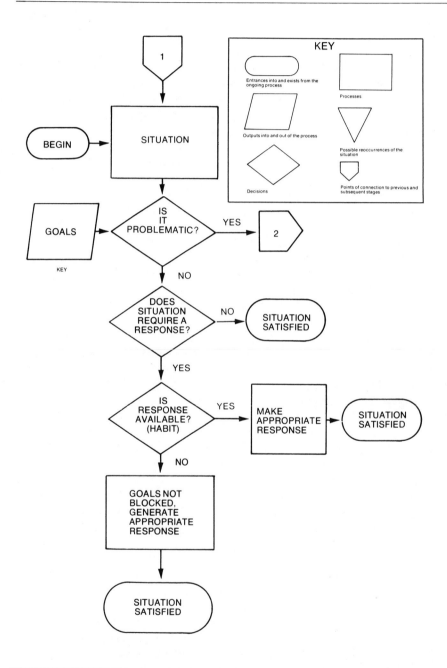

agreed upon ends, rather than on internal conflict over values or goals. This consensus does not imply a lack of value disagreements. Rather, it suggests that *the greater the agreement between spouses on values (what they think is worthwhile in life), the greater the likelihood they will agree on goals (what they want in given situations).*[5] When there are discrepancies, the couple must arrive at some consensus on values before they can agree on goals to implement these values.

The implicit goal of the couple in our example is to apportion their income to maximize other goals. The other goals may be thought of as subgoals, and the extent to which they are agreed upon determines the nature of the overall problem. If both are to be satisfied with the final budget, they have to face such issues as the kind of housing they prefer. Do they want a prestigious location or perhaps a luxury townhouse? Or would they prefer spending less of their total income on shelter and more on savings for vacation travel?

Agreement on the priority of spending is probably the most crucial aspect of budgeting, even when income is insufficient to meet the basic needs of food, clothing, and shelter. In the latter case, survival may be the overriding goal. For those who are more fortunate, the issue is that of a hierarchy or priority of values.

When couples think through and talk about their goals, they are often aware of the barriers which must be dealt with if they are to attain them. In such instances they can define certain situations as problematic, even if they will not occur until some future time. Often, however, people are not conscious of their goals; they have not clearly thought through what must be done to attain them, or perhaps unexpected situations have arisen. Individuals and couples are constantly being presented with a variety of situations which may or may not be problematic. In turn, some situations, regardless of their importance, may arise time after time before they are perceived as being related to the goals of the individual or couple.

A situation can be defined as problematic, as being handleable without difficulty, or as not requiring any kind of action; it may even go unnoticed. By our definition, once a goal is recognized but it is not clear that it can be reached, a problem exists. The problem is to overcome both the barriers which stand in the way of achieving the goal and any unforeseen events that may arise to block achievement. An important element in problem solving is the confidence a person has in his ability to overcome such difficulties; however, confidence is not always easy to achieve. Some people grow up feeling that they are subject to forces outside their control and that their own efforts can have little effect on the course of their life. Such people are not likely to see situations as problematic. To do so would only be distressing, since they believe they can do little to overcome their problems. Other people believe they can be master of their own fate and determine the course of their own life; they are quick to see situations in problematic terms, since they are confident they can overcome obstacles.

Involvement

The crucial decision at this stage of the problem-solving process is whether or not one is motivated to do anything about a situation he has defined as problematic. *Motivation* can be defined for our purposes as the push or drive an individual or couple has toward solving a specific problem. People are motivated for a variety of reasons, such as frustrations resulting from grief and anger, imagination guided by desire, or fear of the unknown.[6]

In the problem-solving process motivation may be thought of as a catalyst; its presence is necesary to get the process going. The greater the motivation, the greater the involvement. (Figure 1-2 illustrates the catalytic nature of motivation in the problem-solving process.) Unless people are motivated, it does not matter how skillful they are at problem solving. If they are not involved they will not be likely to use their skills. Lack of motivation and putting the situation aside to be dealt with later are both classified in Figure 1-2 as ignoring the situation (rectangle). While such

Figure 1-2 *Involvement*

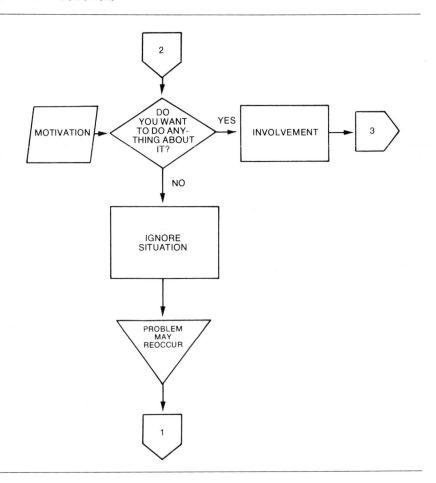

nonaction may seem a solution at the time, it rarely leads to adequate resolution of problems. The situation remains problematic and may have to be dealt with at a later time if the blocked goal is ever to be achieved. (The possible reoccurrence of the situation is depicted by the triangle feeding into the shield—which refers back to Figure 1-1.)

Generation of Alternatives

Once people become involved in trying to solve a problem, they usually examine the alternative courses of action available. Generally speaking, the greater the number of available alternatives, the greater the probability of finding a suitable course of action.

Theoretically, alternative ways of obtaining given goals are infinite. In reality, however, numerous factors restrict the ability to generate alternatives. One of the most important of these is a personality characteristic called *adaptability,* which has been defined in a number of different ways by behavioral scientists. For example, George Karlsson, a Swedish sociologist, sees it as the ability to adjust to changing conditions with a minimum of friction.[7] An even more explicit definition of this concept is stated by Irving Tallman, an American sociologist, who defines adaptability as a person's "ability to deal effectively with problematic situations by changing roles, attitudes, and actions in terms of new or modified understandings of the situation with which he is confronted."[8]

Both definitions imply an ability to "shift gears" when circumstances require a change. Tallman believes that adaptability has three components—flexibility, empathy and motivation. Successful interpersonal problem solving requires all three, as well as the availability of other resources. The importance of each of these three components varies with each stage of the problem-solving process.

In the stage requiring generation of alternatives, flexibility and empathy are most crucial (see Figure 1-3). Flexibility influences the range of alternative behavior available for interpersonal problem solving.[9] It represents the ability to maintain a sufficiently broad range of possible responses so that a person does not respond to different situations in the same way. A flexible person is able to consider a variety of responses to any given situation. Suppose, for example, that a husband becomes moody and his wife wishes to improve the situation. If she is flexible, she will respond according to what she thinks is causing his moodiness. If, for example, she thinks he has been having a rough time at work, she may try to get him to relax and talk about it. If she is not very flexible, she may decide to ignore the situation, hoping it will change on its own.

Empathy is important in the generation of alternatives, because it represents the ability to interpret the behavior of another person in terms of that person's motivations, feelings, and thoughts and to relate this understanding to the specific situation and the person's behavior in that situation.[10] If you can anticipate another's motives, reactions, feelings, and thoughts about a situation, and the consequences for that person of his alternative forms of action, you can use that information as a guide to

Figure 1-3 *Generation of Alternatives*

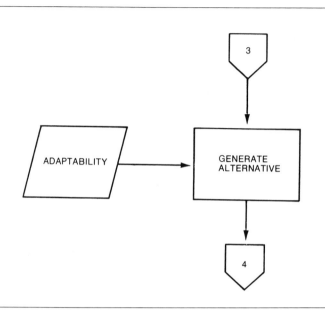

your own behavior. Parental responses to the problem of a three-year-old who continues to write on walls despite frequent admonitions help illustrate the concept of empathy. Sending the child to bed without dinner or spanking him show a lack of empathy. The effort to understand the child's motivation and help him work out alternative ways of expressing himself is indicative of a high level of empathy.

All three components of adaptability are basic to the problem-solving process; they increase a person's ability to deal with the relevant elements of the problem situation. The higher the motivation, the greater the commitment to doing what is necessary to resolve the problem; the more flexible and empathic the person, the greater the likelihood that he will generate a wide range of alternative solutions.

The availability of other resources, such as intelligence, creativity, and past experience, also influences the number and kinds of alternatives developed. Obviously, the alternatives are likely to be more diverse as the quality and quantity of available resources are increased.

Assessment of Alternatives

Once a range of alternatives has been generated, the next step is to assess the acceptability of each one. Figure 1-4 shows three important social and psychological conditions which influence the range and type of choices considered acceptable in a given situation: (1) opportunities available in the social structure, (2) behavioral standards and values (those viewed as acceptable within a particular environment), and (3) available personal, interpersonal, and material resources.

Figure 1-4 *Assessment of Alternatives*

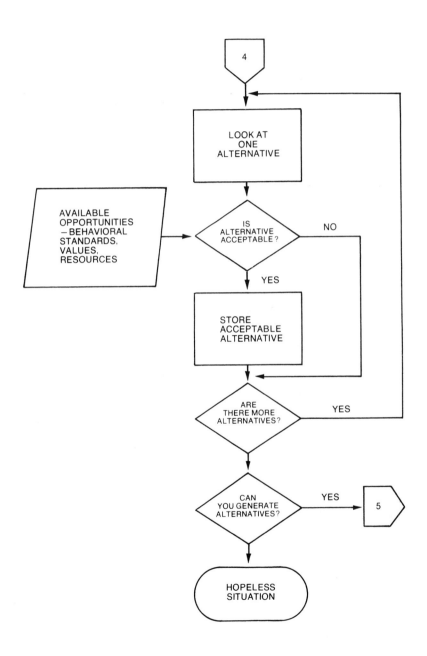

Structural opportunities Opportunities that exist in a particular environment limit the things one can conceivably acquire. For example, a couple may strive for high social status, but if they are poorly educated, black, or physically handicapped, many of the routes for acquiring status will be blocked to them. Those more fortunately situated may be able to choose from a variety of alternative routes to status, including business, professional, or family endeavors.

Behavioral standards and values In the same sense, group behavioral standards restrict the available routes to problem solving. The accumulation of money, for instance, is one way of achieving status; yet, despite the desire to achieve status, many people will not steal or cheat to acquire money. These behaviors are not acceptable because of group standards which label them as immoral. Similarly, married partners may decide not to lie to each other, or not to use manipulative, devious means or threats for getting their partner to accommodate to their wishes because they believe doing so infringes on the right of the other person to behave according to his assessment of the relevant issues. In other words, such behavior would violate their beliefs of how people should live with each other.

Resources Resources are personal, interpersonal, and material means which are available for use in solving problems. *Personal resources* are those possessed by an individual; some are innate, but most are learned skills or traits. They include flexibility, empathy, health, intelligence, creativity, and the power to influence others.

Interpersonal resources are those which involve interaction with at least one other person. One of the most important of these resources is communication—the ability to express one's thoughts and feelings adequately and to correctly perceive the intent of the messages of others. In interpersonal problems, one's inability to communicate adequately can jeopardize the success of any course of action requiring important information exchanges. Other examples of interpersonal resources are kinship or friendship systems and ability to handle conflict.

Material resources consist of time, money, and other goods at one's disposal. Everyone has a finite quantity of time; the amount of time a person can devote to something new depends on current demands and prior commitments. Often, lack of time to carry out various alternatives limits problem-solving ability and is a considerable source of stress. Couples may well have to budget time in the same way that they budget money.

Money is an obvious restricting factor. If income is tied up in securing the basic minimums of food, clothing, and shelter, outlays for extras such as education, material possessions, professional advice, and services that save time and energy will be meager at best.

The process of examining each alternative in the light of available opportunities, behavioral standards and values, and available resources is illustrated in Figure 1-4. If the alternative is acceptable, it is mentally "stored," or set aside for the moment. If there is more than one alternative, each is considered in the same manner. Unacceptable alternatives are discarded. Occasionally a situation arises in which there are no acceptable alternatives; if none can be generated, one is faced with a hopeless situation—at least at that particular time.

Selection of the Best Alternative

Once the number of alternatives has been reduced to those which are feasible, the next step is to select the best one (see Figure 1-5). This is the point where the costs and benefits of the acceptable alternatives are weighed against the probabilities of their solving the problem. It is rare that two alternatives are perceived as equally attractive. Usually the sifting process of this stage will gradually limit the field until only one—the best—is left.

Action

Once the course of action has been decided, the plan for solving the problem is implemented. Usually, action continues until the goal is reached. The length of time necessary is contingent upon such factors as time requirements, the urgency of the situation, and one's hierarchy of goals. Time is an important factor in all problems. For instance, graduating from college requires more time than putting out a kitchen fire. The former is also less urgent. The more immediate the problem, the sooner it is likely to be acted upon. In addition, the more important it is, the greater the motivation, and the more attention it will receive.

Two sources of information are especially relevant during the time of action: (1) negative feedback, indicating that the plan is not solving the problem or that it is having negative, unforeseen consequences, and (2) positive feedback, indicating that the course of action is proceeding smoothly toward the goal.

In the case of negative feedback, the persons involved may try to figure out why the adopted alternative is not producing the desired results. On the basis of this information they may decide to modify the course of action, or to try another one.

Take the case of parents of a two-year-old. In an effort to prevent the child's temper tantrums they have been giving in to whatever he wants. Instead of ceasing his tantrums, the child has become more demanding. The parents see that their behavior, instead of ameliorating the situation, has made it worse. They have been providing positive reinforcement for the behavior they want to eliminate. Realizing this, they start thinking of other alternatives (in Figure 1-6 this is represented by a return to the generation of alternatives stage), and they decide to acquiesce only to those desires he expresses in a nondemanding way and to completely ignore the tantrums.

Positive feedback is validation that the goal is in the process of being reached. Suppose, for example, you are trying to lose thirty pounds. Every time someone tells you how good you look or asks how much weight you have lost, you are reassured that your goal is being realized. Positive feedback tells you that your new eating (actually noneating) pattern is having the desired result. In fact, such messages may provide increased motivation to stick to your diet or even to speed things up!

Figure 1-5 *Selection of the Best Alternative*

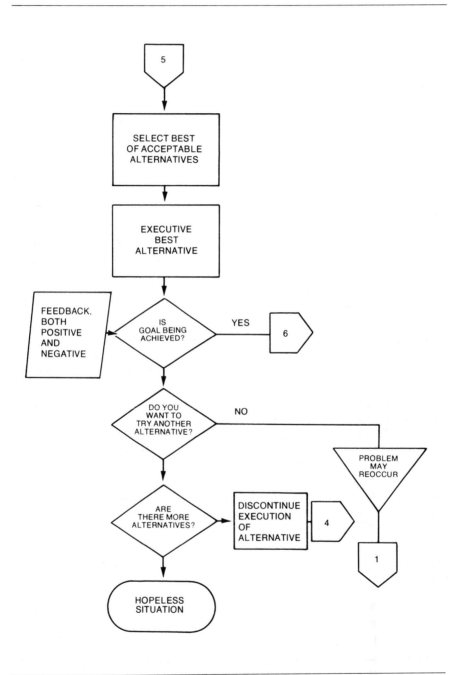

Evaluation

If the goal is attained, there is usually some conscious evaluation of how well the problem has been solved. If the solution is sufficiently unsatisfactory, one must decide whether to try another solution (see Figure 1-6). If one wants to try again, he returns to the generation of alternatives in Figure 1-4. Since a number of alternatives have been generated and assessed, the process should proceed rapidly to the point of selecting the best alternative (unless others have been added). From this step on there is likely to be little repetition. If one chooses not to try another solution, the problem may reappear at a later time.

There are, of course, different gradations of satisfaction. The more adequately the goal is met, the more satisfied one is. Figure 1-6 indicates that relative success in solving problems has several consequences. If an individual has had success in problem-solving endeavors, he is likely to engage in future problem-solving activity, since he is developing confidence in his ability. Thus previous success in problem solving results in both self-esteem and a problem-solving orientation.

Self-esteem plays a critical role in effective problem solving. People with high self-esteem generally are better able to withstand pressures toward conformity,[11] and, consequently, are more likely to utilize a broader range of ideas in seeking solutions to problems. A relationship also exists between self-esteem and risk-taking behavior,[12] and moderate risk taking often brings about positive problem-solving results. For example, any criticism of a partner involves some risk that the partner will grow angry or rejecting. Yet failure to mention a source of irritation may lead to additional strain on the relationship. Without a clear understanding of the reasons for the strain, the problem-solving potential of both partners is restricted. A person with self-esteem is likely to perceive his feelings as important and will point out the irritating behavior to the offender. He is willing to risk his partner's anger or rejection because he realizes that to remain silent would probably in the long run be detrimental to the marital system. On the other hand, resolution of the problem may lead to increased understanding and a stronger commitment to each other. At first glance it seems that in interpersonal relations, such as courtship and marriage, risk taking is dangerous. Relationships are often delicately balanced, and people do not like to rock the boat. However, if problems exist between people, any confrontation of those problems requires some degree of risk taking. Successful resolution increases their understanding of each other as well as their satisfaction with the relationship.

Increased problem-solving orientation As the preceding discussion showed, successful problem solving leads to an increased problem-solving orientation. Over the years a person will tend to use (or go back to) those behaviors he has found to be generally rewarding and will remove from his repertoire those which were unsuccessful or brought about punishment. Thus successful problem solving increases the range of experience one can draw upon in generating alternative ways of solving problems. In addition, past success in problem solving generally leads

Figure 1-6 *Evaluation*

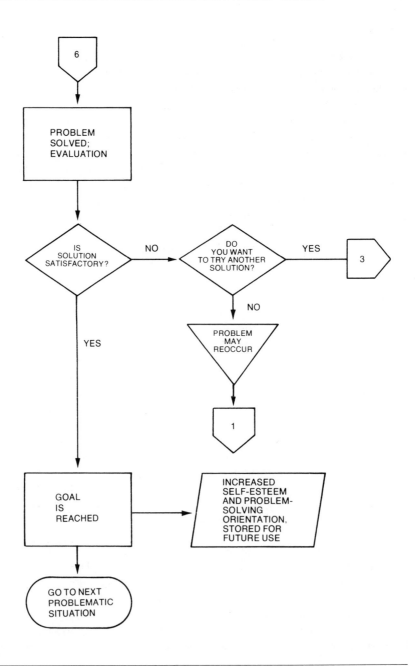

one to expect success in future problem-solving activities, thereby creating a problem-solving orientation toward life.

Individual and Group Problem Solving

Problem-solving activity can be carried on by individuals or groups. The process is essentially the same, except that with the involvement of each additional person interaction patterns become more complex.

Goal consensus is hardly relevant when only one person is involved, but it is critical to effective group problem solving. Once the family group (couple, nuclear family, or commune) arrives at a consensus on the goal and on the role each member is to play in problem solving, the focus shifts to determining the best way to reach the goal.

Research indicates that certain kinds of group organization are more conducive to problem solving than others. For instance, situations requiring creative solutions appear to be more frequently resolved if every group member has the opportunity to help in generating alternatives.[13] Open channels of communication, therefore, are particularly important in this type of group of problem-solving situation—provided, of course, that all share the same goal.[14] Increasing the variety in a couple's sex life is an example of a problem requiring a creative solution. The importance of open channels of communication is evident. Problems whose solutions require the coordinated efforts of all family members are probably best resolved when there is some central authority handling the coordination.[15] For example, the problem of how to pack the family car to maximize passenger comfort for an extended trip is best handled if everyone old enough to understand the situation contributes suggestions (generates alternatives) and one person supervises the actual packing according to his interpretation of the agreed upon way. Without this coordination the packing process is apt to be very confusing.

How well *normative expectations* (the standards of behavior generally expected in given situations) are incorporated into the family's organization is also associated with the success of solving certain kinds of problems. For example, blue collar families appear better able to deal with some kinds of problems if they are husband-dominated and white collar families if they are equalitarian. In each group the family organization is consonant with its expectations of how families should be organized.[16]

The interaction and coordination of efforts required for effective group problem solving increases its complexity. At the same time, the addition of even one person may result in generation of a broader range of alternatives and an increase in the variety of resources that can be utilized throughout the entire process.

Summary

If we view dating and marriage as problem-solving relationships, then the interaction of any two persons in a manner which could potentially draw them toward marriage can be thought of as a problem-solving system. Each person has his or her own goals and resources in addition to those which are mutually shared. We anticipate that individuals and couples who are skilled in problem solving will be more likely to reach their individual or shared goals than those who are less effective problem solvers.

For clarity the problem-solving process has been presented in seven stages—recognition, involvement, generation of alternatives, assessment of alternatives, selection of the best course of behavior, action, and evaluation. Several of these steps may overlap, take place simultaneously, or even occur in some other order. However, in an effort to state the process logically, we presented the stages in their most rational order.

The problem-solving process is essentially the same for individuals as it is for couples. Interaction with another person, as in dating or marriage, results in the organization of a new problem-solving system. Effective group problem solving requires some degree of goal consensus, open communication channels, and agreement as to the roles each member will play in the problem-solving process.

Underlying the problem-solving approach is one important assumption—that people, even those who have a deep emotional involvement, have the capacity to know what they want and to try to get it.

Notes

1. John Cuber and Peggy Harroff, *Sex and the Significant Americans* (Baltimore: Penguin, 1968).

2. Ibid., p. 46.

3. Ibid., p. 55-56.

4. Irving Tallman, et al., "A Taxonomy of Group Problems: Implications for a Theory of Group Problem Solving," technical report, Family Studies Center, University of Minnesota, Fall 1974.

5. Norman R. F. Maier and Allen Solem, "The Contribution of a Discussion Leader to the Quality of Group Thinking: The Effective Use of Minority Opinions," *Human Relations* 5 (1952), 277-288.

6. Gardner Murphy, "Social Motivation," in Gardner Lindzey, ed., *Handbook of Social Psychology*, II (Cambridge, Mass.: Addison-Wesley, 1954), 601-634.

7. George Karlsson, *Adaptability and Communication in Marriage*, 2d ed. (Totowa, N. J.: Bedminster, 1963).

8. Irving Tallman, "Adaptability: A Problem Solving Approach to Assessing Childrearing Practices," *Child Development* 32 (1961), 651-668.

9. Ibid.

10. Tallman points out that the orientation (no recognition or thoughts about causation versus understanding of feelings, motivations, and thoughts) is more important than the accuracy of perception to the problem-solving process, although, of course, the greater the accuracy the more likely the solution will be acceptable.

11. Carl I. Hovland et al., *Communication and Persuasion* (New Haven: Yale University Press, 1953).

12. Irving Tallman, "Family Problem Solving and Social Problems," in J. Aldous et al., eds., *Family Problem Solving* (Hinsdale, Ill.: Dryden Press, 1971), pp. 324-350.

13. Bernard Bass, "Amount of Participation, Coalescence and Profitability of Decision Making Discussion," *Journal of Abnormal and Social Psychology* 67 (1963), 92-94; Richard Hoffman, "Group Problem Solving," in L. Berkowitz, ed., *Advances in Experimental Psychology* (New York: Academic Press, 1965).

14. Irving Tallman, "The Family as a Small Problem Solving Group," *Journal of Marriage and the Family* 23 (February 1970), 94.

15. Ibid.

16. Irving Tallman and Gary Miller, "Class Differences in Family Problem Solving: The Effects of Verbal Ability, Hierarchical Structure, and Role Expectations," *Sociometry,* 37 (March 1974), 13-37.

Suggested Readings

Kenkel, W. R. "Husband-Wife Interaction in Decision Making and Decision Choices." *Journal of Social Psychology* (1961), 255-262. Report of a study of fifty married couples (in which the husband was a university student) given the problem of deciding how to spend a hypothetical gift of $300.

Kenkel, W. R. "Sex of Observer and Spousal Roles in Decision Making." *Marriage and Family Living* 73 (1961), 185-186. The difficulties of observing marital problem solving are reported in this short article.

Shepherd, C. R. *Small Groups: Some Sociological Perspectives.* San Francisco: Chandler Publishing, 1964. A book directed at college students who are beginning their work in sociology and social psychology and who are interested in the dynamics of interpersonal relations and small groups.

Snow, C. P. *The Masters.* Garden City, N. Y. Doubleday, 1959. A novel about a small group of professors at Cambridge University faced with the task of selecting a new Master. A brilliant example of the intricacies of small group interaction.

Tallman, I. "The Family as a Small Problem Solving Group." *Journal of Marriage and the Family* 23 (February 1970), 94-104. An article showing how the principles derived from research and theory of small group behavior apply to the family (which is a type of small group). This is an important work for those with an interest in optional problem solving in family groups.

2

Developing Resources for Problem Solving

Resources are the raw material of which problem solutions are developed. The availability of resources is implied in the problem-solving process described in the previous chapter. In marital problem solving, the type and number of personal, interpersonal, and material resources available to a couple can and do influence the generation of alternatives and whether or not a goal can be reached.

Theoretically, resources are unlimited. Man has not only his own intelligence, personality, and energy available to achieve his goals but also his capacity to create or seek means outside himself. Considering the vast potential of the human body and mind, however, any comparison between a person's potential resources and those he has recognized and developed would probably be disappointing. People typically ignore or underdevelop their potential. Thus achievement of the goal of developing an adequate pool of resources often emerges as a common problem-solving situation for individuals and couples.

People can develop their resources throughout their lifetime, either by maturing physically or by their own concerted action. Because of his cognitive development (physical maturation), the eighteen-month-old child achieves the resource of object permanence when he is able to recognize that although mother is out of sight she is not gone forever. Object permanence is a resource because it helps the child cope with his relationships with important persons and attain his goal of security. The retired person with an interest in art takes lessons and develops skill in painting (concerted action). This skill is a resource in attaining his goal of recognition. While there is little one can do about increasing resources that are a function of physical maturation, many other resources can be developed or enhanced by attention to the process of problem solving.

In this chapter we will focus on the general problem of how to develop personal and interpersonal resources for marital problem solving. While it is obvious that developing any particular resource has its unique features, basic similarities do exist in the overall process. We will use two particular resources—*communication* and *constructive conflict*—to illustrate the process, since these resources play significant roles in resolving marital problem-solving situations.

Our discussion will address itself to *self-initiated resource development*—a rational process which assumes that a person can become aware of his own potential, is desirous of developing more of that potential, and can devise methods to accomplish that objective. Human problem solving also has an unconscious component. Emotions and unconscious desires sometimes unpredictably influence even the best problem-solving strategy. For example, a young woman who experiences doubts about her love for her fiancé decides to break their engagement. However, while she has thought of several methods of telling him, she finds these rational plans hampered by her interpretation of his response and her own guilt feelings.

While such emotions act negatively in problem solving, some emotions, like happiness and joy, facilitate the accomplishment of a goal. Human behavior is indeed complex. Perhaps it is true that rational control of our lives is really similar to the tip of the iceberg, and a great deal of our rational plans are influenced by emotions and other unconscious elements. Nevertheless, the problem-solving process proposed in this book, while recognizing the unconscious component of human behavior, focuses on a rational approach. It does this because rationality is the characteristic that makes man a unique being and because it is this type of influence on human behavior which is most easily described, controlled, and learned.

Recognition of Resource Potential

One's personal resource potential is directly related to certain human characteristics, including the growing, developing nature of the organism, the ability to think rationally, the ability to communicate using symbols, and the ability to adapt behavior to changes occurring inside and outside the body system.

Determination of one's resource potential begins with the ability to understand the capacities of the human organism; it also involves recognition of the personal adaptation of that organism which provides one's uniqueness. Such a self-inventory provides a good starting point for the development of any particular resource.

Self-analysis or confrontation occurs when one person (confronter) does something either purposely or inadvertently to direct another person (confrontee) to examine, question, or change his behavior.[1] This confrontation can be a self-analysis, where the individual himself reflects on a particular part of his behavior, or it can be generated by some other person or group questioning or challenging his behavior. Confrontation is used to determine which resources are assets and which could be made more effective and if one's limitations have the potential to develop into resources. This self-disclosure is a way of communicating with others as well as with oneself. Humanistic psychologist Sidney Jourard writes, "When a man does not acknowledge to himself who, what, and how he is, he is out of touch with reality, and he will sicken and die; and no one can help him without access to the facts."[2] For some people, avoidance of self-disclosure is really avoidance of responsibility. It is difficult to recognize one's areas of deficit, and hard work is needed to change them. People gloss over their limitations because of the behavioral consequences of recognizing them. "Self disclosure commits one to conversion, to the process of restructuring one's life; it demands that a person leave the security of his own house and journey into a foreign land, and most men balk at that."[3]

One way to begin self-disclosure is to analyze your own behavior in past problem-solving situations. Think of the last time you found yourself in a problem-solving situation and describe how you responded. Then, list all the personal and interpersonal resources and limitations which helped you reach a solution or prevented you from reaching one. Make note of any limitations you want to change or eliminate in the future. Repeat this procedure for several other past problem-solving situations. Are there any limitations which have consistently interfered with your problem solving? Do you think these can be changed? This type of exercise can provide basic information about your potential for resource development. However, since it depends solely on information gathered from yourself, it may ignore hidden potentials; thus you should further explore the same situations with other persons. Basically these procedures aim toward data collection—increasing the amount of information you have about yourself.

The methods available for self-analysis fall generally into two categories —*personal* (introspective) and *interpersonal* or *group* (dependent on information from other people as well as oneself). The way these two types of analysis complement one another is illustrated by the "Johari Window" in Figure 2-1. Each quadrant is defined by its coordinates. *Quadrant I* includes those apparent characteristics which are known to others and to oneself, such as eye color, height, and weight. *Quadrant II* includes information which is known to others but not acknowledged by oneself; it is called the blind area. Bad breath, poor communication skills, and insensitivity could be located in one's blind area if they are not recognized as personal traits. One may purposely ignore certain traits as a defense mechanism; but until they are brought into consciousness, problem solving is not likely to occur. *Quadrant III* is the set of characteristics known to oneself but hidden from others. Feelings of insecurity, a desire to commit suicide, or being a homosexual may fall into this quadrant. *Quadrant IV* is a completely unknown area; neither the self nor others are aware of certain potential resources or limitations. Confrontation is one means by which information in Quadrants II and III is moved into Quadrant I (the area of free activity). In our problem-solving model, moving the information to Quadrant I allows for continuous recognition of potential resources and increases the likelihood of establishing goals related to developing these resources. Even though such self-evaluation makes one aware of his potential, problem-solving activity may not occur until one establishes a goal related to his resources and experiences some difficulty in achieving the goal.

The following sections discuss the application of this process to the achievement of specific goals related to communication and constructive conflict.

Developing Communication as a Resource

Good communication is the ability to express one's thoughts and feelings adequately and to perceive correctly the intent of others' messages. Communication does not require that the sender and receiver each interpret behavior in the same way, for merely to behave is to communicate. There is no opposite to behavior, because it is

Figure 2-1   *The Johari Window*

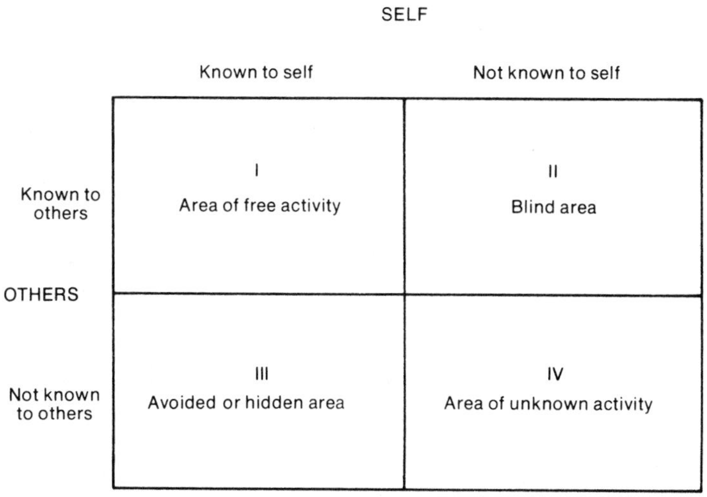

Reprinted from *Group Processes: An Introduction to Group Dynamics* by Joseph Luft by permission of National Press Books, copyright 1963.

impossible to not behave; inactivity and silence have message value just as activity or words do. They influence others, and these others respond, even if the response is silence.[4] Memories of the old "silent treatment" linger on to remind us that we cannot *not* communicate. Maintaining harmonious relationships among people, however, usually requires going beyond this type of communication. We all want others to understand the meaning of our actions or statements; but too often we assume that someone knows the meaning when he really does not know it at all.

The following example by family educator Virginia Satir illustrates this.

A husband says, in an irritable tone, "The dog is on the couch." The wife, in this relationship, may go through the following process:

a. He is telling me where the dog is.

b. But he is doing more than that. He sounds irritated.

c. Why is he telling me about his irritation? Is he criticizing me for the fact that the dog is on the couch?

d. If he is not criticizing me, what does he want me to do? Just listen to him? Sympathize with his irritation? Take the dog off the couch? Or what?

e. I wanted a dog. He didn't. I went ahead and got one without his agreement. Now, when he shows his irritation at the dog, he is complaining about what I did. He is criticizing me for disobeying him. He undoubtedly wants me to take the dog off the couch, but does he also want me to get rid of the dog, and apologize to him for going against his wishes?

Instead of saying, "The dog is on the couch", the husband should say, "Take the dog off the couch and get rid of him. You never should have bought a dog. I told you I didn't want one". The wife in this case would have little trouble assessing his message.

a. He would be telling her specifically what he wanted from her and why. In other words, his request that she agree to obey would be clear.

b. In both cases, the wife is still in the position of deciding whether or not to agree to her husband's request that she obey him. But at least she is in no doubt about what it really is that her husband wants of her.[5]

In the above example, the wife could have checked out the intent of her husband's message by asking him whether she was interpreting him correctly. Sending unambiguous messages and checking out the intent of unclear messages are as essential to good marital problem solving as they are to giving good directions on finding an address.

The problem of grasping the full meaning of verbal messages is sometimes simplified and sometimes complicated by nonverbal cues. A frown, a wink, a smile, or a crossing or uncrossing of legs and arms can add meaning which would not have been noticed if the impact of the words alone were interpreted. Too often words and feelings contradict each other, which demands that the listener become sensitive to the possibility of such contradictions and develop skills for assessing them. When one becomes proficient at this he is less likely to take offense at what people say, because he will react not only to the spoken words but also the nonverbal motivation behind the words.

When read accurately, these nonverbal messages can be meaningful; yet there is an ever present danger of misinterpretation. A woman might say, "He tells me he doesn't love me, that nothing permanent can ever come out of our relationship, but I know it's not true. I can *sense* how he feels." In some cases she is right, but often she wants so desperately for the man to love her that she imposes her own feelings on him and simply will not accept the truth. She misreads the signs, interpreting them according to her desires.

For most people it is risky to rely too heavily on facial expressions, gestures, and the like as a means of communication, without some form of verbal reinforcement—especially with new friends and acquaintances. It is much safer to learn to say what one means as clearly and succinctly as possible and to listen closely to others' responses for accurate interpretation.

Openness of communication between husband and wife is a resource at several steps of the problem-solving process. Judging from marriage counseling situations, when couples discover they can express their feelings without being destroyed, they feel free to utilize communication as a problem-solving resource.[6] One basic prerequisite to good communication is learning to listen in a nonjudgmental fashion.[7] We all want to be listened to when we talk, but the achievement of this end is sometimes quite a difficult accomplishment. Often one asks questions that apparently do not require answers, or so it appears when the inquirer continues on without ever hearing the responses. Others are eager to take issue with expressed opinions or beliefs and don't give the speaker a chance to fully explain himself.

Most of us tend to impose our own thoughts and feelings on others, and we assume everyone else will react to a situation the same way we do. Real communication involves allowing others to be autonomous and accepting them as such. The wise husband or wife soon discovers it is safer not to operate on the basis of unquestioned assumptions; each learns to ask the other to clarify meanings. Phrases such as "Do you mean . . . ?" or "Are you trying to say . . . ?" often serve to help the couple more accurately interpret how each feels.

It goes without saying that some people find it easier to communicate than others. However, in the beginning stages of a relationship it is important that each person learn to send up danger signals in order to at least let the other know something is wrong. This brings to mind the story of a man who reported that his wife had left him, with no warning, after two years of marriage. He had no idea why she had gone; he thought everything was fine. Who was at fault? Should she have told him generally how she felt, even if she couldn't verbalize her problems specifically? Or is there perhaps something strange about a man who lives with a woman for two years without having the faintest idea she is unhappy? Inability to put feelings into words and insensitivity to nonverbal cues left this couple miles apart.

Good communication is tied in with self-esteem. Carl Rogers believes that when you are free from hurt yourself, it is easier to listen to someone else with an open mind.[8] If a husband and wife can freely express their desires and irritations to each other, individual issues can more easily be defined as problematic to one or both. Once goal consensus is reached, openness of communication again comes into play in selecting possible alternatives to reach the goal. It is also useful in evaluating the effectiveness of the couple's efforts along the way and when they arrive at a solution to the problem. This evaluation becomes helpful in resolving future problem situations.

Recognition of the Problem

We define a situation as problematic when goal attainment is uncertain. The goal of attaining good communication in a marriage does not mean the same thing to all couples. However, unless there is a discrepancy between the goal and its attainment, it is unlikely that the situation will be viewed as problematic. If couple A wants to be open and honest *only* in regard to their sexual relationship and are sure they can attain this goal, the situation is not a problem. If, on the other hand, one or both wonder whether this openness can be accomplished, the situation is more likely to be viewed as needing action.

While this seems straightforward, the goal itself may be unclear. Couples rarely sit down together and map out their goals for communication. Instead they informally exchange expectations in bed, at parties, while moving furniture, and so on. If, however, the couple agree to check out each other's feelings before making any assumptions about them, then they have established the goal of better communication.

Setting realistic goals is very important. Goals may be long-term or short-term, inclusive or exclusive, attainable or unattainable. Too often the goal is so inclusive that the task is unending and the progress difficult to assess. One such goal might be the achievement of open, honest communication in all areas of the marital relationship. With this kind of long-term goal, even significant progress toward openness in one area would probably go unnoticed. Short-term goals, which mark progress toward reaching the overall goal, are more useful in learning to use a problem-solving process. Among the short-term goals which might lead to open communication are: expressing three open, honest feelings about the relationship during the next week; checking out one statement where the message was unclear; and allowing one's spouse to complete a train of thought without interruption. Progress toward achieving these short-term goals can be measured by the couple.

Involvement

Once they have identified a problem, a couple must decide whether it is important enough to act on. In other words, is the discrepancy between the goal and the attainment of it interfering with the relationship?

Motivation on the part of both partners is particularly necessary in the area of communication goals, because communication is an interpersonal resource. Unless each person feels moved to act on the established goal, it is unlikely that the goal will be attained. While one partner may develop listening skills and express his feelings more openly, there is no guarantee that communication between the two will improve unless both are motivated to act in a similar fashion. Thus the problem-solving process may be stalemated at this point until one partner can demonstrate to the other that the situation needs action.

Generation and Assessment of Alternatives

Generating alternatives to attain a specific goal, such as marital communication, is the step where a couple can demonstrate their creativity and flexibility. Consider the following example. A couple are discussing the husband's behavior at a party they attended the night before. The wife complains that she tried desperately to signal to him, as he told an incredibly bad story, to change the subject, but he ignored her. He responds by saying he thought she really was enjoying it and couldn't understand her frosty attitude later on.

Obviously this couple misinterpreted each other's nonverbal cues. The upshot of their discussion was that they decided to set a goal of developing skill in interpreting each other's nonverbal cues. In suggesting alternative ways of achieving this goal, they made up the following list.

Alternative	Available Resources	Advantages	Disadvantages
1. Note all nonverbal cues of spouse for period of one day and discuss at end of day.	*Wife* Good memory. Motivated. Good observer, trained in observation techniques. *Husband* Motivated. Relates well to active plans to achieve goals.	Provides basis for discussion instead of rehashing old issues. Could immediately clear up misinterpretations of spouse's cues. Creates the time to talk to one another.	Limited time to observe. Tedious task. Must have way to record cues. Time consuming. Interferes with normal interaction.
2. Note spouse's nonverbal cues and check them out with spouse immediately.	Wife Good memory. Motivated. Good observer, trained in observation techniques. *Husband* Motivated. Relates well to active plans to achieve goals.	Could provide for immediate correction of misinterpretation. Encourages attention to *how* spouse responds as well as to response itself.	Husband defensive when challenged on the spot. Behavior observable only when couple are together. Could be interpreted as criticism instead of checking perception. Time needed immediately—may interfere with interaction with other people.

Alternatives	Available Resources	Advantages	Disadvantages
3. Both spouses sit down and discuss the meaning of the non-verbal clues they send to each other, thus checking their perception.	*Wife* Good memory. Motivated. Good observer, trained in observation techniques. *Husband* Motivated. Relates well to active plans to achieve goals.	Immediately clears away misperception.	No observation. Past interpretation may overrule new evidence. Retrospection rather than focus on here and now. Hostilities may be generated.

It is unlikely that this procedure will be necessary for each problem, but, early in the development of problem-solving skills, writing out this step helps make sure that each proposed alternative is given fair consideration.

Evaluating the alternatives on the basis of available resources, it would appear that all three alternatives are possible. Looking more closely, however, the advantages and disadvantages of each should eliminate some of them. For example, if the couple decide they have time to collect data about their present behavior, the first two alternatives would be preferred over the third one. If, on the other hand, time is limited and there is need for immediate action, number three would be a better choice. There is no single appropriate solution for any problem. Past experience and the ability of the couple to generate alternatives determines how many and varied the alternatives are. The important thing is to determine which solution is most appropriate to achievement of the goal and then to implement it.

Evaluation

The last step of the problem-solving process is evaluation of the chosen alternative. Did it in fact achieve the goal? What problems were involved in executing the solution? Did any resources or limitations emerge which were unknown before? If the goal is still not attained, another alternative can be tried and evaluated or more alternatives can be generated.

Developing communication as a resource is a lifelong process. While our example focused on nonverbal communication, the achievement of goals related to verbal communication would follow a similar pattern. Self-disclosure, self-knowledge, and honesty provide the psychological foundation for good communication. To achieve the objective of improved communication, each person must: (1) become sensitive to the setting and to exactly what is said, (2) decide when to talk about certain things according to the interpretation of verbal and nonverbal cues, (3) separate what is observed from what is felt about a particular situation, (4) become a skilled listener as well as talker, and (5) continually check out what he hears in order to correct misperceptions.

The material resources available to help couples achieve specific communication goals are exciting and worth exploring. Programmed texts,[9] marriage enrichment courses, sensitivity or encounter groups, communication games,[10] kits,[11] and marriage counseling complement the thousands of techniques they can develop themselves.

Developing Conflict as a Resource

Just as in the case of communication, a couple's development of conflict as a resource requires (1) a basic understanding of conflict as a positive tool in interpersonal relations, (2) an understanding of their own conflict techniques, and (3) a shared goal that focuses on developing conflict as a resource.

Evidence from the literature on marriage suggests that marital conflict is widespread. While sociologists Robert Blood and Donald Wolfe,[12] Bernard Farber,[13] Judson Landis,[14] and Clifford Kirkpatrick[15] noted differences in how conflict occurs between spouses, it would appear that conflict is a natural outgrowth of intimate, day-to-day living with another person. In marriage, each spouse brings certain expectations for behavior which may or may not be congruent with that of his partner. Conflict occurs when there is an overt response to the discrepancies between expectations and actual behavior. When one recognizes that the expectations for marital behavior cover everything from providing love and affection to taking out the garbage, it is obvious that a person will probably fail to fulfill one or more of these expectations.

Conflict is a resource because it implies a willingness to bring issues into the open, even though it also places demands on the interpersonal system. If conflicts are not openly expressed, they may smolder beneath the surface, emerging later in the form of much greater demands. Willingness to listen to others and to evaluate the merits of what is said (rather than the person saying it) is important in resolving conflict.

For years family specialists studied the effects of quarreling on married couples and concluded that the more conflict there was, the more unstable the relationship tended to be. These efforts focused on identifying the causes in an effort to help couples avoid conflict or eliminate it if it occurred. Recently some scholars have proposed a more positive view of marital discord, one which recognizes that conflict is a normal part of marriage. We take the position that conflict can be utilized effectively as a resource for enhancing interpersonal relationships. As we view it, conflict is an overt struggle involving any issue. As such it actually is a form of communication representing the process by which one feels intensely, lets others know how one feels, and handles the intensity of others' feelings.

This is not to say, however, that all verbal confrontations promote problem solving.

Certain elements of discord are believed to enhance the relationship, while others are viewed as moving in a more destructive direction.[16] Further exploration of these phenomena reveals that productive quarreling focuses on the *problem at hand*, disregarding extraneous issues, and becomes a valuable asset for the couple if properly handled. Conversely, destructive quarreling does not deal with the issues but instead strikes out at the personalities of the individuals. Destructive quarreling can be devastating to the marriage, and it accomplishes nothing in the way of problem solving. Following is an example of a destructive quarrel.

Wife: We never do anything interesting anymore. Why don't you ever take me out in the evening instead of always wanting to sit at home?

Husband: If you would do a little work once in a while, you would realize that people are tired at night and need some rest.

Wife: Work! You expect me to stay home all day long and get my kicks from cleaning up after you? However, I'll have to admit that keeping house turns into a full-time job when you won't even hang up your own clothes.

Husband: Speaking of clothes, where did you come up with that garb you have on? It looks like something you slept in.

At the onset one is led to believe that the problem is a discrepancy between the husband's and the wife's inclinations to go out in the evening. However, no progress has been made toward resolving this problem because of other disturbing factors which interfered.

Explicit problem definition is essential to the development of conflict as a resource. According to their dialogue, however, this couple not only identified the original problem but also came up with three others: (1) the husband's belief that his wife didn't work during the day, (2) the wife's anger at her husband's lack of neatness and/or help around the house, and (3) the husband's opinion that his wife's appearance is unattractive. If they had focused their anger on any one of these problems instead of playing the "I can hurt you worse than you can hurt me" game, they might have gained something. As it turned out, resentment and hostility were all they had to show for their anger.

It is frequently difficult to stick to the issues during a quarrel. Although conflict is a means of getting problems out in the open, it is also an emotional response that emerges when one is tense and irritable. When two people disagree, each tends to become defensive about his views and tries to attack the other person by saying something to hurt him. This does not mean that conflict as a problem-solving technique is less effective when an individual is emotional; instead it suggests the importance of learning how to think and act well in the midst of furor. The wounds inflicted by words uttered in the heat of battle cannot always be healed by saying, "I'm sorry."

Patterns of conflict in individual marriages emerge as the relationship develops and grows. They are influenced by past experiences with conflict and conflict management (including observation of conflict among parents and friends), personality characteristics, and the goals established for the relationship.

Awareness of marital conflict patterns is an important adjunct to the development of conflict as a positive resource. To achieve awareness the couple must assess which areas of the relationship produce conflict, why it occurs, when it is likely to occur, who initiates it, how each reacts in the conflict situation, and how it is eventually resolved.

Couples may establish a goal to develop conflict as a positive resource when the pattern of conflict is harmful to the relationship or when there is no pattern available to express frustrations. This constitutes the recognition step of the problem-solving process. If there is sufficient motivation by both partners to achieve the goal, the generation and assessment of alternatives follows.

If the overall goal is to establish some ground rules for disagreeing "agreeably," we propose the following alternatives.

Alternative	Available Resources	Advantages	Disadvantages
1. Analyze present conflict pattern and make recommendations for general rules.	Openmindedness of both spouses. Motivation. Open communication. Relationship important to both. Support from friends.	Uses own interaction for basic information. Doesn't draw in outside information or resources. Keeps conflict private.	No specific situation to focus on. Discussion tried before with little success.
2. Read *The Intimate Enemy* by George Bach and Peter Wyden and set up own ground rules for conflict.	Same as above. Both enjoy reading.	Brings in professional resources to complement personal ones. More enjoyable than number 1.	Takes time to develop rules, though they are needed immediately.
3. Analyze last conflict situation and discuss rules which would have directed conflict to the issue rather than the person.	Same as above.	Could increase variety of alternatives proposed. Uses own relationship in positive way. Situation recent.	Sensitivity remains from last conflict.
4. Enroll in marriage enrichment program.	Same as above. Positive orientation to education.	May enrich other areas of marriage.	Lack of time—immediacy of situation. Course may not necessarily discuss conflict.
5. Engage professional counselor to assist in developing guidelines for conflict.	Counselor available. Positive orientation to outside help.	May stimulate new ideas for alternatives.	Money limited. May depend too heavily on someone outside of relationship.

Obviously these suggestions are not all-inclusive. They serve only to illustrate the possibilities for reaching a proposed goal. If, for example, alternative 2 is elected, the couple will discover that George Bach and Peter Wyden's proposed method of "learning to fight"[17] is a useful one to assist them in setting up their own ground rules for conflict management.

After they read the book and discuss the authors' suggestions, they can decide which of them are relevant to their situation and conflict style. The major limitation of this alternative is the relatively large outlay of time required to read the book. However, if both enjoy reading, respect the opinions of the authors, and are not in a rush to immediately develop ground rules for their conflict, it may be an enjoyable experience which not only helps them attain the conflict objective but also encourages them to develop communication as a resource.

People forget that there is usually more than one answer to any problem. As spouses become more adept and comfortable with the problem-solving process, however, they find it easier to search for a variety of possible solutions. Conflict, when used openly and honestly, can provide a stimulating and vital way of communicating intense feelings and beliefs.

Summary

Personal, interpersonal, and material resources are important elements in the generation and assessment of problem-solving alternatives. Even so, it is fallacious to assume that one's human resource potential is equal to one's realized human resources. Because of this discrepancy, most couples view the development of problem-solving resources as problematic. Resolution of this major problem is essential to problem solving in other areas of the marital relationship. We have discussed the basic process of developing resources as problem-solving tools and have utilized the development of communication and constructive conflict to illustrate the problem-solving process.

Many material resources in the form of kits, marriage enrichment courses, books, and workshops are available to supplement the skills that spouses already have in achieving goals related to resource development.

Notes

1. Gerard Egan, *Encounter: Group Processes for Interpersonal Growth* (Belmont, Calif.: Brooks/Cole, 1970), p. 293.

2. Sidney M. Jourard, *The Transparent Self* (Princeton, N.J.: Van Nostrand, 1964), p. 25.

3. Egan, *Encounter*, p. 209.

4. Paul Watzlawick, Janet H. Beavin, and Don D. Jackson, *Pragmatics of Human Communication* (New York: Norton, 1967), p. 49.

5. Virginia Satir, *Conjoint Family Therapy,* rev. ed. (Palo Alto, Calif.: Science and Behavior Books, 1967). p. 80.

6. Gordon Bolte, "A Communications Approach to Marital Counselling," *Family Coordinator* 19 (January 1970), 32-40.

7. Carl R. Rogers, "Some Elements of Effective Interpersonal Communication," unpublished speech, California Institute of Technology, Pasadena, 1964.

8. Ibid.

9. Human Development Institute, *Improving Communications in Marriage,* 3rd ed. (Atlanta: Human Development Institute, 1967). Use of this book is reported in Mary Hickmann and Bruce Baldwin, "Use of Programmed Instruction to Improve Communication in Marriage," *Family Coordinator* 20 (April 1971), 121-125.

10. Two examples of communication games are *Two to One* (Edmonton, Alberta, Canada: Hyphen Inc., 1970), $7.95; and *Body Talk* (Del Mar, Calif.: Psychology Today Games, CRM), $5.95.

11. Thomas P. Malone, Mark Vlosky, Daniel Memen, Nancy Miller Phillips, *Intimacy: An Encounter Program for Couples*, Atlanta: Human Development Institute. Cassette tape and activity kit.

12. Robert O. Blood, Jr., and Donald M. Wolfe, *Husbands and Wives: The Dynamics of Married Living* (Glencoe, Ill.: Free Press, 1960).

13. Bernard Farber, "An Index of Marital Integration," *Sociometry* XX (June 1957), 117-133.

14. Judson T. Landis, "Length of Time Required to Achieve Adjustment in Marriage," *American Sociological Review* XI (1946), 666-667.

15. Clifford Kirkpatrick, *The Family as Process and Institution* (New York: Ronald Press, 1963).

16. George Bach and Peter Wyden, *The Intimate Enemy* (New York: Random House, 1969).

17. Ibid.

Suggested Readings

Bach, George R., and Wyden, Peter. *The Intimate Enemy*. New York: Random House, 1969. Discussion of conflict as an integral part of marriage, with a cathartic value. Includes method of "fight training" that uses conflict constructively.

Mehrabian, Albert. "Communication without Words." *Psychology Today,* September 1968, pp. 53-55. Takes the stance that the total impact of communication is 7 percent verbal, 38 percent vocal, and 55 percent facial. Suggests applications of these findings to interpersonal relations.

O'Neil, Nena, and O'Neil, George. *Open Marriage*. New York: Avon Books, 1973. Suggests that the marriage contract can be reformulated to enhance independent living, personal growth, individual freedom, flexible roles, mutual trust, and increased openness. Instead of proposing that marriage be done away with, the authors maintain that change within marriage is possible.

Satir, Virginia. "Communication: A Verbal and Nonverbal Process of Making Requests of the Receiver." *Conjoint Family Therapy*. Rev. ed. Palo Alto, Calif.: Science & Behavior Books, 1967, Chapter 9, pp. 75-90. Straightforward discussion of the process of human message sending and receiving, including numerous

Part Two
Premarital Problem Solving

3

Dating as a Resource for Marriage

The initial pairing of male-female couples in our society usually occurs through a casual type of involvement known as dating. While dating appears to be a *solution* to the age-old problem of interacting with a member of the opposite sex, it is often a *problem* instead, because of artificiality and unrealistically high expectations for this interaction.

The goals individuals set for dating are many and varied. Most people date because of the sheer fun and good times they anticipate. Some (particularly college students) find the sexual component of dating (necking, petting, or sexual relations) a large part of its attraction. Others date to achieve educational goals, to learn the social and emotional skills required to get along with a member of the opposite sex. Still others see dating as the means by which they can gain prestige through sexual conquests or through dating popular people within their peer group. While this goal is not in vogue at present, the game-like quality of dating interaction still persists. Some dating is consciously and deliberately directed toward mate selection, and all dating indirectly assists in the attainment of this goal.

This chapter addresses itself particularly to dating as it relates to the goal of mate selection. Dating has the potential of being a resource for marriage because it provides the opportunity for individuals to informally interact with persons of the opposite sex in a variety of settings. Sociologist Robert Winch suggests that just as people look at merchandise in a store window and assess its potential worth, dating lets people look at other people with the same critical eye.[1] Winch considers this kind of window shopping both an enjoyable recreation and a useful "sorting out process," a way of determining likable and unlikable characteristics in a person of the opposite sex. It also helps people determine the criteria on which to base future judgments and more intense involvement. Winch also sees dating as a means of learning appropriate behavior in association with members of the opposite sex. Closely related to this idea is what he calls "trying out your personality" to see how others react.

Depending on motivation, any one or all of these goals of dating, if achieved, should be valuable, in that they reveal the identity of the participants. People not only learn about their specific dating partners, but they also become more aware of their own identity.

We have elected to focus on the problem of making dating a resource for marriage. The process proposed, however, is adaptable to the many individual problem-solving situations surrounding dating.

Birth of the Anonymous Man

Most people in our society take for granted that at a certain age, usually during adolescence, an individual begins to date. A typical sequence begins with casual relationships, sometimes in groups or on double dates, followed by more serious stages of involvement such as dating steadily, going steady, or "engaged to be engaged," and engagement itself.[2] Variations of this sequence (casual to serious involvement) generally are accepted as normal, and questions are seldom raised about the implications of dating or why it is needed at all.

Dating patterns have emerged as responses to specific conditions of society. Casual dating, as it is known today, was essentially unheard of until the twentieth century. Before that time interaction on a one-to-one basis between members of the opposite sex was limited mostly to premarital circumstances referred to as *courtship*.[3] (Courtship, in contrast to dating, implies marriage intent.)

Settlement patterns of early North American life were such that there was a high degree of homogeneity among family groups in a given community. The agrarian setting dictated the occupational structure and encouraged early marriage since land was cheap and a family was of great assistance in its development. Freedom of choice of a mate was possible but modes of transportation were limited, which discouraged travel and perpetuated intergenerational continuity as children grew up. As a result, young adults met their potential mates and made their homes in the same geographic area as their parents.[4]

The similarity of family backgrounds and the restricted mobility of the society generally assured an individual that he would marry someone who could help create the type of home and community life they were both used to.[5] Since practical considerations such as these were of major importance in mate selection, divorces were rare, and many couples spent their whole lives in close proximity to their families, sharing in community activities and gaining comprehensive knowledge about friends and acquaintances.[6] While companionship between boys and girls before marriage was expected the development of a love relationship was usually tightly controlled by the parents, thereby ensuring parental approval of a match.[7] From this historical background comes the word *courting*, which implies controlled, marriage-oriented premarital interaction.

Needless to say, times have changed. There is little doubt that the technological innovations which prompted specialization in the labor force have been some of the most influential factors affecting change in group interaction patterns.[8] Families from different geographic areas, possessing diverse value systems and attitudes toward life itself, began to congregate in the city. The isolation of farm living and its comfortable familiarity among neighbors became a thing of the past. It was replaced by a way of life that threw together an assortment of people who had little in common, people with no names—only faces. The frame of reference used for judging individuals on first meeting was outmoded, because none of the old assumptions fit. A new person possessed no identity; indeed, he actually possessed an anonymity which required a new method to erase.

Today, children attend modernized educational institutions which keep them out of the home many hours each day. They continually interact within a heterogeneous group which exposes them to alternatives to their accepted traditional behavior patterns. The result of these changes is that the characteristics sought in a marriage partner cannot be identified in the traditional manner. Mate selection has become much less oriented toward finding a partner who will provide assistance in making a living. Instead it has focused on finding someone whose personality is compatible.[9]

Our contemporary dating system has been a natural outgrowth of this society of anonymous men. Decentralization of activities out of the home has served to place much more responsibility on the individual to choose his own friends and to obtain adequate knowledge to select a future spouse.

Little has been written to describe dating patterns in the late sixties and early seventies. While there was considerable research interest in dating in the fifties and early sixties, a perusal of the *Social Science and Humanities Index*, which lists over two hundred professional periodicals, turns up ten articles on dating from April 1968 to March 1973. Of these, only one deals with the nature of current dating patterns or stages of involvement.

This is not to suggest that changes have not occurred. Informal observation and conversations with young people indicate that dating patterns today are less structured than they were in, say, the fifties, and that there are fewer observable landmarks in the stages of involvement.[10] The practice of wearing a boyfriend's high school ring to indicate "going steady" or his fraternity pin to indicate "engaged to be engaged" appears to have died a natural death. The stages (playing the field, going together, engaged) appear to have less definite end points, and dating interaction is much more casual and informal. One young woman described the inter-sexual relationships she had observed as loosely following this pattern:

"initial encounter, during which attention is felt; generally the male follows up with usual phone calls or visits during which the couple seeks to establish rapport. This phase is generally introspective and characterized by cautious honesty . . . ; the third phase continues mutual discovery but is intensified by sexual encounters, and so it goes until some couple discover incompatibility or boredom or are attracted by another person. Those couples who maintain their relationship may consider living together, living together as a preliminary to marriage, or simply marriage."

Perhaps the most significant change in the dating pattern is the added sexual interaction, which undoubtedly is a result of the liberalization of premarital sexual codes, at least among young persons. (We will discuss these changes in detail in Chapter 5.) As a result of this liberalization both men and women face the decision of whether or not to have sex as part of their dating interaction.

We predict that some form of dating will remain popular for many years to come. Not all the changes that will occur will necessarily focus on making dating a resource for marriage. Persons with this goal will still be faced with making choices to encourage such a development. The next section discusses some of the factors which limit the usefulness of dating as a resource for mate selection.

Recognizing the Limitations of Dating

Recently a popular approach to describe dating has been to call it a "game." Sociologist Gerald Leslie describes it as a courtship game in which the language and gestures are identical to true lovemaking.[11] He states that theoretically anyone can play the dating game as long as he is not involved in courtship. Even so, it is usually more fun when played by two partners of comparatively equal status and skill, since it is too easy to beat an inferior player. Although certain dating rules are fairly widespread, it is doubtful that any are universal. Rules depend on the composition of the group from which one selects his dates.

As rules of the dating game are examined, it becomes evident that the "satisfactions sought are not, in the first instance, sensual but self-regarding."[12] This emphasis on the self becomes evident as soon as attempts are made to present oneself in a more favorable light to members of the opposite sex. For example, many women let the telephone ring at least twice before answering. While some are unaware of why they do it, others freely admit that they cultivate this habit in an effort not to appear as if they were sitting by the phone waiting for it to ring (even though they may have been doing just that). A male student revealed that some men have what they call weekend and weeknight dates. Since the more important events take place on weekends, the women they generally take out then are more likely to be higher status dates.

If a date is a matter of taking someone out to a certain place to be seen by certain people, the self again becomes the center of attention. This practice is more common for those individuals who have the goal of achieving status through dating. Sociologists Willard Waller and Reuben Hill, writing in the 1930s about campus dating, identified a *rating and dating complex*.[13] They described college dating as being structured around one person who was trying to get the other person to fall in love *harder* and *earlier* than he. The authors believed that the objective was to establish oneself in an advantageous position that would permit one to maneuver the relationship. They contended that couples were operating on the *principle of least interest*, meaning that the person who cared the least about maintaining the relationship was the one who would control it. Examples of this principle were observed when popular men on campus dated women who were not so popular, and vice versa. The "not so popular" individual had more to lose from the standpoint of dating prestige if the two broke up and was therefore more interested in keeping the relationship intact. This practice allowed the more popular person to make demands, because he had nothing to lose if the demands were not met and everything to gain if they were.

Dates are often characterized by what family sociologists H. R. Lantz and E. C. Snyder call meaningless interaction.[14] Instead of endeavoring to discuss matters of significance, so that a better understanding of each other will occur, couples avoid any serious topics and dwell on the superficial. In fact, this superficiality is part of the game, tied in with the principle of least interest. Talking about anything besides highly superficial matters implies the desire for a more intense relationship, and committing oneself to the possibility of that desire puts one at a disadvantage. The outcome of dating conversations is often designed not to expose one's identity but to hide it. It is almost like living behind a mask, with each person acting out roles in a play—trying to be what he thinks the other person wants him to be instead of showing himself as he really is. The situation is humorous but a bit tragic as well. Dating partners try to impress each other with facades, when the real personality would serve as well (if not better) in most instances.

Among other devices, dating couples use *lines* to hide their true feelings or to avoid having to devise new responses for new situations. Lines are routinized ways of getting into interaction. They provide the light banter between partners which eases tenseness in new situations. They also provide support for an insecure ego; without a line, some people might never enter into communication at all. For example, if a woman is unsure of her partner's feelings but wishes to express her affection for him, she may talk in such a way that he thinks it is a line. By doing this, she has protected her ego in case he does not reciprocate her feelings. The damaging part of using a line is the dishonesty, which makes it difficult to recognize the truth when it is spoken. Whether the man uses "everyone does it" or "we're getting married anyway" lines[15] in order to bargain for sexual favors or the woman uses fencing comments to keep her partner interested but maintain her own involvement at a low level, the effect is similar—their communication is closed and deceptive. How frustrating it becomes to hear words of tenderness and love and never dare believe them for fear they are a "put on."

Problem Solving: Assisting the Decline of the Doorstep Routine

If the preceding description of the modern dating system is accurate, in the process of accommodating short-term personal goals, dating may also be encouraging attitudes and behaviors that are dysfunctional for marriage preparation. Several authors have warned of this possibility, expressing concern over the future of the dating system in its current state.[16]

The most limiting factor in dating is the superficiality of the relationship, one result of which is that individuals are not given the opportunity to expose their true selves. Thus, if dating is to be used as a resource for marriage, some of the superficiality of the relationship must be eliminated.

What are the elements which provoke superficiality in dating relationships? They include unrealistic expectations for the relationship, limited opportunities for exposure of one's real self, and stilted communication patterns illustrated by the "line." In order to change the dating pattern, one or both partners must see it as a problem and must establish goals to change whatever superficiality they can identify in their relationship. The goals initially may focus on one area of superficiality, so that progress will be easier to assess. For example, a man may decide to stop comparing every woman he dates to the *Playboy* ideal. Though this goal will be difficult to reach, given the strength of peer pressure and the portrayal of the ideal date in the media, he feels it is worth striving for. He remembers the enjoyment he had in his few spontaneously arranged dating relationships, and he hopes to find this enjoyment again. He finds that two alternatives come to mind:

1. He could decide that all women are pretty much the same, that as long as a woman meets his needs, beauty doesn't really matter.
2. He could decide to redefine his idea of beauty to include more than physical attributes.

After mulling the two alternatives over in his mind, he decides that the first one is really no better than the situation which prompted his problem-solving action in the first place. By electing this alternative he would be just as stereotypic and impersonal as he was in following the *Playboy* ideal. The second alternative has more appeal for him, because it allows him to think about his own concept of beauty. Through this alternative he could decide which particular characteristics of a dating partner are most important and satisfying to him. Then he could consciously attempt to date partners with these characteristics. Finally, he could evaluate whether this practice is more satisfying than his past practice. Of course, these alternatives do not exhaust the possible solutions to the problem.

To determine the potential usefulness of any alternative, one should try to identify the resources available to carry it out and its advantages and disadvantages. Acting on the alternative in the above example may not immediately solve the problem of establishing realistic expectations for dating, but the rewards possible from even the least attempt at this goal can encourage future problem-solving action.

Looking at the other two areas of superficiality—limited exposure of the real self and stilted communication patterns—we find that the problem-solving method can generate solutions here as well. The fact that dating is structured almost entirely around leisure-time activities greatly restricts what one can learn about another person. Encounters of this type seldom permit individuals to be seen under pressure. In fact, any serious thoughts one might have are likely to be shoved aside, since one of the rules of the dating game is that the couple should be carefree and have a good time. To resolve this problem, one must set a goal of creating the kind of dating interaction which potentially can reveal something about the dating partner's nature and interests; then one must establish alternatives to achieve the goal. Planning a picnic when rain is certain may seem a contrived way of seeing how a person reacts to stress, but it does make an attempt to reach the stated objective. Other alternatives may include planning more spontaneous, informal dates, going on a weekend camping trip together, or visiting with his or her parents over a weekend. One important alternative is taking the risk of expressing true feelings so that the dating partner is encouraged to do so as well. Creative dating involves this kind of risk taking. It means doing away with the routine that presents a fully scrubbed facade to a dating partner. The routes to accomplishing this objective follow two major themes—changing and broadening the situations experienced in dating and developing self-confidence and courage so that risk taking is not an ego shattering or even an upsetting experience.

Social philosopher Rollo May has suggested that "courage is the capacity to meet the anxiety which arises as one achieves freedom."[17] For dating this can mean the courage to experiment with techniques which might achieve more valid exposures of the self to a dating partner even though taking this position may not be rewarded initially by society. The possible benefits center on the inner growth of the self; this growth is necessary before one can give oneself to another person in a close interpersonal relationship.

The last superficial aspect of dating we have noted for problem solving is coping with stilted communication patterns. This problem relates directly to the general problem of developing communication as a resource (which was outlined in Chapter 2). The overall goal is to develop a more open, honest communication pattern. Where the "line" has become an established interaction technique and honest feelings are difficult to express, there is some degree of urgency to generate alternatives which will effect an immediate solution. One alternative would be to use a behavior modification technique and reinforce honest, open communication with tokens redeemable for, say, a steak dinner (a real incentive at today's prices). Obviously this technique has limited usefulness. Only some dating partners would agree to the goal and see the point of the exercise. In addition, there is no guarantee that any change in behavior accomplished by the technique would be retained once the rewards stopped. Furthermore, most people would soon tire of the artificial situation. The major advantage of trying this alternative is that it vividly identifies the degree of superficiality present (one can count the tokens) and it provides a necessary motivation to continue developing a more open communication pattern.

A second dysfunctional aspect of dating as a precursor to marriage is the fact that some people never find a dating partner. One can be a genuine, warm person, possessing admirable qualities for a marriage partner, but still be unable to find an eligible partner. An analysis of who rates as a good date has undoubtedly changed over the years. Waller and Hill discovered that during the thirties good looks, nice clothes, a car, and fraternity or sorority membership characterized a good date.[18] Sociologist Robert Blood's restudy at the Univerity of Michigan of the Rating and Dating Complex (or how dating partners are evaluated by each other), however, revealed that attitudes had changed significantly.[19] Much more emphasis was being placed on personality traits such as considerateness and a sense of humor. Even so, observation of who gets the dates shows again and again that those who can "play the game" are the ones most desired.

Kenneth Cannon expresses the fear that dating can be problematic for both the daters and the nondaters.[20] Those who want to date but are unable to do so may suffer serious damage to their self-esteem. At the same time the "popular date," who has good looks and sex appeal and can carry on the light banter which is a part of dating, may possess few of the characteristics necessary to maintain a continuing relationship. Cannon believes that popularity based on superficial standards may contribute to an inflated sense of self-worth. The system itself is becoming more and more flexible, probably as a by-product of changing male-female roles and of increased informality of interpersonal relationships. Even so, change in a system as intricate as the dating system is accomplished over time. Waving banners and writing folk songs decrying the unavailability of dating partners won't suffice to resolve a person's immediate problem of getting a date. What he needs are alternatives which center around increasing his exposure to potential dating partners and developing his interpersonal skills so that when he does meet someone he can develop a relationship. Whether he joins a dating service or joins some new activities is his choice. Evaluation of these choices, however, may require that he assess not only his progress toward the goal but also whether the goal is a realistic one for him.

Finally, the tendency for dating interaction to encourage exploitation is also dysfunctional. Women particularly feel they must compromise their values in order to keep the relationship alive. To cope with this problem, one must first recognize the values he holds and then express them to the dating partner.

More important, one must attempt to do away with ego-protective bargaining techniques. Self-confidence and courage help resolve this problem. When a person has confidence in his ability to think, respond, and communicate openly with someone, he has little need to exploit that person.

All this discussion sounds rather discouraging on the surface, but it does not have to be. The accomplishment of almost anything depends largely on one's motivations and persistence in carrying out a plan of action. Awareness of potential hazards in dating can itself be a positive step toward avoiding them. If one has a real desire to make dating experiences into resources rather than limitations, the goal can be reached.

Signs of unrest have already become evident among people who are fed up with the present system. The trend appears to be moving toward more unstructured dating. It may be a spur-of-the-moment affair that gets away from "the phone call a week in advance, negotiating for a car, dressing up, trying to impress the parents, holding hands in the movies, parking on the way home. You call her up because you feel like flying a kite or going for hamburgers . . . At least you get away from the doorstep routine."[21]

Although what a couple does on a date is not our primary concern, it seems that breaking away from the traditional things might allow more expression of individual personality. It is natural to want to please each other, but why should people be so afraid to try something different? Instead of going out to dinner for a first date, how about an ice cream and a long walk? Would the date be insulted? And if so, what could this tell you about the person?

There are numerous ways to improve our chances of viewing members of the opposite sex more realistically. For example, we are now doing away with segregation of the sexes in college living units. (This segregation increases the discomfort people often feel when they finally do get together.) Journalist Martha Lear believes that separation is abnormal and could be remedied somewhat by establishing coeducational dormitories on college campuses.[22] Where coed dorms have been established, indications are that the romantic aspect of a man-woman relationship are often set aside, and men and women get to know each other as friends. Lear also reports that manners and appearance improve, noise level goes down, building destruction decreases, and conversational level is higher.[23]

It appears obvious, on the basis of these suggestions alone, that with a little initiative and ingenuity young couples could significantly alter existing conditions in the dating system. Society may have to look a long time before finding an alternative that would provide more freedom or be more fun, but it might not be that difficult to make improvements within the system.

Summary

Changes occurring in courtship and mate selection over the past century have centered around increased freedom of choice of a mate and increased contact between young men and women without parental supervision. Dating patterns have reflected a similar trend. While companionship between young men and women was expected before marriage in an earlier time, dating as we know it today is a necessary adaptation to economic and social changes. The move from rural to urban living altered patterns of interaction and produced a situation whereby people from every conceivable background were thrown together. Lack of knowledge about each other created the need for some system to help them get acquainted and make intelligent choices of marriage partners.

The dating system emanating from this background has the potential to satisfy many goals, both long-term and short-term. While most persons date for sheer fun and enjoyment, dating can also be considered a resource for marriage. Emphasis on superficial traits, however, has led family sociologists to describe dating as a game, possessing characteristics that are dysfunctional to marriage preparation. Persons with valuable personality traits but who lack some of the more superficial qualities, such as good looks or dating skills, are unable to enter the dating system; others achieve popularity based on superficial standards. This situation may cause a misinterpretation of self-worth. Concentration on leisure activities, along with the casual nature of dating conversation, can serve to hide rather than reveal identities, and exploitation is often encouraged.

Efforts are now being made by some young people to do away with the more traditional forms of dating and move toward more spontaneous interchange. What is needed is continued individual goal setting and problem solving to stimulate further evolution of dating practices.

Notes

1. Robert F. Winch, *The Modern Family* (New York: Holt, Rinehart and Winston, 1958).
2. Jack Delora, "Social Systems of Dating on a College Campus," *Marriage and Family Living* 25 (February 1963), 81-84.
3. Ernest W. Burgess and Harvey J. Locke, *The Family–from Institution to Companionship* (New York: American Book, 1960).
4. Ibid.
5. W. F. Ogburn and M. F. Nimkoff, *Technology and the Changing Family* (Cambridge, Mass.: Houghton Mifflin, 1955).
6. Herman R. Lantz and Eloise C. Snyder, *Marriage: An Examination of the Man-Woman Relationship* (New York: Wiley, 1969).
7. Ogburn and Nimkoff, *Technology*.
8. Talcott Parsons, "The Social Structure of the Family," in Ruth Anshen, ed., *The Family: Its Function and Destiny* (New York: Harper Brothers, 1959), pp. 241-274; and Ogburn and Nimkoff, *Technology*. Both discuss technology and family structure.
9. Ogburn and Nimkoff, *Technology*, and Burgess and Locke, *The Family–from Institution to Companionship*, report this trend.
10. E. Gilliam, "Is Dating Outmoded?" *Seventeen*, March 1973, pp. 106-107.
11. Gerald Leslie, *The Family in Social Context* (New York: Oxford University Press, 1967).

12. Geoffrey Gorer, *The American People: A Study in National Character*, rev. ed. (New York: Norton, 1964).

13. Willard Waller and Reuben Hill, *The Family: A Dynamic Interpretation* (New York: Holt, Rinehart and Winston, 1951).

14. Lantz and Snyder, *Marriage*.

15. Charles Shedd, "Lines Guys Use," *Teen,* October 1967, pp. 51-53.

16. Gorer, *The American People*.

17. Rollo May, *Man's Search for Himself* (New York: Norton, 1953).

18. Waller and Hill, *The Family: A Dynamic Interpretation*.

19. Robert Blood, "A Re-Test of Waller's Rating Complex," *Marriage and Family Living* 17 (1955), 41-47.

20. Kenneth Cannon, "An Evaluation of Dating," unpublished paper.

21. F. Maynard, "New Rites for Old," *Seventeen*, March 1969, pp. 154-155.

22. Martha Weinman Lear, "When College Dorms Go Coed," *Reader's Digest,* February 1970, pp. 27-32.

23. Ibid.

Suggested Readings

Combs, Robert H., and Kenkel, William F. "Sex Differences in Dating Aspirations and Satisfaction with Computer-Selected Partners." *Journal of Marriage and the Family* 28 (February 1966), 62-66. Compares male and female expectations and satisfactions with blind dates arranged by an IBM computer for five hundred male and five hundred female students.

Heiss, Jerold S., and Gordon, Michael. "Need Patterns and Mutual Satisfaction of Dating and Engaged Couples," *Journal of Marriage and the Family* 26 (August 1964), 337-339. An attempt to discover need patterns associated with mutual satisfaction in dating and engagement, the article focuses on Winch's theory of complementary needs.

McDaniel, Clyde. "Dating Roles and Reasons for Dating." *Journal of Marriage and the Family* 31 (February 1969), 97-107. One of the few studies to explore the current pattern of dating stages. The pattern of random dating, going steady, and becoming pinned/engaged was supported for this sample of college women.

4

Love
Problems

Unlike people in most cultures around the world, North Americans are expected to marry for love, and when they are in love they are expected to marry.[1] Love is a vague and amorphous concept which seems to defy definition, probably because it means different things to different people.

Most individuals who are romantically involved with someone are faced with two basic questions: (1) Am I in love? (2) If I am, what should I do about it? Answering these to one's satisfaction are major problems for many young people because of the varied and ambiguous definitions of love and because of society's expectation that people in love will marry. This chapter is an attempt to help people understanding the relationship between these issues and their own needs and desires.

The Nature of Love

Most people are convinced that love is as legitimate an emotion as joy or hate. Unfortunately, few can agree on how to capture the essence of love, although poets and novelists seem to have been far more successful than social scientists in this regard.² Despite the lack of a clear definition, we can proceed with some assurance that an emotion involving positive feelings of people toward one another exists and that this emotion can, on occasion, be a powerful force in people's lives.

Cultural and Societal Constraints

People in all societies experience the emotion of love; yet research data clearly indicate that heterosexual love is rarely the basis for marriage in non-Western countries.³ Although love as a basis for marriage is more prevalent in the United States than probably anywhere else in the world, even here it is not the only criterion for selecting a mate. A person's freedom to fall in love with and marry anyone he wishes is curtailed by social and cultural norms specifying certain characteristics the chosen person should have. As sociologist William Goode puts it, love is "one final or crystalizing element in the decision to marry, which is otherwise structured by factors such as class, ethnic origin, religion, education, and residence."⁴ One's pool of eligibles (the group from which a mate is chosen) is restricted by a sifting process that tends to eliminate people of different racial, ethnic, social class, educational, and religious background. (This process will be discussed in more detail in Chapter 7.) The more marriage is seen as a link between families, and the more power, prestige, property, and the like are believed to be passed by kinship, the greater is the parents' desire to restrict their children's field of eligibles. Parents with racist attitudes, for example, may restrict their children's contact with members of other races, often by carefully selecting which schools their children will attend.

Although the *nuclear* family system, mother, father, and their children, is regarded as the ideal living arrangement in North America, it is by no means an isolated system.⁵ (The very fact that most people know who their grandparents, aunts, uncles, and cousins are, and have some idea of the relationship between themselves and each of these people, is evidence that extended kinship ties do exist.) According to Goode, the importance of the husband-wife subsystem to the solidarity of the kinship system varies directly with concern over the maintenance of acceptable and intact *kin lines*. In North America the upper social stratum is most concerned with the social implications of kin lines; therefore, kin groups in this stratum exert considerable control over marital choices of their young. They are apt to be fairly successful, as not only do they have considerable resources available to use in their efforts to restrict their children's pool of eligibles, but "wayward lovers" have more to lose in terms of prestige, property, and power if kinfolk are alienated. This does not mean that a person cannot marry whomever he chooses; what it suggests is that there are certain costs involved in marrying out of one's pool of eligibles, however it is defined. Anyone contemplating such a marriage should be sensitive to the potential costs. In particular, he should assess his own strengths in being able to withstand pressures from relatives and friends who have been close to him in past years.

Psychosocial development of love   Most behavior, including the patterns of love and sexual expression, are products of our past and present socialization experiences. Significant persons (parents, friends, siblings) and groups (family, church, peers) in one's life provide role models of approved behavior. They are supportive if one adopts this behavior, and they withhold rewards or apply negative sanctions if one behaves in an unapproved manner. Through interaction with these "significant others" and through contact with the larger society via the mass media (love songs, movies, and television, for example) the individual acquires a notion of what love is, how to act when in love, who to love, and when love should occur.

The family provides one of the first opportunities for love relationships. In infancy, positive emotional feelings are associated with reduction of the primary drives of hunger, thirst, and pain. The person who meets these needs is th e child's first object of attachment. In North America this person, at least in the past, has been the mother. Bottle feeding and the emergence of less distinct role definitions for men and women provide increasing opportunities for either parent to be the first love object of a child.

Many parents do not realize how crucial these early years are for children in developing an ability to love and how lasting an influence parent-child relationships have on later relationships. Basic attitudes regarding the self are developed early in life, and there is considerable evidence that a positive sense of self-worth is required before one becomes capable of loving another person.[6] During early childhood, parents and other significant people provide a sounding board upon which the child tests his ability to express and receive love and affection. If the child's significant others are loving and accepting of him and administer firm and consistent discipline, he has a good chance of deciding he is an "all right person." If, however, significant others are hostile, rejecting, and inconsistent in their disciplinary efforts, the child may experience difficulty in developing a positive self-concept. A child who is developing self-esteem and autonomy has greater resources to draw upon than a child who lacks self-esteem and autonomy. He will therefore be more likely to enter into new relationships, since his sense of worth is less dependent upon validation by others.

While it is important for a child to experience the emotion of love, it is also important that he learn how to be loving. Learning theorists suggest that generosity and other love-related behavior parents express to their children and to other people is important. One of the ways children learn is by imitation. If they grow up in a loving home, they are likely to relate to those they care about in unselfish, caring ways.

As children play together and attend school, they begin to establish attachments to peers of the same sex.[7] By the time they reach late adolescence, however, they usually have turned to members of the opposite sex for love. Psychologist Lawrence Casler describes this series of events in the development of love from cradle to adulthood as a progression from the infant's emphasis on touch (skin love) to relationships with parents (kin love) and culminating with attachments to the opposite sex (in love).[8] Healthy love experiences during early and late childhood and adolescence produce a person who is secure in his sexual identity, who can relate well to both men and women, and who is confident that he is a worthwhile individual. When a person's significant others perpetuate rather than retard his growth toward these objectives, he can move from childhood to full adulthood with relative ease. As psychiatrist George Preston explains it in *The Substance of Mental Health,* if parents are successful, they will lose their children.[9] This expresses the need for parents to encourage their children to become independent and to allow them freedom to grow.

Some definitions of heterosexual love One reason people have so much difficulty deciding whether or not they are in love is that there is little agreement, even among the experts, of what love is.

Definitions of love by social scientists are lackluster in comparison with the descriptions by novelists and poets. After all, it is terribly difficult, if not impossible, to capture passion, tenderness, eroticism, caring, and sharing in a single definition that will help us understand how these components fit together—if indeed they do.

Psychologists' and sociologists' definitions of love all have shortcomings. All involve value judgments which reflect whatever they think is important. Sociologist Robert Blood, for example, writes: "Love is an attachment between people, not a 'free floating' feeling. It is a cathexis to an object, a personal object."[10] He prefers *attachment* to *attraction* because the former connotes reciprocity. One-sided *love*, according to Blood, does not exist, and he calls this type of unilateral affection a *crush*.

Reciprocity in the love relationship is also central to sociologist Lyle Larson's definition of love as "the mutual perception of positive affect between male and female."[11] Larson believes that positive emotional feelings indicates the extent to which two people are drawn or attracted to each other. It develops in identifiable steps through interaction with another, but it varies in expression from person to person. One's value orientation therefore influences his heterosexual love relationships.

According to Larson, all heterosexual positive affect has the potential of the three basic heterosexual orientations—the sexual, the companion, and the altruist—although usually one of these takes precedence in a person's value hierarchy. The person with a *sexual orientation* feels that love cannot exist unless sexual needs are met. This person has self-gratification rather than mutual satisfaction as his primary object. The person holding a *companion orientation* places highest priority on comradeship, communication, or just being together and places sex as a secondary element in human expression. This person depends on mutual feeling and response. The *altruist*, on the other hand, reflects a completely other-centered philosophy; his expressions of love are offered regardless of whether he anticipates any response by the loved one. (Although Larson claims that love must be reciprocal, it appears that his "altruistic" lover has no need for reciprocity. This is just one example of the problems created by social scientists who try to define love.)

Needs, values, goals, and situational factors such as proximity influence whether or not two people are drawn to each other. Psychologist Abraham Maslow, for example, has suggested that love is associated with satisfying primary drives.[12] Those individuals who are responsible for reduction of the basic drives of hunger, thirst, or sex become love objects.

According to sociologists Snell and Gail Putney, love is an attraction toward a person upon whom one has projected some alienated quality or potential he would like to experience in himself.[13] They suggest that a person usually admires a number of qualities that are, for one reason or another, contradictory to his self-image and that he projects these qualities onto someone else and therefore loves that person. For example, every culture assigns certain characteristics to each sex. In our society femininity connotes dependence and submission. A man, therefore, may see in his sweetheart his own desire to be dependent and submissive. A woman, on the other hand, learns not to be assertive and independent. She may, therefore, love masterful men, because these attributes reflect her own repressed desires to be dominant.

The Putneys suggest that another reason for projecting valued traits onto another person is a false conviction that one lacks something. For instance, an attractive woman may have been labeled "beautiful but dumb" enough times that this has become part of her self-image. She may cherish brainpower; but having been told often that she hasn't any, she denies her intellectual potential and projects it onto someone who appears witty and bright. Thus, according to the Putneys, "each individual makes idiosyncratic alienations which fill in details on the cultural specific 'Ideal.' "[14] This suggests that when a person falls in love, he hangs his ideal image on someone and loves it. If the image doesn't fit very well, he may withdraw his projection and believe he was only "infatuated." If, however, the projection fits fairly well, he is able to acknowledge love feelings.

One of the broadest definitions of love is that of Goode: "a strong emotional attachment, a cathexis, between adolescents or adults of opposite sexes, with at least the components of sex desire and tenderness."[15] Because the institutionalization of love varies from society to society, differences may exist between the intensity of a couple's love relationship and the culture's expression of love as a basis for marriage. To deal with this, Goode differentiates between what he calls a love pattern and the romantic love value complex. A *love pattern* reflects a norm where love is permissible and may be a usual element in courtship and an expected prelude to marriage. The *romantic love value complex* includes not only the elements in the love patttern but also an "ideological prescription that falling in love is a highly desirable basis of courtship and marriage."[16] This complex is rare. In the 1950s Goode suggested that possibly only the urban United States, Polynesia, northwestern Europe, and the European nobility of the eleventh and twelfth centuries possessed the romantic love value complex. (If this indeed is true, we would suggest that the complex spread rapidly during the 1960s, at least in North America and urban Latin America.) On the other hand, Goode suggested that the love *pattern*—love viewed as a basis for the final decision to marry—is probably relatively common.

An important point in Goode's writing is that a deep love relationship does not necessarily reflect extreme romanticism. In other words, the romantic complex and love patterns may be separate dimensions, and a person could place himself anywhere from high to low on either one. Goode's view differs greatly from the more common allegation that romantic and conjugal love are on opposite ends of the same continuum.

Our society's definitions of romantic love suggest that it is highly emotional and intense. Ultraromantic love attachments, common among teenagers,[17] are often referred to as *infatuations,* implying that they are "a flash in the pan"—enjoyable, intensely involving at the time, and of short duration. An infatuation is highly ego-centered, as is revealed by the girl who complains she is so much in love that she can't eat, can't sleep, can't study. Who gets the benefit? Certainly not the object of her love! Another important characteristic of infatuation is its emphasis on physical attraction. It is possible to be highly infatuated with someone whom you have never met. The mere sight of the person or his picture is pleasing and often leads to fantasies about what this person must be like and what the two of you would do together.

Conjugal love, sometimes referred to as mature or rational love, connotes the love between a stable, happily married couple. For the unmarried couple, conjugal love involves an analysis of their relationship and the possibilities of satisfying each other's needs in the future.

According to family sociologist Ira Reiss, defining love involves identification of the cultural forms given to a love relationship and of the cultural backgrounds that tend to promote love relationships.[18] Accordingly, one could analyze the characteristics and consequences of different types of love in various segments of a particular culture and society. This approach, coupled with Goode's notions, would lead us to expect social class, ethnic, and gender differences in expressions and meanings of love.

In an attempt to conceptualize a theoretical framework to deal with the various types of heterosexual love relationships (such as romantic and conjugal) and their cultural and societal differences, Reiss developed the "wheel theory."[19] The underlying assumption of this theory is that our major cultural types of love develop through four interrelated processes—rapport, self-revelation, mutual dependency, and need fulfillment. When two people first meet, each sizes up the other. What is there of mutual interest that they can do or talk about? How open and free can they be in conversation? To what extent do they feel they understand each other?

During their initial interaction they will either experience *rapport* (characterized by a comfortable feeling in which they are at ease with each other), or they will fail to develop this rapport and feel ill at ease. Good rapport is likely to lead to further interaction, while poor rapport lessens the likelihood that they will seek each other out again for further conversation. Development of rapport is facilitated by the similarity of the couple's background, since members of the same social class and same religious, educational, and ethnic groups share many similar experiences. Another factor contributing to rapport is the specific way each person views and defines his social roles. For example, those who define the female role similarly are more apt to feel rapport for each other than are those who hold divergent opinions.

The development of rapport between two people is usually accomplished by a relaxation of guard, which results in an openness where each reveals more about him or herself than previously. Reiss calls this second process in the love cycle *self-revelation.* When one is at ease, he is more likely to talk about his important experiences, feelings, attitudes, and goals. However, his social and cultural background determines what he thinks is proper to reveal to an interesting member of the opposite sex at a particular time in the relationship. Some groups are more formal than others, and certain topics may be taboo. For example, is it proper to talk about one's ambitions? Are sex related topics permissible subjects of conversation?

The third stage in the love cycle is *mutual dependency*. As a couple with good rapport spend more and more time with each other, they tend to reveal more of themselves, and in doing so they build interdependent habit systems—consistent ways of responding to each other in certain situations. The development of these habit systems creates a mutual dependency. Each needs the other to joke with, to confide in, to fulfill his sexual desires. When such habitual expectations are not fulfilled, the couple experience frustration and loneliness. The habits that are developed are culturally or socially determined to the extent that the content of self-revelation is contingent upon the couple's cultural and social background.

Need fulfillment is the fourth and final stage in the love cycle. Basically, one needs a confidant, respect, and love. Clearly these needs require the active participation of another person, and the extent to which that person fulfills the needs, the love relationship flourishes. Reiss reports, however, that while 70 percent of the women college students in his study considered it very important to have a loved one whom they could look up to, only 22 percent of the men felt this to be very important.

The four-step process is circular; Reiss suggests that the rapport one feels upon meeting someone for the first time is partially due to an awareness of the potential of the other person to meet one's personal needs. If one needs recognition, for example, and senses that the other will give it to him, he will feel rapport, will reveal (often unconsciously) something about himself designed to elicit the desired response, will become dependent upon the other if that person's response is one of recognition, and will find his needs at least somewhat fulfilled. Figure 4-1 depicts the process that is constantly occurring if the love is growing, as the four stages continually feed into each other.

The wheel theory provides one conceptualization of the various types of love. For example, ultraromantic love goes through the processes in very rapid order. In the course of one short encounter, for instance, a person may feel rapport, reveal himself, become dependent, and feel fulfilled! In the case of someone madly in love with a person he has never met, the theory suggests that he fantasizes the entire process. Conjugal love involves a number of turns of the wheel (as well as a larger number of rapport, revelation, dependency, and fulfillment factors) as it emphasizes the need to know one another in a number of circumstances. In addition, before one allows himself to become too involved, he evaluates the relationship in terms of its capacity to fulfill his future needs. Erotic love, on the other hand, emphasizes the sexual component through all four stages.

The process is also reversible. If, for example, the sharing which goes on in self-revelation produces arguments, shame, or guilt, this will probably lead to a decrease in rapport, and, as the wheel turns in the opposite direction, unfulfilled needs. Thus the model provides a framework for describing the deterioration of a love relationship. It also explains multiple loves, in the following manner:

Figure 4-1 *Graphic Presentation of Reiss's Wheel Theory of the Development of Love*

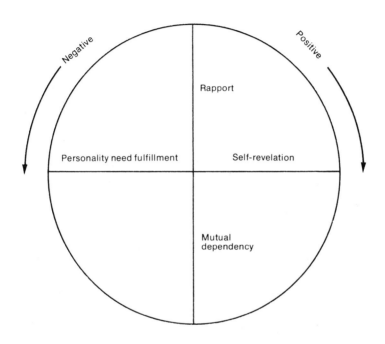

Ira Reiss, "Toward a Sociology of the Heterosexual Love Relationship," *Marriage and Family Living* 22 (1960), 139-145.

. . . if love does not develop through the culturally directed processes of a primary relationship involving rapport, revelation, dependency, and need fulfillment, then one would expect that there would be wide differences in the amount of needs which were fulfilled in any one relationship; and it also follows that although one has fulfilled some of his needs in one love relationship, he may fall simultaneously in love with another person who is capable of fulfilling different combinations of needs.[20]

Considerable harmony exists between Reiss's conception of the wheel moving in a positive direction and psychologist Nelson Foote's conception of the mutual development of a love relationship. "Love," Foote contends, "is the relationship between one person and another which is most conducive to the optimal development of both."[21] According to Foote, optimal development can be measured in terms of the growth of competence in interpersonal relations. He suggests that the growth of love can be charted as a developing process which continually progresses with the mutual satisfaction and increased interpersonal competence of the partners.

From this viewpoint, one values a partner not only for what he is at the moment but also for his potentialities of development. This is a commitment to a dynamic future rather than to a static present, and trust and appreciation accumulate through the partners' mutual development. Each is committed to helping the other develop as a love partner, a parent, or a competent citizen in terms of whatever values or goals are mutually agreed upon.

Foote believes that the relationship of lover to loved one can be likened to the relationship of an artist to his audience. Almost any artist is acutely conscious of the influence of his audience upon his performance and development as an artist. To attain an audience that is critical but appreciative, objective but hopeful, and neither patronizing nor condemning nor overly sentimental in its adulation is the ideal which can assist him in improving his performance. The ideal audience expects a performance from him as good or better than he has given before. It expects him to work hard, but at the same time it identifies with him and is sympathetic in an informed, understanding way. Thus the ideal audience never unrealistically demands that he exceed his abilities, be what he is not, or achieve a result he never aimed for. When a wife refers to her husband as "her best friend and critic," she implies that he is playing a role involving acceptance, encouragement, and realism. Such a relationship is conducive to continued growth and development.

This kind of relationship can best be described as one of social equality and reciprocity. Equality is indispensable if genuine discussion is to occur between people,[22] and discussion and sociability are invaluable in the kind of creative criticism from which personal development derives.

Equality does not imply sameness. The practice of equality is a sharing of certain valued experiences. For example, Foote posits that it would be ruinous for parents to insist that each child reach the same standard of performance. Loving parents instead expect each child to move toward a standard that is reasonable for his capacities. The same thing is possible for married couples. Each can achieve and strive for creative performance in his own skills, interests, and abilities. The role of the partner is to understand, encourage, and serve as a critic. This practice reinforces the individuality of each partner.

Reciprocity involves the right of each partner to play the role of the helper and of the helped. It implies mutual dependency and mutual assistance. To deny a person opportunities for reciprocating is to forestall his respect for himself and to invite resentment. Each partner should try to facilitate the creative and autonomous development of the other partner. The closeness that develops in this kind of relationship involves the mutual dependency of equals.

It is obvious that Foote's definition reflects what he considers to be the optimal kind of love for marriage. In contrast to the conception of romantic love as a violent emotion which can be stabilized only by ritual and pretense, Foote's conjugal love is known by its works—by its loving behavior.

None of the theories of love discussed above are adequately supported by research findings; rather, they provide educated speculations. As such, they may furnish some means for understanding love feelings. Unfortunately, we have a tendency to shy away from examining many of the important aspects of love.[23] We seem to feel that an understanding of love might destroy it. However, if love cannot withstand the scrutiny of analysis, it is probably not a firm foundation for building a long-standing relationship.

Apprehending Love

Most people are able to acknowledge love for their parents, siblings, and friends of the same sex; yet these same people are often anxious about their feelings toward someone of the opposite sex. "Am I enough in love to get married?" is a common question and often a crucial problematic situation. Even though love is culturally defined in terms of how intense one's feelings should be before they are called "love," some people are satisfied with relatively shallow feelings while others require feelings so intense that they may never think they are in love. Each person must decide how many "turns of the wheel" are necessary before he is in love. If the person is interested in marriage, however, it is just as important that his feelings be conducive for building a good marriage.

Many marriage counselors and some psychiatrists emphasize conjugal love as the only worthwhile emotion, disparaging romantic love as immature and a poor basis for marriage; some even question whether romance can survive in marriage. In his article "In Defense of Romance," philosopher Thomas S. Knight contrasts viewpoints held by de Rougement and Kierkegaard, who disagree about the likelihood that marriage can sustain romance.[24] Both believe that romance thrives on obstacles. However, de Rougement feels that if romance exists, the marriage cannot (for example, separation may enhance romantic situations for a couple, but few people want to build a marriage on separation). Kierkegaard, on the other hand, views the "obstacles" as *internal* struggles with which the people must deal. To him, romance makes a marriage more complete, more alive, more rewarding. Neither philosopher believes, however, that romantic love alone is a sufficient condition to warrant being married.

Others argue that romantic love is important to the stability of the monogamous marital system.[25] Although not an entirely realistic approach toward life, romantic love does provide impetus for the couple to overcome obstacles that sometimes warn against the advisability of getting married at all. From this standpoint it may be dangerous. On the other hand, some authors contend that the romantic love attachment promotes mutual loyalty, which may be very useful in keeping the couple together, especially during the first year or so of marriage, when each is trying to adjust to the other. Romantic love thus appears to be a mixed blessing. On the one hand, it provides impetus for freedom of choice in selecting a mate, recognition of the potential for human ecstacy, and freedom from restraint; but on the other hand it leads to an unrealistic and demanding relationship that is difficult to attain and nearly impossible to maintain.

If, however, as Goode posits, romantic and rational love are actually two dimensions instead of one, a balance of the two would probably be optimal at the time of marriage. The conjugal component would provide a basis for a developing relationship, and the romantic would keep the couple together long enough for them to begin a marriage.

Love and the Fulfillment of Marital Goals

Our romantic ethos suggests that love is everything, that nothing else matters because love conquers all. In fact, there are many valid reasons for marriage; love is simply one of them. In most of our society it is mildly shameful to marry without being in love, but too strong a love is viewed as a laughable or tragic aberration.[26] Perhaps the crucial questions are: What does one really want from marriage? and Is the kind of love one feels likely to hinder realization of these desires?

Of course, these questions introduce a rational element that may be very difficult to cope with when one is certain he just can't live without his beloved. Although it is difficult to realize at the time, most people do survive broken love affairs and go on to love again. In fact, a study of University of Minnesota students indicated that 85 percent of the men and 69 percent of the women adjusted to the breakup of a relationship in several weeks.[27] The reasons for the breakups no doubt affected the recovery time. Those who instigated the split and those who broke up because of mutual loss of interest adjusted most readily. The fact, however, that only about 7 percent of the men and 12 percent of the women reported that it took them over a year to recover is indicative of the high recuperative powers of these students.

Some people believe that other things are more important than love in marriage and that if the other needs (such as security, stability, and prestige) are met, love will develop. This orientation is more likely to be held by women than by men. In a recent study of over a thousand white students from five colleges in the Philadelphia area only 24 percent of the women (compared to 65 percent of the men) replied no to the question, "If a boy (girl) had all the other qualities you desired, would you marry this person if you were not in love with him (her)?"[28] Other studies suggest that women are less romantic than men,[29] although this should not be interpreted to mean that women generally do not love romantically or conjugally. The pattern of decreasing romanticism for women as they approach marriage—in contrast to the steadiness or increase in romanticism for men— is commensurate with their belief that marriage is the woman's career while for the man it comes second to his occupational career. Given the concerted effort of virtually all our society to socialize women throughout their childhood, adolescent, and adult years to become wives and mothers, it seems logical that women emphasize conjugal love more and romantic love less than their future spouses—despite the media's emphasis on the romantic love complex.

Studies of marital happiness stress the importance of shared expectations. One of the issues to consider when deciding whether or not one's love will flourish in marriage is whether both have compatible expectations for marriage. If expectations and/or goals are not compatible, one or both partners will feel frustrated and cheated.

Those who want a companionship relationship that will grow with the passage of time may want to rationally examine their feelings in terms of Foote's definition of love as "that relationship between one person and another which is most conducive to the optimal development of both." The Putneys, for example, suggest that successful marriages are more likely if both expect to enjoy the self rather than the other.

Because the expectation is different, the interaction is different. As each partner seeks to maximize his own enjoyment of the marriage, he assists his spouse in doing the same. Each is seeking candor and warmth, and the exploration of self-potential (sexual capacities and many others), all of which is facilitated by the cooperation of someone else engaged in a similar development. Such persons are not preoccupied with being loved or with maintaining romantic illusions. They are trying to enjoy life—together.[30]

What of those who expect the romance to continue? Most evidence to date suggests that the excitement and thrill in each other's touch gradually diminishes with the familiarity of living together. The evidence, however, is not clear that *romance dies out,* although the persistence of intense excitement after many years of marriage is rare. If a person's romantic feelings are directly related to his sexual fulfillment, he is likely to consider sexual compatibility as the key criterion of a good love relationship.[31] If not, as the romance gradually fades and there is no growing component of conjugal love, he will probably find the marriage unsatisfactory. For many, however, the words of Amy Lowell strike a resonant chord.

When you came you were like red wine and honey,
And the taste of you burnt my mouth with its sweetness.
Now you are like morning bread,
Smooth and pleasant.
I hardly taste you at all, for I know your savor;
But I am completely nourished.[32]

Objectivity is one of the most valuable resources available to an individual as he tries to assess his love relationship—even when he feels consumed by passion or when he is afraid that an objective examination of love will cause it to lose some of its mystery. People make different demands on their love objects, and it is helpful to be aware of what actually can be lived with and what can cause trouble. People raised in different family environments have decidedly different expectations about how one shows love and affection. Thus signs of love assurance can be anything from a hug to a spanking, depending on its interpretation.[33] A common complaint of newlyweds is that the spouse's family shows affection differently from their own. One woman reported, "When we visit my husband's parents, one would think we haven't seen each other for a year, and it may only have been the day before." Her husband says, "When we visit her parents, they may be glad to see us, but one would never know it from the way they act." Though time takes care of a great many misunderstandings about how love should be expressed, each person must decide early whether he can accept the other's love in the manner in which it is given. Before marriage one young man stated, "She isn't a very affectionate person. I don't like it, but I can live with it." As it turned out, he couldn't.

Likewise, love may be viewed differently at different times. Considerable evidence exists that men and women view love differently, at least in the early years of dating. According to Mary Calderone, Director of SIECUS (Sex Information & Education Council of the U.S.), "the girl plays at sex, for which she is not ready, because fundamentally what she wants is love; and the boy plays at love, for which he is not ready, because he wants sex."[34] She also sees a major difference in the way males and females play at love. "The boy can do so consciously; the girl cannot. In this sense, the boy can play at love in a more profound and vulnerable way, since the person the girl must mislead—if she is to obtain what she wants—is herself."[35]

Becoming a More Loving Person

People who feel unlovable or incapable of loving another sometimes wish they could become more loving and lovable. Psychiatrist Thomas Harris points out three things that make people want to change: (1) they hurt inside, (2) they experience a slow type of despair or boredom, and (3) they believe change is possible and desirable.[36]

In a world where everyone asks for love but few seem to provide it, it should be obvious that there are no easy ways to become more loving. Indeed, if one accepts the perspective of behaviorists such as B. F. Skinner, it is no use to try to change.[37] Many other social scientists and philosophers, however, feel that people have choices and can exercise them. Individuals often find it difficult to break away from old habits ("that's the way I am—I'll never change"), but according to Harris and others[38] it can be done. Harris, for instance, might recommend that if you feel you are unlovable, think through the kinds of things you do which you believe annoy people. For instance, if you are a grouch before your morning coffee, you may find that you are using that excuse as a license for abusing others. Anything goes (usually the people around you) until you have the first cup of coffee. It is your excuse to grouch all you want. After all, it's not your fault. Or is it?

Another approach is to look at loving as a form of intimacy. According to human relations consultants Muriel James and Dorothy Jongeward intimacy has to do with expressing the feelings of warmth, closeness, and tenderness. It involves genuine caring.[39] Many people lack the ability to be intimate—to risk feeling affection for someone and to express affectionate feelings. A person who tries to change may feel awkward or even phony at first. But in the process of developing a capacity for openness, he becomes more open and reveals more of himself. He refrains from interacting with people in ways which prevent the development of closeness. He attempts to relate to each individual in terms of that person's uniqueness and not through his distortions of past experiences. He allows his own capabilities to unfold and encourages the same in others. He is concerned with *being* more, not getting more. Obviously, James and Jongeward's ideas on intimacy fit nicely into Reiss's wheel theory of love.

Psychoanalyst Erich Fromm takes a somewhat different approach to the problem of becoming a more loving person. In his foreword to *The Art of Loving* he states that all

attempts for love are bound to fail, unless he [the reader] tries more actively to develop his total personality so as to achieve a productive orientation; that satisfaction in individual love cannot be attained without the capacity to love one's neighbor, without true humility, courage, faith and discipline. In a culture in which these qualities are rare, the attainment of the capacity to love must remain a rare achievement.[49]

His basic premise is that love is an art and that anyone who wants to learn how to love must proceed in the same way he learns any other art, such as music or sculpture. First one must understand the theory of love, and then one must put it into practice. All this, he cautions, requires a great deal of time, effort, discipline, patience, and concentration. The meaning of these concepts and their relationship to the art of loving are carefully spelled out in his book.

Underlying all the above ideas for becoming more loving and lovable is an acceptance of oneself as a worthwhile person. A person who feels good about himself will probably find it much easier to reach out to others in a giving rather than a taking way. For some people who don't like themselves at a basic level, books such as *I'm OK–You're OK*, or *Born to Win: Transactional Analysis with Gestalt Experiments,* or *The Art of Loving* may be helpful. Others may wish to go into therapy if they desire to become more loving to others and comfortable with themselves.

Summary

Unfortunately, social scientists know very little about the nature of heterosexual love. It exists throughout the world, but its expression is, to a large degree, culturally determined. In our society it is viewed as part of the mate selection process and as the "glue" that holds a couple together over the course of their married life.

The types of love detailed in this chapter generally describe the kinds of relationships which exist predominantly in our middle class society, although we have pointed out that other types of love also exist. Research on love, as is true of so many other areas of study, has been restricted primarily to this class. As observations are made among other groups, the basic philosophy of love will probably remain the same, but we may be able to recognize the various cultural manifestations.

The first problem for some people is the mere recognition of whether their feeling is temporary infatuation or a more enduring kind of love. Having decided that it is love, the next problem is to decide what to do about it. If the answer is to marry, the question arises as to whether this is the kind of love which can grow and develop in a marital relationship. There are no reliable guidelines to help one come to grips with these issues. Each person must decide for himself if his feelings are composed of an adequate blend of romantic and conjugal love, if the loved one has the potential to fulfill his needs in marriage, and if he can accept the loved one as is.

Notes

1. William J. Goode, "The Theoretical Importance of Love," *American Sociological Review* 24 (February 1959), 38-47.

2. Not only have social scientists experienced difficulty in defining love, but empirical investigations of physical responses associated with love have been futile. No evidence to date has substantiated the existence of love on the basis of irregular heartbeat, swooning sensations, or other indications more commonly referred to in writings about love. See, for example, Lawrence Casler, "This Thing Called Love Is Pathological," *Psychology Today*, December 1969, p. 20.

3. Goode, "Theoretical Importance of Love."

4. Ibid., p. 39.

5. See, for example, Marvin Sussman, "The Isolated Nuclear Family: Fact or Fiction?" *Social Problems* 6 (1959), 333-340, and Marvin Sussman and Lee Burchinal, "Kin Family Network: Unheralded Structure in Current Conceptualizations of Family Functioning," *Marriage and Family Living* 24 (1962), 231-240.

6. Erich Fromm, *The Art of Loving* (New York: Harper & Row, 1956), and Bonaro Overstreet, "The Unloving Personality and the Religion of Love," in Simon Doniger, ed., *Religion and Human Behavior* (New York: Association Press, 1954, pp. 73-87.

7. M. S. Breckenridge and E. Lee Vincent, *Child Development: Physical and Psychological Growth through Adolescence* (Philadelphia: Saunders, 1965).

8. Casler, "This Thing Called Love," p. 20.

9. George H. Preston, *The Substance of Mental Health* (New York: Holt, Rinehart and Winston, 1943).

10. Robert O. Blood, *Marriage*, 2d ed. (New York: Free Press, 1962), Chapter 4.

11. Lyle Larson, "Toward a Conceptual Model of Heterosexual Love: An Exploratory Study," *Family Life Coordinator* 15 (October 1966), 200.

12. Abraham Maslow, *Motivation and Personality* (New York: Harper and Row, 1954).

13. Snell Putney and Gail Putney, *The Adjusted American: Normal Neuroses in the Individual and Society* (New York: Harper & Row, 1966).

14. Ibid., p. 112.

15. Goode, "Theoretical Importance of Love," p. 41.

16. Ibid., p. 42.

17. Albert Ellis, "A Study of Love Relationships," *Journal of Genetic Psychology* 75 (1949), 61-71, and Ira Reiss, "Toward a Sociology of the Heterosexual Love Relationship," *Marriage and Family Living* 22 (May 1960), 139-145.

18. Ibid.

19. Ibid.

20. Ibid., p. 144.

21. Nelson A. Foote, "Love," *Psychiatry* 16 (August 1953), 247.

22. Durkheim cited in Foote, "Love."

23. Rhona Rapaport and Robert Rapaport, "New Light on the Honeymoon," *Human Relations* 17 (1964), 33-56.

24. Thomas Knight, "In Defense of Romance," *Marriage and Family Living* 22 (May 1959), 107-110.

25. See, for example, Hugo Beigel, "Romantic Love," *American Sociological Review* 16 (June 1951), 326-334, and W. L. Kolb, "Family Sociology, Marriage Education, and the Romantic Complex," *Social Forces* 29 (1959), 65-72.

26. Goode, "Theoretical Importance of Love."

27. Clifford Kirkpatrick and Theodore Caplow, "Courtship in a Group of Minnesota Students," *American Journal of Sociology* 51 (September 1945), 114-125.

28. William Kephart, "Some Correlates of Romantic Love," *Journal of Marriage and the Family* 29 (August 1967), 470-474.

29. Ellis, "Study of Love Relationships"; Charles Hobart, "The Incidence of Romanticism during Courtship," *Social Forces* 36 (1958), 362-367; and Kephart, "Correlates of Romantic Love."

30. Putney and Putney, *Adjusted American,* p. 124.

31. Reiss, "Toward a Sociology."

32. Amy Lowell, *Love Is Now: The Moods of Love Today,* ed. Jane Morgan (Kansas City, Mo.: Hallmark Cards, 1972), p. 68. Reprinted by permission of Houghton Mifflin.

33. J. Joel Moss, "The Modern American Family as a Struggle Center," in Paul E. Dahl, ed., *Supplementary Readings for Family Relationships* (Provo, Utah: Brigham Young University Press, 1968), pp. 82-90.

34. Mary S. Calderone, Adaptation of the address "How Young Men Influence the Girls Who Love Them," *Redbook,* July 1965, p. 45.

35. Ibid.

36. Thomas A. Harris, *I'm OK–You're OK* (New York: Harper & Row, 1969).

37. B. F. Skinner, *Beyond Freedom and Dignity* (New York: Knopf, 1970).

38. See, for example, Muriel James and Dorothy Jongeward, *Born to Win: Transactional Analysis with Gestalt Experiments* (Reading, Mass.: Addison-Wesley, 1971).

39. Ibid.

40. Fromm, *Art of Loving,* p. 1.

41. See notes 6, 36, and 40 for complete citations of these books.

Suggested Readings

Casler, Lawrence. "This Thing Called Love Is Pathological." *Psychology Today,* December 1969, pp. 18, 20, 74-76. Suggests that the emphasis on lovingness in our society is misplaced. Love is both an effect and a cause of the insecurity, dependency, and conformity exhibited by men and women today. As such it is pathological in that it impedes personal potential for growth.

Ellis, Albert. "Romantic Love." In William Stephens, ed. *Reflections on Marriage.* New York: T. Y. Crowell, 1968, pp. 63-84. Section taken from Ellis's book *American Sexual Tragedy.* Written in the sharp manner characteristic of Ellis, it identifies the incongruities of romantic love and marriage.

Fromm, Erich. *The Art of Loving.* New York: Harper & Row, 1956. Espouses belief that love is an art and must be understood and practiced if we are to become loving people.

Fullerton, Gail Putney. "Love as Myth." In *Survival in Marriage.* New York: Holt, Rinehart and Winston, 1972, Chapter 15, pp. 341-353. Thesis of this provocative and thoughtful chapter on love is that romantic love does not contribute to marital happiness or stability and that love is essentially a reflection of the feelings one has toward oneself.

Harris, Thomas A. *I'm OK–You're OK.* New York: Harper & Row, 1969. Written in a very light style. A translation of transactional analysis into easily understood language.

How do you feel about yourself and what you feel about the most important people in your life strongly influences your relationship with others.

James, Muriel, and Jongeward, Dorothy. *Born to Win: Transactional Analysis with Gestalt Experiments*. Reading, Mass.' Addison-Wesley, 1971. Easy to read book presenting an interpretation of transactional analysis (based on Eric Berne) and integrating Gestalt therapy (based on Frederick Perls) in an effort to help readers discover themelves and to foster awareness, self-responsibility, and genuineness.

Kogan, Benjamin. *Human Sexual Expression*. New York: Harcourt Brace Jovanovich, 1973. Central concept is human sexuality as an expression of the total personality. Covers a wide variety of topics related to human sexuality. Interesting and informative, with technical terms explained clearly, so that even one with little knowledge of physiology can understand the technical aspects of sexuality.

5 Premarital Sexual Decision Making

Premarital sexual decision making in our society is a confusing and complex undertaking. If we define problematic areas as those in which behavior is uncertain, questionable, or doubtful, this area probably looms as the primary problem to solve. In this chapter we will present information to help students make decisions about physical involvement in dating and courtship.

Every known society has established norms to channel the maturing sexual impulses of its youth into acceptable behavior. Our society, however, has been particularly ambivalent in both the overt and the covert conveyance of its standards. This is illustrated by our permissive attitudes toward sexual content in the communications media and a participant-run dating system on the one hand and our restrictive standards for premarital sexual expression on the other.

While the overt societal norm continues to be disapproval of premarital sexual involvement, young people are faced with two major contradictory forces: (1) liberalized nonmarital standards and attitudes toward sexual activity among their peers and (2) improved contraception techniques. These two factors weaken the societal stance and increase the range of possibilities for personal decisions.

Premarital sexual interaction involves any and all sexually stimulating behavior occurring between two people before marriage—including kissing, petting, petting to orgasm, and coitus. Today's problem is not a clear-cut one of determining right or wrong behavior based on societal norms; it is much more a unique personal decision guided by a complex of factors including norms, values, and the relationship in which the person is involved. As sociologist Lester Kirkendall aptly comments:

> Dogmatic definitions of right-wrong, which rule out all concern with circumstances and the motivations or feelings of the persons involved, break down very shortly. The real problem for premarital sexual decision making is determining appropriate types and levels of sex activity based on the interaction of personal, interpersonal, family and societal influences on the individuals concerned.[1]

In terms of our approach, the problem is to determine the level of intimacy and sexual expression desired and possible, taking into account the needs, values, goals, resources, and limitations of both individuals. We do not claim that problem solving in this area is entirely a conscious, rational process, but we do suggest that factors that help in the search for an appropriate level of intimacy can be isolated. According to Reiss, "the area of sex is one in which all humans are daily confronted with choices—to engage in coitus with their mate or sweetheart, or to make advances toward some sexual object. These are everyday human choices. The choices here are often important determinants of self satisfaction. Thus sex is relevant to both individuals and to social scientists."[2]

Changing Sexual Standards

Our cultural tradition undoubtedly has been a primary force in shaping sexual standards and behavior. Several authors have done extensive studies of the major historical developments influencing North American premarital sexual standards.[3] They have noted that the Judeo-Christian tradition, Protestantism, and a patriarchal family organization have been the major forces contributing to the definition and support of a relatively conservative pattern of sexual morality—abstinence and the "double standard" as the basic premarital sexual norms. However, with the movement toward a more mobile and industrialized society, and with increased freedom in dating and courtship interaction, there has emerged a shift in sexual attitudes, values, and behavior.

The fact that sexual values are changing and that contradictory forces are at work in society compounds the difficulty of sexual decision making. In addition, there is presently a reluctance on the part of the adult world to acknowledge that the traditional mores are today more theoretical than actual. One explanation for this attitude is that adults hesitate to reject the old standards before new ones have been developed to take their place. Family educator Richard Hettlinger has said:

They (the adult generation) are in a near panic at the prospect of this generation reproducing and extending the trend toward promiscuity, for which they bear responsibility. They still enjoy their liberation from Victorian conventions and yet are terrified at the emptiness of freedom without purpose, of lust without love, of independence without discipline. Quite unable to put the genie back into the bottle, our society, on the one hand, enjoys a vicarious second youth in its encouragement and stimulation of adolescent sexuality, and on the other hand, attempts to relieve its senses of guilt and failure by imposing on the young those same conventional taboos from which it broke away.[4]

A more comprehensive explanation of society's view of contemporary sexuality has been suggested by sociologist Jetse Sprey, who explains that sexuality today "is becoming institutionalized autonomously, that is, in its own right, rather than primarily within the institutional contexts of reproduction and childrearing."[5] Although the parents of today's youth have been instrumental in initiating a broader view of sex, they are still subject to the pressures under which their personal moral codes were established, and they continue to support a standard consistent with those codes.

A Summary of Present Sexual Standards

Sexual standards are the end product of the ordering of values related to sexual behavior. These values include satisfaction or pleasure, love, autonomy, independence, and religious beliefs.

The formal overt standard for our society is a single standard forbidding coitus outside of marriage for both sexes. However, three other standards have been identified as operational standards. Reiss states that even though many of us have leanings toward more than one standard, we generally can be placed in one of the following categories:

1. Abstinence   Premarital coitus is unacceptable for either sex regardless of situation.
2. Permissiveness with affection   Premarital coitus is acceptable for both sexes where there is a stable relationship such as engagement, love, or strong affection.
3. Permissiveness without affection   Premarital coitus is acceptable for either sex regardless of the precondition of affection or stability of the relationship, providing there is physical attraction.
4. Double standard   Premarital coitus for men is acceptable; however, for women it is wrong and unacceptable.[6]

The above standards can be placed on a continuum. *Body centered sex,* with emphasis on the physical nature of sex, is at one end; *person centered sex,* with emphasis on the emotional relationship between sexual partners, is at the other. (See Figure 5.1.)

Of the four emergent premarital standards, the *double standard* is perhaps the most traditional belief. Reiss suggests two types of double standard—the *orthodox*, which holds true regardless of the premarital relationship of the couple, and the *transitional*, which makes some exceptions for a woman if she is in love and/or engaged.[7]

Following is a description of a student who adheres to the transitional double standard adherent:

John had always planned to marry a virgin. Although he had had at least ten premarital sexual experiences, he was not willing to accept such freedom for his future wife—until he met Mona. They had been going together for over a year and wanted to get married. Her parents were opposed to the marriage, and out of frustration with the situation they engaged in intercourse. Both felt that they needed to be close to each other and that this was the best way to achieve closeness. John now says he can accept his fiancée's participation because of her deep love for him and their sincere plans to be married. However, he still does not accept a single standard of premarital freedom for both of them.

Under the double standard, in order for a woman to gain society's approval of her premarital intercourse, an examination of her motivations must be made. If it is determined that she is deeply in love with her sex partner, this "cleans the slate" for her. While a man's premarital sexual behavior continues to be condoned either enthusiastically or with a shrug of the shoulders, regardless of his motives, a woman is allowed no such freedom. Those who believe the double standard is vanishing

Figure 5-1 *Continuum of Premarital Standards*

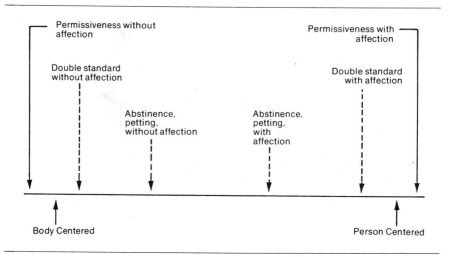

simply because young men are less likely today than previously to insist that they want to marry a virgin might be enlightened by doing some follow-up questioning: You say you would have no reservations about marrying a nonvirgin. Would you care if she had two affairs instead of one? How about five? Or ten? Would you be concerned about why she got involved in these relationships? What if she initiated sexual involvement solely for physical pleasure? Or to make herself popular?

Although the double standard involving virginity per se may be declining, we continue to see two distinct standards for the sexual involvement of men and women. This unequal treatment is contradictory. How can one allow sexual freedom to men without similar freedom to their potential partners? Historically, prostitution was the answer to this dilemma by providing "bad" girls for men's exercise of sexual freedom. Now, however, sexual relations are more likely engaged in with dating and courtship partners. This contributes to sexual mobility and the virginity paradox. Men seek premarital sex partners outside their neighborhood "pool" of possible marital partners, since they want to marry a virgin. At the same time women often date outside their own neighborhood in order to escape the double standard restrictions placed on them. The operation of this sexual standard has been weakened, but it still is informally accepted by large groups of people.

Of the four standards, _permissiveness without affection_ is probably the least prevalent in our society.[8] As can be seen in Figure 5-1, this standard is at the body-centered extreme of the sexual standard continuum. Reiss pinpoints two types of believers in this standard. The _orgiastic_ believer is highly promiscuous and considers precautions of little importance. Describing his experience with pick-ups, a young man says, "I don't mind having intercourse with any of them, because you can't hurt those kind anyhow. If they don't know their business that's their fault." Interestingly enough, this is the standard supported by many women for their prospective husbands. It shows up in answer to the question: "If you could choose the conditions under which your husband acquired his premarital sexual experience, would you prefer that he had loved the woman or that she had been a "pick-up?" Frequently young women choose the latter, simply because they feel there will be less competition for their husband's affections. Seldom do they realize that they are perpetuating a body-centered standard for men and that the kind of experience it encourages is poor preparation for marriage. (Another example of proponents of the body-centered standard are "groupies"—teenage girls who follow various rock groups with the intention of having intercourse with them.)

The Playboy philosophy, propounded by Hugh Hefner, illustrates the second type of adherent to permissiveness without affection—the _sophisticated believer._ Basically, the philosophy recognizes sexual pleasure as a given right for both men and women. While Hefner refutes a purely hedonistic orientation, his philosophy recognizes that sex without love or affection exists and that it is neither evil nor purposeless: "We are opposed to wholly selfish sex, but we are opposed to any human relationship that is truly self oriented—that takes all and gives nothing in return."[9]

Albert Ellis also defends body-centered sexual behavior:

Assuming that it might be better if men and women refrained from coitus without affection, the fact is that such a general change in human behavior is not going to take place for decades or centuries to come. In the meantime, whether we like it or not, we are going to continue to live in a world where countless individuals do have and enjoy loveless affairs. If this is so, why should we create needless guilt and despair among the residents of our existing society by scorning or penalizing them for having sex without love?[10]

Permissiveness with affection implies that premarital coitus is dependent on the partner's strong affection and/or love. This standard is probably most congruent with young people's emphasis on freedom and responsibility in human relationships. It assumes that precautions against pregnancy and venereal disease will be taken and that each partner has a concern for the psychological wellbeing and reputation of the other. In Reiss's terminology, this standard exemplifies person-centered intercourse. Among the adherents to the permissiveness with affection standard are: (1) those who demand love and/or engagement as the affectionate prerequisite and (2) those who accept strong affection alone as a prerequisite. (The second type is more likely to accept occasional instances of body-centered coitus.)

The one totally restrictive standard prevalent today is *abstinence*. While abstinence implies less intimacy, survey data indicate that today's adherents of this standard support more permissive attitudes toward other forms of premarital sexual behavior—namely kissing, necking, and petting. Reiss breaks the abstinence standard into four groups: (1) petting without affection, (2) petting with affection, (3) kissing without affection, and (4) kissing with affection.[11]

It is apparent that those who accept *petting without affection* are the ones who define virginity as a purely physical condition. This group is similar to that of permissiveness without affection. in its emphasis on body-centered behavior. Petting without affection is a relatively new variant of abstinence and has produced a group of women who are labeled "promiscuous" or "technical" virgins; while they have not engaged in intercourse, they have experienced a whole range of sexual intimacy, including petting to orgasm. *Petting with affection,* particularly among middle-class college students, is a widely accepted variant of abstinence. Sociologist Winston Ehrmann suggests that the commitment of going steady and the subsequent shared affection for each other is related to the increased incidence of petting, *particularly for women.*[12] It seems that the going steady relationship facilitates females entering into petting with clear consciences.

As a standard, *kissing without affection* is probably limited to younger people who want to explore sexual activity but are reluctant to go beyond kissing in their temporary relationships. Some girls justify their kissing without affection on a casual date by saying that the boy has paid for the evening, and they are, in a sense, paying their share. The adherents of *kissing only with affection* make up the most conservative group of the abstinence standard. Both these last two groups of the abstinence standard could be construed as early levels of premarital permissiveness through which all persons pass to reach more permissive levels. There are, however, wide ranges in the speed with which people move from this point and some never proceed beyond kissing in premarital relationships.

Social Class Differences

Social class is a sociological term used to rank people on any dimension of stratification. Common determinants of social class in our society are income, education, occupation, or a combination of these.

Research data on premarital sexual permissiveness have been incomplete in regard to social class differences, in that middle-class respondents have been overrepresented and lower-class respondents have been underrepresented.

A. C. Kinsey, a zoologist, noted social class differences in the reported sexual behavior of his male respondents as far back as 1948.[13] However, the validity of his findings was challenged recently when it was discovered that his lower-class sample was composed largely of ex-convicts and his middle-class sample was composed largely of college students. Kinsey should have concluded that male ex-convicts report more premarital coitus than male college students, instead of concluding that lower-class men report more premarital coitus than middle-class men. Reiss, on the other hand, using a *national* sample of adults and a *college* sample of students, reported initially that among white respondents there were no clear-cut social class differences in the acceptance of premarital coitus for either the student or adult sample.[14]

Upon further examination of his social class data, Reiss later reported that actually there were some interesting class differences in premarital sexual activities that had been undetected in his earlier analysis.[15] When the sample was divided into liberals and conservatives in politics, education, and religion, a clear-cut social class difference appeared. He found that among the conservatives lower-class people were the most permissive (as many previous studies had indicated). Among the liberals, however, he found that lower-class people were the least permissive and that upper middle-class, college educated people were the most permissive. When he analyzed the data on white and black lower-class respondents, Reiss noticed that social class and race operated in complex ways to produce a large range of acceptance of premarital coitus within a particular class (see Table 5-1).

Noting the distinct differences in responses between white and black lower-class individuals, Reiss concluded that the black lower-class culture is different from the white lower-class culture in the area of sexual permissiveness. He felt that because of racial discrimination black lower-class individuals might believe more firmly than whites that they cannot control environmental forces around them, and thus they might take a more body-oriented view of sex and love.

In 1972 researchers for the U.S. Commission on Population Growth and the American Future reported marked racial differences between blacks and whites in incidence of premarital coitus for teenagers.[16] Teenage blacks reported more premarital sex at every age. For example, at age fifteen, 32 percent of the black

Table 5-1 *Within-Class Differences in Accepting Premarital Coitus*

	Lower Class Adults* (Percent)	Sample Size	Lower Class Students† (Percent)	Sample Size
White women	5	221	17	109
Black women	33	63	42	90
White men	32	202	56	96
Black men	70	49	86	88

* Drawn from national adult sample.
† Drawn from five-school student sample.

From *The Social Context of Premarital Sexual Permissiveness* by Ira L. Reiss. Copyright © 1967 by Holt, Rinehart and Winston, Inc. Reprinted by permission of Holt, Rinehart and Winston, Inc.

sample reported having experienced coitus, compared with 11 percent of the white sample. At age nineteen, 81 percent of the black sample reported having coitus compared to 40 percent of the white sample. Although these data point to race as the crucial factor, the differences may actually be due to variation in life-style.

These explanations must be viewed as tentative. Much more research is needed to describe the complex interaction of class, race, and environmental factors in influencing the acceptance of different premarital sexual ethics.[17]

Measuring Premarital Sexual Permissiveness

A number of methods are used by researchers to assess the sexual standards of their respondents. These also can be used by an individual to help him more clearly understand his own sexual standard. One technique calls for a direct evaluation of this standard. For example, one might ask oneself: Which of the following statements best describes your attitudes toward premarital sexual interaction? Check the one closest to your present beliefs.

1. Kissing acceptable when strong affection felt for partner.
2. Kissing acceptable even without affection.
3. Petting acceptable when strong affection felt for partner.
4. Kissing and petting acceptable when in love or engaged.
5. Kissing and petting acceptable without affection.
6. Kissing, petting, and coitus acceptable when strong affection felt for partner.
7. Kissing, petting, and coitus acceptable when in love or engaged.
8. Kissing, petting, and coitus acceptable even without affection.

A second technique uses a scale composed of a set of questions designed to give information from which a person's standard can be deduced. One example is the

Male and Female Premarital Sexual Permissiveness Scale developed by Reiss in the late fifties. It consists of one scale for men and another for women and is intended to measure acceptance of premarital permissiveness. Each succeeding statement in the scales indicates a more permissive attitude toward premarital sexual interaction (see Table 5-2).

Respondents are divided into six types, on the following basis:

Zero Scale Type   accepted only items 1-4
Scale Type I   accepted items 1-6
Scale Type II   accepted items 1-7
Scale Type III   accepted items 1-10
Scale Type IV   accepted items 1-11
Scale Type V   accepted items 1-12

Zero Scale Type represents a respondent with a highly restrictive standard, and Scale Type V represents one with a highly permissive standard.

Assessing Behavior Trends

Survey data from the fifties and sixties do not reveal that a revolution in sexual behavior actually took place. However the poor methodology of some studies leaves them suspect, and it appears that major shifts occured during this period.[18] For example, sociologists Robert Bell and Jay Chaskes, using comparable samples in 1958 and 1968, reported that the percentage of college women experiencing premarital coitus in a dating relationship went up from 10 percent in 1958 to 23 percent in 1968. The percentage of girls experiencing premarital coitus in a steady relationship went up from 15 percent in 1958 to 23 percent in 1968.[19]

In 1958, 31 percent of engaged girls reported experiencing coitus, as compared to 39 percent in 1968. The authors noted particularly the increase in the percentage reporting coitus in a dating relationship and a relative decrease in reported guilt for all ages. This implies women are more accepting of premarital sexual experiences for themselves even in casual types of involvement.

In 1967, a *Seventeen* survey of 1,166 teenage girls aged thirteen to nineteen indicated that 15 percent had experienced coitus; the survey also showed that 25 percent of those aged eighteen and nineteen had experienced coitus.[20] The most recent national sample by the U.S. Commission on Population Growth and the American Future of 4,611 black and white girls reported that 14 percent had experienced intercourse by age 15, 21 percent by age 16, 27 percent by age 17, 37 percent by age 18 and 46 percent by age 19.[21] The obvious conclusions are that many teenage girls are experiencing coitus, and, of course, that the older they are, the greater the probability that they will experience premarital coitus.

These data provide some insight into the occurrence of premarital coitus, but it is somewhat misleading to look to unmarried women for an assessment of premarital

Table 5-2 *Reiss Premarital Sexual Permissiveness Scale*

First decide whether you agree or disagree with the view expressed. Then circle the degree of your agreement or disagreement with the views expressed in each question. We are not interested in your tolerance of other people's beliefs. Please answer these questions on the basis of how YOU feel toward the views expressed. Your name will never be connected with these answers. Please be as honest as you can. Thank you.

We use the words below to mean just what they do to most people but some may need definition:

Love means the emotional state which is more intense than strong affection and which you would define as love.

Strong affection means affection which is stronger than physical attraction, average fondness, or "liking"—but less strong than love.

Petting means sexually-stimulating behavior more intimate than kissing and simple hugging, but not including full sexual relations.

MALE STANDARDS (Both Men and Women Check This Section.)

1. I believe that kissing is acceptable for the male before marriage when he is engaged to be married.

> Agree: 1) Strong,   2) Medium,   3) Slight
> Disagree: 1) Strong,   2) Medium,   3) Slight

2. I believe that kissing is acceptable for the male before marriage when he is in love.
   (The same six-way choice found in Question 1 follows every question)
3. I believe that kissing is acceptable for the male before marriage when he feels strong affection for his partner.
4. I believe that kissing is acceptable for the male before marriage when he is engaged to be married.
5. I believe that petting is acceptable for the male before marriage when he is engaged to be married.
6. I believe that petting is acceptable for the male before marriage when he is in love.
7. I believe that petting is acceptable for the male before marriage when he feels strong affection for his partner.
8. I believe that petting is acceptable for the male before marriage even if he does not feel particularly affectionate toward his partner.
9. I believe that full sexual relations are acceptable for the male before marriage when he is engaged to be married.
10. I believe that full sexual relations are acceptable for the male before marriage when he is in love.
11. I believe that full sexual relations are acceptable for the male before marriage when he feels strong affection for his partner.
12. I believe that full sexual relations are acceptable for the male before marriage even if he does not feel particularly affectionate toward his partner.

Ira Reiss, "The Scaling of Premarital Sexual Permissiveness," *Journal of Marriage and the Family,* 1964, **26**. Reprinted by permission.

sexual trends. A more accurate account of premarital behavior probably comes from reports of married women, in that all married women have passed through the premarital period, thus eliminating the possibility that reports about their sexual behavior prior to marriage could change at a later date. Whereas with single women, they can state they have not had sexual intercourse at a given time, but that fact may change in the future, consequently, falsifying the original information presented.

Reiss suggests that when all women having gone through the premarital period are taken into account, the proportion of nonvirginal women would approximate 70 to 75 percent.[22] Although the rates have increased, he believes that women have not and will not reach full sexual equality with men until a change in their priorities comes about:

If females think that getting married and starting a family is their first priority in life and place occupational ambitions secondary to this, then they will view sex in terms of these goals. This means that they will consider whether copulating with a boy will waste time in their search for a mate; whether this boy will tell others what happened and hurt their chances of getting married; whether having interourse will make a boy more seriously committed to marriage or less; and so forth. These concerns are nowhere near as potent to a male, for he is not so strongly oriented toward marriage as his primary life goal. In the middle class his primary goal will be an occupational career and having premarital intercourse is not very likely to matter one way or the other in terms of that goal. Surely men today are oriented toward marriage but the immediate pressures felt by such a marriage goal are considerably less than those felt by females. A male is not that concerned with the time wasted in an affair, nor is he so worried about the impact of the word getting around that he is having an affair. In fact, in many circles news of such an affair might enhance his image as an exciting date or a romantic interest for females.[23]

For those who have begun to believe there are no male virgins left, we report the contrary. There appears to be little change in the number of men who are experiencing coitus today as compared to ten years ago. Sociologists Harold Christensen and Cris F. Gregg studied individuals from three groups that differ in their degree of "liberalism"—Mormons, midwesterners, and Danish.[24] Among the Mormons and midwesterners (the "conservative" groups) there was actually a slight decline in coital experience among men (39.4 percent of the Mormon men studied had experienced coitus in 1958 as compared with 36.5 percent in 1968, and 50.77 percent of the midwestern men studied had experienced coitus in 1958 as compared with 50.2 percent in 1968). Among the more liberal Danes, however, male coital experience increased from 63.7 percent in 1958 to 94.7 percent in 1968.

It is apparent from the available data that the changes which have occurred are in the direction of achieving equal percentages of men to women in a given sample who are participating in premarital sexual activity. To get an accurate representation of the fact, however, we need studies that are based on modern, acceptable sampling techniques which utilize carefully planned and tested measurement devices. At present we can say with certainty only that there have been *increases* in coitus rates in recent years (particularly for women) and in less intimate forms of premarital sexual behavior.

Making Premarital Sexual Decisions

Our discussion of premarital standards and behavior patterns should help the student by identifying the outside pressures that impinge on sexual decision making. Since personal decisions are made within the social-cultural environment, the factors previously discussed will influence the individual's choice.

A person's definition of a situation as problematic depends upon his needs, values, and goals. *Needs* are potent forces. Sexual satisfaction, recognition of sexuality and sexual capacity, success in interpersonal relationships, self-esteem, and approval from peers are a few of the needs that are relevant to sexual decision making. A need for approval from peers can be so great as to push a person into a sexual decision that he later regrets. Bob, a student, feels that prostitution is disgusting and definitely a waste of money. One night, on a dare, he had intercourse with a prostitute. Although he is convinced he will never go again, he has not described his feelings to his friends. In bull sessions he pretends that he really enjoyed it. He says that "fitting in with his group" is more important than venting his frustrations with that experience.

Our discussion of the relationship between values and standards for sexual behavior suggests that some kind of value framework operates to allow each person to reach decisions on the behavior that is acceptable to him. Kirkendall suggests that there are two problems in sexual decision making: (1) identification of the value framework and (2) determination of the behavior and attitudes that are congruent with the framework.[25]

Developing a Value Framework

Valuing is now recognized as an active process which continues over the entire life cycle. Thus two persons in a dating or courtship relationship each bring a value system which they have been developing for a considerable period of time. *Morality* is simply the manifestation of these values. Because values change as a result of physical, mental, and emotional development and interaction with others, morality will be different at different times in one's life.

Using the definition proposed by family educator James Maddock, sexual morality consists of "the appropriate expression of one's sexuality in relationship with others with whom one shares a common humanity."[26] Maddock's developmental view of sexual morality is useful to our discussion of sexual decision making, since it provides a basis for examining some common elements of moral experience that transcend the specific content of moral beliefs.

Maddock suggests that "a major part of man's moral task is to come to grips with his development—with the fact that this life is characterized by movement and change—from little to big, from young to old, from something he potentially is to something he must struggle in his lifetime to become."[27] The fact is that ethics, and specifically religious ethics, has ignored the possibility of a gradual development of individual morality. Instead it assumes a fully developed mature self when dealing with moral decisions. A developmental approach, however, recognizes the many forces which are a part of moral experience—perception, emotion, logic, and social circumstances, as well as religious belief.

Utilizing Erik Erikson's stage theory of development, Maddock outlines the following step-by-step process. The quality of morality changes through interaction with one's environment as well as with other persons. New elements are added to the existing pattern of morality, and old elements are revised or discarded.

Moral perception in infancy and early childhood is characterized by conscious perception or recognition of value in the child's world. Carl Rogers,[28] a psychologist and counselor, sees the infant's approach to value as a clear and honest process. Each object is evaluated on the basis of whether or not it maintains, enhances, or develops the potential of his being. For example, confining snowsuits are negatively valued, and romps in the nude are positively valued. The child is the center of the evaluating process. At first his body provides the clues for evaluation. Later, interpersonal relationships gain importance in this assessment; at this point in his development, a child's moral feelings are not *his* evaluations but those of significant people in his life who provide moral guidance for him. The child thus takes on the basic value beliefs of his social setting even before he can communicate verbally. Maddock suggests that this process is a form of behavior conditioning that occurs as love and security are exchanged between the child and his parents, resulting in the child's development of moral feelings about how things are and how they should be. There is no rational basis to these feelings. The child identifies with his parents' values, and through his interaction with them he develops his sense of identity and self-worth.

During the school years the child learns that he is accountable to others for his behavior. He feels morally obligated to make choices and have his judgment accepted by others. At this stage the child uses information (in the form of rules and suggestions) provided by parents, friends, and others to arrive at his decision. The school years carry with them many demands for the child. He is sent out to interact widely with his environment. This very fact increases the likelihood he will be called on to respond to things over which he has little control. Through trial and error he increases his skills in problem solving—learning to recognize problem situations, assessing his resources and the consequences of his actions, make decisions, and evaluate his decisions.

Morality is still oriented to particular situations at this stage; only slowly does it become generalized to universal ethical principles. Abstract ethical concepts like responsibility have little meaning until the child has had enough life experiences to see how they fit into his own life.

Moral intentionality (acting morally for one's own purposes) characterizes the adolescent years. The adolescent's moral goals are both part of his identity and a way of expressing this identity. The adolescent tests out individual goals to see how his moral perceptions fit into those of the rest of society. By discovering the benefits of acting in certain ways, he makes a moral commitment to these actions.

Commitment is the desire to act in accord with one's beliefs and to accept responsibility for one's actions. Moral commitment develops during adulthood; it suggests that an act is worthwhile because it has future significance in one's life. Through commitment to a particular value, individuals are able to risk acting decisively. Moral commitment thus provides the foundation for a personal philosophy of life. According to Maddock, "moral development comes to fruition in adulthood with the emergence of an ethical sense in which fulfillment is sought by directing one's energies toward others and toward the struggle to come to grips with the meaning of life itself."[29]

Solutions to the problem of developing a value framework for sexual behavior differ from adolescence to adulthood because of the developmental differences during these two periods. Adolescents should be allowed to experiment with alternate value systems in order to gain practice in problem solving. This, however, requires a situation in which there are indeed choices. If, for example, the community or parents have an extremely strict framework regarding physical intimacy, there is no chance for the adolescent to realistically assess the consequences of his behavior and to evaluate various value alternatives. This is not to suggest that adolescents be allowed unlimited experimentation. Adults can and should set limits; but they should also recognize (1) the variety of available value systems, each with its own limitations and advantages, and (2) the impact of the child's early moral training, when he accepted parental norms as his own. They should see also that in order for the adolescent to develop a value framework for sexual behavior, he must be allowed a certain degree of testing and evaluating in real life experiences.

Values in Action

Developing a value framework is just one problem to be solved in premarital sexual decision making. Others include finding a dating or courtship partner with a value framework similar to one's own and making decisions congruent with one's value framework. The remainder of this chapter addresses itself to the resolution of these problems.

Because our basic value structure influences the development of specific goals for behavior, finding a dating or courtship partner with a similar value framework facilitates goal achievement. If, for example, your value framework is one which rejects any form of sexual intimacy before marriage, and your dating partner's value framework allows for considerable intimacy, achieving goal consensus will be time-consuming and difficult (perhaps impossible).

Most young persons share general goals for sexual interaction, namely, to understand and achieve confidence in their sexuality and to develop styles of sexual behavior in line with personal, family, and societal values. Other goals, however, may override the general goals. These goals include attaining peer recognition, gaining sexual experience, or finding a mate. Where goals between partners in a relationship are divergent, exploitation is likely to occur. A male college student describes such a relationship: "We began having intercourse after going steady for four months. I'm sure she felt more for me than I did for her. I was out for a good time and she was willing. She might have consented to intercourse because I threatened to leave her but really I think she continued because she wanted to marry me."

Finding a person with a similar value framework may occur in the normal dating process if open communication patterns are developed. It is also realistic to expect individuals in a close interpersonal relationship to take on some beliefs of the other partner. However, as we have indicated, many values are so deeply integrated into our personality that they are extremely difficult to change. Even sharing a similar value framework does not eliminate the need for problem solving. The intense emotional nature of sexual interaction creates many situations where value frameworks are challenged to the limit. At such times, all aspects of the situation should be assessed—commitment to the value framework as well as immediate and future consequences of the sexual behavior on the persons and the relationship.

Discussion provides one method of identifying a partner's value framework for sexual behavior. Other methods include observation of the partner's behavior in decision-making situations, of his attitudes toward other persons, and of his ability to accept responsibility for negative as well as positive actions.

The crux of premarital sexual decision-making, however, is the selection of behavior patterns in specific situations. You may wonder how you can use a calm, cool, rational approach for developing a value framework when your sexual desire and opportunity shout, *yes*, while a weak, small voice from within whispers, *no*.

First of all, we suggest that the time factor be considered. Important decisions, such as those related to sexual morality, should not be made impulsively but should be thought through *prior to* the time when action is required. It is a matter of deciding what your goal is and then assessing possible alternatives for reaching it. If the goal is to discover various ways to enhance a premarital relationship, one immediate question may be whether or not sexual intercourse would add a positive or negative dimension.

Several factors have been studied in relation to premarital sexual behavior. One that is particularly relevant to the decision of what sexual intercourse will do to a relationship is the degree of involvement. Often, men and women feel differently about sex, and each partner should be aware of his own and the other person's feelings. Because of the double standard, many men have depended completely on the woman to "draw the line," while they pursued the aggressor role to the limit. These men do not necessarily relate sex and love as women are inclined to do. It is helpful therefore to know what the other person's degree of involvement really is.

Many of us tend to assume that others feel as we do in a given situation. This is a dangerous practice. In a study of premarital sexual conduct, Ehrmann found that 56 percent of the men, as compared with only 2 percent of the women, had experienced coitus with individuals they would classify only as "acquaintances."[30] Therefore, although a woman may think love and sex are constant companions, she should be aware that when her boy friend wants to have sex with her, he may or may not have love feelings similar to her own. And men too may feel more concern about making a sexual decision if they understand better what motivations prompt women's behavior.

Maddock has suggested that the value system each person develops is a product of experiences with significant people. Religiosity has been studied in relation to sexual permissiveness, and research findings of family educators Mary E. Heltsley and Carlfred E. Brokerick reveal that when sexual abstinence is supported by one's church, then degree of permissiveness declines for the individual.[31] These results suggest that one's value stance is influenced by association with various groups. We can then expect that if relatively conservative values have been internalized and the individuals involved defy these norms, the probability of their experiencing guilt feelings is greater than if they had internalized more liberal values.

Reports dealing with the aftermath of premarital coitus have presented conflicting evidence. Recent studies indicate a trend toward *fewer* feelings of remorse or regret among those who participate in premarital sexual intercourse than was the case with earlier studies. Bell and Chaskes, for example, found that in their 1968 sample, 36 percent of all women who had experienced coitus while dating and 20 percent who had done so while engaged felt they had gone too far.[32] This was a marked change from their 1958 sample, when 65 percent of the women in dating relationships and 41 percent who were engaged felt regret after experiencing coitus.

If premarital orgasm is used as a measure of sexual adjustment in marriage, the following findings are noteworthy. In 1953 Kinsey reported that of those virgins who had not achieved orgasm from any source premaritally, 40 percent failed to achieve orgasm in the first year of marriage; however, of those virgins who had achieved orgasm by petting or masturbation prior to marriage reported only 15 percent failed to do so in the first year of marriage.[33] Kinsey also reported that of those women who were not virgins when they married and had not experienced an orgasm, 56 percent failed to reach orgasm in their first year of marriage. In the same nonvirgin group, however, where the women had experienced orgasm in coitus 25 times or more, the failure rate was only 3 percent. Thus women who had failed to achieve orgasm in premarital coitus had the highest rates of orgasmic failure in marriage. Kinsey's data support the notion that premarital orgasm from any source contributes to marital orgasm. Reiss suggests that the high failure rate among nonvirgins may be explained by possible guilt feelings and a view of the sex act as primarily for male satisfaction.[34] Virgins' failures, on the other hand, may be explained by their being so conditioned to nonreaction to sexual stimuli that a single year of marriage may not facilitate the unlearning of this response.[34]

Sociologists Ernest W. Burgess and Paul Wallin reported a negative influence of premarital coitus on individual assessments of how well their engagements prepared them for marriage,[35] but the trend appeared slight. Eugene I. Kanin and David H. Howard found instead that sexually experienced women reported better sexual adjustment on their honeymoon than did nonexperienced women. However, more of the experienced women indicated that they had sexual difficulties early in marriage.[36]

Although the findings are inconsistent, the knowledge obtained from these carefully planned research studies can be integrated into one's problem-solving scheme. The studies provide no definitive answers, but they can be useful in placing one's particular situation in perspective.

Assuming that our values regarding sexual behavior are influenced by forces both within and outside the family system, they must reflect the subtle and not so subtle pressures exerted by the society. We can conjecture that even the person holding extremely liberal sexual values is somewhat influenced in his decision making by the existing value stance of society. Thus premarital sexual decisions will always take into account the effect of the pervading value stance—either through the alternatives available or through the consequences for a particular choice.

The question is not simply one of whether or not to engage in premarital coitus. While this has been the primary issue debated in the literature for years, the real question must consider the persons involved and the nature of their relationship, their value framework, and the perceived consequences for their behavior.

A decision not to have premarital sex   Joan and her fiancé had been dating for nearly a year and had recently become engaged. After considerable discussion they decided they would not have intercourse before they were married. Joan had been raised in a strict, religious family, which had instilled in her a high value for premarital chastity. Her fiancé was not as strict in his beliefs, but he respected her feelings. It was difficult at first, but after talking through their alternatives they decided they'd rather not create a wedge between them by the secrecy and guilt each was afraid of feeling. "We had to set up a program to help us through," Joan reported. "We addressed wedding invitations, participated in new activities with other couples, and really worked at developing other parts of our relationship. It was purely a value decision. I had access to contraceptives, and, heaven knows, we had the opportunity. It was our first real success in solving an important problem."

Looking at this example, there are three important factors contributing to the couple's satisfactory solution: (1) they shared a similar (though not the same) value framework, (2) they expressed a long-term commitment (engagement) to each other, and (3) they understood each other's feelings.

There are no clear answers as to whether premarital coitus improves or weakens a relationship. Kirkendall argues that "the effect of intercourse in and of itself, on the strengthening or weakening of a relationship is indirect and minimal. The outcome is more a function of other factors which are a part of that relationship and make it unique."[37] For example, one young man in the study from which this quote was taken indicated that intercourse had weakened the relationship with his partner because the act itself had the symbolic significance of turning the "nice" girl into a "bad" girl in his mind. Though he tried to overcome the feeling, the relationship deteriorated. In another situation, both partners reported that intercourse actually made the relationship more complete and honest.

Because the consequences of premarital intercourse are often unpredictable, it is not a decision to be taken lightly. As we mentioned earlier, the outcome may be influenced by the level of involvement of the relationship. Intercourse takes on a different meaning with a casual date than with an engaged partner. Engagement normally carries with it a commitment to future development of the relationship. Still, the evidence regarding the effect of premarital intercourse on the relationship leans toward the negative. Fear of discovery and pregnancy, exploitation, guilt, and loss of self-respect, illustrate the possible negative effects of premarital intercourse even among engaged couples. In summary, Kirkendall suggests that the following four factors have considerable bearing on the effect of premarital intercourse on engagement relationships:

1. The partners' ability to create a relationship, and the progress they make before intercourse begins, determines the outcome. If communication is still limited and impersonal, they may be unable to cope with the strains which are often a consequence of premarital intercourse.
2. A similar view toward engagement contributes to good effects of intercourse on a relationship. If both believe the engagement period is a time for achieving sexual adjustment, this will favor a positive attitude.
3. Attitudes toward sexual behavior influence the effect of sex on the relationship because of guilt feelings associated with breaking the moral code.
4. Personal maturity allows premarital intercourse to be placed into the context of the whole relationship, inferring that the risks of this behavior, if they occur, can be coped with.[38]

A Change of Plans   When Louise and Ted were at the university, they were involved in an increasing amount of physical intimacy and, likewise, an increased desire for intercourse. They did engage in some petting but agreed they would not engage in coitus. To achieve their goal they decided they would limit petting and late dating. The early leavetakings began to frustrate both and spoil the entire date, without doing anything for decreasing their sexual desire. They discussed the problem again and decided to have intercourse.

While this couple approached the reversal of their decision in a rational way, many couples who are unable to live up to a decision prohibiting intercourse make an impulse decision based on an immediate sexually stimulating situation. "It just happened" or "I can't explain what it was, but one night we just couldn't stop" are common descriptive statements. Reactions following such an emotional reversal may be considerably stronger than those following a more rational reversal, particularly since contraceptives often are not used, thereby creating a threat of pregnancy. In addition, a general feeling of disappointment and guilt may be present.

Guilt is a feeling commonly expressed by persons who have engaged in sexual behavior that is more permissive than their previous behavior had been. Therefore, guilt may be felt at any level, even as a person moves from a kissing only standard to a petting standard. After studying 248 single undergraduate students, Reiss noted that guilt was associated with any new form of sexual behavior but that it did not prevent a person from later accepting that behavior and even moving on to more permissive levels.[39] While most behavior is repeated rather than discontinued, the speed of overcoming guilt differs among individuals. Reiss found that more women than men expressed guilt over increasing permissiveness. Perhaps this is because until a woman falls in love, relations with her parents or other significant persons promote values opposed to sexual permissiveness. The tendency for parents to allow their sons more sexual freedom than daughters may help males to avoid such restrictions.

Even though guilt can be overcome, it is not an easy task. Reiss suggests that societal taboos, and parental taboos in particular, account for persistent guilt.[40] An interesting aspect of guilt is that it has an intellectual component as well as an emotional one. While those in Reiss's study who went beyond their personal limits expressed the most guilt, those who reported doing less or just what they had decided on also reported guilt. This finding demonstrates that while some people can intellectually agree with permissive standards, emotionally they are unable to accept them and thus feel guilty.

Coping with exploitation "Mary Ann didn't want to have sexual relations but I persuaded her. We'd been petting heavily for months, and one night she finally agreed to have intercourse. We broke up shortly after that, and I will always attribute it to my coercion."

Experience tells us that one partner is often more desirous of adding sex to a relationship than the other and may use undue persuasion to get his or her way; this is using sex in an exploitative way. Unless the decision is a shared one, the effect is likely to be negative and lead to increased guilt on the part of both partners.

These examples serve to illustrate the complex interrelationship of societal, family, and personal factors in arriving at an acceptable premarital sexual decision. Society's value stance is still premarital chastity; yet we propose that premarital sexual decision-making is best judged according to one's personal value framework (which will also encompass to some degree the standards approved by society). Where partners share similar value frameworks, have established networks of friends, acquaintances, and so on to support the use of this framework, and share common goals for sexual interaction, sexual decision making is less likely to be fraught with difficulties. All alternatives for behavior should be assessed in the light of immediate as well as long-term consequences on the relationship. The result of integrating sex into a relationship depends on the nature of the persons making up that relationship, whether or not the decision is to have premarital coitus. Insecurity, purposelessness, and immaturity interfere with the development of a satisfying, long-term relationship. Self-confidence makes it easier to arrive at decisions which are congruent with a particular value framework. Working to develop that level of self-confidence is necessary to achieving adequacy in premarital sexual decision making.

Summary

Premarital sexual decision making is complicated by the fact that our society is ambivalent toward sex—standards are in transition, and social and personal factors interact in unusual ways in the decision process.

Three basic problems have been proposed: (1) developing a value framework for sexual behavior, (2) finding a partner with a similar value stance, and (3) making behavioral choices congruent with this value framework. As part of socialization, a child acquires a value framework congruent with his develoment. Through dating and courtship, individuals have the opportunity to seek out partners with value frameworks similar to their own. They also acquire experience in testing out alternative value frameworks. However, arriving at behavioral choices congruent with values takes concerted action. Sexual decision making is complicated by the nature of the setting, the strength of the impulses involved, and the severity of the consequences. Important parts of the problem-solving process are goal setting and evaluating the consequences of each potential alternative, honestly and openly.

Notes

1. Lester Kirkendall, *Premarital Intercourse and Interpersonal Relations* (New York; Agora, 1966), p. 3.

2. Ira Reiss, *The Family System in America* (New York: Holt, Rinehart and Winston, 1971), p. 129.

3. Robert Bell, *Premarital Sex in a Changing Society* (Englewood Cliffs, N.J.: Prentice-Hall, 1966), gives a particularly good account of the historical factors which have influenced premarital sexual standards.

4. Richard Hettlinger, *Living with Sex: The Student's Dilemma* (New York: Seabury Press, 1966), p. 11.

5. Jetse Sprey, "On the Institutionalization of Sexuality," *Journal of Marriage and the Family* 31 (August 1969), 432.

6. Ira Reiss, *Premarital Sexual Standards in America* (New York: Free Press, 1960), p. 83.

7. Ibid., p. 97.

8. In a pilot study done by Reiss in 1956, including over a hundred students, only one respondent fully advocated this standard.

9. Hugh Hefner, *The Playboy Philosophy*, Part II, installments 8-12 (Chicago: Playboy Press, 1963, p. 51.

10. Albert Ellis, *Sex without Guilt* (New York: Lyle Stuart, 1958), Chapter 5, p. 83.

11. Reiss, *Premarital Sexual Standards in America*, p. 196.

12. Winston Ehrmann, *Premarital Dating Behavior* (New York: Holt, Rinehart and Winston, 1959), p. 141.

13. A. C. Kinsey, *Sexual Behavior in the Human Male* (Philadelphia: Saunders, 1948).

14. Ira Reiss, "Premarital Sexual Permissiveness among Negroes and Whites," *American Sociological Review* 29 (October 1964), 688-698.

15. Ira Reiss, "Premarital Sexuality: Past, Present and Future, " in Ira L. Reiss, ed., *Readings on the Family System* (New York: Holt, Rinehart and Winston, 1972).

16. The Commission on Population Growth and the American Future submitted its final report in September 1972. It is available from the U.S. Superintendent of Documents, Washington, D. C.

17. An interesting discussion of the sexuality of black women is found in Robert Staples, "The Sexuality of Black Women," *Sexual Behavior* 2 (June 1972), p. 9.

18. By poor methodology we refer to the fact that most studies have utilized nonrandom samples of middle-class college groups, which cannot be generalized to the entire population.

19. Robert Bell and Jay Chaskes, "Premarital Sexual Experience among Coeds—1958 and 1968," *Journal of Marriage and the Family* 32 (February 1971), 81-84.

20. Alice Lake, "Teenagers and Sex: A Student Report," *Seventeen,* July 1967.

21. *Time*, May 22, 1972, pp. 48-49.

22. Reiss, "Premarital Sexuality," p. 171.

23. Ibid., p. 168.

24. Harold Christensen and Christina F. Gregg, "Changing Sex Norms in America and Scandinavia," *Journal of Marriage and the Family* 32 (November 1970), 616-627.

25. Kirkendall, *Premarital Intercourse*.

26. James Maddock, "Morality and Individual Development: A Basis for Value Education," paper presented at the annual meeting of the National Council of Family Relations, Estes Park, Colorado, 1971, p.4.

27. James Maddock, "Morality and Individual Development: A Basis for Value Education," *Family Coordinator* 21 (July 1972), 291-302.

28. Carl Rogers, "Toward a Modern Approach to Values: The Valuing Process in the Mature Person," *Journal of Abnormal and Social Psychology* 68 (1964), 160-167.

29. Maddock, "Morality and Individual Development," p. 17.

30. Winston Ehrmann, "Premarital Sexual Behavior and Sex Codes of Conduct with Acquaintances, Friends, and Lovers," *Social Forces* 38 (December 1959), 161.

31. Mary E. Heltsley and Carlfred B. Broderick, "Religiosity and Premarital Sexual Permissiveness: A Re-examination of Reiss' Traditionalism Proposition," *Journal of Marriage and the Family* 31 (August 1969), 441-443.

32. Bell and Chaskes, "Premarital Sexual Experience," p. 83.

33. A. C. Kinsey et al., *Sexual Behavior in the Human Female* (Philadelphia: Saunders, 1953), p. 406.

34. Reiss, *The Family System in America*, p. 124.

35. Ernest W. Burgess and Paul Wallin, *Engagement and Marriage* (Philadelphia: Lippincott, 1953), p. 355.

36. Eugene J. Kanin and David H. Howard, "Postmarital Consequences of Premarital Sex Adjustments," *American Sociological Review* 23 (October 1958), 556-562.

37. Kirkendall, *Premarital Intercourse*, pp. 197-199.

38. Ibid., p. 196.

39. Ira L. Reiss, *Premarital Sexual Standards in America;* 87 percent of the women and 58 percent of the men in his sample had accepted behavior that made them feel guilty.

40. Reiss, *The Family System in America,* p. 167.

Suggested Readings

Brenton, Myron. "Sex Therapy for College Students." *Sexual Behavior*, June 1972, pp. 52-55. Review of what is happening on United States campuses where sex counselling is available.

Ellis, Albert. *Sex Without Guilt*. New York: Lyle Stuart, 1958. Open discussion of the positives as well as the negatives of premarital sex.

Kirkendall, Lester. "Ethic and Interpersonal Relationships." *The Humanist* 16 (November-December 1956), 261-267. More on sexual decision making and its effects on the interpersonal relationship.

Packard, Vance. *The Sexual Wilderness*. Toronto: Pocket Books, 1970. A look at the wilderness created in male and female relations by changing social forces.

Student Committee on Human Sexuality, Yale University. *The Student Guide to Sex on Campus*. Chicago: Signet Books, 1971. A book on human sexual behavior written for and by students.

6 Examining Alternative Life-styles

Recent attacks on marriage by people in all walks of life echo age-old criticisms of that venerable and remarkably resistant institution. In a recent study, 60 percent of the Canadian high school students interviewed reported that their greatest concern about monogamous marriage is that it is not meeting the needs of people today.[1] This, however, is only a contemporary version of complaints about the system voiced long ago by Plato, Marx and Engels, and the suffragettes, and more recently by authors such as Robert Rimmer (in *The Harrad Experiment* and *Proposition 31*), Alvin Toffler (*Future Shock*), and women's liberationists such as Shulamith Firestone (*The Dialectics of Sex*). Despite these critiques, most people do not consider alternatives to marriage as viable.

Our Western ways of thinking and inadequate knowledge of our own history, as well as that of other cultures, gives us the impression that our way of life is universal or at least dominant. It comes as a shock to many people to learn, for instance, that even though monogamous marriages outnumber all other types, only a few decades ago a noted anthropologist found monogamy to be the ideal cultural norm for only 135 out of the world's 554 known societies.[2]

When we talk about life-style choices, we are referring to the various types of commitments and living arrangements which influence how one spends time, money, and energy. The most common life-style for adult men and women in our society emanates from monogamous, nuclear marriage (that is, a commitment to and residence with one's spouse and children, apart from friends and other relatives).

We do not know how many people in our society have willingly participated in life-styles other than the contemporary monogamous relationship since the European colonization, but it is probably a larger number than most of us suspect. Some communal societies, such as the Moravians and the Hutterites, were transplanted from Europe to the United States and Canada. Others, such as the Shakers, the Owenites, the Oneida Community, and the Mormons, originated in the New World.

Despite increasing expertise in data collection we still lack adequate estimates of the numbers of people currently involved in alternative life-styles. The existence of a few group marriages has been acknowledged, as have what appears to be growing numbers of communal and cohabitation systems. A 1971 New York Times inquiry uncovered two hundred thousand communes in thirty-four states, and the National Institute of Mental Health estimates that there are more than three thousand urban communes operating in the United States.[3] In 1967, a sampling of a dozen U.S. universities revealed that 9.3 percent of their student bodies were cohabiting at that time. In 1971, almost 20 percent of the students in a large, urban, northeastern U.S. university were cohabiting, and nearly 80 percent of the student sample said if they had the chance they would do so.[4] Floyd Levin, a marketing consultant, predicts that "by the year 1975, one-third of the age group 18-35 will cohabit without marrying."[5]

While the actual numbers of people involved in systems of close interpersonal relationships other than the contemporary monogamous nuclear system are still small when compared with the total population, they are sizable enough to attract considerable public attention and are sufficiently important to include in a book on marriage—especially one with a problem-solving orientation. Increasingly, one of the problems individuals will face is the selection of a system most appropriate for and compatible with their needs, values, and goals.

The Nature of the Problem

In North America, the expectation of marrying is so thoroughly ingrained that most of us blissfully sail into the sea of matrimony without much consideration of the nature of the ship or the implications of the long voyage with another passenger who is pretty much a stranger at the start of the journey. Somewhere in the back of our minds the course has been charted, and when we meet the "right" person we set sail. Few of us seriously question the advisability of setting sail, let alone which kind of vessel to board!

Indeed, the expectation to marry is so strong that only about 10 percent of all North Americans never marry. According to census data, 92 to 95 percent of the United

States population marry at some point in their lifetime.[6] The Canadian percentage is somewhat lower than the U.S., but still considerably higher than that of most other countries in the world.[7]

Reasons for marrying are numerous, as will be pointed out in the chapter on selecting a mate. What appears clear is that, increasingly, a general goal for North Americans is one of self-fulfillment, contentment, and self-realization. For most people, interacting with a person of the opposite sex is perceived as one way of working toward this personal goal. For a growing number, however, contemporary monogamous marriage is viewed as only one of a number of alternative ways of seeking these ends. Since the primary focus of the remainder of the book is the monogamous nuclear dyadic relationship, in this chapter we shall explore a number of other alternative life-styles which seem viable at this point in time.

Alternate Routes to Happiness

A major goal for many young people is to attain that vague and illusory state called happiness. It is generally believed that interacting with people is one way of achieving this state. The vast majority of people consider monogamous marriage the best way to interact closely with someone to attain a happy life. In addition to legitimizing the pleasures of sexual intercourse and protecting access to a loved partner, marriage offers security, companionship, mutual support, affection, intimacy, and social approval.

People change, however, and what contributes to their sense of happiness at one point in time may be interpreted as tedious or unsatisfying at another. The belief that permanence means contentment has recently been subject to reevaluation by some scholars and radical youth. Even among contemporary married couples there is a growing minority that tends to view the commitment as open or even temporary. "I have never had an unhappy marriage," replied a woman on a late night television talk show when asked about her five previous marriages. "They were all good marriages, but after a certain point they ceased to provide what I wanted out of life." The increase in divorce rates can be interpreted to suggest that a sizable number of people feel that their marriages are standing in the way of personal happiness. To allow people more freedom in pursuit of their personal goals, Margaret Mead, the noted anthropologist, has suggested that marriage be a five-year renewable contract. Two women legislators introduced a bill attempting to implement Mead's ideas in the 1971 Maryland legislature. Although the bill failed to pass, it created considerable controversy over a norm that has up to this point been taken pretty much for granted.

The life-styles discussed below, while presented as alternatives to contemporary monogamous marriage, are not mutually exclusive; that is, a person could enter into several of these systems over the years and later marry in the conventional sense. It is also conceivable that a more conventional marriage might evolve into a group marriage or communal arrangement.

The choices discussed in this chapter by no means exhaust all possibilities for living arrangements which might meet one's needs. The selection is presented merely to reflect the growing concern of people for a variety of viable systems in addition to marriage. Good problem solving, as we have stated earlier, requires both an awareness of alternatives and a tolerance for conflicts of ideas. The following discussion is presented for the purposes of increasing the reader's awareness of the available choices.

Remaining Single

An obvious alternative to marriage is to remain single. This alternative, always acceptable for men in our society, is becoming increasingly more viable for women. Education and occupational training have expanded the possibilities for women to exist independent of the financial support of fathers, husbands, and brothers.

A person planning to devote himself to a certain cause or professional career involving considerable travel, odd hours, or little free time may find remaining single more advantageous than marriage. In addition, one is freer to use his resources as he chooses if he does not have to take into consideration another's desires, values, and needs. On the other hand, some careers involve social and community activities which, for a male at this point in history, are more easily managed if he has a wife who will represent him in the community and organize, prepare, and be hostess at parties or other work-related functions. Conventional marital status can also be useful in advancing certain careers. For example, in an intense political campaign a man who displays a public image of being a devoted husband and father seems to have an edge over a single person. Marital status may not be related to one's ability on the job, but it does carry an aura of respectability. If this kind of reputation is important to a person psychologically or professionally, it should be considered in the decision of remaining single or marrying.

The life-style a single person develops depends to some extent upon whether or not he is residing with someone else; one can come and go and bring friends in irrespective of the hour, spend time and money as one chooses, and live in as much or as little clutter as one likes if there is no need to be considerate of others. There are other advantages to living by oneself, but there are also disadvantages. For instance, it is less expensive to share housing costs, and one is less lonely if he lives with others.

A number of residential alternatives to living alone are available to the single person whose happiness is increased by living with others. One of the more popular is a friendship arrangement such as apartment sharing among college students and working adults. Different kinds of communal and cooperative arrangements are also becoming increasingly common. We will discuss some of these in more detail later on in this chapter. Kinship provides another basis for forming household units. Cousins, brothers, and/or sisters may share living quarters, or the single person may prefer living with his or her parents or lover. Each of these arrangements and the extent and type of commitment to the other people involved will affect one's life-style. These alternatives are often more casual and temporary than contemporary marriage. The possibility of someone finding a better job elsewhere or marrying and moving out, for example, may affect the quality of the interpersonal relationships between residential members by restricting their commitment to the relationship. The closeness, warmth, and emotional support available in a system defined as both temporary and casual may not be sufficiently satisfactory for some people.

Cohabitation

One of the most familiar nonmarital heterosexual living arrangements is cohabitation. This particular alternative ranges from a casual arrangement where the couple decides to share living space—no ties, no responsibilities—to one of trial marriage. The difference between these two extremes is essentially one of goals. Trial marriage implies a testing of the couple's compatibility. It involves sense of commitment to the other as well as to oneself, a trying out of the system to see how well each can relate to the other, with the goal of a more permanent union if they are successful. Cohabitation, on the other hand, is a more open-ended system. There is no commitment to the future of the couple. The goal is more likely to be one of enjoying each other on a day-to-day basis, with the implicit assumption that when the relationship ceases to be enjoyable the couple will split up.

The nature of the relationship—that is, the boundaries of the system—determines one's life-style the same way as in a conventional marriage. Although some people might behave identically in cohabiting circumstances and marriage, others would live quite differently. Marriage laws and normative expectations define to some extent what a "good" wife or "good" husband does. These definitions don't exist for cohabitants, and they therefore have greater freedom to define their relationship on the basis of individual wishes, although there may also be more pressure for both to contribute financially to the household. Certainly, there is less pressure for them to stay together than in the case of a legal marriage.

One of the problems of cohabitation is that of mutual understanding and equality of input into the system. The exploitation possibilities of one partner by the other are least when both have similar expectations of the union and similar intensity of commitment to each other. Although this statement could also apply to marriage, generally we expect marriages to be based on love and mutual commitment. In addition, in marriage the expectations of the rights and responsibilities of each spouse are traditionally and legally defined, providing guidelines for appropriate behavior. The results of a study conducted in Boulder, Colorado, during 1969 and 1970 illustrate the problem of commitment. A comparison of unmarried couples living together with those going together and involved in what they considered to be a serious relationship revealed that the going-together couples held more traditional orientations toward each other. Commitment to marriage formed a strong part of this orientation. The living-together couples appeared to have moved in with each other while holding varied expectations, and they were in greater disagreement about what the relationship meant to them. Men were more likely to view the arrangement as an alternative to marriage, while women were more likely to desire the security of marriage. On the basis of these data the authors suggested that if the woman's commitment to marriage resulted in her pressuring the man to marry her, he might respond by leaving, by finding a new partner, or by marrying her. They speculated that if the latter occurred, unless there were changes in the degree of reciprocity of feelings and an increase in positive feelings, the possibility for a happy marriage was low.[8]

Since cohabitation implies a sexual relationship, we can include homosexual living arrangements under this heading, as Canada and most states in the United States do not issue marriage licenses for this type of union. Here, also, the nature of the commitment affects the closeness and the emotional content of the relationship. Outside pressures to dissolve the union are likely to be much stronger if the relationship is homosexual. If the cohabitants are of the opposite sex, outsiders may be shocked at their not possessing the necessary license to have intercourse; in the case of homosexuality, the reactions of outsiders to what they consider perverted behavior are likely to be more extreme. Such reactions are not only hostile; they tend to be punitive and have the intent of eradicating the behavior.

Polygamy

Polyandry (one wife, two or more husbands) and polygyny (one husband, two or more wives) appear to be viable alternatives, at least in the abstract, when a person finds himself in love with several people of the opposite sex. If all involved are compatible and can encapsulate themselves from the hostility and sanctions of outsiders, such solutions are feasible. The hostility and negative sanctions of the community, however, constitute serious problems. Polygamy is illegal in the United States and Canada, and participants in this form of marriage are subject to fines and imprisonment. It was primarily the legal pressures from the United States government that forced the Mormons to give up polygyny as their preferred marital system.

A polyandrous system may well be an attractive alternative to widowhood, especially for elderly women, since they outnumber widowers.[9] The loneliness and depression of old age brought on by the deaths of spouse and friends might be considerably alleviated if the elderly had the alternative of forming a polygamous system which would provide them with a system of meaningful relations on a daily basis and with sex, personal attention during illness, and an improvement in diet (people who cook only for themselves have notoriously poor eating habits). Such persons also could pool their incomes and possessions, which would raise their general level of living above what most could afford on their own at this stage of life.

Probably there would be less public outcry against polygamy for the elderly than for the young, since people seem to be more threatened by the under-thirty group than by the over-sixty crows. Since homes for the aged and retirement villages bring the elderly together and improve personal care and services, the idea of polygamy may be viewed as an extension of these practices. It would enlarge the limited range of alternatives for the elderly and might very well maintain self-esteem among those who feel strongly about not becoming a burden on their children.

One of the problems people interested in this option would face at this time (in addition to negative social and legal sanctions) is that of finding others compatible with themselves and willing to adjust to the habits and idiosyncracies each has accumulated over a lifetime. In addition, the age-old problems of jealousy and competition among co-wives or co-husbands in polygamous systems would have to be recognized and adequately dealt with if harmonious relationships were to be maintained.[10]

Communal Living

As an alternative life-style, communal living is growing in popularity. Historically, the communal movement reflects a search for utopia. The utopian believes that man is basically good but that society corrupts him. If societies are the cause of human problems, it should be possible to bring about a higher order of living by establishing the correct environmental conditions.

Utopians, particularly those of nineteenth century North America, can be characterized by their commitment to human perfectability; conscious planning for the welfare of all members; brotherhood; merging of values, ideals, and spiritual matters with physical events; experimentation; and uniqueness as a group.[11] Human perfectability, they believe, can be achieved by discovering the natural laws regulating the universe and establishing communities according to these laws. The welfare of every member can be assured by conscious planning and coordination. From this perspective, brotherhood embodies the idea that people can be brought into harmony with each other, just as the social world can be brought into harmony with the laws of the universe. This is basically translated into a sharing of property, regardless of ownership, and prohibitions against the accumulation of wealth. Monogamous marriage is seen as possessive and a source of tension and jealousy. In the nineteenth century this tenet resulted in the formation of a number of what we might call communities of lovers and communities of families. Adults did not "belong" to each other, nor did biological parents have exclusive "rights" over their children. In many communities such social practices and less constricting styles of dress had the effect of relieving women of sole responsibility for care of the home and children. Women found an equality unknown in the larger society.

Utopian communities represent major social experiments in human relations. They seek to implement their goals through new ways of doing things. Because they are so different from the world surrounding them, some of their practices may be illegal as well as deviant; in such instances they run the risk of reprisals from the law. It is very important for a utopian community to have a clear sense of itself as a closed or semiclosed system. Utopians want to live life as an expression of their ideals. They object to what they view in the outside world as hypocritical divergence between values and the way people live. "Utopian communities offer to members life's services—food and shelter, a job, education for the children, care in old age—in the context of an explicit set of shared beliefs about how people should live."[12] It should be borne in mind that these are the expectations, not necessarily the realities. It is not surprising, considering their radical departure from prevailing norms, that such communities are often short-lived. As sociologist Rosabeth Kanter points out in her book *Commitment and Community*:

The experiences of the few successful ones indicate the kinds of social organization that are important to implementing a utopian dream, as well as the limitations to utopian theory inherent in these very practices. For example, interpersonal harmony is in many communities often purchased at the price of limits on personal choice and on creative dissension. Full commitment and unequivocal belief, central to the viability of a utopia, involve the individual in giving up some of his differentiated privileges and attributes, at the same time that he gains belonging and meaning. Even when potential inter- or intra-personal conflicts are resolved in favor of the group, tensions often arise between two pulls in a community—for example, between maintaining the group as an expression of shared beliefs and operating an effective organization in servicing and providing for members, that is, between communal values and the practical realities of running a production organization. The dream of utopia must be compared with the realities of creating viable utopian communities.[13]

Oneida: A utopian attempt   Integration of the utopian principles discussed above is illustrated in the case of the Oneida Community. Of the numerous groups in the eighteenth and nineteenth centuries attempting to create a more perfect society, the Oneida Community in upstate New York was one of the more successful.[14]

John Humphrey Noyes, a graduate of Yale Theological Seminary, established a community in Putney, Vermont, based on his interpretation of "Perfectionism." When irate townspeople broke up the community in 1848, Noyes and his followers were invited to join a small band of Perfectionists in New York. This small group, inspired by a speech given by Noyes at a Perfectionist convention several years before, had united their families on their farms on Oneida Creek to form the type of community he had advocated.

Almost from its conception the Community was self-sufficient. This was one of the forces solidifying the group; the outside community was literally and figuratively outside, and was referred to as "The World."[15] The wide range of skills of its members resulted in a relatively high level of living. From the applicants Noyes had carefully selected only those deeply committed to his teaching; in addition, these people were responsible skilled craftsmen and good farmers. Among the first members were an architect, a lawyer, a minister, a doctor, a machinery manufacturer, a bookkeeper, a trap maker, several clerks and teachers, and many farmers.[16] Members turned over all their belongings and possessions to the Community upon joining. This not only gave the Community sizable assets, but insured the total commitment of the joiners. In the beginning farming was the sole means of support, but soon the Community became involved in commercial enterprises, several of which—such as the manufacturing of steel traps and silver table service—became world renowned.

The Community was organized economically, socially, and sexually around the

Perfectionist religious philosophy as espoused by Noyes. He preached that Christ had already returned to earth and that all were redeemed from sin. The spiritual world, therefore, was free, independent, and autonomous of the temporal world. A person could improve his character, spirit, and intellect, however; and the sharing of all things by all members of the commune was a way of achieving this perfection.

To further the sharing notion all activities were devised to stress the group rather than the individual, even in the economic sphere. Work was shared by all, and jobs rotated so that each member participated in most of the Community's activities. Individual skills and aptitudes were taken into account on job assignments whenever possible, and there were a few jobs which were not rotated because of a particular skill requirement (such as that of shoemaker). Women worked at many jobs which at that time were considered for men only; among these were putting up laths when the first large house was built and administering certain enterprises of the Community.

Communal living arrangements also served to promote group cohesiveness. The Mansion House, a spacious brick building constructed in 1862 and added to as needed, provided each adult with a small room of his own. All other rooms were communal, including the dining hall, library, recreation rooms, concert hall, and outdoor picnic area. Members were active in the performing arts, frequently organizing plays, symphony concerts, recitals, and other entertainment. Artists were occasionally brought in to perform, but most talent was drawn from the membership. Dancing and card playing were permitted, as they were considered social activities. Smoking and coffee drinking were not, as they were considered appetitive and individualistic in nature.

Although the members were well behaved, hardworking people, generally respected by those who came to know them as well as by the surrounding community, it was the Community's sexual and marital practices which apparently outraged outsiders. Monogamous marriage and romantic love were believed by Noyes to be selfish and tinged with possessiveness. Focusing one's attention almost exclusively on one's spouse was felt to deprive God and one's fellow man of adequate attention. As spiritual leader of the community Noyes taught that all men and women should love one another. Group marriage, or "complex marriage" as they called it, was practiced as long as the Community existed.

As everyone lived in the Mansion House, sexual relations were easy to arrange through a third party.[17] A man would simply ask the go-between to express his desire to a certain woman, who had the choice of refusing or accepting. Special love between two people was highly undesirable because it supposedly caused selfishness; therefore couples were not allowed to spend the night together for fear they might develop romantic feelings. Coitus reservatus (the withdrawl of the penis before ejaculation) was successfully utilized as the contraceptive method to control the population of the Community. Special permits had to be obtained to have children. After approximately a year and a half of breast feeding, in the care of the mother, children were reared communally. Parents treated their children lovingly, but an effort was made to treat all children equally. Noyes, impressed with the writings of Galton and Darwin, prescribed a method of scientific propagation referred to as stripiculture. Committees were set up to make the selection of parents, or strips, as various people requested permission to have children. The program was an apparent success, providing healthy, vigorous children with a lower death rate than that experienced in the surrounding community and a longevity figure substantially higher than actuarial expectancy.[18]

What happened to put an end to the Community after more than thirty vigorous years? Various writers seem to agree on two points: (1) hostility from the outside, and (2) the loss of their charismatic leader, John Humphrey Noyes. Although many who were in contact with the Oneidans respected them, outsiders must have wondered about their strange behavior, some of which would appear radical even today. For instance, Oneidan women bobbed their hair and wore a type of pantalet trousers. This was quite a change from the long hair and cumbersome floor-length dresses of the day. In addition, their economic success and equalization of sex roles must have appeared threatening to some. Also, their religion was different in that they believed that Christ's second coming was an accomplished fact. Perhaps all of this could have been overlooked, however, if the Community's sexual behavior had not differed so radically from the monogamous norm. It is said that the practice of the older men and women initiating the young girls and boys into the Community's system of complex marriage was difficult for even some of the members to cope with. The fact that some of these young girls were undoubtedly under New York's statutory age limit provided the outside world with a way of legally coercing the Community. Noyes, probably one of the older men involved, presumably desiring to avoid scandal and prosecution, resigned as the leader of the Community in 1877 and two years later moved to Canada.

Noyes was a remarkable man with tremendous personal appeal. Apparently he was, to use sociologist William Kephart's words, "much more than the extraordinary leader. He was the indispensable man."[19] When he left the Community, the void could not be adequately filled. In the face of renewed hostile attacks by the local clergy, the question of continuing with their religious and social experiment arose. The matter was studied, discussed, and then voted upon by a committee of the whole, as was their life-long custom. In 1880 the old Community was dissolved and a joint stock company, Oneida Ltd., was formed with the assets. Members were given shares commensurate with the number of years they had lived in the Community and the amount of property they had contributed upon joining. Some moved away, but many remained at the Mansion House.

The enthusiastic testimony of the descendants of the Community, some of whom still live in the old Mansion House, seems to reflect a certain nostalgia for their parents' way of life. Yet today Oneida is more likely to bring to mind quality silver service than thoughts of a relatively successful experimental community.

Retreat from utopia   The recent twentieth century renewed search for utopia and a sense of community appears to differ from the nineteenth century movement in several important ways. Kanter suggests that in general the contemporary communal movement encompasses fewer visions of social reconstruction, less hope for permanence, fewer institutions, and fewer demands on its members than was typical of the nineteenth century utopian communities. She attributes much of this change to the differences in American society, in the 1840s to 1860s and the 1960s to 1970s.

Although the periods are similar in many aspects (for example, social movements involving women and blacks, religious revivalism, and dissatisfaction with capitalism), there appears to be more emphasis on individual fulfillment, extended families, and turning to the past in the 1960s and 1970s. Personal fulfillment was considered important but secondary in the nineteenth century movements. Many contemporary communes, however, see individual growth as more important than economic and political change, social reform, or the community's welfare. The ethic of "doing one's own thing" frees a person to leave when he is no longer satisfied. It also has the effect of limiting a person's involvement with the group.

Kanter suggests that the names of contemporary communes and the ways in which they recruit their members reflect a change of focus from that of an alternative society to that of an alternative family style. Oneida Community and Harmony Society were typical names a century ago, while the Lyman Family and the Family of the Mystic Arts seem more representative of the current movement. Many contemporary communes develop out of friendship rather than out of a shared ideology, and as a result, group goals probably reflect a greater emphasis on individual growth than on the realization of a particular ideology.

Nineteenth century communes were future oriented in that the members believed they were capable of creating a better society, perhaps even anticipating human evolution. Present-day communes are more likely to romanticize about the past, as is reflected in the "back to the earth" movements to get in touch with nature, each other, and themselves. The sense of impermanance of many contemporary communes might also be interpreted as lack of a future orientation; terms such as *trip*, *scene*, and *into*, frequently used to describe communal experiences, convey an episodic quality. Kanter suggests that communal living for many people today may represent a way of making do during a particular phase of a peron's life rather than a commitment to a way of life oriented toward the future.

In brief, as one social observer put it, many contemporary communes seek "Eden rather than Utopia."[20] Instead of a designed and imposed social order, many of today's communards strive for an order that is spontaneous, flowing, and natural.

Contemporary communal arrangements Communes are becoming so numerous that it is difficult for someone who might be interested in this life-style to know which kinds of arrangements are most likely to be compatible with his goals. Distinct types, however, seem to be emerging. We will look at two systems of classification in the hope that this information will be not only interesting but useful for anyone desiring to seek out a type of commune that will meet his needs.

After visiting thirty communes in various parts of the United States, Herbert Otto, chairperson of the National Center for the Exploration of Human Potential, categorized eleven different types.

The agricultural subsistence commune   The main thrust is to farm or till the soil (mostly organic farming) so that the land will provide most, if not all, needs and make the commune independent and self-supporting. Many of these communes cultivate such specialized crops or organically grown grain, vegetables, and other produce, which are then sold to health-food stores, health-food wholesalers, or supermarkets.

The nature commune   Emphasis is on supporting the ecological system and on the enjoyment of nature. Buildings and gardening or farming plots are designed to fit into the landscape to preserve its natural beauty. Everyone "does his own thing," and economic support for subsistence usually comes from such varied sources as sale of produce and handicrafts, wages from part-time work, welfare support, etc.

The denominational commune   There is a religious emphasis with membership restricted to those of a particular denomination. Examples are the Episcopalian Order of St. Michael, in Crown Point, Indiana, and the Catholic Worker Farm, in Trivoli, New York.

The church-sponsored commune   Such a commune may be originated or sponsored by a church. There is usually a religious emphasis, but denominationalism is not stressed.

The political commune   Members subscribe to or share a common ideology. They may identify themselves as anarchists, socialists, pacificists, etc. Emphasis is on the communal living experience with others sharing the same role in the life of the commune. All adults are considered to be parents of the members' children.

The homosexual commune   Currently found in large urban areas, with admission restricted to homophiles. The aim of these communes is to afford individuals who share a common way of life an opportunity to live and communicate together and to benefit from the economics of a communal living arrangement. Some of the communes subscribe to the principles of the homophile liberation movement. From a recent ad in *Kaliflower*, the bi-weekly information journal for communes in the San Francisco Bay area: "OUR GAY COMMUNE HAS ROOM FOR TWO MORE. CALL AND RAP."

The growth-centered commune   The main focus is on helping members to grow as persons, to actualize their potential. There are ongoing group sessions; sometimes professional are asked to lead these. The commune continues to seek out new experiences and methods designed to develop the potentialities of its members.

The mobile or gypsy commune   This is a caravan, usually on the move. Cars, buses, and trucks provide both transportation and living quarters. Members usually include artists, a rock group, or a light-show staff. The mobile commune often obtains contributions from "happenings" or performances given in communities or on college campuses.

The street or neighborhood commune   Several of these communes often are on the same street or in the same neighborhood. Ownership of property is in the hands of commune members or friendly and sympathetic neighbors. Basically the idea is of a free enclave or free community. For example, in a recent *New York Times* article, Albert Solnit, chief of advance planning for California's Marin County, was reported at work "on a city of 20,000 for those who wish to live communally."

The craft commune   One or several crafts, such as weaving, pottery making, or carpentry (including construction or work on buildings outside the commune), occupy the interest of members. They often spend considerable blocks of time enjoying the exercise of their craft with the income contributed to the commune. Many of the craft communes sell directly to the consumer as a result of local, regional, or sometimes national advertisements and publicity. Profit margins vary since the vast majority of such communes do not subscribe to the amassing of profits as the primary aim of their enterprise. Included in this category are the multi-media communes that specialize in light shows, video tape, and film-making.

The spiritual-mystic commune   The ongoing spiritual development of members is recognized to be of primary importance. There may be adherence to a religious system, such as Buddhism, Sufism, or Zen, and a teacher or guru may be involved. Studies of various texts and mystical works, use of rituals, a number of forms of meditation (such as transcendental or Zen meditation), and spontaneous spiritual celebrations play key roles in the life of the commune. Several of these communes also describe themselves as Christian and have a strong spiritual, but not denominational, emphasis.[21]

A broader and perhaps more heuristic typology is offered by Kanter. On the basis of three years of research and personal experiences, she classifies contemporary communes into three types according to their goals and boundaries—traditional utopian, retreat, and service. Traditional utopian communities are those which are committed to developing a new society on the basis of the utopian principles of human perfectability, order, brotherhood, unity of mind and body, experimentation, and coherence as a group. Such communities may be thought of as having fairly closed systems; that is, they relate very little to other societal systems. Boundaries are very clear; a member knows who is and who is not a community member and relates differently to each. Outside influences appear to have little impact on the organization of these communities; in other words, outside systems effect little change on traditional utopian communities. The Bruderhof, Amish, Hutterites, and Twin Oaks belong to this category. Twin Oaks is based on behaviorist B. F. Skinner's *Walden Two*, although it incorporates some features of the Oneida Community.

Retreat communes are characterized as having weak, "negative" boundaries.

They tend to be small, anarchistic, youth-oriented, and predominantly rural. They are easily dissolved because they lack a common ideology and defined patterns of behavior, rules, or organization. Without a common ground of interest to unite members, rules for joining (for instance, a membership fee or relinquishment of private property), or some kind of organization for maintenance of the commune (for example, all work may be voluntary), it is difficult for members to distinguish between themselves and nonmembers, and consequently to define themselves as a group. Kanter reports that the looseness of boundaries and organization characteristics of these groups frequently contribute to failure to complete jobs, lack of success in working out conflicts, and difficulty in developing a "family feeling." Otto's nature communes belong to this category.

Service communes have boundaries which tend to be more "positive" than "negative," more strict than permissive, and more exclusive than inclusive. They tend to be larger and less youth-oriented than retreat communes and are frequently found in urban settings. Service communes have an ideological orientation which is integral to their organization. They tend to have definitions of appropriate behavior and a distinctive life-style which members are expected to adopt. Rules are clear and explicit, if not always formalized. There is sufficient organization to accomplish the necessary work and some system of decision making. A clearly defined membership makes it possible for members to know at any given time who is a member and who is not. Visitors are not admitted to service communes as often as is the case in retreat communes, and when they are, their activities are frequently controlled or watched. For example, one commune runs a coffeehouse once a week as a place where visitors and members can interact. The coffeehouse has the added advantage of insuring that nonmembers at least partially pay their own way. Synanon, a drug rehabilitation community, and Esalen, a permanent service community which takes in people for certain periods of time to help them grow as individuals, are examples of this type of commune.

Pluses and minuses of communal life The advantages and disadvantages of communal living compared to conventional monogamous marriage are numerous. One of the more important advantages is an increased sense of community, which affords opportunities for greater intimacy with a variety of people. The availability of multifaceted love, sex, childrearing, and other human relationships are much greater in communal arrangements than in the monogamous situation.

An inherent disadvantage is the loss of privacy and time for oneself. This is frequently aggravated by overcrowding, which Otto reports is a major problem for most communes. Another disadvantage is the frequent hostility expressed by unfriendly neighbors, local authorities, and the larger community. Many communes, aware of this, are actively working to promote good community relations. The use of narcotics occasionally leads to difficulties, although some communities forbid the use of drugs, including alcohol. The casual use of marihuana and hashish is common in many communes. Heroin is rarely encountered, reports Otto, who also feels that the use of many hallucinogens such as LSD is on the decline.

Other advantages and disadvantages have been alluded to in the course of the discussion on communal living, and naturally these vary by type of commune. For instance, the looseness of organization characteristic of the so-called "retreatist" communes provides maximum freedom to "do your own thing." One might starve to death, however, if he had to rely on complete communal cooperation to get a meal on the table.

Longevity Many view communal living more as an experience than as a commitment to a particular way of living. Others, however, desire to adopt this life-style on a long-range basis. Predictions of longevity for any particular kind of commune are risky. Many are short-lived, while a few, such as the Hutterites, have existed for over a century—far exceeding the life-spans of their founders.

When talking about longevity of communes, we make the assumption that a fundamental difference between communes and monogamous marriage is the relationship between these systems and the larger society. In addition to the members' desire to maintain or break up a marital or communal system, there are outside forces acting to *maintain* monogamous marriages (for example, strict divorce laws, the stigma of divorce, and so on) and to *break up* communes (for example, residential zoning ordinances specifying kinship or legal relationship as a condition for occupancy of single family dwellings or rental units). As a result a communal system probably cannot endure as much internal dissension as monogamous marriages.

In an attempt to ferret out the factors that contribute to longevity, Kanter compared nine successful (lasting over thirty-three years) with twenty-one unsuccessful (lasting under sixteen years) nineteenth century U.S. communes. She argues, on the basis of her research, that the primary issue a community must deal with is human organization—how people arrange to do the work essential to group survival and how the community involves and satisfies its members over time. The idealized vision of communal living must be integrated with the reality of necessary work. Kanter states the issue graphically by asking, "In utopia . . . who takes out the garbage?"[22]

The organizational issues are essentially facets of commitment reflecting how members relate to the work of the community, to its goals, and to one another, and how much independence members are willing to relinquish in the interests of the commune.

A person is committed to a group or to a relationship

when he himself is fully invested in it, so that the maintenance of his own internal being requires behavior that supports the social order. A committed person is loyal and involved; he has a sense of belonging, a feeling that the group is an extension of himself and he is an extension of the group. Through commitment, person and group are inextricably linked.[23]

Commitment can be promoted and sustained in a variety of ways. Turning one's property over upon admission to the community with no way of getting it back and abrogating the right to accumulate additional personal property appear to be important in assuring that members will be committed to trying to realize the ideals of the commune. For instance, the data in Figure 6-1 indicate that all the successful communities required members, upon joining, to turn over all their property to the commune. Kanter also points out that these communities were more likely to own the land, the building, the furniture and tools, and even the clothing and personal effects each member wore. None of the successful communities gave any compensation for labor or charged for community services. They set up daily routines, and everyone worked for the good of the community. This was the case in less than half of those which were unsuccessful.

Table 6-1   *A Comparison of Nine Successful and Twenty-one Unsuccessful Utopian Communities*

	Successful Communities	Unsuccessful Communities
Financial Investment		
Property signed over at admission	100%	45%
Irreversibility of investment	30	0
Boundary Maintenance		
Nonresidential members prohibited	86	41
Self-contained	100	55
Different dress	89	30
Different language, jargon	56	14
Ritual		
Songs about the community	63	14
Group singing	100	73
Special community occasions celebrated	83	50
Communal Family Structure		
Free love or celibacy	100	29
Parent-child separation	48	15
Biological families not living together	33	5
Mutual Criticism		
Regular confession	44	0
Mutual-criticism sessions	44	26
Daily group meetings	56	6

Data from Rosabeth Moss Kanter, *Commitment and Community: Communes and Utopias in Sociological Perspective,* Cambridge, Mass.: Harvard University Press, 1972, pp. 82, 92, 105, and 112. Copyright © 1972 by the President and Fellows of Harvard College; by permission of the author and publishers. Reprinted from *Psychology Today* Magazine, July, 1970. Copyright © Ziff-Davis Publishing Company. Reprinted by permission.

Ways of differentiating members from outsiders which seem to have contributed to longevity were differences in dress, language, use of jargon or other special terms, calling outsiders by a specific term, considering outsiders as wicked or evil, ignoring outside newspapers, and being able to sustain all members' needs within the community itself. These mechanisms had the effect of creating fairly closed systems, with distinct visual and verbal boundaries.

The establishment of group solidarity is also related to longevity. Those communes who did not gather together for group singing and special community celebrations had a substantially higher failure rate than those who used these mechanisms to promote "family togetherness," feelings of good times, and brotherly love among themselves.

The systems of sexual relations which seemed most successful in the nineteenth century communes were group marriage (such as that of the Oneidans, who coined the term "free love") and celibacy (as practiced by the Shakers and others). Forty-eight percent of the successful communes compared to 15 percent of the unsuccessful communes adhered to collective child-rearing arrangements, usually deemphasizing the biological aspects in favor of all adults and all children belonging to one another. The emphasis on the group as family was ever-present at meals, work, and leisure.

Successful communes emphasized personal growth in line with ideas of human perfection much more strongly than did unsuccessful communes. Almost half of those surviving thirty-three years or more had some system of feedback to members concerning their behavior and attitudes. For example, the Oneida Community established an elaborate system, called mutual criticism, which required members to submit themselves periodically to a committee of six to twelve peers for criticism. An individual could express his inner secrets, his doubts, problems, weaknesses, and so on to this group, which, in turn, would attempt to help him in his struggle to attain perfection.

How do today's communities measure up to these criteria? Unfortunately, there is a dearth of systematic research on present-day communal living. Evidence suggests that a number of the types listed by Otto incorporate principles of the successful nineteenth century communes, such as group marriage, collective childrearing, and sharing resources and work. One notable exception is prevalent particularly in retreat communes—the lack of central coordination of work arrangements. Otto feels that one of the major problems communards encounter is that of authority and structure. Many members feel that ideally no one should tell anyone else what to do. Often, however, those with strong personalities assume some degree of responsibility. In many communes so much opposition exists to any form of organized structure that not only is there little cooperation with other communes in terms of joint undertakings, but at times the members are unable to cooperate to reach any common goal.

On the basis of Kanter's data we suggest that two kinds of utopian communities will have a long-term future—those organized around religious beliefs (such as the Hutterites, the Bruderhof, and the Oneida communities) and the well-organized growth and learning centers structured around small group interaction, which generates strong group ties and a feeling of family.

Growth centers provide a temporary experience in expressive involvement and intimacy for guests and total involvement for permanent staff members of the community. They tend to have philosophies and explicit sets of values that must be accepted and shared by all members. In addition, they usually have fixed routines and assignments, as well as articulate and forceful leadership.

The small, anarchistic communes, on the other hand, although seeking involvement and intimacy, have little definable pattern, group structure, or rules. Most lack any kind of integrating philosophy. A rather vague desire for group living and closer personal relationships holds members loosely together. These communes do not appear very stable or permanent. However, as Kanter suggests, these small, dissolvable, and unstructured communities may successfully meet the needs of members for a temporary home and family.

Group marriage Strictly defined, communal living involves a sharing of labor, goods, and services. Group marriage refers specifically to sexual relationships among members of a group, consisting of sexual access to all consenting members and implying shared childrearing. Group marriage, then, is only one of a varity of ways, ranging from nonexclusive sex to celibacy, in which people relate to each other in a communal setting.

Two major types of group marriage can be distinguished according to the focus of the members' commitment. If the focus is on the group's philosophy of human society, group marriage is likely to bear some resemblance to that practiced in the Oneida Community. If the commitment to self-fulfillment and other group members take precedence, group marriage will probably resemble what Larry and Joan Constantine defined in the early sixties as multilateral marriages. *Multilateral marriages* are relatively small group marriages of usually more than three men and women. The Constantines estimate that there are somewhere between a hundred and a thousand such marriages in the United States today.[24] They report great diversity in the few they have been able to locate and study. For example, they have found that the participants are between twenty-three and sixty years of age, with about half under thirty; incomes range from somewhat below $10,000 to $100,000 annually; and the only occupational duplications are those of student and housewife.

Multilateral marriages appear to evolve from monogamous units. Usually one married couple acts as a core to which singles or other couples are drawn. Among the more frequently mentioned reasons the participants give for entering a group marriage are those of seeking an expanded family identification and a sense of community, a system beneficial to children (most groups have three or fewer children), sexual freedom, and economic efficiency. Multilateral marriage through a larger "community of intimates" is offered as potentially providing exactly the size and diversity lacking in autonomous, nuclear monogyny.[25] By simply enlarging the group, each individual has a greater number of people to satisfy his needs while he, alone, does not have to satisfy *all* the needs of any particular person.

Implicit in the goals of those involved in multilateral marriages is the notion of self-realization and self-actualization. The Constantines report that the groups appear to operate much like continuous, leaderless encounter groups, with very intense and intimate interaction among all members. One immediate consequence of this, according to the members, is a pressure for growth, with the inherent problem of keeping all group members growing at a compatible rate. The most insecure or the youngest is likely to feel more pressure than the others as the rest of the group impatiently admonishes the laggard to catch up.

The Constantines found that although sex appears to be a fairly central issue, the participants *deemphasize* the sexual dimensions of their multilateral marriages. Sex is not a strong factor for forming a group marriage; rather, the respondents feel it a "retrospective benefit." The majority of both women and men participants appeared to enjoy the sexual variety afforded by their marriage. Certainly, group marriage provides the maximum variety of sexual partners for both sexes within the marriage itself.

Working out sleeping arrangements and sexual sharing, however, is often reported as problematic. Most people involved in multilateral marriage desire natural, spontaneous sexual relations but have found this goal to be elusive.

Even after possessive jealousy recedes into the background, insecurity is manifest in the difficulty of deciding the sleeping arrangements. Unfortunately, immediate preference for one partner is too easily read as sexual rejection of another, and in our society that is tantamount to personal rejection. We would not describe the sexual sharing in any of the groups as truly spontaneous, although clear progress toward this is evident.[26]

Fixed rotation, or the switching of partners every week, enthusiastically espoused by Rimmer,[27] in practice has been found to destroy spontaneity and avoid confrontation of the issue of unequal demand for all partners.

Group sex, or simultaneous sexual activity among three or more participants, appears rare, even though it is considered acceptable and even desirable in some cases. When it does take place, usually one man and two women are involved. Multiple couple sex is very infrequent, perhaps because it has been found by the participants to trigger destructive jealousy and competition, especially among the men, occasionally resulting in temporary impotence.

In order to survive, a multilateral marriage must deal with the jealousy, possessiveness, and competition which arise out of close interactions with one another and out of its sexual arrangement. Participants appear to feel that jealousy is often a behavioral manifestation of other emotional difficulties rather than an *affect* in and of itself. For instance, jealousy may arise when a person desires the exclusive love and affection of another, when a person desires to control or own another as an object (possessiveness), or when a person fears losing the other, whether or not the threat is real. The most common form of jealousy in multilateral marriage seems to be possessiveness, but it is frequently overcome. The Constantines report that most families have found effective ways to deal with these issues so that they are no longer problematic, although all groups reported some residual difficulty.

Participants in these marriages generally hope for greater freedom, especially role freedom, but this desire has been largely unfulfilled. The Constantines found participants to be highly equalitarian in principle but without much reduction in traditional sex roles. The researchers, however, do report greater success in other areas. The participants strongly feel that group marriage is an improvement over monogamous marriage for childrearing. They also express more meaningful self-insight in personal growth as a result of the group experience.

What are the prospects for group marriage? As with all forms that deviate from the monogamous norm, great hostility exists. The survival of group marriages today depends to no small degree on how well the group can maintain anonymity from the outside world. Whether outside hostility stems from resentment over the increased freedom of others, guilt, or "righteous" wrath over extramarital sexual involvement is an interesting question; it is less serious, however, than the question of how to survive without any external support in the face of such hostility.

Selecting a Life-style

In the beginning of this chapter we pointed out that people in our society increasingly share the general goals of self-fulfillment, self-realization, and contentment. For most, one way of working toward these goals is by interacting with the opposite sex. What happens when two young people in college fall in love and then wonder whether or not they should get married? A typical couple might ask themselves if they are right for each other, if their hopes can be realized in marriage, if they are ready for marriage, and if marriage will block the achievement of other important goals.

If both want to have satisfying occupational careers, they are faced with the possibility that after graduation their respective jobs might well separate them geographically. Moreover, they have seen many friends' marriages break up, with considerable expense and distress to the couple, their parents, and their friends.

Being good problem solvers, they try to think of all possible alternatives, and they end up with a list of possibilities:

1. marriage
2. communal living
3. continue dating
4. split up
5. trial marriage
6. live together

They examine each alternative to see if it requires any opportunities or resources which they do not have or any behavior modification which they think is unethical or which will block their goals.

In discussing the first alternative, marriage, it becomes evident that neither wants to marry at this point in time. Both have been brought up to view marriage as a very serious and permanent step involving considerable responsibility. Neither wants children right now, and neither is certain about being able to live compatibly with the other. Each is worried that the other might not change as rapidly, or as slowly, or in the same direction as he does. In addition, the woman views marriage as confining and detrimental to personal growth. Both are afraid that marriage as they envision it will not help them attain their individual goals of personal fulfillment and happiness and, indeed, may impair their efforts. Therefore, they decide to discard this alternative.

Their discussion of communal living brings out some revealing information. Both feel that their commitment to each other is stronger than their commitment to any utopian ideal, so they agree that if they were to live cooperatively or communally, the basis for forming a group would be that of friendship. Although both are intrigued with the idea, they cannot agree on even one other person they would both like to live with, so they eliminate communes as a viable alternative for the present.

They admit that continuing to date or splitting up are both viable—although they don't like these alternatives. In the back of their minds lurks the realization that if they cannot come up with something to which they will both agree, they are likely to continue dating until graduation, at which time they will probably split up.

Because neither feels ready to marry at this time, they reject the idea of a trial marriage. They agree that if they set a time when they will have to make a decision about getting married, their goals of personal fulfillment will be distorted. In addition, they are afraid of falling into the trap of defining their relationship to each other according to the normative roles of husband and wife; they feel this will stifle their efforts to relate to each other as distinct individuals.

After considerable discussion, they determine that simply living together might be an acceptable alternative, although they wonder if it will be any more viable than marriage. Projecting themselves into the situation of living together, they try to anticipate the difficulties they will probably encounter. They decide that the two most important issues to be faced are the reactions of their parents and their own fears of falling into the very interaction patterns they are trying to avoid by not getting married.

The woman is more concerned about her parents than the man is, although he shares much of the same anxiety. Both feel very strongly that they have to tell their parents about their plans to live together in order to keep them from being hurt by finding out from someone else. He feels that once he has worked up the courage to tell his parents, they will probably accept the idea, although they might not agree that he is acting wisely. In fact, he thinks they might even be relieved, since they have expressed concern about the possibility of his settling down with the responsibilities of a wife and family before he becomes established in his career. She, however, feels that her parents will not be as understanding. She has been brought up, like most girls in our society, to be more dependent on her parents than he is on his, and she is very concerned about how her parents might react. She knows they will try to talk her out of it, but what she fears more is that they will reject her. Although she does not anticipate being disowned, she feels that living with her boy friend would definitely alter her relationship with her parents. After much thoughtful deliberation, she decides that she has to do what she feels is best for herself and hope that her parents will understand and accept her decision. If they do not, she feels that she is strong enough to withstand whatever pressures they might exert on her to conform to their wishes, even if they ultimately break off their relationship with her.

As for friends and prospective employers, both feel that their private lives are their own business and that friends and employers will have to accept them as they are.

But can they define their relationship in such a way that their personal goals will not be thwarted? She is particularly concerned about the possibility of subtle exploitation in the house. She intends to have a career and does not believe that just because she is a woman she has any particular expertise, desire, or duty to cook, clean, or do laundry. They finally resolve the issue by drawing up a list of every chore they can think of, from emptying the garbage to paying the bills, and working out schedules which they will rotate. After some estimation of living expenses and income, they decided to pool 60 percent of the take-home pay of each to cover housing, food, entertainment, and other shared expenses. The remaining 40 percent is to be spent as each sees fit. They agree that after the first few months they will evalute their division of labor and financial situation to see how adequate their planning is.

Both are still worried about the expectations each has of the other and of the relationship. This proves to be the hardest issue to resolve. They try to think of what might get in the way of their goal of individual fulfillment and come up with the following questions. How much privacy does each expect? How possessive and jealous is each, and how can such feelings be handled? How much independence does each have a right to or want? What are the responsibilities each has to the other? Why does each want to live with the other, and what are their visions of togetherness? And are these goals shared, or at least not contradictory?

After many interesting evenings of debate, they decide that they have answered these questions adequately and that living together is preferable to continued dating or splitting up. Clearly this is a temporary solution. Graduation will bring them face to face with the problem of seeking jobs in the same or different communities. At this point they may have to examine the depth of their commitment to each other compared to their careers. Again they will have to consider whether marriage or any other alternative is a possible solution.

The Probabilities of Marriage

Recent census data indicate that almost 90 percent of all North Americans marry at some point in their lives, and there is little evidence at present to suggest a strong downward trend in marriage rates. Conventional monogamous marriage, therefore, is likely to be the major marital arrangement for some time to come—accompanied by an increasing tolerance of alternative life-styles.

Each of us, in the final analysis, must make up our own mind on the basis of what we know about ourself and the people who are important to us. Our purpose in this chapter, as throughout the book, has been to provide relevant information and possible ways of thinking about problems, which, however, must be solved by the individual.

Summary

A growing number of individuals are looking at marriage as only one alternative and are considering other life-styles to meet their needs. We cannot predict what forms marriage will take in the future, but we can predict that humans will desire some type of close interpersonal relationship to meet their needs.

The people who are experimenting with alternative systems are those who do not find enough satisfaction in the usual arrangements. A small but growing number of people, many over thirty years old and many from the more traditional and respectable occupations, are struggling and experimenting to find a better fit between the demands of the larger society and their personal desires than contemporary monogamous marriage seems to offer them.

On an actuarial basis it appears that the likelihood of success in the near future for most alternatives is lower than for more conventional marriages. This prediction is based on the lack of appropriate models and modes of behavior as guidelines. Persons electing these new ways of living generally seem to know more about what they do not want than about what they do want. Developing appropriate modes of behavior, defining boundaries, and the like require substantial amounts of time and therefore necessitate a tremendous amount of commitment on the part of the people involved. In addition, some of the life-style values of particular groups conflict with those of the larger society, and when translated into behavior, collisions are inevitable. It is safe to say that the stronger the negative sanction against a particular system, the less likely it is that the system will survive over time.

Notes

1. Dianne Kieren, "Marital Role Expectations of Canadian High School Students," mimeographed interim research report, June 1971.

2. George P. Murdock, "World Ethnographic Sample," *American Anthropologist* 59 (1957), 686.

3. Figures cited in Herbert Otto, "Communes: The Alternative Life Style," *Saturday Review*, April 24, 1971, pp. 16-21.

4. Statistics from research cited by Sam Newlund, "Cohabitation—A Growing Reality," *Minneapolis Tribune*, June 10, 1973, p. 1E.

5. Floyd M. Levin, "Life Styles and Life Insurance," *Best Review*, Spring 1973, p. 22.

6. Dan Golenpaul, ed., *Information Please Almanac 1970* (New York: Dan Golenpaul Associates, 1969), p. 637.

7. The *Demographic Yearbook* for 1970 indicates that, based on 1968 data, the Canadian marriage rates are 8.6/1000 persons compared with 10.6/1000 persons for the United States.

8. Judith Lyness, Milton Lipetz, and Keith Davis, "Living Together: An Alternative to Marriage," *Journal of Marriage and the Family* 34 (May 1972), 305-312.

9. Victor Kassel, "Polygyny after Sixty," in Herbert Otto, ed., *The Family in Search of a Future* (New York: Appleton-Century-Crofts), 1970), pp. 137-144.

10. William N. Stephens, *The Family in Cross-Cultural Perspective* (New York: Holt, Rinehart & Winston, 1963), chapter 2.

11. Rosabeth Moss Kanter, *Commitment and Community: Communes and Utopias in Sociological Perspective* (Cambridge, Mass.: Harvard University Press, 1972).

12. Ibid.

13. Ibid., p. 56-57.

14. In upper New York state alone, the following groups were among those established in the eighteenth and nineteenth centuries: the Bloomfield Association, the Ontario Union, the Moorhouse Union, the Jefferson County Phalanx, and the Shaker Community at New Lebanon. Maren L. Carden, *Oneida: Utopian Community to Modern Corporation* (Baltimore: Johns Hopkins Press, 1969).

15. William Kephart, "Experimental Family Organization: An Historical-Cultural Report on the Oneida Community," *Journal of Marriage and the Family* 25 (August 1963), 261-271.

16. Carden, *Oneida*.

17. According to Kephart, it is not known if a woman could also take the initiative. Kephart, "Experimental Family Organization."

18. Ibid., p. 268.

19. Ibid., p. 268.

20. Judson Jerome, quoted in Kanter *Commitment and Community*, p. 168.

21. Otto, "Communes," pp. 17-20.

22. Kanter, *Commitment and Community*, p. 64.

23. Kanter, *Commitment and Community*, p. 66.

24. Constantine, Larry and Joan. "Where Is Marriage Going?" *The Futurist*, 4 (April 1970) 44-46.

25. The Constantines define *monogyny* as one spouse at a time as opposed to *monogamy* (one lifetime mate). Monogyny is more frequently referred to by other writers as serial monogamy.

26. Larry and Joan Constantine, The Group Marriage in Michael Gordon (ed.) *The Nuclear Family in Crisis: The Search for an Alternative* (New York: Harper & Row, 1972), p. 215.

27. Robert Rimmer, *Proposition 31* (New York: Holt, Rinehart and Winston, inc., 1971).

Suggested Readings

Baker, Luther, Jr. "The Personal and Social Adjustment of the Never-Married Woman." *Journal of Marriage and the Family* 30 (August 1968), 473-479. Disputes current contemporary stereotypes picturing the never-married woman as deficient in personal and social adjustment. Also presents data indicating that marriage and motherhood are not necessary to feminine fulfillment.

Gordon, Michael, ed. *The Nuclear Family in Search of a Crisis: The Search for an Alternative.* New York: Harper & Row, 1972. Book of readings which focuses primarily on past and present communal living patterns.

Kanter, Rosabeth Moss. *Commitment and Community: Communes and Utopias in Sociological Perspective.* Cambridge, Mass.: Harvard University Press, 1972. For those interested in communal living this book presents an objective view of the nineteenth and twentieth century communal movements in the United States, detailing their successes and failures.

Kinkade, Kathleen. "Commune: A Walden-Two Experiment." *Psychology Today,*

January and February 1973, pp. 357 and 717 *respectively.* A member's candid and intimate account of communal life at Twin Oaks, a five year old community founded on the philosophy of B. F. Skinner.

Keller, Suzanne. "Does the Family Have a Future?" *Journal of Comparative Family Studies* (Spring 1971), 1-14. One of the more thought-provoking articles on the subject to date. Refutes the universality of the family and the notion that the family is *the* basic unit of society, discusses challenges to the contemporary industrial family, and suggests implications for the family of recent biological discoveries.

"The Future of Women and Marriage." *The Futurist* 4 (July 1970). An issue of the magazine which raises many pertinent questions about women's roles and alternate family forms.

7

Selecting a Mate

Marriage is widespread in our society, and mate selection is a problem faced by most young adults. In fact, people have been marrying earlier than they used to. During the last part of the nineteenth century, the median age at first marriage was approximately 26.1 for men and 22.0 for women. In 1959 it was 22.5 for men and 20.2 for women. (By 1970 the median age had risen to 23.2 for men and 20.8 for women, still below the median age for the last century.)[1]

Pressures for marriage have been strong ever since the Puritans settled in New England in the early seventeenth century. These people believed that God had ordained marriage for man, and His law was enforced by their regulations. Those who did not marry were fined or placed in some other familial living arrangement. In Massachusetts, for example, if a single man could not afford to hire servants, and in this manner set up a household (family) for himself, he was required to enter another family as servant or boarder.[2] Other colonies taxed the single man more heavily than the married man.[3] Living alone was considered sinful.

Subtle and not-so-subtle pressures continue today. For instance, the U.S. federal income tax structure favors married couples who file jointly rather than individually. The "harmless" teasing of a young boy about his girl friend intensifies over the years, so that by the time he is out of school, friends and relatives are questioning him about whether he has a girl, and *if* not, *why* not! And senior panic, the fear that "everyone will be engaged but me," is illustrative of group pressure to marry within a certain time period. Group pressures would not be terribly successful if marriage provided little personal gain; in fact, however, it offers (or seems to offer) the solution to a number of problems.

As we showed earlier, people marry for a variety of reasons; that is, they see marriage as a way of achieving a number of goals. Some marry to obtain emotional support. As society becomes increasingly urbanized and mobile, relationships with fellow workers, neighbors, and tradespeople become less personal and more transitory. Under these conditions, close personal relations become more important. Since warmth, understanding, intimacy, and loyalty are not easily found in the everyday world of work or even play, marriage is seen as one possible way of obtaining them.

Others marry to gain status—the status of adulthood, "maturity," and responsible citizenship, as well as the status of wealth if the partner has money. Moreover, through marriage one can attain the social approval which comes of having a beautiful or handsome spouse, admission into a desirable family, and sexual accessibility.

Kirkpatrick suggests several additional motives for seeking a mate.[4] One of these he calls awareness of economy of effort. Any dating situation, even if it is very casual, makes demands upon one's time and energy. It is not always easy to find a date when a person wants one, and making and breaking even casual commitments involves some inconvenience. In addition, various preliminaries are necessary before satisfaction can be gained from contact with the opposite sex. Sooner or later the thought arises that life would be more secure, less competitive, and simpler if a single serious relationship could be established to gratify a variety of needs.

Another motive is the need for a love-companionship relationship. This is often difficult to obtain without either marriage or commitment leading to marriage. Kirkpatrick feels that we have a need for love and another need for companionship; and often we try to have both needs met by one person. Today, middle-class attitudes toward marriage reflect the expectation that one's partner should be the person responsible for meeting most of one's needs; particularly in the area of love-companionship. Whether, in actual fact, this expectation can realistically be met is another matter entirely.

According to Kirkpatrick, a more subtle motive for marriage is the family situation and parental roles that provide models which the child is likely to adopt as an adult. Since our norms decree that reproduction and childrearing take place within the context of marriage, people wanting children usually find a partner so they can raise a family.

Other reasons for marriage include escaping from an unhappy home, from loneliness, or just from being single; acquiring material possessions, wealth, and/or prestige; living vicariously through others; and legitimizing a child.

Whatever an individual's motivations for marriage, the satisfaction of those objectives lies in his ability and willingness to carefully deliberate over the selection of his spouse and to become confident of their compatibility. Our primary purpose in this chapter is to suggest means by which the potential compatibility of marriage partners can be evaluated.

It has been said that those decisions which are the most important in our lives also create the greatest amount of ambivalence within us. Since the choice of a marriage partner is probably one of the most significant decisions that a person will ever make, it should also follow that this decision may be one of the most difficult to make.

In terms of problem solving, it is unlikely that one will have to choose among several prospects at a given time. Rather, the problem will more likely be whether one specific person is the "right" one or if it would be better to wait for someone else to come along. All too frquently individuals do not give enough serious consideration to this problem and merely assume that they are making the right choices without facing up to the hard issues.

We suggested in Chapter 4 that love is usually one prerequisite to marriage. However, some of the magical, mystical misconceptions about love which have been perpetuated over time (such as "love at first sight" and the myth of the "one and only") have been uncovered, and it has been found that the romanticism of a strong love relationship does not just happen with anyone who initially attracts us. Instead, we are attracted to certain types of people, and given the opportunity we interact with them over time and eventually end up loving them.

Similarly, in the matter of mate selection it is a mistaken belief that young people in North America enjoy unlimited freedom. Even in this society we find there are certain constraints on "free choice." These constraints begin subtly long before one's first date and usually manifest themselves most strongly when the young adult becomes "serious" about a member of the opposite sex.

For those who deny the existence of indirect controls within our society, let us visualize the effects of random dating. For instance, considering the proportions of various groups in the total population, Catholics and Jews would marry Protestants more often than not; blacks, Indians, Orientals, and Spanish Americans would be more likely to marry whites than members of their own groups; college graduates would be more likely to marry high school dropouts than other college graduates; and the old would marry the young. The fact that this does not occur suggests the existence of controls that define boundaries within which individuals are free to choose their marriage partners.

This being the case, if one is to make a sound judgment about whether he can possibly have a successful marriage with a given person, perhaps it would be wise to stop and consider what boundaries exist and how they can influence his chances for a satisfactory relationship.

Field of Eligibles

All individuals who are potential marriage partners for a person make up his *field of eligibles*. Theoretically, this field may include almost anyone. Realistically, however, certain patterns of association seriously restrict actual possibilities.

Mating Gradient

One of our society's cultural sanctions governing mate selection is the tendency of men to marry downward (and women upward) on a number of characteristics such as age, height, education, and intelligence.[5] While there is nothing inherently sacred in any of these notions, they are subtly ingrained in us. For instance, the idea that a man should be taller than a woman has no relation to marital happiness. But if we pass a couple on the street and the woman is taller than the man, we do a double take. Furthermore, women who go out with shorter men consciously try to minimize the height difference, for example, they might wear flats instead of heels or change to a hairstyle that makes them look shorter.

With education the matter has been much more serious than just concern over how people react to the taller woman. Women in the past have had to be concerned about how much education they could acquire without jeopardizing their chances for marriage. Before the improvement of contraception, marriage was often followed automatically by pregnancy, which frequently called a halt to educational pursuits. For many women, therefore, it became a matter of continuing with their education and running the risk of narrowing their field of eligibles or marrying and postponing their educational pursuits indefinitely.

The age variable of the mating gradient also favors men. Since men are expected to be older than their wives, a man who is eighty years old theoretically can consider every unmarried woman under eighty as a potential mate. This is a little extreme, of course, but the odds are particularly unfavorable for women as they become older. A thirty-five-year-old woman who wishes to marry is faced with finding a man who is thirty-five or older, who is not married, and who would be a desirable partner. Many people would say that by that age most of the "good prospects" are already married. If, on the other hand, a man decides to delay marriage until he is thirty-five, the younger women who compose his field of eligibles include those who are just approaching the marriageable age and are of high desirability. It is easy to see the basis for the "senior panic" referred to earlier in the chapter.

Propinquity

Another factor which operates in the mate selection process is proximity, or nearness (frequently referred to as *propinquity*). This factor is obvious, but its very obviousness often allows it to be overlooked. Since it is the strongest determinant in defining one's field of eligibles, it merits explicit mention here. With rare exceptions (such as computer matchmaking or mail-order brides(propinquity is a precondition for engaging in interaction with others and, therefore, for selecting a mate. Your choices are limited to people you know.

When our society was made up of rural communities, the chance of meeting and getting to know people other than those from nearby communities was extremely small. But even in urban environments choices are limited. Studies of Italian communities in New York, for example, indicate that opportunities to meet members of the opposite sex are greatly restricted to the immediate Italian community. This is a reflection of choices based not on ethnicity but on geographical propinquity.

Even the university and college systems served a very restricted group of white middle-class people until after World War II. Since then the base of education has broadened to include many more groups, particularly in the United States. This has increased the probabilities of persons of diverse cultures marrying by bringing them together in a single locale.

Although the propinquity factor can be used to explain why individuals choose certain mates, it is not a concern for conscious deliberation except as it relates to other factors, such as ethnicity.

Ideal Mate

One further determinant in the process of mate selection is one's image of the ideal mate. Nearly every young person cherishes in his imagination a picture of the mental, moral, termperamental, and social traits (as well as the appearance and physical attributes) of the person he hopes to marry. For some the image is vague; for others, it is clearly defined.

The roles of men and women and the nature of the marital system in a particular society influence one's conception of the ideal mate. Ideal traits change to keep pace with the sex role differentiation within the society. Since the turn of the century, the ideal husband in the U.S. has changed from a rugged individualist whose main role was family provider to one who interacts well with his wife. The ideal wife has changed from one whose major tasks were to keep house and bear and rear children to one who relates to the interpersonal needs of her husband. These changes have paralleled the decline in importance of physical strength for survival, the action of the feminist movement of the early twentieth century, the continued sex role differentiation following that era, and the current push for equality of women. Notions of masculinity and femininity are influenced in much the same manner.

Society's definition of the ideal mate influences our choice by conferring status on those who most closely approximate the ideal.[6] The person who gets such a mate also acquires esteem and admiration, because the "ideal mate" would not have married that person unless he got something in exchange. In addition, since the set of desirable traits to be found in a mate are culturally specified, these characteristics are often attributed to the person with whom one is in love, regardless of whether or not the person possesses them. This process has been called "idealization of the mate."

Another aspect of the ideal mate image is the personality makeup of the individual holding the image. Sociologist J. Richard Udry found that ideal mate descriptions obtained from unmarried subjects were heavily influenced by their own personalities.[7] This finding supports the notion that mates are important sources of need gratification.[8]

How much influence does the image of the ideal mate have on the actual selection of a mate? A person's preconceived ideas about such social characteristics as religion, race, socioeconomic status, and education frequently (and often unconsciously) narrow the number of people he would marry. In terms of physical and personality traits, the image appears to operate more "ideally" in the initial stages of mate selection; it changes in the course of one's interaction with persons of the opposite sex until it finally becomes more a product of one's experiences than a determinant of the choice of a mate.[9]

Parent Image

Closely related to the available evidence linking an ideal with a chosen mate is the impact of the parent image. Anselm Strauss contends that the "ideal image" originates in childhood as the individual develops feelings about the parent of the opposite sex—feelings which are basically general in nature and which constitute influences that are seldom dealt with on a conscious level.[10] Some individuals, however, are aware of their feelings, as can be illustrated by this interview reported by Strauss:

Dad's a very accommodating soul. He's lenient, understanding. And I've always been his favorite—I suppose that's something, too. My dad and I were always very close. With my dad it was always more or less a playful relationship. He was always pampering me no end. Naturally I liked that. My ideal has been based on him to some extent: generosity, likability, jovial, sense of humor. My fiancé is very close to the ideal. He comes the closest to it of any boy I ever met. The fact that he was understanding was the primary factor; and the sense of humor was second. He was talkative and jolly. My father and he resemble each other as far as personality is concerned: generous, loyal to friends and family. They're very much the same. My fiance and I act toward each other very much the same as my father and I: companionship, laughter, gaiety. He's always had my interest at heart. He and dad think I'm tops.[11]

This is a good example, we believe, of a young woman who relates positively to her father and makes no excuses about comparing him with her fiancé. This attitude is encountered often in the classroom, particularly among women. Men seldom claim they would like to marry a woman similar to their mother. It is not clear whether fewer men than women idealize the parent of the opposite sex or whether the reaction is merely a reflection of men's efforts to "cut the apron strings," in keeping with societal expectations.

We do not intend to belabor this parent image issue, especially since empirical supportive evidence is scarce. On the other hand, knowing how influential the early parent-child relationship is on the mature child, there seems to be a good case for giving the idea at least passing consideration. In sum, positive experiences with the parent of the opposite sex may encourage one to wish to recreate a similar situation with one's spouse, while negative experiences encourage one to look for characteristics opposite to those of the parent. Positive or negative, the impact is there.

Many young couples are sensitive to the factors in their experiences which constitute a basis for their feelings and know that much of their emotional makeup originates with the family. They are aware that extreme parental attachments which interfere with the development of normal heterosexual relationships are unhealthy, and they control their emotions accordingly.

Complementary Needs

An additional factor influencing one to become attracted to certain types of people is known as *personality needs*. In a study involving a small sample of college students, Robert Winch collected data in support of a mate selection theory of complementary needs.[12] He discovered that the final choice of a mate is based on whether the couple have needs that complement each other (assuming that the individuals are interacting with eligible mates from a restricted cultural boundary).

The basic idea is that individuals with dissimilar needs will be attracted to each other and marry. More specifically, if one person has a strong need to dominate then we would expect him to marry someone who preferred playing a more submissive role.

Numerous studies have been done to retest Winch's results, and the majority have not supported the original findings.[13] There are, however, indications that these investigations do not all represent accurate replications, and there continues to be a great deal of interest generated by the complementary needs theory. Although the empirical evidence supporting this theory is undoubtedly weak, the complementary needs idea still appears in one account after another when factors related to mate selection are discussed. This must be due at least partly to the frequency with which this phenomenon is observed in the real world. Comments such as "they are nothing alike" or "I wonder how those two ever got together" or "they are as different as night and day" are typical descriptions of married couples. Thus we feel that the complementary needs theory has potential explanatory power, though at this point in time the degree of its utility is uncertain.

Homogamy

In the preceding section we discussed complementary needs. Now we will focus on *homogamy*, the tendency for a person to marry someone similar to himself in many social characteristics. We will give this explanation special attention, since it appears to constitute the major force in choosing a marriage partner.

In one way homogamy seems to be closely associated with propinquity, since where people live, play, and work usually corresponds with social class, race, education, religion, and ethnicity. It is difficult, therefore, to determine whether someone dates a particular person because he or she lives nearby or because they are alike. For example, in the United States from 50 to 80 percent of all marriages are class endogamous;[14] this means that one's field of eligibles usually is restricted to members of the same social stratum as his family. Propinquity, however, also plays a large part in mate selection. Public school districts generally have geographic boundaries; as the size of a city increases, the schools serve fairly homogeneous areas. As one goes up the social ladder, residential areas become more homogeneous, especially in the suburbs. In addition to adequate education, the concept of "good schools" implies some regulation of the kinds of students who attend them. Since this generally is a geographic factor, parents with sufficient resources may move into a residential area which meets their requirements of a good school in a good neighborhood. Parents also select colleges in part by the race, wealth, and religious and family backgrounds of the students attending them.

Social homogamy serves in a general way to conserve traditional beliefs and values. This is important to a society's preservation and perpetuation. It is also important to parents, who want their children to cherish the same values, beliefs, goals, and ways of living that they have always believed in. As a result, subtle boundaries are maintained, with the object of directing the young into homogamous marriages.

Whatever the reason, by design or accident, an overwhelming majority of individuals choose mates who live nearby.[15] Since urban communities are populated with people who are alike on important social variables, most people marry individuals like themselves. Thus there appear to be realistic *structural* factors influencing homogamy.

Homogamous pressures may have worked even more effectively in the past than today. North America used to be more rural, and people were less mobile and had fewer contacts with diverse groups. Today, however, increasing education (particularly college education) provides opportunities for people to meet and work with a variety of others.

To a certain extent this is an economic as well as a propinquity issue, because the opportunities for going to college or traveling are greater among middle and upper-class groups as a direct result of their greater access to resources. Since middle and upper-class groups are psychologically more open,[16] given the liberalizing effect of college, they tend to have a larger group from which to choose a mate than do the lower classes. A tolerance for individual differences and a more accepting attitude toward interaction with a variety of personality types seems to be a by-product of a college education for many. Logically, then, there is a greater propensity today for certain people to marry exogamously (out of their particular group), although the proportions are relatively small and the risk factor is generally greater.

Heterogamy

Heterogamous marriage is also known as "exogamous" or "mixed" marriage.

Whether or not a couple is inolved in a mixed marriage can be decided only according to their specific social milieu. A marriage that is considered to be exogamous in one region or subculture may not be considered so in another. Exogamy can refer to social class, ethnic group, race, religion, and age. Subcultures which maintain a strict set of values are usually not in favor of intermarriage.

Social Class   Within social class levels, marriage is more apt to occur between two people of closely related classes.

The number of cross-class marriages in our society is next to impossible to obtain, since a woman's social status typically is determined by her father's or husband's education, income, or occupation. This information is rarely found on marriage license application forms. We suspect that the percentage of such marriages is low, since people tend to marry within their own social stratum,[17] especially if they are living with or near their parents at the time of their marriage.[18]

Ethnic Group   Mixed marriages across ethnic lines generally are not problematic by the time the third generation is residing in the new country. With the first and second generations, however, not only are there differences in values but frequently there is also a language barrier to conquer.[19] However, many of the differences attributed to these two factors are actually more a product of social class diversity than ethnicity.

Race   Racially mixed marriages have been the object of much controversy in recent years, despite their small number. Interracial marriages in the U.S. generally are estimated as less than 1 percent of all marriages,[20] though the rate seems to be rising slightly (perhaps because of greater similarities in socioeconomic status, less job differentiation, and less residential segregation).[21] According to sociologist David Heer, miscegenation will have very little effect on the racial composition of the U.S. within the next hundred years.[22] According to Gunnar Myrdal, racial intermarriage is the form of integration that whites are least willing to grant and in which blacks have the least interest.[23] Myrdal's statement is supported by the fact that until 1967, when the U.S. Supreme Court declared unconstitutional a state law prohibiting interracial marriages (Loving vs. Virginia), nineteen states had laws banning marriage between people of various races.

With the increase in racial consciousness and racial pride, blacks at this time do not appear to be encouraging interracial marriages either, although one study reports that the family of the black spouse appears more willing than the family of the white spouse to accept the couple.[24] Sociologist Rosalind Wolf feels that blacks have adopted the stereotypes created by whites: "They had so fully accepted their imposed role of inferiority, that they believed (like White society) that any White woman who had a Black boy-friend had to be a tramp."[25] Thus a racially mixed couple may find themselves socially isolated, ostracized by both racial groups. On the positive side, however, individuals in an interracial union may become stronger and more self-reliant by learning that their self-image need not depend totally on the reactions of others.

Religion Only about 10 to 15 percent of all marriages in the U.S. and Canada are interfaith.[26] However, the rate in recent years has been increasing.[27] Canadian data indicate that as the percentage in a population of a minority group decreases, their interreligious marriage rates increase.[28] For example, in Quebec, where almost 90 percent of the people are Catholic, there is strong encouragement to marry a Catholic. In fact, the chance of mixed marriage occurring is very slim. In the western province of British Columbia, however, where the proportion of Catholics is less than 20 percent, the interfaith marriage rate for Catholics is close to 50 percent.[29] These differences, of course, are largely the product of the availability of like mates.

The values each partner holds and the couple's individual and combined resources will affect their response to the pressures resulting from intermarriage. The negative sanctioning of mixed marriages by most denominations, especially Jews and Catholics, probably will not be a source of friction unless both are devout or feel strongly against the spouse's faith. Usually the most problematic situations revolve around children, particularly when specific guidelines regarding marital and childrearing responsibilities are indicated by one or the other religion. In addition, jealousy and competition may arise over which children are to be raised in which religion.

In clarifying or interpreting the risk involved in an interfaith marriage, however, one must look carefully at all the factors involved. For instance, it has been asserted frequently that interfaith marriages are unstable. Upon examination of the statistics, however, it is apparent that the people who most frequently marry across religious boundaries are the very young, the rather old, and those in the lower social strata.[30] Looking within these groups we discover that for high status couples marrying in their twenties, religion makes little differences; but for couples where the bride is under nineteen and the groom is of low status, interfaith marriages are considerably less stable.[31] It may well be the case that two sets of beliefs *in addition to* the problems caused by lack of education, inadequate income, and the lack of experience correlated with young marriages may be too much for the couple to cope with. While cultural differences can be a source of misunderstandings, the bringing together of two cultures—each with its particular set of attitudes, beliefs, and behaviors—also provides an opportunity for many new experiences and a chance to choose the best aspects of each culture.

Age The norm in our society is for the man to be the same age or slightly older than the woman he marries. Large age differences either way are frowned upon, although various studies disagree about whether a discrepancy in age has any effect on marital happiness and stability.

Some researchers even report that marriages running counter to the age norm seem to be more durable. For example, a study of divorces in Iowa found proportionately fewer divorces among couples where either the husband was ten or more years older than his spouse or the wife five or more years older than her husband as compared with couples with small age differences.[32] Two other studies found fewer divorces and greater marital happiness among couples where the wife was older.[33]

For some, age differences present no problems. However, people who are sensitive to societal norms may find certain negative sanctions upsetting. These sanctions often appear as comments, such as "she's robbing the cradle," "he wants a mother, not a wife," and "she must have married him for his money."

Some couples have difficulty finding mutual friends, since each is likely to have friends closer to his or her own age. Though this can be a source of friction, time should ease the problem. Differences in outlook tend to be less between the ages of forty and fifty, for instance, than between twenty and thirty. On the positive side, the age difference provides a wide variety of people with whom to make friends. The couple's life may be enriched by the differences in opinions and in the activities engaged in by such range of individuals. It is also possible that maintaining separate friendships from those of one's spouse may provide a healthy basis for individual growth and development in the marriage.

Certain people are less concerned with the present than with the future. They worry, for example, that differences in their physical abilities will increase. It is true that the older person may show an earlier decrease in physical activity, but efforts to maintain physical fitness can do much to retard this phenomenon.

An accompanying fear is that as the older partner ages, the younger will start roaming. Albert Ellis says there is little validity in this belief. In most cases, if a person is going to be unfaithful, he or she will be, regardless of any age difference. "If a deeply satisfying relationship is built up through the years, instead of crumbling as time goes on, it can grow stronger."[34]

Concluding Evidence   While it is true that *proportionately* more heterogamous than homogamous marriages terminate in divorce or are rated by the participants as unhappy, the majority of such marriages remain intact[35]—an important point! Unfortunately, the characteristics of the people who succeed in these marriages have not been adequately studied. It is conceivable that some people are not faced with any of the problems attributed to mixed marriages. Some may have parents who can accept their potential mates regardless of color, religion, or background. They may also associate with peers who either encourage or do not have strong feelings about heterogamy. Such attitudes seem to be more popular among young people now than was true of previous eras, at least in the United States.

Nevertheless, for some the problems will be very real. A strain toward conformity exists in our society. People who attempt heterogamous marriages are subjected to sanctions ranging from criticism and ridicule to social ostracism. They also face internal problems arising out of misunderstandings of the other culture.

Exposure to the total homogamy-heterogamy issue clearly suggests how essential it is that couples face up to their differences and try to resolve any problems as soon as possible.

Predictive Factors of Marital Success

In addition to knowing what restrictions are imposed upon individuals by their field of eligibles in choosing marriage partners, it is also valuable to be aware of those factors which in the past have been found to characterize successful marriages. After reviewing the available literature, sociologist William Stephens categorized the various predictors of marital success as A, B, and C classes.[35] He explains, "In the Class A predictors I have the highest confidence. For the Class B predictors, evidence seems a bit less persuasive. With the Class C predictors I am impressed, but still less confident."[36]

Class A Variables   Stephens listed six predictive factors as Class A variables. One of these, *similarity of faith,* has already been discussed in the previous section, with indications that interfaith marriages generally involve greater marital risk than intrafaith unions. A second factor, *religiosity*, although closely related to similarity of faith, deserves additional mention here. Stephens' survey of existing studies revealed that those individuals who attend church and Sunday school frequently or who at least manifest a religious preference, are better marital risks than nonreligious individuals. He found from reports of three studies that marriages performed by a clergyman also had higher probabilities of success. It should be noted here, however, that there is some indication that a civil ceremony is not predictive of marital failure if the couple are not religiously inclined, and the marriage by a Justice of the Peace is not reflective of rebellious attitudes.[37]

Stephens's third major predictor is *age at marriage*. It has been suggested by some that the age at which one marries may have as much effect on his marital happiness as whom he marries. The relatively high divorce statistics for teenage marriages suggest that teenagers contemplating marriage should take the following things into account: (1) the effects on education and career aspirations; (2) the risk that a choice made too early may restrict potentials for growth; (3) the danger of one or both partners changing substantially over time; and (4) the possibility of each changing in different directions because of different experiences and maturational factors.

Marrying before completing school may create stresses and strains within the marriage, as the couple struggle to live on a shoestring budget while one or both finish school. Of course, monetary support from parents may alleviate much of this problem, although strings attached to such aid may provoke a different set of problems. If one or both drop out of school because of financial pressures, eventually they will probably find that this restricts the kinds of jobs they can get and, correspondingly, their income.

The matter of income itself seems to be significant enough to predict marital success or failure. According to Stephens, "It is best not to be poor. Fourteen studies return a positive correlation between social class (signified by income or by husband's occupation) and a marital adjustment index."[38] *Social class,* then, we recognize as his fourth Class A predictor. He further suggests that certain occupations (particularly those of traveling salesman, railroad worker, and transcontinental truck driver) appear especially hazardous for marriage. Interclass marriages, too, hold considerable risk for the couple.

Premarital pregnancy is the fifth predictor, and Stephens suggests, "Don't let it happen to you."[39] A national natality study published in 1968 states that 56 percent of the firstborn children born to girls aged fifteen to nineteen were conceived out of wedlock.[40] (See Table 7-1.)

Problems associated with many premarital pregnancies include lack of time to adjust to spouse, forced marriage, an unwanted child, and the kinds of problems found in some teenage marriages. For example, one California study revealed the modal age for premaritally pregnant brides was eighteen; usually the groom was younger.[41] These couples, customarily from homes which are run and maintained by their parents, are thrust into adulthood abruptly, without an interim period of being on their own and relying on their own resources. This is accompanied by a lack of time to adjust to each other as a couple. One study found that the sooner a baby is born after the wedding, the more difficult the adjustment and the shorter the duration of the marriage.[42]

Studies of age falsification at the time of marriage for the premaritally pregnant and

Figure 7-1 *Percent of First Births Conceived out of Wedlock for Women Aged 15-19 and 15-44, by color (United States, 1964-1966 National Natality Survey)*

	Age of Mother at First Birth					
	15-19			15-44		
	Total	White	Non-white	Total	White	Non-white
Number of first births (in thousands)	442	348	94	1,180	1,008	171
Percent of first births which were:						
Illegitimate	24.0	15.0	57.3	14.5	9.3	45.5
Born less than 8 months after marriage	32.2	33.9	26.0	18.5	17.7	22.6
Conceived out of wedlock	56.2	48.9	83.3	33.0	27.0	68.1
Percent of legitimate first births which were conceived out of wedlock	42.4	39.9	60.8	21.6	19.5	41.6
Percent of first births which were conceived out of wedlock and were later legitimized by marriage	57.2	69.3	31.1	55.9	65.6	33.3

Table from U.S., Department of Health, Education, and Welfare, Vital Statistics of the United States, 1968, Vol. I—Natality (Washington, D.C.: Government Printing Office, 1970), tables 1-49 and 1-51. Unpublished data from National Center for Health Statistics, 1964-1966 National Natality Survey.

the higher frequency of civil over religious ceremonies[43] indicate probable lack of parental consent, as well as a hasty decision. Parental approval is evidently more important than most of us realize. A marriage involving a pregnancy often cuts the length of acquaintanceship short. Premarital conceptions are accompanied by brief engagements, if any, suggesting that there hasn't been enough time for an extended acquaintance and knowledge of each other.

This brings us to the final Class A variable, *length of acquaintanceship.* Succinctly stated, the longer you've known the other person, the longer you've gone together, the longer the engagement—the better your chances. Lengthy dating and courtship in themselves, however, do not necessarily prevent unsuccessful marriages in our society. What appears important is getting to know what the other person is like. An extended time period allows each to confide in the other, to see if either is greatly disturbed by any of the beliefs and attitudes of the other, to test their compatibility, to express affection and tolerate hostilities. People need time to discover if they can be happy together and work for the same or compatible goals in marriage.

Class B Variables In an effort to present major trends of the marital prediction studies, Stephens's Class B variables will be mentioned briefly, along with the available evidence he has collected for each: (1) level of education—the more years of schooling, the greater the chance for success; (2) previous divorce—previous divorce constitutes a greater chance for failure in current marriage; (3) divorced parents—children have higher divorce probabilities themselves; (4) where they will live—more marriage failures among city dwellers; (5) parents' approval—helpful for successful marriage; and (6) sociability—people who like and interact well with others are better marital risks.

Class C Variables The following Class C variables conclude Stephens's findings: (1) differences in age—extreme differences in either direction for the couple appear to be problematic; (2) brothers and sisters—only children have more marital failures than those with siblings; (3) relationship with parents—high conflict indicates greater chance of marital difficulties; (4) relationship before marriage—engagements characterized by many difficulties and conflicts are unfavorable for success in marriage; and (5) mental health—good mental health correlates positively with marital success.

These factors are not claimed to be surefire predictors. There is evidence that some of the variables might not be related to successful marriage. Refinement of research techniques and new interpretations of findings will be of continued value in improving our knowledge in this area.

At the same time, however, the studies conducted to date do show a surprising degree of agreement. Although any single variable may or may not hold accurate predictive possibilities, as a group they are likely to be quite useful.

Thus, for a contemplated marriage: if the signs are unfavorable on only two of the predictors, this is very good, because it means that the signs are favorable with respect to the other fifteen. If, on the other hand, the prospective marriage rates bad on ten of the predictors, this is a reason to pause.[44]

Summary

The choice of a mate is dependent upon what the individual wants out of marriage. The clearer the individual's goals, the more easily he can evaluate whether or not a particular person will help him realize his goals.

In our society mate selection is subject to numerous restrictions imposed by societal expectations (mating gradient), where we live, and the types of friendships that are encouraged by significant people around us. We also have an affinity toward those individuals who fulfill our ideals for a mate (sometimes based on the image of the parent of the opposite sex), who complement our personality needs, and who are similar to us on specified social characteristics. The homogamous variables of social class, ethnic group, race, religion, and age are examples of qualities to be paralleled.

Knowledge about factors which in the past have been predictive of marital success is also important in mate selection. Religious similarity, religiousity, age, social class, length of acquaintanceship, and premarital pregnancy are considered critical variables.

Notes

1. U.S., Bureau of the Census, "Social and Economic Variations in Marriage, Divorce and Remarriage: 1967," *Current Population Reports* Series P-20, No. 223 (Washington, D.C.: Government Printing Office, 1971).

2. Edmund Morgan, *The Puritan Family* (New York: Harper & Row, 1966).

3 Panos D. Bardis, "Family Forms and Variations Historically Considered," in Harold Christensen, ed., *Handbook of Marriage and the Family* (Chicago: Rand McNally, 1964), pp. 403-461.

4. Clifford Kirkpatrick, *The Family as Process and Institution* (New York: Ronald Press, 1963).

5. The results of this mating gradient are that, with the exception of the very top and the very bottom, men have a larger pool from which to select an eligible mate. This results in a disproportionate number of unmarried high-status women and low-status men.

6. J. Richard Udry, *The Social Context of Marriage*, 2d ed. (Philadelphia: Lippincott, 1971), Chapter 9.

7. J. Richard Udry, "Ideal Mates, Real Mates, and Autistic Perception" (Paper presented at the annual meetings of the American Sociological Association, Los Angeles, California, 1963).

8. Anselm Strauss, "Personality Needs and Marital Choices," *Social Forces* 24 (1947), 332-335.

9. J. Richard Udry, "Influence of the Ideal Mate on Mate Selection and Mate Perception," *Journal of Marriage and the Family* 27 (1965), 477-482.

10. Anselm Strauss, "The Ideal and the Chosen Mate," in Marvin B. Sussman, ed., *Sourcebook In Marriage and the Family* (Boston: Houghton Mifflin, 1963), pp. 120-124.

11. Ibid., p. 123.

12. Robert F. Winch, "The Theory of Complementary Needs in Mate Selection," in Sussman, *Sourcebook*, pp. 112-115.

13. See, for example, Charles E. Bowerman and Barbara R. Day, "A Test of the Theory of Complementary

Needs as Applied to Couples during Courtship," *American Sociological Review* 21 (October 1956), 602-605; Jan Frost, "Some Data on Mate Selection: Complementarity," *Journal of Marriage and the Family* 29 (November 1967), 730-738.

14. Bruce Eckland, "Theories of Mate Selection," *Eugenics Quarterly* 15 (1968), 71-84.

15. Alfred Clark, "An Examination of the Operation of Residential Propinquity as a Factor in Mate Selection," *American Sociological Review* 27 (1952), 17-22; William Kephart, *The Family, Society and the Individual* (Boston: Houghton Mifflin, 1961), p. 269.

16. Joel Nelson, "Clique Contacts and Family Orientations," *American Sociological Review* 31 (October 1966), 663-672.

17. Ernest Burgess and Paul Wallin, "Homogamy in Social Characteristics," *American Journal of Sociology* 49 (September 1943), 117-124; Richard Centers, "Marital Selection and Occupational Strata," *American Journal of Sociology* 54 (May 1949), 530-535; August Hollingshead, "Cultural Factors in the Selection of Marriage Mates," *American Sociological Review* 15 (October 1950), 619-627; Philip A. Sundal and Thomas McCormick, "Age at Marriage and Mate Selection: Madison, Wisconsin, 1937-1943," *American Sociological Review* 16 (February 1951), 37-48.

18. Gerald Leslie and Arthur Richardson, "Family versus Campus Influences in Relation to Mate Selection," *Social Problems* 4 (October 1956), 117-121.

19. Ruth Shonle Cavan, "Subcultural Variations and Mobility," in Christensen, *Handbook* pp. 535-581.

20. Hugh H. Carter and Paul C. Glick, *Marriage and Divorce: A Social and Economic Study.* (Cambridge, Mass.: Harvard University Press, 1970).

21. David Heer, "Negro-White Marriage in the United States," *Journal of Marriage and the Family* 28 (1966), 262-273.

22. David Heer, "Negro-White Marriage in the United States," in Robert F. Winch and Louis W. Goodman, eds., *Selected Studies in Marriage and the Family* (New York: Holt, Rinehart and Winston, 1968), pp. 481-486.

23. Gunnar Myrdal, *An American Dilemma* (New York: Harper & Bros., 1944).

24. Larry Barnett, "Research in Interreligious Dating and Marriage," *Marriage and Family Living* 24 (May 1962), 191-194.

25. Rosalind Wolf, "Self-Image of the White member of an Interracial Couple," in Jaqueline Wiseman, ed., *People as Partners* (San Francisco: Canfield Press, 1971), p. 59.

26. Eckland, "Theories of Mate Selection."; Gerhard Lenski, *The Religious Factor: A Sociological Study of Religion's Impact on Politics, Economics and Family Life* (New York: Doubleday, 1961), p. 49; Ira Reiss. *The Family System in America* (New York: Holt, Rinehart and Winston, 1971), pp. 326-327. 27. Data from the *Official Catholic Directory* as reported in Ernest W. Burgess, Harvey J. Locke, and Mary M. Thomas, *The Family,* 4th ed., (New York: Van Nostrand Reinhold, 1971), p. 306; Calvin Goldscheider and Sidney Goldstein, "Generation Changes in Jewish Family Structure," *Journal of Marriage and the Family* 29 (1967), 267-276; John L. Thomas, "The Factor of Religion in the Selection of Marriage Mates," *American Sociological Review* 26 (August 1951), 487-491.

28. David Heer, "The trend of Interfaith Marriages in Canada, 1922-1957," *American Sociological Review* 27 (April 1962), 245-250.

29. Robert O. Blood, *Love Match and Arranged Marriage* (New York: Free Press, 1967).

30 Lee Burchinal, "Proportions of Catholics, Urbanism and Mixed-Catholic Marriage Rates among Iowa Counties," *Social Problems* 9 (1962), 359-365.

31. Lee Burchinal and Loren Chancellor, "Survival Rates among Religiously Homogamous and Interreligious Marriages," *Agricultural and Home Economics Experiment Station Research Bulletin 512* (December 1962), pp. 743-770.

32. Thomas Monahan, "Does Age at Marriage Matter in Divorce," *Social Forces* 32 (1953), 81-87.

33, Paul H. Landis, *Making the Most of Marriage* (New York: Appleton-Century-Crofts, 1965), pp. 310-313; L. M. Terman, *Psychological Factors in Marital Happiness* (New York: McGraw-Hill, 1938).

34. Albert Ellis with Lester David, "Should Men Marry Older Women?" *This Week Magazine*, July 6, 1958, p. 8.

35. William N. Stephens, "Predictors of Marital Adjustment," *Reflections on Marriage* (New York: Crowell, 1968), pp. 119-129.

36. Ibid., p. 123.

37. Gerald Albert, "Marriage Prediction Revisited,"*Journal of the Long Island Consultation Center* 5 (Fall 1967), 38-46.

38. Stephens, "Predictors," p. 124-125.

37. Ibid., p. 124.

40. U. S., Department of Health, Education, and Welfare, *Vital Statistics of the United States, 1968, Vol. I.–Natality* (Washington, D.C.: Government Printing Office, 1970), tables 1-49 and 1-51.

41. Horace Gray, "Marriage and Premarital Conception," *Journal of Psychology* 50 (October 1960), 383-398; see also H. Christensen and Hanna H. Meissner, "Studies in Child Spacing III: Premarital Pregnancy as a Factor in Divorce," *American Sociological Review* 18 (October 1953), 641-644.

42. Edward Pohlman, "Timing of First Births," *Eugenics Quarterly* 15 (December 1968), 252-263.

43. Harold Christensen et al., "Falsification of Age at Marriage," *Journal of Marriage and Family Living* 15 (1953), 301-304; Harold Christensen and Olive P. Bowden, "Studies in Child Spacing II: The Time Interval between Marriage of Parents and Birth of Their First Child," *Social Forces* 31 (1953), 346-351.

44. Stephens, "Predictors," p. 128.

Suggested Readings

Cuber, John, and Harroff, Peggy. *Sex and the Significant Americans*.Baltimore: Penguin, 1968. Sections on types of marriages and on intrinsic and utilitarian marriages particularly present several marital arrangements. They give insight into the kinds of implicit marital contracts spouses make with each other, as well as showing how individuals work out differences between their marital expectations and reality.

Foote, Nelson. "Matching of Husband and Wife in Phases of Development," In Marvin Sussman, ed. *Sourcebook in Marriage and the Family.* 2d ed. Boston: Houghton Mifflin, 1965. An excellent article, proposing that dynamic variables (such as changing personalities) rather than static variables (such as race or religion) are the crucial factors in marital happiness.

Klemer, Richard. "For or Against Endogamy?" and "The Case Against Endogamy." *Marriage and Family Relationships*. New York: Harper & Row, 1970, chapters 9 and 10, pp. 95-120. A somewhat biased but interesting case study approach to the issue of homogamy versus heterogamy.

8

Making a Commitment: Engagement

The problems confronting engaged couples today are different from those of the past. Traditionally, engagement was the last stage on the dating and courtship continuum. It represented a kind of preliminary contract to marry and indicated, with a fair degree of certainty, that the couple had completed the mate selection process and were making preparations for marriage. It involved a formal request to the girl's father for her hand in marriage, a gift to her of an engagement ring, and a public announcement of the couple's intention to marry.

Contemporary engagement can still be interpreted as a promise to marry; however, Burgess and Wallin's data on broken engagements reveal that engagement no longer indicates with certainty that a marriage will actually take place. In their sample of a thousand couples, 24 percent of the men and 36 percent of the women reported they had experienced a broken engagement previously.[1] Despite the breakups of so many engagements, it is rare that either of the partners is sued for breach of promise (as was frequently done in the past). Marriage used to be viewed much more as an economic arrangement, with built-in expectations for the woman's lifetime financial support; today, other factors take precedence. With more employment opportunities for women, engagement has taken on a new look. Breach of promise suits have no relevance when the loss incurred due to a breakup involves nothing tangible. These days it may even be difficult for some engaged couples to remember *when* or *if* they formally promise to marry; many also seem to forego the engagement ring (though there are no statistics available on the number who do this).

It appears that engagement is less formal today than in the past and has fewer public and community status implications. There is less emphasis on symbols and more on the interpersonal aspects of the relationship. As far as problem solving is concerned, this means that the problems have changed somewhat and have expanded significantly in number. Although people still must resolve problems involving the mechanics of planning and preparing for a wedding and honeymoon, the emphasis, particularly in the early stages of engagement, is on the fulfillment of other goals.

Throughout this book we have referred to the *courtship process*. The word *process* implies movement, and the engagement part of courtship exemplifies this quality. A couple's decision to marry changes their relationship significantly. Once their plans have been made known, they no longer appear to themselves or to others as separate individuals; though they are not yet married, they are not really single either. They have entered a period of transition, during which they can test out what it will be like to interact as married partners while maintaining the status of the unmarried.

The new relationship is one of social exclusiveness. Engagement usually marks the beginning of a noncompetitive period in which potential spouses can determine whether or not they are suitable for one another. Since they are no longer in the "marriage market," they assume new roles (as potential spouses) which can be practiced with a certain degree of security. With this increased security comes the freedom to be more relaxed both in the relationship and with members of the opposite sex in general. Engagement also provides added opportunities to promote the development of the four spokes in the wheel of love (see Chapter 4)—rapport, self-revelation, mutual dependence, and psychological need fulfillment.[2] Within the relationship, the needs for recognition, affection, sharing, security and excitement should be apparent. By exploring each other's needs during the engagement, the couple can determine whether or not it will be possible to meet them in a marital relationship.

Thus the major goal of the engagement period is not preparation for the wedding but rather preparation for the marriage. It involves a thorough analysis of the relationship and an effort to see if both are ready for marriage—interpersonally and physically.

Analyzing the Interpersonal Dimension

In early North American society, a broken engagement caused enough social trauma to make many couples ignore the most glaring incompatibilities. Today's more casual interpretation of engagement encourages a real appraisal of the other person and provides an opportunity to break the relationship if it is unsatisfactory. This approach does not detract from the seriousness of the situation; instead it affords the opportunity to explore personal and interpersonal compatabilities which may, until now, have gone unattended. We have suggested earlier that dating often provides an artificial setting in which people present only their better sides. Engagement, because it allows more frequent and more intense interaction, should remove the "game-like" quality of the date and begin a period where the couple reveal more about themselves.

Evidence exists that critical analysis does, in fact, occur during engagement. Burgess and Wallin indicate that two-thirds of their sample experienced some strain in the relationship during engagement, and 15 percent actually broke the engagement.[3] Many of the disagreements that occur during engagement are resolved and the relationship is strengthened.

Disagreements are fairly common between two persons who interact frequently. If they involve important aspects of life (such as basic beliefs, values, and goals), and if they appear unreconcilable, the only recourse may be breaking up. Burgess and Wallin found that the five major factors in broken engagements are slight attachment, geographical separation, parental opposition, cultural differences, and personality problems.[4] However, since the authors did their study in 1946, we suspect it is more representative of the parents of today's college students. We believe, for example, that cultural differences probably are less influential in broken engagements today than they were during World War II. The value of these data is their indication that engagement can serve an analytical purpose, allowing two individuals to assess whether their values, goals, and resources are sufficiently compatible to establish a workable marital system.

The mere fact of being engaged does not, however, guarantee that any analysis is occurring. When two persons are in love and planning to be married, they may find it boring to talk about values, attitudes, or potential finances. With concerted effort, though, they can arrange opportunities to see each other in a variety of settings and to develop and use the art of open and honest communication. Although they are bound to discover certain differences, they will be able to decide which of them they can tolerate and which they cannot.

Compatibility is the maintenence of a harmonious relationship; inherent in this definition is the assumption that two persons can mesh positive and negative characteristics to develop a satisfactory working system. While some writers have focused on specific personality traits, such as dominance or submissiveness, as the primary characteristics to explore in establishing compatibility, we suggest that couples should also analyze each other in terms of personal habits, values, goals, and resources which will be input to the marital system. It is sometimes very difficult to accept dominating characteristics or irritating personal habits of another person; yet compatibility implies that the two will coexist in harmony in spite of these characteristics. If irritation or antagonism are apparent in the relationship as a result of incompatibilities, serious questions should be raised about whether the couple will do well to marry.

The close relationship of marriage often intensifies the spouse's irritating personal habits. While you might find it amusing to hear talk of your fiancé's messiness from his roommate, you may be less amused when it means stepping over his shoes and socks in the living room. In a recent study involving problem-solving situations for married couples, 32 percent of the 195 spouses reported disagreements over irritating personal habits of their spouse.[5] What may seem a minor irritation now has the potential of becoming important in the future. No magic reformation occurs at marriage; thus differences should be discussed, and attempts should be made to resolve them, prior to marriage. *Clinical* records give further indication that irritating personal habits can become issues in marital discontent. The following vignette is illustrative.

I am furious at my wife. She is lazy and ungiving to me and the children. I can't count on her for anything. I have the feeling that any man who treated her decently and nicely could have been her husband. No affection given and apparently none expected. I have to make my own breakfast. She usually gets up about ten in the morning. It's a good thing we have a cook or the children wouldn't be fed either. She wants to be a 'free agent' with all the benefits of being a wife but none or few of the responsibilities.[6]

Values should also receive considerable attention in the engagement period. Couples do not need identical values in order to develop a cooperative pattern of life, but they must understand and respect each other's values in order to prevent problems which are damaging to the relationship. Couples would do well to determine the relative importance each partner attaches to such things as religion, material goods, humanitarian efforts, culture, power, status, and individual freedom. There is little chance for a relationship like the following one to survive troublefree.

We have different values. I believe we need to make some firm decisions on how we wish to live and what we wish to do with our income and then stick to it. He is always wanting to keep up with the Joneses and be like some of our neighbors who are very wealthy. He never invites his parents to come to our home because they speak with an accent and I can't understand his attitude toward money. It's not like his parents, who lived in the basement and rented the other part of their home until they paid off their mortgage. I think we should make some long range financial plans, discuss what our mutual and individual desires are, reach a compromise and try to keep within this framework. I met him when I was teaching school and he was the handsome maintenance man there. Besides, I had just turned thirty and thought I had better get married before it was too late.[7]

Since our society is a mobile one, many couples meet each other and decide to marry in an environment which is far different from what they are used to or even what they want. The realization that the foreign student you are engaged to intends to return to his home country after your marriage or that the girl you intend to marry would never be able to accept the mobile life of an up-and-coming business manager are important facts to discuss and recognize before marriage. Life-style is more than place of residence and mobility; it also refers to basic patterns of recreation, entertaining, and working. The transition to thinking of "we" rather than "I" is more difficult for some than for others; yet marriage implies that thinking and acting will be along these lines. Individuals who are flexible and empathetic are usually able to adapt their style of life to that of their spouse. Those who are inflexible may continue to express dissatisfaction and disagreement throughout the marriage.

She knew when we married we would always live in small farming towns, since I manage a chain of feed stores. But she always harps on moving to the city—an impossibility for me. She even refuses to buy a home here although we have lived here for five years.

It is important for engaged couples to investigate the problems which concern them the most and attempt to work out ways of coping with them. While adjustment is a lifelong process, some incompatibilities are too severe to warrant continuing the relationship. The couple should attempt to isolate these areas prior to marriage. For this reason, the engagement should be of *sufficient length* to provide enough varied experiences over a period of time so that a complete analysis of the relationship can be made. For some this may mean many months; others may be able to accomplish the goal in less time..

Analyzing the Physical Dimension

Although the primary emphasis in preparing for marriage has been placed on the interpersonal aspects of a relationship, one should not overlook the importance of physical problems as well. While most marriage license requirements involve only a blood test to check for venereal disease, it is wise for both partners to have a complete physical examination prior to marriage. Physical readiness for intercourse and conception, as well as the general health of the both, can thereby be assessed. At the same time, the physician can advise the couple regarding conception and contraception.

Birth planning includes deciding whether or not to have children, when to have them, and so on. Even those who want children should probably avoid having them early in the marriage, so the couple have time to adjust to each other first. According to sociologist Gerald Leslie, one out of every two married couples have a child during the first year of marriage.[8] While some of these couples decided to have a child, many more were surprised that they conceived one so soon. Birth planning is a way of increasing the probabilities of achieving personal and couple goals. For instance, if one or both partners are students or if they are just beginning careers which should not be interrupted, the birth of a child might be better delayed. If the goal is not to have children or to have them only at a particular time, the problem is one of controlling conception.

Selecting a Birth Control Method

It is likely that no single contraceptive method will be appropriate for all the years of a couple's fertile period; as circumstances change (frequency of intercourse, number of children already in the family, and so on), so will the nature of the contraceptive method used. Thus both husband and wife should be well acquainted with methods of birth control and how they are used.

The ideal contraceptive has yet to be marketed. If one judges by users' desires, it will be difficult to achieve the ideal in a single product. People want their contraceptives to be easy to get, easy to use, inexpensive, 100 percent effective, long lasting, not dependent on memory, noninterfering with sexual pleasure, and congruent with their religious or cultural sensitivities. Though no contraceptives currently available meet all these criteria, there are many to choose from. We will discuss the following methods and types of contraception: sterilization, mechanical, natural, chemical, hormonal, and experimental. Each of the available methods has advantages and disadvantages, but our major concern is with their degree of effectiveness. Regardless of how easy a method is to implement, if it does not effectively prevent pregnancy, it is a poor choice.

The effectiveness of a particular contraceptive is generally expressed in terms of its failure rate. The *Pearl Formula*[9] is a method to determine the contraceptive failure rate:

$$\text{Failure rate per 100 woman years of exposure} = 1300 \times \frac{\text{total number of conceptions}}{\text{total months of exposure}}$$

This formula assumes that ovulation occurs 13 times a year (that is, there are 13 chances for conception); 13 is multiplied by 100 to obtain a percent figure; 100 woman years refers to the pregnancy rate in terms of the number of times conception is possible in a year. If 36 women use a particular contraceptive method for 30 months, and 6 pregnancies occur, the formula would show a failure rate of:

$$1300 = \frac{6}{30 \times 36} = \frac{7800}{1080} = 7\% \text{ failure rate}$$

This means that 7 pregnancies occur among the 100 women using this method for one year. Table 8-1 summarizes the failure rates for the major contraceptives used in North America.

Sterilization Sterilization is permanent fertility control. For many couples who have completed their reproduction period, it provides a long-term method which is

Table 8-1 *Known Methods of Contraception and Failure Rates*

Method	Rate per 100 Woman Years
1. *Sterilization*	
Vasectomy	nil
Tubal ligation	nil
2. *Mechanical*	
Condom	13.8
Diaphragm	14.4
Intrauterine device (Lippes Loop "D")	2.7
3. *Natural*	
Rhythm	38.5
Withdrawal	16.8
4. *Chemical*	
Douche	40.8
Foam	7.6-13.0
5. *Hormonal*	
Sequential pills	1.02
Combined pills	.02-.2
6. *Experimental*	
Injectables	Not yet determined
Implantation	Not yet determined
Morning after pill	Not yet determined
Day 25 pill	Not yet determined
Male pill	Not yet determined

Adapted from William Rashbaum, "A Review, Evaluation and Forward Look at Contraceptive Technology," in Florence Hadelkorn, *Family Planning: The Role of Social Work*, vol. 2, no. 1 (Garden City, N.Y.: Adelphi University School of Social Work, 1968), 31-32. Pregnancy rates are from a variety of sources and results vary, depending on when the study was done, the sample size and the number of cycles investigated. The numbers are not absolutes and are not really comparable but serve as a rough index of effectiveness.

highly satisfactory. The procedure is rarely reversible. Therefore, this method is advised only for people who are certain they have completed their family.

Vasectomy The term *ligation* means cutting and tying. *Vas ligation (vasectomy)* involves cutting and tying of the vas deferens (the tube leading from the testes to the urethra in the male) under local anesthesia. This procedure has no effect on potency, the amount of semen, or any other masculine characteristic. What it does accomplish is to prevent the sperm from entering the semen. The operation takes only a few minutes and is ordinarily done on an out-patient basis. The couple is usually advised to continue using a contraceptive for a six week period, at which time a test of semen for sperm will indicate if the vasectomy was successful.

Follow-up studies have indicated that some men do experience psychological problems after the operation. While these may be attributed to attitudes or concerns about masculinity prior to the operation or other factors, it suggests that counseling the couple prior to and after the operation is worthwhile. Frederick Ziegler, a medical doctor who conducted a longitudinal study of forty-eight men who had had vasectomies, suggests that the "potential adverse effects of vasectomy can generally be effectively avoided by counselling focused on aspects of the sexual and marital relationship."[10]

Figure 8-1   *Vasectomy*

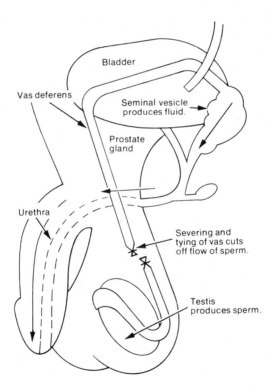

Tubal ligation   A more complicated procedure than vasectomy, *tubal ligation* is performed on women. The Fallopian tubes are cut, separated, and tied. (The tubes are the means by which the egg is transported from the ovary to the uterus.) Since fertilization occurs in the tube, this procedure can be done either abdominally or vaginally. A technique has also been developed whereby a needle is injected through the abdomen to cauterize the tubes.

Mechanical contraception   Mechanical contraceptives are products designed to block the meeting of sperm and egg. They include condoms, diaphragms, and intrauterine devices.

Condom   A *condom* is a rubber sheath used by the man to cover the entire penis and collect the ejaculate during intercourse. To be effective condoms must be used correctly. They must be put on prior to any entrance into the vagina, since even the pre-ejaculatory fluid contains viable sperm. Space must also be allowed at the end of the condom to provide room for the ejaculate. Condoms must be held in place when withdrawing the penis to prevent slippage of sperm into the vagina.

While the condom has one of the lower rates of failure (13.8) and provides protection from venereal disease, many men complain about having to interrupt foreplay to put it on. Some men also report a dulling of sensations when they are wearing it. Physiologically, this claim is suspect, since modern condoms are approximately .0025 inches thick and transmit sensation very well. The condom is probably one of the most commonly used contraceptives in North America; eight hundred million are sold each year in Canada and the United States. The major advantages are its harmlessness, simplicity of use, and ready availability.

Diaphragm   The *diaphragm* is a rubber, half moon-shaped device that fits over the cervix of the uterus and the anterior wall of the vagina (see Figure 8-2). Each diaphragm must be fitted to the woman by a physician and must be refitted periodically. A virgin can be fitted with a diaphragm, but because sexual intercourse stretches the vagina slightly, she should be refitted soon after her first act of intercourse. Fitting should be checked at least every few years and after the birth of a baby, miscarriage, or a gain or loss of ten pounds. Women who use a diaphragm should also use a spermicidal agent such as a vaginal jelly or cream. The diaphragm is constructed to hold these agents over the cervix at all times and can be inserted with a small amount of the spermicidal jelly on the rim.

The diaphragm can be inserted up to two hours before intercourse, but additional jelly must be inserted into the vagina before each act of coitus; the diaphragm should remain in place for at least six hours following intercourse. It costs about $15 to $25 to have a diaphragm fitted by a private doctor but less at a family planning clinic.

Intrauterine device   The *intrauterine device (IUD)* promises to be one of the better new techniques for contraception. It generally involves little time and discomfort for

Figure 8-2 *The Diaphragm*

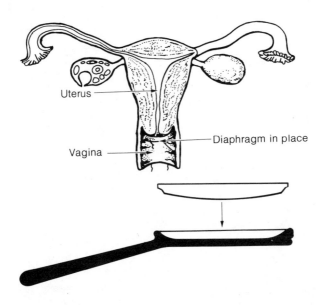

Uterus

Diaphragm in place

Vagina

From *Birth Control* by Garrett Hardin, copyright © 1970 by Western Publishing Company, Inc., reprinted by permission of the publisher, The Bobbs-Merrill Company, Inc.

insertion, has long-term effectiveness, is relatively inexpensive, and has few side effects. IUDs come in various shapes and are usually made of a plastic-like material (see Figure 8-3).

There is little evidence to explain how the IUD works in preventing conception in humans. In monkeys, it causes the ova to move more rapidly through the Fallopian tubes so that, in spite of contact with sperm, conception does not occur.

There are some problems with the IUD, including poor retention by women who have not borne children, spontaneous expulsion, excessive menstrual bleeding, and cramping and pelvic infection. In one study, spontaneous expulsion occurred in 15.5 percent of the women. Expulsions, however, generally occur early in the use of the IUD and are more common among younger women and among those who have had few pregnancies.

Use of the device involves insertion and removal by a physician. Each device has an attached thread which can be felt in the vaginal canal, so a woman can check prior to sexual contact to see if the device has been misplaced or expelled. Insertion of the device is usually a simple and painless procedure (see Figure 8-4).

Figure 8-3 *Intrauterine Devices*

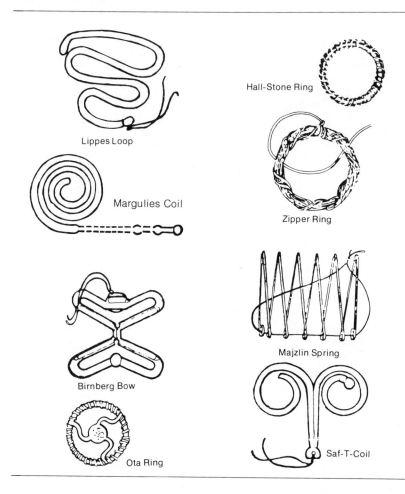

Lippes Loop

Hall-Stone Ring

Margulies Coil

Zipper Ring

Birnberg Bow

Majzlin Spring

Ota Ring

Saf-T-Coil

Natural contraception *Rhythm*   The *rhythm* system of contraception is an avoidance technique. By avoiding intercourse at the time of ovulation, conception is controlled. This is the only contraceptive method formally sanctioned by the Roman Catholic Church. It is based on the fact that there is only a brief period each month when a woman can become pregnant. The period for conception ranges from forty-eight hours before to forty-eight hours after ovulation. For women who menstruate regularly, in a perfect pattern, ovulation occurs fourteen days before the first day of the next menstrual period. Thus conception could theoretically take place two days before and two days after this time. Most calculations of the fertile period include two extra days at either end to allow for cycle variation.

Figure 8-4   *Insertion of Intrauterine Device.*

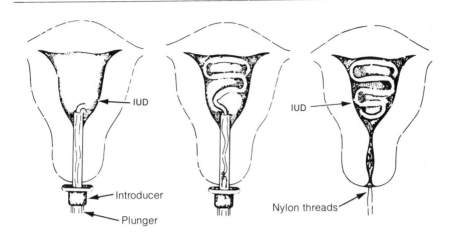

Adapted from Donna Cherniak and Allan Feingold, eds., *The Birth Control Handbook* (Montreal, Quebec:
Montreal Health Press, 1971), p. 23. Reprinted by permission. Copies available from
Montreal Health Press, Box 1000, Station G, Montreal, Quebec, Canada.

Women are not perfectly regular in their cycle. However, with a small amount of
irregularity, the rhythm system offers limited protection—if several estimates of the
fertile period are made. For greater accuracy two estimates of the fertile period
should be made by using both the earliest and the latest day menstruation might be
expected to begin. Subtract fourteen days to get the date of ovulation, and do not
allow intercourse on the four days prior to and the four days after this date. The
double estimation lessens the number of days which are "safe" for sexual relations
but greatly increases the success of this technique.

There are also several newer and more effective methods of calculating
ovulation. One international educational organization, Serena, Inc., emphasizes a
sympto-thermal method which includes observation of signs and symptoms of the
ovulatory period (cervical mucus discharge at the vulva, pink discharge, or
ovulatory pain) as well as records of basal temperature variations to indicate fertile
and infertile days.[11] While this combined method improves the effectiveness of the
rhythm technique, it still requires a dedicated effort to record basal temperature
each day and to observe symptoms of ovulation. Serena utilizes teacher-couples to
provide instruction in using the method and encouragement in developing the
observation techniques necessary to accomplish the objective—contraception.

Rhythm requires a motivation on the part of both partners to determine the safe
period and to refrain from intercourse on those days which conception could occur.
It also requires an extended period of recording the exact time of menstruation.
Because ovulation is sometimes precipitated by sexual relations, and because

human beings do not always act rationally in an emotionally charged situation, rhythm has a fairly high failure rate (38.5).

Withdrawal   *Coitus interruptus* (withdrawal) is an old and somewhat unsatisfactory method of contraception, by present standards. It involves a great deal of skill and willpower on the part of the man, who has to withdraw in time to prevent ejaculation into the vagina. Because the drops of fluid which are emitted prior to ejaculation can also contain sperm, this method has little dependability. Psychologically, the technique can be very unsatisfactory for the woman because it usually involves interruption prior to her orgasm. Withdrawal can lead to frustration unless masturbation or clitoral stimulation is used to bring the woman to climax.

Chemical contraception   *Douche*   The *douche* should not be considered a contraceptive technique. Since it is a postcoital method, and since it consists of a relatively mild liquid in order not to damage the vagina, it has very little effectiveness in either preventing sperm from reaching the uterus or killing them in the vagina. Since sperm can lodge in the folds of the vagina, care must be taken to distend the vagina by retaining the fluid in for a short time. Douches generally are used to cleanse the vagina rather than prevent conception.

Foam   Along with jellies and suppositories, spermicidal foams provide a film over the surface of the vagina and cervix prior to intercourse and act as a mechanical barrier to the movement of sperm. To use a foam, the woman inserts a full applicator into the vagina (see Figure 8-5). The foam flows out of the applicator near the cervix and blocks the sperm. One application is needed for each act of intercourse. If the woman gets up from bed or goes to the toilet before intercourse, an additional application should be made.

Common complaints about this method are that it is messy and short lasting, and the excessive lubrication limits sexual satisfaction. Some men and women are also allergic to spermicides. If this is the case, treatment should be sought and use discontinued. The advantages of the technique are its easy availability and low cost.

Hormonal contraceptions   Since its discovery, the contraceptive pill has been widely used throughout the world. It is estimated that over 8.5 million North American women currently are using some form of "the pill." In terms of effectiveness it is the most foolproof technique available, and it is free from the negative application characteristics of foams, jellies, and diaphragms.

The pill operates by providing the body with hormones that inhibit the gonadotrophic secretions of the pituitary gland (which normally stimulates the ovaries to secrete estrogen and cause ovulation).[12]

Pills normally are taken for twenty days, from the fifth to the twenty-fifth day of the menstrual cycle; then they are stopped so that the menses will occur; and after five days another set of pills is begun. A second type of pill, called the sequential pill,

Figure 8-5 *Application of Contraceptive Foam*

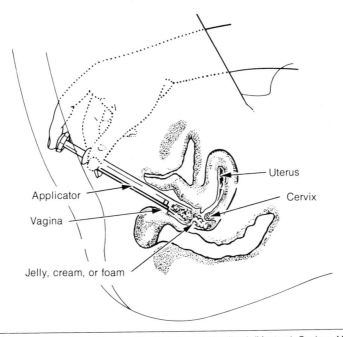

Donna Cherniak and Allan Feingold, eds., *The Birth Control Handbook* (Montreal, Quebec: Montreal Health Press, 1971), p. 23. Reprinted by permission. Copies available from Montreal Health Press, Box 1000, Station G, Montreal, Quebec, Canada.

inhibits ovulation by administering estrogen alone during the first two weeks. Then combined hormones are given to stimulate withdrawal bleeding.

The main complaint about oral contraceptives has been the side effects which they produce. While some women experience weight gain, nausea, and retention of fluids while on the pill, of much greater concern has been the reported association of pill taking and blood clotting. Dr. William Rashbaum suggests, however, that many of the reported associations do not include comparisons with non-pill takers, are on limited samples, and do not take cognizance of mortality rates for women who become pregnant using less effective methods. While long-term effects have not been adequately assessed, the pill continues to be one of the most popular contraceptive methods in history.

Women who have had a blood clotting disease (or who have a family history of such diseases), stroke, heart disease, severe endocrine disorder, or any form of cancer should not take the pill.

Experimental devices Several contraceptive techniques are still in the experimental phase or at least are available only on a limited basis. Injections of hormones, minidose pills, the male pill, and the morning after pill are examples of experimental methods which may become available on a limited basis in the very near future.

One of the most publicized of the experimental methods is the morning after pill, which consists of a synthetic female hormone (estrogen) called diethylstilbestrol (DES). The dosage includes two tablets each day for five days, beginning within seventy-two hours of exposure.[14] The drug is believed to prevent implantation of the fertilized egg, but it does not interfere with an existing pregnancy.

A controversy currently surrounds the use of DES as a contraceptive. While the U.S. Food and Drug Administration initially approved DES as a postcoital contraceptive for rape or medical emergency cases, later research revealed a high incidence of vaginal cancers in teenage daughters of women who had taken DES early in pregnancy to prevent miscarriage. Late in 1974 the FDA reassessed and qualified its endorsement of DES and ordered doctors who prescribed it to warn their patients of these possible side effects. DES is a contraceptive technique to be utilized only on an emergency basis.

While most family planning has been directed at the woman, the attitude and support of the man is necessary to successful contraception. A contraceptive is utterly useless if left in the drawer. During engagement or prior to any sexual commitments, a couple should explore the attitudes they have about marriage and children, the acceptability of various contraceptive techniques, and the motivation they have for birth planning.

Resolving Disagreements

The interpersonal and physical dimensions constitute all that exists between a couple. The process of working through some of the incompatibilities discovered during engagement may be their initial problem-solving ventures in the marriage.

Disagreements encountered in the engagement period provide the couple with the opportunity to develop a problem-solving pattern for their life together. Two individuals come to marriage with different viewpoints on many subjects, yet the competitive dating environment often emphasizes giving in to the other person rather than working through a problem. Because engagement implies a commitment to one another toward marriage and a future perspective for the relationship, motivation for problem solving should be higher than in other periods before marriage. A recent study investigated areas of disagreement in marriage by comparing groups of engaged couples with couples who very happily married, happily married, and unhappily married. Preliminary findings pointed overwhelmingly to the fact that engaged couples, more than any of the other three groups, reported relatively low levels of disagreement in most areas (see Figure 8-6).[15] This might be interpreted as showing that engaged couples tend to idealize their relationships more and ignore more problems than do married couples. It is

Figure 8-6 *Agreement of Partners in Sixteen Areas of Partner Relationship as Reported by Women*

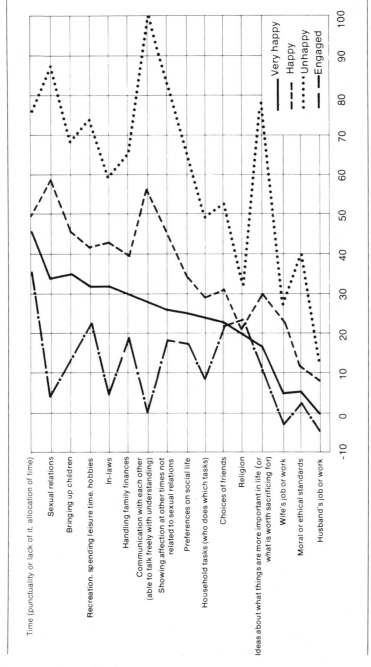

Adapted from Judson T. Landis, "A Study of Disagreements and Conflicts during Engagement and in Marriage," paper presented at the annual meeting of the National Council on Family Relations, Chicago, October 7-10, 1970. Reprinted by permission.

also possible that the romantic element of the relationship camouflages areas of potential disagreement.

People encounter various types of problems during engagement. The engagement period places special emphasis on such problem-solving areas as money, demonstration of affection, wedding plans, religion, future in-law relations, selection of friends, sexual intimacy, and birth planning. Burgess and Wallin indicate that only 1.7 percent of the couples they interviewed claimed to agree on all topics; four fifths noted disagreements in one or more areas.[16]

One of the most prevalent problems of engaged couples undoubtedly concerns sexual decision making. While North American society does not overtly sanction any premarital intercourse, a number of engaged couples do engage in coitus. Vance Packard, among others, suggests that the more intense and formalized the relationship, the greater the likelihood of sexual activity (see Tables 8-2 and 8-3).[17]

Burgess and Wallin indicate that approximately half their couples had intercourse with each other prior to marriage.[18] Kinsey has indicated a similar trend.[19] These statistics substantiate the trend toward permissiveness with affection and weakening of the double standard.

Sexual interaction can overpower other interaction during the engagement period; however, if it is allowed to take over the relationship so fully that other areas cannot be explored, it is not good for the relationship. Kirkendall suggests that if, on the other hand, the addition of the sexual component enhances what has already been established without concurrent guilt or threat of pregnancy, it may be a positive force for the couple.[20]

Working through any of these problems means recognizing the problem, delineating the factors involved in the situation, communicating effectively, and acting to explore possible solutions. With regard to making decisions about premarital intimacies, the engaged couple should have resources beyond those

Table 8-2 *Age Level and Type of Relationship that U.S. College Males Viewed as Appropriate for Considering Coitus*

Type of Relationship	Age Level 14-17	18-20	21-23	24 and over
Only if married	67.6%	33.5%	23.4%	18.9%
Officially engaged	10.7	14.8	15.0	13.9
Tentatively engaged	06.7	15.5	16.1	11.5
Going steady	08.5	20.5	19.0	18.1
Good friends	02.1	08.1	14.3	13.9
Casually attracted	04.4	07.6	12.2	23.7
	100	100	100	100
Number of respondents	(469)	(540)	(566)	(501)

Table 8-3 Age Level and Type of Relationship that U.S. College
Females Viewed as Appropriate for Considering Coitus

Type of Relationship	Age Level 14-17	18-20	21-23	24 and over
Only if married	86.5%	58.6%	46.0%	38.3%
Officially engaged	07.7	16.7	19.2	17.4
Tentatively engaged	02.1	11.7	15.4	14.0
Going steady	02.5	09.7	13.6	19.2
Good friends	00.8	01.2	03.2	06.1
Casually attracted	00.4	02.1	02.6	05.0
	100	100	100	100
Number of respondents	(530)	(580)	(624)	(557)

which would have been available earlier in their relationship. One resource is the "couple" orientation that evolves as they prepare to be married. The change in perspective arises from the knowledge that they have a future to share and that unwise decisions are likely to have a detrimental effect on their marriage. Consequently, problems which in the past have been viewed as more individually based are now faced from the perspective of "What will be best for us?" What are our goals?"

In addition, the security of engagement ordinarily opens communication channels that allow each person to let his or her feelings be known. Communication is one of the most powerful resources available to couples; they can begin to talk about more meaningful topics without fear that their seriousness will scare the other person away.

During engagement the couple learn to depend on each other for support and suggestions in problem-solving situations. In this sense, too, their resources are increased. However, those who are not used to having help in solving problems may find this "sharing" a difficult adjustment to make. Others may find that the acquisition of a future spouse involves a transference of dependence patterns from someone else, possibly parents, to the partner.

Problem Solving for Others Besides the Engaged Couple

Prior to the marriage, time is needed not only for the engaged couple to adjust to each other but also for their parents to adjust to the situation. Although a couple may have dated for more than two years, engagement marks a definite change in their status, as viewed by themselves and by others. Parents suddenly are confronted with what it will be like to have another person as a family member. Intensely negative initial reactions by parents toward the prospect of their child's marriage may change significantly as they accustom themselves to the idea over time.

The engagement period helps the family adjust to the prospect that a marriage will be occurring and that in some ways the parent-child relationship will be altered. Once again, if sufficient time is provided for this transition period, parents usually become accustomed to their child's shift in dependence away from them toward the marital partner. They can also take the opportunity to integrate the prospective in-law into their family as they get to know him or her better and begin to visualize what the situation will be like after marriage.

Parental disapproval of the marriage can create real obstacles to a harmonious relationship between the marriage partners. A head-on confrontation of this problem during engagement, however, may relieve the couple of numerous in-law difficulties later on. When parents do not approve of the match, the couple can pursue any number of alternatives, including the severance of family ties. However, a more reasonable possibility would be an effort to change their opinions of the situation.

How can the goal be accomplished? A brainstorming session may prove beneficial if the couple can get their heads together and come up with some plausible alternatives. To change parents' attitudes toward a future in-law will obviously involve either a change of behavior by the person to fit the parents' expectations or an effort at helping the parents change their expectations to fit more closely with the person's present behavior.

Although some behavioral changes can be made, greater probabilities for success lie with generating a change in the family's expectations. To do this, the couple may decide to overtly confront the parents about the matter. Profitable input for a solution might include: (1) having both parents and couple admit the problem openly; (2) give-and-take conversation on what the issues are; and (3) explanation of both sides, doubts about dealing with the problem honestly for fear of hurting feelings.

Another viable possibility would involve dealing with the problem covertly. Instead of approaching the parents about their disapproval, the couple can simply continue their interaction and try to provide additional opportunities for the parents to see them together and to become accustomed to the partner's personality. Parents frequently comment about how much the other person has changed since marrying their child. Perhaps what has actually happened is that the parents are only beginning to really know what the person has been like all along.

In trying this possibility, consequences such as the following may be expected: (1) not making an overt issue of the disapproval may help keep this problem from taking over the whole relationship; (2) parents, however, may not make a conscious effort to adapt their attitudes, since they may not have dealt with their feelings themselves; (3) additional time will likely be required if this more subtle route is selected; (4) this avenue could avoid the necessity of resorting to the use of ultimatums; and (5) an atmosphere free from overt conflict can be maintained.

Let us assume that the couple decides to proceed on the covert course of action, and satisfactory progress is made toward the goal. In this case the selection can be considered appropriate. If, however, nothing happens to improve the parents' feelings toward the future in-law, the couple may have to resort to attacking the problem overtly. At any rate, it is reasonable to assume that unless a satisfactory solution is found, the problem is likely to continue, or recur, either before or after marriage.

Problems of this type can cause a great deal of tension in a relationship. Situations created by the problems are particularly revealing of important aspects of each partner's personality—honesty, warmth, acceptance of others, escape mechanisms commonly used, and manner in which situations are handled or ignored.

Couples probably will not agree on all problem situations, but they may wish to have basic agreement on the major issues of finances, demonstration of affection, selection of friends, religious matters, plans for the wedding, and birth planning. Kirkendall and Adams have developed a set of questions to be used as a guide in evaluating problem areas:

1. Have you visited in each other's homes to the point that normal family behavior is practiced even though the prospective in-law is there?
2. Has each of you become well enough acquainted with the other's friends that you are clear about your attitudes toward them?
3. Have you seen each other in a crisis, or under tension, or at a time when strong feelings were involved?
4. Have you checked financial costs by actually looking at living quarters, shopping together, and by pricing and examining furniture?
5. Have you arrived at premarital sex standards acceptable to each cooperatively, and through open discussion?
6. Do you feel free and relaxed in expressions of affection?
7. Have you from time to time enjoyed being together when you were not occupied with doing something or being with other people?
8. Have you been in situations where you had to work together as a team, e.g., caring for children, entertaining your families or friends, working on a committee?
9. Have you worked through some definite difference of opinion in a manner satisfactory to both of you?
10. Is your fiancé(e) able and willing to accept you as you are?
11. Are you able and willing to accept your fiancé(e) as he (she) is?
12. Have you spent a prolonged time together when each had to be his honest, unadorned self?
13. Have you discussed in detail your ideas on:
    discipline of children
    when to have children
    future relations with each other's families
    attitudes toward sex in marriage
    feelings toward each other's friends
    attitudes toward religious practices and church attendance
    attitudes toward your initial sexual experiences.[21]

In conclusion, success in problem solving can contribute to a "security bank" which, for engaged couples, represents confidence in their ability as a couple to meet unforeseen circumstances. Even though the nature of the problems will differ throughout life, the couple will be confident that they are acquainted with a method of attacking problems and can expect future success with similar endeavors.

Summary

The major goal of the engagement period, whether it is defined formally or informally, is to provide the time for two persons who have pledged to marry one another to carefully analyze both interpersonal and physical dimensions of their relationship. The transition from "I" to "we" is not always easy. Personalities, values, plans, and ambitions must be meshed in order to establish patterns which are satisfactory for both persons in the relationship. Engagement provides the opportunity for couples to develop problem-solving techniques which will facilitate marital interaction. While problem situations are specific to each couple, most couples experience disagreements in one or more areas. Engagement cannot be expected to provide time to resolve all disagreements, but it should be long enough to allow couples to work through major problems and determine their compatibility.

Notes

1. Ernest W. Burgess and Paul Wallin, *Engagement and Marriage* (Chicago: Lippincott, 1953).

2. Ira Reiss, *Premarital Sexual Standards in America* (New York: Free Press of Glencoe, 1960).

3. Burgess and Wallin, *Engagement and Marriage*, pp. 136, 246.

4. Ibid., p. 273.

5. Dianne Kieren, "Adaptability: A Measure of Spousal Problem Solving and Its Relation to Child Rearing Practices" (Ph.D. thesis, University of Minnesota, 1969); June Henton, "Problem Solving through Conflict in Marriage" (Ph.D. thesis, University of Minnesota, 1970).

6. Bernard Greene, *A Clinical Approach to Marital Problems: Evaluation and Management* (Springfield, Ill.: 1970), p. 52.

7. Ibid., p. 88.

8. Gerald Leslie, *The Family in Social Context* (New York: Oxford University Press, 1967), p. 512.

9. Raymond Pearl, "Contraception and Fertility in 2000 Women," *Human Biology*, 4 (September 1932), 363-407.

10. Frederick Ziegler, "Male Sterilization," *Sexual Behavior*, July 1971, p. 73.

11. Claude Lanctot and Suzanne Parenteau-Carreau, "Studies of the Effectiveness of Temperature Methods" (Ottawa, Ontario, Canada: Serena, Inc., n.d.)

12. Edward Tyler, "Current Methods in Conception Control: Oral Techniques," in Edward Tyler, ed., *Birth Control: A Continuing Controversy* (Springfield, Ill.: Charles C. Thomas, 1967), pp. 133-141.

13. William Rashbaum, "A Review, Evaluation and Forward Look at Contraceptive Technology," in Florence Haselkorn, *Family Planning: The Role of Social Work*, vol. 2, no. 1 (Garden City, N.Y.: Adelphi University School of Social Work, 1968).

14. Kenneth Jones, Louis W. Shainberg, and Curtis O. Byer, *Sex,* 2d ed. (New York: Harper & Row, 1973), p. 53.

15. Judson T. Landis. "A Study of Disagreements and Conflicts During Engagement and in Marriage". Paper presented at the Annual Meeting of the National Council on Family Relations, Education Section, October 7-10, 1970, Chicago.

16. Burgess and Wallin, *Engagement and Marriage.*

17. Vance Packard, *The Sexual Wilderness* (New York: David McKay, 1968).

18. Burgess and Wallin, *Engagement and Marriage.*

19. Alfred Kinsey et al., *Sexual Behavior in the Human Male* (Philadelphia: Saunders, 1948); Alfred Kinsey et al., *Sexual Behavior in the Human Female* (Philadelphia: Saunders, 1953).

20. Lester Kirkendall, *Premarital Intercourse and Interpersonal Relationships* (New York: Julian Press, 1961).

21. Lester Kirkendall and Wesley Adams, *The Student's Guide to Marriage and Family Life Literature* (Dubuque, Iowa: Wm. C. Brown, 1971), p. 89.

Suggested Readings

Havemann, E. *Birth Control.* New York: Time-Life Books, 1967. A factual account of birth control in the 1960s.

Kirkendall, Lester. *Premarital Intercourse and Interpersonal Relationships.* New York: Julian Press, 1961. A good discussion of the effect of sex relations on engaged couples.

Pierson, Elaine. *Sex Is Never an Emergency.* New York: Lippincott, 1971. Written by a gynecologist at the University of Pennsylvania, this booklet is an informative and nonjudgmental review of contraceptive techniques.

Part Three
Marital Problem Solving

9

Celebrating the Union

The wedding ceremony is a public announcement of a change in the couple's relationship. The honeymoon is a more private celebration of their new status, during which the couple more clearly define the boundaries of their marital system. In this chapter we will look briefly at some of the problematic situations which frequently arise over wedding plans and during the honeymoon.

Planning the Wedding

The emphasis placed on the wedding ceremony varies according to the interpretation given it by the bride, the groom, their families, and peers. While some approach this day with great anticipation, others view it merely as a needless preliminary to the significant relationship which comes later—the marriage. The extent to which the wedding presents a problem hinges primariy upon how difficult it is to: (1) set the wedding date, and (2) plan a ceremony satisfactory to all persons involved.

Setting the Date

Young persons of moderate means who are contemplating marriage must face the difficult question of when to marry. Optimal timing assumes physical, emotional, social, and financial readiness for marriage. For college students, this state of readiness frequently coincides with graduation.

While a number of studies suggest that people who marry relatively late have better chances for marital happiness than those who marry early, these data do not account for a variety of individual differences and conditions. Rather, they represent general trends indicating greater problems in youthful marriages. This does not mean that problems will not exist for some who marry later or that all youthful marriages are disastrous. Waller and Hill suggest that the factors which propel young people into early marriages may be the very ones which cause later difficulty in their marriage.[1] Those who marry relatively late probably are more able to live comfortably outside of marriage and perhaps are less likely, for this reason, to place unrealistic expectations on the marriage.

Utilizing the problem-solving approach in arriving at the decision of when to marry involves taking one's hierarchy of goals into account—that is, examining one's goals in terms of their relative importance. If marriage at a particular time will block the attainment of other important goals, it probably is best to postpone the marriage. If, however, postponing the marriage will jeopardize the fulfillment of more important goals, it might be in one's best interest to marry.

Unfortunately, there are no clear answers to the question of when to marry. Each individual is usually faced with deciding between immediate gratification of some goals at the possible expense of others or deferring this gratification with the hopes of maximizing the attainment of other goals. It is a tough problem to solve, especially since concern about and passion for the beloved increases the difficulty of putting life goals into a logical order of preference. A person will be emotionally better off if he realizes that whatever choices he makes will have costs which he will have to endure.

Planning the Ceremony

In the eyes of the law, marriage is a civil contract established between two people which cannot be altered or broken except by court action. All fifty states and Canada require a license, an officiant, witnesses, and mutual consent; all have restrictions pertaining to unsound minds, certain diseases, blood ties, and minimum age levels for both sexes with and without parental approval; all have laws regarding inheritance rights and traditional privileges and obligations. These requirements evolved basically to fix financial responsibility, so that the financial burden of supporting dependent women and children would not fall to the state or province, and to confine sexual activity within the boundaries of a unit likely to produce acceptable offspring. Once a couple prove that both meet the requirements of the marriage laws where they plan to marry, they are issued a license, which becomes valid when signed by the officiant and the witnesses.

Some couples encounter few difficulties in planning the celebration. Religion, cultural background, and/or social status may determine the type of wedding they will have. Traditionally the bride and her parents plan the ceremony. Recently, however, more couples are doing the planning. While this may greatly relieve some parents, it may well upset others, especially if they do not agree with the kind of ceremony the couple are planning. Many couples feel that since it is their wedding, they should be able to get married their way; at the same time, some parents (particularly those of the bride) feel left out or hurt by such an arrangement. In many ways the wedding is a rite of passage for parents as well as children. It represents a change for all of them and involves a transition which requires a proper ceremonial event to acknowledge the new status for the child as well as for the parents. However, difficulties in this area are not as common as one might think. Most parents and children have sufficient affection for each other and share enough similar values to reach compromises. When such compromises cannot be reached, it is usually indicative of other long-standing problems between the parents and the child.

There are three basic types of weddings—elopement, civil ceremonies, and religious ceremonies. Elopements bypass the normal wedding procedures and are certainly less formal. For those whose marriage is opposed by one or both families, elopement provides a way of avoiding friction at the time of the ceremony; however, it may only add to whatever parental disapproval is already present (see Chapter 12 for a more detailed discussion of this problem). Couples with limited finances may find that marrying away from relatives and friends will save them money. Civil ceremonies, or those with a Justice of the Peace or some other duly authorized person as officiant, are usually less expensive than religious ceremonies, mainly because they tend to be less elaborate.

The church takes an interest in weddings because of the concerns it shares with the family and because strong family life is a value of most of the major religious groups. While marriage is not a sacrament in all denominations, it is usually considered an important religious ceremony. For many (if not most) people religious marriage is a commitment made in the presence of their God.

Many marriage ceremonies today have distinct personal touches. The standard procedures have been altered or eliminated to meet personal preferences. The changes include rephrasing the marriage vows, adding poems or ballads, using contemporary music, and changing the site from churches to gardens, meadows, and seasides. An article in a popular magazine suggests that "as the ceremony itself is changing, so is the spirit of the celebration. Spontaneity is replacing formality, and joy is replacing play acting."[2] One young woman expressed her desire for an old-fashioned wedding, but not with old-fashioned restrictions. She said, "I don't want it to be another multiple-choice, fill-in-the-blanks affair. I want to take part—to sing a song to my husband, to dance, to be seen. . . a flute solo when I come down the aisle, and country tunes on the way back."[3]

Even the marriage contract may be altered if the couple wish to define their relationship in a way different from the definition provided by the government. In general, state and provincial laws specify that the husband is responsible for supporting his wife and children, that the wife must set up a home where the husband chooses, that each has the right to sexual intercourse with the other and with no one else, that each retains some individual identity, and that each has some claim on the personal possessions acquired before and after the marriage by the other. The legal procedures necessary to change the marriage contract differ from place to place. However, as more people make use of them there are more models from which one may draw ideas,[4] and the civil authorities are more likely to know the appropriate legal procedures to take.

While not all clergy view changes in the contract and/or ceremony with favor, there has been a trend to view marriage changes in religious services as an example of the church's flexibility and vitality. Rev. A. Myron DeLapp of Philadelphia, an official of the United Presbyterian Church, says:

Some of our ancient language simply doesn't express the meaning these kids want to express to each other when they take marriage vows. Their great concern is for the honesty of the human relationship; the sense of personhood is to be honored and respected. They don't view marriage as simply entering into a contract, nor the wedding as a performance. They want their marriage to have the fullest possible meaning, validity and integrity.[5]

Changes in the religious ceremonies appear to be interdenominational. In the case of mixed religious marriages, many churches now allow dual officiating by clergy from both faiths. With this increased emphasis on individualizing weddings, civil ceremonies have in many instances replaced the traditional religious rites. Although studies investigating the relationship between type of marriage ceremony and marital stability indicate that couples who are married by a clergyman have a better chance for future success,[6] this does not imply that the mere presence of a minister, priest, or rabbi automatically makes the marriage a better one. What is important is that their presence is also indicative of other factors; a religious ceremony often indicates that a certain amount of planning has preceded the wedding, usually including assistance from parents, which suggests that they support the action being taken. A civil ceremony for those whose religious convictions are weak or nonexistent should suffice equally well, given supportive partents and sufficient thought about the marriage.

Even with these changes, weddings can still be costly. The bride and groom's attire, the flowers, the rings, and even the simplest of refreshments can add up to more than a couple can afford. While it is traditional for the bride's family to shoulder most of the expenses, the groom or the couple themselves may be responsible for some major costs. A large or elaborate wedding can place undue strain on the budget allowed for setting up housekeeping. While it is possible to get married on credit, couples faced with this alternative might well ponder the advisability of going into debt for the wedding and honeymoon. Setting up housekeeping requires expenditures way above the normal costs of living, especially if major purchases such as appliances or furniture are necessary. Possible alternatives include a simpler wedding and less costly honeymoon, postponing or eliminating the honeymoon, and saving the money in advance.

The Honeymoon

The change in status from single to married is celebrated publicly at the wedding and privately during the honeymoon. Those who have already had sexual relations or who have lived together will find that the boundaries of their relationship before and after marriage will be blurred. They may have already worked through some of the problems still awaiting those without such experiences. For the latter, the honeymoon will have more intense meaning and greater excitement and anxiety than would be the case if they had had previous sexual relations togther.

Although the honeymoon period has been somewhat slighted as a topic of research, the few studies which have been done suggest the likelihood of at least four problems—relating to each other sexually, relating to each other intimately in other ways, learning how to spend money together, and resolving unrealistic expectations of each other. We will explore each of these problems briefly, in the hopes that an awareness of the issues will lead to a speedy recognition of the problems if they arise. The sooner situations are defined as problematic, the quicker the problem-solving process can begin. Because the honeymoon for most is the beginning of living together, it is often seen as a transitional period from singlehood to couplehood. Critical role transitions occur at this time, characterized by changes in relationships not only between the new husband and wife but between others in the environment. During times of significant change, a person's perspective of what is or is not problematic may be altered. If, however, he is aware of various problematic situations which might occur, he is more likely to be able to recognize them as they arise.

Developing Sexual Competence

The honeymoon provides a couple with special opportunities to focus on their sexual relationship without the interference of other day-to-day responsibilities. The wedding night is emotionally charged. Somehow, the virginal are expected to overcome all inhibitions that have been previously built up and, throwing their fears to the wind, indulge themselves in the experience of simultaneous orgasm. If only it were so easy! Social anthropologists Rhona and Robert Rapoport suggest that honeymooners are often worried about their sexual abilities.[7] Women without any previous experiences may be afraid of the pain of intercourse[8] and may wonder whether they will be able to satisfy their new husband or whether he will be patient, gentle, and understanding. Men are apt to worry about whether or not they can be potent with their wives and if they will satisfy them. In addition, the couple are often tired from last minute wedding preparations and parties, as well as from the wedding and reception itself. Once at their destination they must face the awkward problem of undressing and sharing bathroom facilities, perhaps for the first time. Their exhaustion and discomfort contribute to the likelihood that one or both of them may not reach orgasm. The extent to which all of this is unsettling is directly proportional to the couple's sexual naivete.

Our intent in the above paragraph is not to minimize the joy and excitement of the occasion, but only to point out that this joy is too often mitigated by the couple's unrealistic expectations of what should happen on the honeymoon. The following comments of a young newlywed illustrate a typical problem:

I was a virgin when I married, although Joe and I had petted to climax many times. I felt like I had been in a thousand "dry runs," yet I worried that intercourse would not be as pleasurable as petting. I worried about this a lot during our honeymoon. Fortunately, I was wrong.

Not all sexual problem-solving situations are this simple. In many cases, lack of information about human sexual response patterns and physical problems require the use of other resources. Communication, both verbal and nonverbal, is a key resource in enabling spouses to identify and resolve problems.

Only recently has human sexuality become a topic of exploration, but all kinds of authors have risen to the challenge. There are many books and articles on the market dealing with varying aspects of human sexuality. Interested buyers, however, should check to make sure that what they buy is based on fact and not on someone's moral conviction. (An example of such a factual book is Dr. Benjamin A. Kogan's *Human Sexual Expression*.[9]) In addition, counseling services are becoming more available.

During the honeymoon, couples who have not lived together may feel the need to clarify some of their ideas about the place of sex in their marriage; this can involve frank discussions as to frequency and types of sexual activities which the partners prefer. For others, the honeymoon may mean coping with differences in sexual desire and with each spouse's ability to express feelings. Satisfactory sexual adjustment does not rely entirely on intellectual processes, however. The honeymoon provides an opportunity to explore each other physically and emotionally. The heat of love and passion provides the right atmosphere for building a relationship that is both free and secure. Sex also involves some thought and decision in regard to family planning or preparation for children. These issues are examined in greater detail in Chapters 8 and 11. It should be pointed out that despite any disappointments the couple experience, there is little evidence that sexual difficulties during the honeymoon will be carried over into long-term difficulties. Most difficulties encountered during this time are worked out satisfactorily over the years.[10]

Relating to Each Other Intimately

A recent study conducted by two of the authors found that some of the most salient everyday problems for married couples are those relating to irritating personal habits of the spouse.[11] For many, the honeymoon is the first time they have had a chance to "let their hair down." The realities of halitosis and untidiness are often difficult to adjust to. One young woman, who had been married for a month, said about a weekend she spent alone, "I was really happy to get away for a time so that I could have the whole bed to myself." Sometimes people don't realize how much they enjoy certain aspects of their lives until they have to change their patterns of behavior.

Rapoport and Rapoport suggest that a person's ability to live closely with another person depends upon his needs for dependence, unity, autonomy, and separation.[12] For instance, a person with a strong need to retain a separate identity may experience great difficulty in living closely with his spouse. Honeymoons in our society involve a great deal of strain for people who have difficulty relating to others intimately, as the honeymoon is seen ideally as a time when the newlyweds are to be alone together. In addition to being with each other constantly during the daylight hours, at night the pressure on the husband to prove he is a good lover and the pressure on the wife to be alluring and responsive is for many too much to bear for very long. Because of these strains, many couples in Rapoport and Rapoport's studies were anxious to return much sooner than originally planned. The young couples they interviewed indicated that the intimacy situation was the cause of their anxiety. A return to ordinary day-to-day life was one means of resolving the intense intimacy situation, as it provided a larger potential for other relationships. The return to familiar surroundings also provided the opportunity to test their new relationship with people they knew.

Money Matters

The financial accommodations each begins to make during the honeymoon plague many individuals.[13] Before marriage, each person usually spent his *own* money, but now he is spending the *couple's* money. Adjusting to the way one's partner spends money is not always easy, especially if the "wealth" is limited. One of the problems all newlyweds face is working out satisfactory joint spending patterns.[14] This issue will be more fully discussed in Chapter 13.

Unrealistic Expectations

Our folklore depicts the honeymoon as an ultraromantic, fun-filled time when newlyweds get to know each other intimately for the first time. This glorification of the honeymoon leads to high expectations. To the extent that these are not met, the couple are confronted with reality shock.[15]

The following comments from disillusioned honeymooners illustrate some of the unrealistic expectations people have. One young wife complained, "Our honeymoon was most unsatisfactory in all areas. When I couldn't have an orgasm, he reacted and made a big deal of it. He even sent me to see a doctor. Besides, he was paying more attention to his friends than to me." A husband tells of his problems with his virgin wife, "Our honeymoon was not successful as far as being intimate. My wife's vagina was not large enough for me to enter. She didn't disrobe or attempt any relations the first night. She had absolutely no knowledge of what intercourse was about."

Such complaints are indicative of people expecting too much from their first prolonged attempts at intimacy. Rapaport and Rapaport suggest that at least part of this problem is due to our cultural tendency to deny the existence of strains inherent in making initial adjustments to each other.[16] The emphasis on "love conquers all" plays down these complexities and may delay the couple's facing them and dealing with them, even during the honeymoon. The expectation of perfection is rarely realized. For instance, according to one study, the site picked for the honeymoon was a major source of complaint.[17] One sociologist suggests the possibility that some couples use the honeymoon location as a scapegoat for disappointing interpersonal experiences. He goes on to suggest that young married couples frequently blame their first troubles on external conditions, only gradually realizing that "most of their problems are their own making—they are *relationship problems,* and the surroundings are not to blame."[18]

We would predict that to the extent that couples have already developed close, intimate relationships, including sex, they will be less likely to encounter problems in this area on their honeymoon, only because they will have dealt with these issues at an earlier time. Orientations to intimacy before and after marriage differ, and couples have to work this out to their mutual satisfaction. The shift from primarily personal gratification in the present to a concern for the present and future happiness of oneself and one's partner in marriage may require the attention of both partners. Think how much fun working this through could be!

A honeymoon can be a memorable experience that brings the couple closer together and provides fond memories for later recall. In order to avoid disillusionment resulting from unrealistic expectations and instead enjoy a honeymoon which meets their needs, the couple will want to decide what the honeymoon means to themselves as individuals and as a couple. Consideration of what the honeymoon means to each can avoid such complaints as, "All we did was drive for three whole weeks. He wasn't interested in me or even sex; he just wanted to see the country." "We both like camping, but can you imagine spending your wedding night climbing into your flannels and swatting mosquitoes!"

Traditionally, the groom makes the honeymoon plans. If, however, he wants to be certain the honeymoon fulfills both his and his bride's expectations and needs, he certainly should talk over his ideas with her. Together they might discuss their fears and desires and plan accordingly. The more empathetic each is, the more sensitive each will be to the needs of the other. The more flexible each is, the more likely each will be able to adapt the plans to minimize the fears and maximize the desires of both. This will leave them freer to concentrate on having fun and enjoying each other.

From the standpoint of the journey, the honeymoon may vary from one night in a local motel to a trip to a famous honeymoon resort, depending on the interests and finances of the couple. Couples who have lived together or who have experienced sex may feel they don't need a honeymoon,[19] or they may view the honeymoon as a vacation and seek out whatever diversions they enjoy—camping, night life, travel, and so on.

Those who fear intimacy may seek out places such as resorts frequented by honeymooners, where the couple can opt for lots of group activity. Rapaport and Rapaport note that the peculiarly North American custom of honeymooners converging on one spot (such as Niagara Falls) is seen by Europeans as a way to avoid intimacy.[20] Another way to relieve strain is to shorten the duration of the honeymoon.

Those who like less structure might prefer what Rapoport and Rapoport refer to as the "perpetuum mobile honeymoon." Honeymoons of this variety involve lots of traveling, a budget, and a date of return, but often include no predetermined plans, itinerary, or reservations. Spontaneity and creativity are great assets on this type of honeymoon.

While it is important to recognize potential sources of strain in planning the honeymoon, eliminating the strain altogether by keeping too busy and worn out to spend much time alone only puts critical issues off until after the honeymoon. The problems of gaining confidence in one's sexual abilities and learning to live intimately with one another will have to be worked out sooner or later. Ignoring them on the honeymoon won't solve them, but straining to solve them all at once during the honeymoon can be devastating. The fun-filled and loving atmosphere of the honeymoon offers an opportunity under better than average circumstances to *begin* work on these issues.

Weddings and honeymoons are special occasions which cannot be recaptured at a later date. Like other happy times the couple will share, they provide warm memories which may help sustain them through times of stress.

Summary

The wedding ceremony is a public announcement that the couple have initiated a new relationship. Usually the biggest problem couples face is planning a ceremony satisfactory to their parents as well as themselves, given their financial situation. A growing number of weddings are more individualistic and less formal and ritualistic than the traditional wedding.

The honeymoon is seen as a time free from normal responsibilities in which the couple can concentrate on relating to each other intimately as husband and wife. Many people are disillusioned by their honeymoon experience because of unrealistic expectations. To the extent that the change from being single to being married does not concur with these expectations, people may experience reality shock. The areas most likely to be problematic are achieving personal sexual competence, establishing the basis for a satisfactory sexual relationship and developing the ability to live closely with another person, including working through such issues as money management.

Above all, the honeymoon is set aside as a time when the new husband and wife learn how to give each other pleasure. Such pleasure provides a solid foundation for future relationships. Despite the potential difficulties, we hope you have a good time.

Notes

1. Willard Waller and Reuben Hill, *The Family: A Dynamic Interpretation* (New York: Holt, Rinehart and Winston, 1951), Chapter 11.
2. Barbara Lee Diamonstein, "Here Come the Brides," *Good Housekeeping*, June 1971. p. 93.
3. F. Maynard, "New Rites for Old," *Seventeen*, March 1969, p. 155.
4. See for example, the marriage contract printed in the June 1973 issue of *Ms*.
5. Diamonstein, "Here Come the Brides," p. 93.
6. H. J. Locke, *Predicting Adjustment in Marriage* (New York: Henry Holt, 1951).
7. Rhona Rapoport and Robert Rapoport, "New Light on the Honeymoon," *Human Relations* 17 (February 1964), 33-56.
8. Virginal women are advised to see a medical doctor before marriage, among other reasons to have their hymens cut and possibly stretched in order to avoid pain during the first intercourse.
9. Benjamin A. Kogan, *Human Sexual Expression* (New York: Harcourt, Brace, Jovanovich, 1970).
10. Eugene Kanin and David Howard, "Postmarital Consequences of Premarital Sex Adjustments," *American Sociological Review* 23 (October 1958), 556-562.
11. June Henton, "Problem Solving through Conflict in Marriage," Ph.D. thesis, University of Minnesota, June 1970; Dianne Kieren, "Adaptability: A Measure of Spousal Problem Solving and Its Relation to Child Rearing Practices," Ph.D. thesis, University of Minnesota, December 1969.
12. Rapoport and Rapoport, "New Light."
13. Stanley Bran, "Note on Honeymoons," *Marriage and Family Living* 9 (Summer 1947), 60; Theodore Johannis, Jr., "Married College Students and Their Honeymoons," *Family Life Coordinator* 7 (March 1959), 39-40; and Rapoport and Rapoport, "New Light."
14. Bran, "Note on Honeymoons;" Johannis, "Married College Students."
15. Bran, "Note on Honeymoons."
16. Rapoport and Rapoport, "New Light."
17. Bran, "Note on Honeymoons."
18. Leonard Benson, *The Family Bond* (New York: Random House, 1971), p. 198.
19. Kanin and Howard found that couples who had already experimented with sex were much less likely to take a honeymoon than couples who had not had premarital intercourse.
20. Rapoport and Rapoport, "New Light."

Suggested Readings

Rapoport, Rhona, and Rapoport, Robert, "New Light on the Honeymoon." *Human Relations* 17 (February 1964). 33-56. One of the few analytical articles written about the honeymoon, it is both readable and enlightening.

Maynard, F. "New Rites for Old." *Seventeen*, March 1969, pp. 154-155. A look at the current changes in wedding ceremonies.

10 Establishing the Marital System

The excitement and joy many newlyweds feel when setting up their first home together—be it apartment, house or trailer—reflects a dream come true. At last they are together, nestling into a stronghold from which they will sally forth to take on the world. They feel confident that together they will be able to accomplish whatever they want, despite all obstacles.

Each brings to the marriage a unique set of past experiences and philosophy of life. Each comes with expectations of what marriage is all about, including ideas about how the couple should go about getting what each thinks they want out of life. Generally speaking, the more similar their experiences, values, and expectations, the more likely their expectations will coincide and the easier it will be for them to live together as husband and wife. Some people, however, may welcome the adventure of exploring each other's differences, since it opens up an opportunity for new experiences and broadening perspectives. Nevertheless, when two individuals who love each other start living together, they are bound to find that some things simply do not happen as planned.

In the first year or so of living together most

people struggle to work out satisfactory ways of relating to each other and to the outside world. In essence, they are defining the boundaries of their marriage to each other and to others with whom they come in contact. This chapter will explore some of the problems couples encounter in working out mutually compatible ways of relating to each other and to outsiders; it will also examine alternative ways of approaching the problems.

Becoming A Cohesive Unit

Permanence in marriage depends upon the success the couple has in creating a special type of social group. Many of the general properties of social groups, therefore, are applicable to the marriage unit. People form a group when they are talking, playing, loving, or even fighting with each other. When individuals influence the thoughts and actions of each other, they form a bond—a distinct collective identity which distinguishes them from others.

Usually newlyweds desire to become a cohesive unit, to establish "we" feelings instead of "I" feelings. The "we" feelings provide the "glue" that enables them to see themselves as a single unit. These feelings consist of pride in identity, mutual attraction and affection, and some consensus as to goals.

Marriages in our society generally are voluntary mergers, and certain conditions must be met to create cohesive feelings between the partners. First, each must feel *affection* for the other; this involves a commitment to the happiness, welfare, and development of the other. Second, the couple must want to be affiliated with each other because their togetherness provides them with a *source of satisfaction*. In other words each expects certain needs to be fulfilled or goals realized in the marriage. Third, the individuals *do not feel more attracted to alternative groups*, such as their family. Fourth, the individuals must *share each other's values*; this involves subordinating certain personal goals if they conflict with mutual goals.

Consensus is something which often comes about through group pressure. If an individual is attracted to the group and does not have more satisfying alternatives, he will be more subject to pressure to accept the values and norms of the group than would be the case if he had other options. This has implications for the power relations within a marriage. The partner who is least attracted or who perceives more alternatives can influence the other partner. Four basic patterns of power relationships can be discerned in marital systems—husband-dominant, wife-dominant, syncratic, and autonomic.[1] The first two patterns are self-explanatory; one of the spouses has greater control than the other over the family's resources and greater influence in decision making. The other two patterns depict types of equalitarian marriages, the difference being whether decisions are made jointly (syncratic) or whether each partner handles an equal number of decisions independently (autonomic). "We" feelings are more likely to be fostered in a marriage where decisions are made together and responsibility for them shared.

Alternative Marital Roles

Most marital relationships are variations of three major types—*traditional, companionate,* and *egalitarian.* Each of these types illustrates a particular way husbands and wives relate to each other, based on their expectations of how husbands and wives *should* behave. The advantages and disadvantages of a particular set of expectations or of role relationships, therefore, will be different for husbands and wives. In the words of sociologist Jessie Bernard, "There are two marriages in every marital union—his and hers."[2]

Traditional Marriage

A *Traditional* marriage is essentially patriarchal—(husband dominated). As family head, the husband is the major breadwinner and the family's representative in the larger community. His roles include providing his wife with financial security and making decisions affecting the marriage and family. His economic success determines the social position of the family. The wife in this type of marriage is committed to domesticity; her chief roles are mothering, homemaking, and catering to her husband.[3] She is responsible for running the home and raising the children.

The advantages of a traditional marriage appear to be greater for the husband than for the wife. He enjoys all the privileges accorded to the head of the household; he has the power to put his needs first. Indeed, part of his wife's role is to care for his needs. *Power*, as the term is used here, refers to the influence and authority which one person (in this case the husband) exerts over another (in this case the wife). However, the duties of the traditional husband are heavy. He is totally responsible for his family's well-being. He is expected to solve all problems and make all important decisions. In return he expects gratitude from his wife and children and status from significant others commensurate with his success.

The major advantage of a traditional marriage for the wife is security. The understanding in this type of arrangement is that the husband will provide for his wife and children. Thus the better his economic position, the greater her economic security. The major disadvantage is the effect upon her mental and emotional state. She is particularly susceptible to psychological distress, sometimes known as the *housewife's syndrome.* More married women than married men experience physical and psychological anxiety; more feel they are about to have a nervous breakdown; more have feelings of inadequacy in their marriage; and more blame themselves for their own lack of adjustment to marriage[4] Married men show fewer symptoms of psychological distress than unmarried men, regardless of age,[5] whereas married women have poorer emotional and mental health than unmarried women. More married than unmarried women, for example, feel people are watching them, perform poorly in the presence of others, are depressed, feel unhappy, are bothered by aches and pains, have nervous breakdowns, suffer insomnia, have nightmares, worry over possible misfortunes, are nervous, faint, and have headaches and dizziness.[6]

Comparisons of married housewives with married working women indicate that housewives do not fare well. While many married working women are neurotic, they are less likely than housewives to be psychotic.[7] Summarizing these studies, Bernard concludes, "In nearly all symptoms of psychological distress—from headaches to heart palpitations—the working women are overwhelmingly better off."[8]

In the traditional system the wife often unconsciously chooses to live vicariously through her husband and her children. Studies reveal that when a woman's family is her only source of fulfillment, her own needs frequently take over and create interference for her children in their struggle for independence.[9] People fight to maintain a reason to exist, and in many instances the single most important reason for a traditional mother's existence is her children. Even after they leave the family home she strives to be a part of their lives and often finds herself in the role of the domineering mother or the interfering mother-in-law. Not only is she doing her children an injustice by not establishing interests outside the family, but her husband will also be affected by her dependence on him for fulfillment. Women who are active outside the home experience increased self-esteem and a greater sense of equality with their husbands.

Companionate Marriage

In the second type of marriage the wife is a companion to her husband, helping him in his chosen endeavors. According to sociologist Clifford Kirkpatrick, besides managing the home (and perhaps a couple of children), the woman in the companion role

may play the glamour girl, stake her fortunes upon personal charm, and live as a parasite, consuming much and producing little save immediate satisfaction in her husband. She might, however, be a helpmate companion, even applying her social graces to the advancement of her husband. She may identify with her work, share his troubles, and give him a sense of security resulting in higher achievement. The woman playing the companion role might likewise be a civic leader, representing her husband in worthwhile enterprises for which he lacks the time.[10]

The advantages to the husband of this kind of role include having a companion who devotes herself to him. He may show her off as a beautiful possession to enhance his ego or utilize her talents in advancing his career.

The wife may find romance, a variety of experiences, and a satisfying identification with her husband. She may enjoy his satisfactions vicariously and perhaps find her own by directing her energies into civic and community activities where she may make real contributions. She may even pursue a career. However, the woman who subscribes to a full-fledged career in this type of marriage may suffer intense role conflict. Kirkpatrick suggests that the struggle between two roles with corresponding aspirations is more acute than the clash between a major and a minor role.[11] In addition, tremendous quantities of energy and time are required to perform both jobs adequately. Her career is seen by her husband as secondary to her main role of wife and mother, even though she is equally committed to both. "She can work if she wants to, as long as the house and kids don't suffer" is a companionate husband's view of his wife's career.

The disadvantages of a companionate marriage are directly related to the advantages. A wife who relies on her beauty, for example, to keep her husband charmed will find her success fading with the passing years. Women with talent who have subordinated themselves to their husband's career may, in time, feel a great personal loss. There appear to be few obvious disadvantages for the husband in this type of marriage.

Perhaps most disastrous in both companionate and traditional marriages is the wife's personality subordination. Functioning as her husband's appendage, her character and personality may dwindle. She makes more adjustments in the marriage than her husband does,[12] and as a result of her voluntary redefining of her image and the reshaping of her personality, as time goes by she frequently suffers loss of self-esteem and lack of personal development.[13]

One of the basic differences of wives and husbands is that of life-style. After marriage, the husband continues to spend much of his energy on his job. Marriage, however, often involves a complete change in occupation for the wife. Her first job is that of housewife, even if she works outside the home. In addition, the low status accorded to housewives means that the husband's needs have to be catered to first because his work has higher status than hers, involves a greater degree of competition and produces higher earnings. Eventually alienation may result from these differences, particularly on the part of the wife.[14]

Egalitarian Marriage

In egalitarian marriage, the household roles are shared. Each spouse has equal status, equal decision-making power and economic independence. This is not the same as role reversal, which is also a viable option for husbands and wives. In egalitarian marriages, sharing is based on the tenet that all who benefit from the services supplied in the household should contribute to them and that both partners should share in supporting their home.

Many women like the idea of equality as long as the privileges alone are under consideration. They like the idea of gaining respect as wife and mother, financial support as companion, and an equal voice in decision making as partner. The only trouble is that they do not always favor the responsibilities that correspond to the privileges. The corresponding responsibilities in a partnership require that the wife be successful in a career of her own and share in all the legal obligations of the family. Nevertheless, an increasing number of women are no longer content to be formally educated in the same manner as men and then upon marriage assume the more traditional (low status) female roles of wife/mother/homemaker. They want to pursue their own careers and share the housekeeping and child-care responsibilities equitably with their spouses, as well as contribute to the financial security of the family. These truly egalitarian marriages organize the division of household labor by rotation or on the basis of interest and equality rather than by sex. For example, routine tasks such as cooking and the laundry may be delegated to the individual who most likes to do these things, taking into account the time schedules and commitments of each. Disagreeable tasks such as emptying the garbage and cleaning the bathroom may be rotated on a weekly or monthly basis. Mending and ironing, figuring out income tax, keeping financial records, and making purchase decisions for such things as health and life insurance, rather than falling to the spouse with the most expertise, may be done jointly at first. The spouses can thereby learn from each other until neither is totally dependent on the other for any of the tasks of living. This particular organization requires adaptability and flexibility on the part of both partners, as well as a commitment to communication, sharing, and supportive behavior.

For the husband this type of marriage entails less power than he exerts in traditional or companionate marriages and increased expenditures of time and energy in sharing tasks which are performed for him in other types of marriage. On the positive side, the husband may be gratified knowing that his children are receiving the care of both parents and that he is not exploiting another human being for his own gain. He may also feel relieved because his responsibility for the financial and emotional well-being of the family is shared equally with his wife.

Egalitarian roles encourage the wife and the husband to utilize their occupational training and permit both to seek fulfillment of other personal goals. According to Foote, one key to maintaining a satisfying relationship is the matching growth and development of both partners over the years.[15] Active involvement on the job and outside interests contribute to the intellectual growth of both over the course of their life together. Such growth and development is not exclusive to egalitarian marriages, but only in marriages of this type are both spouses equally free to pursue their own interests.

Among the disadvantages of this type of marriage are a lack of emotional support from many individuals and groups in the society, as well as a lack of support systems ranging from equal employment opportunities to professional child care facilities and flexible work scheduling. In addition, our expectations in marriage reflect some aspects of the traditional or companionate families in which most of us were raised. Overcoming internalized expectations and patterns of behavior, with few visible egalitarian role models, is quite a challenge.

Factors Influencing Choice of Marital Roles

The traditional, companionate, and egalitarian marital roles represent basic ways husbands and wives can choose to relate to each other. Each is distinguished by a particular set of reciprocal role relationships. The selection of one of these, certain aspects of each, or some other set of role relationships is dependent upon the expectations each spouse has for the marriage. In turn, these expectations are influenced by a variety of factors including cultural norms, sex roles, parental influence, whether or not the wife plans to work, children, and the husband's occupation.

Cultural Norms

The prototype of the traditional North American family system is that of the WASP (white Anglo-Saxon, Protestant) middle-class nuclear family. According to sociologist John Sirjamaki, it is structured according to a set of cultural norms called cultural configurations.[16] These configurations are the dominant shared moral values and sentiments which rationalize and motivate the behavior of people in our society. Although the prototype, including its cultural configurations, only approximates the average value system of the middle-class nuclear family, it undoubtedly influences the behavior of families in all classes, regardless of religious and ethnic affiliation.

Sirjamaki believes that one of the pervasive cultural configurations is the division of labor by gender within the family, with the man being in a superior position. Men who are good providers, faithful husbands, and loving fathers fulfill the major role expectations of our society. Women who are good mothers, responsive wives, and affectionate companions likewise live up to their reciprocal responsibilities. Biological and cultural conditioning over a lifetime provides the structure for all types of heterosexual relationships, with the presumption of dominance consigned generally to the men.

The double standard of morality (discussed at length in Chapter 5), with its expectations of greater masculine enterprise, exists not only in the sexual arena but in other spheres of life. Sirjamaki says:

Women live, in male estimation, under a blanket of oppressive mores which restrains their ordinary everyday movements. Where men have a relative freedom of action, women must cater to a public opinion of what is womanly behavior. In social life women are under greater disapproval than men when they smoke or indulge in narcotics. On the job they may encounter much male prejudice which affects their pay and possibilities of promotion. They are more protected by social legislation which governs their hours and conditions of employment.[17]

These cultural attitudes persist despite legislation and widespread sentiment in favor of sexual equality. Women in our rapidly changing society are restrained to traditional roles by the cultural configurations, even though economic and social forces are offering them new roles.[18] One of the results is role confusion; that is, it is not always clear what behavior is expected or appropriate in certain situations.

The husband-dominant norm in North America is based on a belief in the inequality of the sexes. The stronger the belief that a woman's place is in the home, the greater the likelihood that marital role expectations will be based on a division of labor according to gender. The classical argument explaining sex-role differentiation is rooted in the assumption that pre-historically a division of labor grew out of the biological functions of reproduction. Women, tied down during pregnancy and lactation, maintained the house and cared for the children, while men secured the means of subsistence.[19] From this point on there is a divergence of opinion. Some feel the subordinate status of women is derived from supposedly innate psychological dispositions or physical weakness. Others hold to religious beliefs. Still others believe that the inequality of women is the result of men exercising control of vital political and economic resources. Whatever the rationale, the traditional sex-role distinction relegates the breadwinning role to the man and the roles of housekeeper and primary child rearer to the woman.

Assigning marital roles on the basis of gender may limit a couple's resources, thereby restricting their problem-solving capabilities. Instead of assessing alternative solutions according to the expertise each person brings to the marriage, some couples cling to rigid notions of what men and women should do. The following hypothetical example illustrates the problem.

Ray and Juanita bought a house which needed a lot of minor repairs. Ray felt that fixing it up was his responsibility because he was the husband. However, he was all thumbs and usually succeeded in making an even worse mess. Eventually it got to the point where Juanita insisted that either they call a repairman when repairs were needed or that she, because of her greater dexterity and experience in fixing and building things, be allowed to try to do the minor repairs. After considerable discussion they concluded that Ray's inability to repair things was no reflection on his masculinity nor on his ability to be a good husband. Instead of rigidly clinging to what Ray considered was a man's job, they were both able to accept Juanita's skills as resources they could utilize in solving certain home maintenance and repair problems.

Changing Sex Roles

Advocates of sexual equality have stressed that feelings of masculinity and femininity are not rooted in what a person *does* but rather in *how he feels* about what he does. Chances are that a man who does not feel threatened by doing a so-called feminine task is more secure in his masculinity than one who refuses to do anything not considered man's work. When couples realize that to be *equal* is not to be the *same*, significant strides toward achieving equality in marriage are made. One can maintain one's own sexual identity and still be given equal consideration with a member of the opposite sex regarding both *privileges* and *responsibilities*.

Feminist groups have pointed out that from birth girls are guided toward marriage and motherhood. They believe that because of this pattern of socialization, many women are robbed of any potential they might have for pursuing other creative endeavors. Feminists do not ignore the possibility that being a wife and mother offers a creative challenge for some women, but they suggest that this type of socialization limits alternatives and restricts the potential of women to function in other spheres.

The present feminist movement represents a change in attitude on the part of an increasing number of women toward their traditionally defined roles as wife and mother. In 1970, a study conducted for the Institute of Life Insurance reported that 57 percent of the young women interviewed thought a woman's place was in the home. By 1972, only 48 percent agreed. In the same time period, the percentage of these women who perceived the housewife role as the most appealing life-style fell from 42 to 35 percent. Marotz reports that this disillusionment with the wife-mother role is also evident among married white-collar mothers of teenagers. When asked to rank ten pictures representing a variety of occupational choices on the basis of what job they would most like their daughter to have if it were a perfect world, white-collar mothers of twelve to fourteen-year-old daughters in Minneapolis, Minnesota, ranked the role of wife-mother significantly lower than did their husbands or the blue-collar mothers and fathers in the study. Significantly more white-collar fathers, however, preferred the role of wife-mother for their daughters than did any of the other three groups of parents. On the basis of these data Marotz predicts a high conflict potential between white-collar husbands and wives over appropriate career roles for their daughters.[21]

Further support for this prediction comes from a recent study by sociologist Mirra Komarovsky of sixty-two college seniors randomly selected from an Ivy League men's college. She reports that these male students profess many egalitarian notions about women in general—but they prefer traditional wives.[22] For instance, questions about the occupational roles of future wives reveal that the men pay lip service to liberal attitudes about working wives, but at the same time, many of them qualify their answers, sometimes to the point of almost negating their original views. One respondent reported that it was appropriate for a mother of a preschooler to take a full-time job "provided, of course, that the home was run smoothly, the children did not suffer, and the wife's job did not interfere with her husband's career."[23] Almost half these male students (48 percent) favored the pattern of a wife working until the advent of children, not working during the childrearing years, and eventually returning to work. The majority felt that there was no substitute for the mother's full-time presence at home during the preschool years and that during their school years she should be home when they returned. If they planned on their future wives working, the respondents were willing to aid them in varying degrees; the more important the wife's work, the more willing they would be to help. On the other hand, these men frequently detailed certain tasks they would not help with, such as the diapers or the laundry.

The data reveal an emerging problem. Despite the weakening support for sharp sex-role differentiation in marriage, the role ideals have not been relinquished. We might surmise that people can tolerate a high degree of value inconsistency until they have to transform it into behavior they must live with, as in marriage.

Parental Influence

During the early years of a child's life his basic instruction in marital roles comes from his parents. In some families the parents consciously instill what they feel is appropriate sex-role behavior in their children (a boy is *taught* the ways a man should behave). In other families the behavior is *inferred* by the child on the basis of how his parents behave. The boy learns the roles of a man through his identification with his father and through his mother's interpretations of the roles of men. A girl learns how a woman should behave in much the same way.

Children also tend to absorb the authority patterns enacted by their parents. In the traditional family the father is dominant and aggressive and the mother subordinate and submissive. In some families the roles are reversed, with the wife dominating and the husband playing the subordinate role; in others both parties are aggressive; and in still others, both are meek and submissive. When the children marry, they usually try to establish in their own marriage the roles they learned from their parents. This generally leads to some role conflict, because the parents of each spouse have worked out different sets of roles, depending upon *their* parents' marital roles, their own social class, and their ethnic and regional backgrounds. Every family takes on unique cultural characteristics, so even couples from similar backgrounds are not immune to role conflict.

Working Wives

The expectation that the wife will or will not work after marriage may have considerable effect upon a couple's marital roles. Women have moved into the labor force in large numbers in the last two decades. They comprise 37 percent of the entire U.S. labor force and 32 percent of the total Canadian labor force. Approximately 60 percent of all U.S. and 18 percent of all Canadian women employed in the labor force are married, many with small children.[24] One of the primary reasons married women work is to supplement the family income.[25] According to a recent estimate, in the U.S. only one-third of the two-income and one-fifth of the one-income households make a little more money than they absolutely need to live on.[26] Nevertheless, for many married women, working is a matter of personal preference.[27] Statistics indicating that the higher the educational level, the more likely a woman is to work[28] probably reflect two major factors: (1) the salience of her job and (2) her husband's approval of her working. The higher her husband's social class, the more likely he is to be pleased that his wife works if she wants to. Marotz, for instance, reports that 41 percent of the blue-collar husbands in her study felt that the husband should decide whether or not the wife should work, as compared with 23 percent of the blue-collar wives, 18 percent of the white-collar husbands, and 21 percent of the white-collar wives.[29] White-collar husbands probably feel much more secure in their ability to provide for their families and therefore are less likely to find their masculinity threatened if their wives work.[30] It could also be argued that one's expectations about marital roles determine to some extent whether or not the wife will work. Some men may feel derelict in the performance of their economic role as provider if their wives are in the labor force, and some women prefer not to work outside the home.

Children

There is considerable support today for women to select the role which best suits their personality and to pursue it until children come along. Today's young woman often has a life plan that includes a career with a temporary retirement period built in to accommodate full-time motherhood, at least while her children are young. We refer to *her* children advisedly. The traditional division of labor requires that there be a breadwinner and someone to care for the home and children. Since the husband traditionally has assumed responsibility for providing financial support, and since the wife bears the children, people have expected that she will also rear them. The belief that "biology is destiny" has placed women in this position and reinforced it over the years.

Sociologist Alice Rossi complains that this role definition for women has been upheld even by social scientists.[31] She points out that investigations of parent-child separation have been labeled as "maternal *deprivation*" and "father *absence*" studies (note which one implies damaging effects).

Some individuals are adamant about the predetermined role patterns which have been imposed on husbands and wives. A "good" mother is defined as always placing her children first in making decisions about her activities. A common attitude is that she should not have children if she does not want to care for them. Children need good care, and the demands upon their parents vary with their ages and individual personalities. Parents also have needs and rights, however, and when these are in conflict with those of the child, the resulting interaction may not constitute a healthy situation for either. Most research studies report few, if any, adverse influences of maternal employment on children's personalities or social interaction.[32] What appears more crucial than the *quantity* of time the child spends with his mother is the *quality* of the mothering.[33] This is undoubtedly true of fathering too, although quantity versus quality of fathering has not been studied. The assumption in the past has been that the father will be working and therefore quantity is not an issue.

Empirical evidence suggests that although the family may be exposed to more TV dinners if the wife works, both husband and wife will experience less tension and more sociability if she is doing what she wants to do.[34]

Occupation

White-collar couples are more likely to opt for companionate roles and blue-collar couples for traditional roles. The ultimate goal of many middle and upper middle-class wives is to enhance their husband's professional and social status and thus further the couple's goal of upward mobility. The wife of a blue-collar worker, however, can do little to further her husband's career. (What, for instance, can the wife of an assembly line worker do to help her husband become foreman?) Under such circumstances the blue-collar couple are likely to develop more traditional marital roles, with the husband as provider and the wife devoting herself to caring for the children, keeping the house in order, and providing an emotional haven for her husband.

The dedication a man has to his career affects the kinds of roles he wants his wife to play. Some husbands are so dedicated that they resent any loss of time from their work. This kind of man is unwilling to curtail his dedication, though he expects his wife to do so—even when she would like to spend as much time with her exciting job as he does with his.[35] If such a man marries a wife also committed to a career, the two of them are likely to have difficulties deciding who does what at home, unless the wife is willing to subordinate her career to his and be a "super mom" (one who manages the home, rears the children, and works, asking no sacrifice of male privilege).[36] This kind of situation illustrates how important it is for two people planning to marry or even to live together to talk over the expectations each has for the other. The probabilities of getting your spouse to change after marriage in order to meet your expectations, whatever they are, are slim, unless your spouse *wants* to change.

Developing A Satisfying Relationship

Each person entering a marriage has a preconceived image of what he would like his marriage to be and how husbands and wives behave. In other words, each comes into marriage expecting that the wife will perform certain activities and the husband others. Many of the joys and sorrows of marriage arise from the ability or inability of the participants to measure up to the role behavior expected of them. Consequently, one of the problems most people in marriage face is how to deal with the discrepancies between what they expect their wife or husband to do and what she or he actually does.

Role Conflict

Discrepancies between the way a person expects another to behave toward him and the way the other actually behaves result in strain. Strain provokes anxiety; if left unchecked, it can lead to a disruption of the role relationship and, consequently, of the marital system. A considerable amount of this strain, called role conflict, is not unusual during the first year or so of marriage, as couples work through their adjustment to living intimately with each other. Role conflict also occurs periodically as partners relate to each other in new or different ways because of intellectual and emotional growth or regression. Role conflict is a problematic situation. The couple have no guarantee that either partner can make the necessary adjustments to alleviate the situation satisfactorily, nor are there established formulas they may follow to relieve the strain.

John Spiegel, a psychiatrist, feels that the restoration of compatible reciprocal roles is a complicated process.[37] He distinguishes eleven steps, which can be divided into two categories. The first five are forms of *manipulation*, and the last five involve *behavior modification*. The sixth step forms a connecting link between the two groups. The major difference between the two categories is the method by which the role conflict is handled. In the first five steps one person attempts to get his partner to comply with his desires. If his partner complies and adopts the complementary role, the strain is eased—with one partner doing all the changing. In the last five steps, compatible roles are worked out through changes in the roles of *both* spouses. These steps are based on mutual insight instead of manipulation.Spiegel calls this category *role modification*, because the change in role expectation occurs with both partners, and the modifications of their roles are based on interchanges and mutual identification between the partners. The sixth step can go either way.

1 *Coercion* involves present or future punishment. It ranges from overt attack to the threat of attack or of deprivation ("shape up or you won't get something"). None of the coercive techniques guarantee success. They can be responded to by a passive kind of defiance or by counter-coercion ("if you do that, I'll do something else").

2. *Coaxing* includes tempting, bribing, or seducing ("please do this" or "be a dear and do that"). Coaxing is actually a subtle form of coercion and has limited usefulness. It is probably effective only for a short period of time, and its effect can be neutralized by the partner refusing or withholding.

3. *Evaluation* represents praising, blaming, and shaming; it is the procedure of applying a moral or value judgment and can be either positive or negative. The motive behind positive evaluation/is the same as behind negative evaluation—to induce the other person to adopt roles which do not conflict with one's own.

4. *Masking* includes such behavior as pretending, evading, censoring, distorting, lying, hoaxing, and deceiving, in order to manipulate the spouse into adopting an appropriate role. It may also be used to elicit positive responses. The woman who tells a man he is *so strong* and *intelligent* may not believe it but may say it to elicit a certain response. Masking provides only temporary relief from role conflict, as there is usually a period of unmasking at some future point in time. At that point the role partners confront each other with what has been concealed or disguised.

5. *Postponement* is usually undertaken with the hope or belief that "in the interval he will change his mind." The phrases "think it over" or "I'll think about it" imply a postponing process. This technique may result in an attempt at role modification, or it may simply postpone confronting the conflict to a later date.

6. *Role reversal* is an attempt to get the other person to assume your role so that he will better understand how you feel about his behavior. Such questions as "How would you feel if *I* kept calling *you* stupid?" are attempts to create role reversal. This can lead to effective role modification. If done mutually, both can gain insight as to why they respond as they do.

7. *Joking* is an outgrowth of role reversal. If role partners have successfully exchanged places and obtained some insight into each other's feelings and perceptions, they are able to laugh at themselves and each other. In this way playfulness is introduced into what was previously an extremely tense commitment to playing certain roles. Joking or playfulness loosens up the situation and often reduces social distance.

8. *Referral to a third party* assumes that the third party can be objective and has information or skills which may be of help. The third party may be a member of the

family, a friend, a counselor, or an organization. The dangers in this are that the third party may steer the process back to manipulation (perhaps by suggesting such things as "Why don't you try to get him to do this?") or may form a coalition with one partner against the other.

9. *Exploring* is an element of mutual problem solving. This is the point where modified roles are tested. They may have been undertaken to some extent in the joking phase, but at this point they become much more serious. In this process both persons propose and reject possible alternatives. An important aspect of exploring is that it is not done through talk but through actual behavior; that is, it involves an actual test of the alternatives, with evaluation seen in terms of negative or positive.

10. *Compromise* involves some change in the goal each desires or in the values which support the particular goal. People usually are more amenable to compromise after a period of exploration than before if it becomes clear to them that somewhat different complementary roles are necessary to end the conflict.

11. *Consolidation* is required to establish compromise role behavior. In compromising, an adjustment is made in terms of goals and values. Consolidation involves working through and internalizing the modified roles as the couple discover how to reward each other in their new roles.[38]

Spiegel implies that individuals do not have to go through these processes to alleviate role conflict but that they frequently do. He suggests that the second set is more conducive to a long-range solution, because if role modification is successful, the new behaviors are incorporated into the couple's habit system, and the problem is solved. Manipulation, however, is primarily defensive behavior. It may ward off the role conflict for a time, but the conflict is likely to reappear at a later date. In other words, manipulation as a solution may be likened to a bandage on a cancer. Unless the problem is exposed and understood, it is likely to fester below the surface.

Summary

Most people enter marriage with high expectations. Unfortunately, the expectations one person brings into the marriage may not coincide with those of his spouse. One of the problems most marriages face, then, is working out satisfactory role relationships to each other and to outsiders. Part of this process consists of developing cohesiveness as a marital group or unit, which requires mutual attraction and affection and shared values and goals.

Spouses relate to each other in many ways. In an effort to look at the reciprocal nature of roles, we have described three basic marital systems. In the traditional marriage the husband is the provider and head of the house, and the wife cares for the home, rears the children, and caters to her husband. In the companionate marriage, the wife assumes a less subordinate position. She is her husband's companion, and part of her role is to help him in his occupational endeavors. In a sense, both share the husband's career. In egalitarian marriages there is equality between the spouses, mutual decision making, and mutual contributions to maintaining the home. The marital system of most couples is some variation of these types. One's choice of marital roles is influenced by cultural norms, changing sex roles, parental marital roles, childrearing, and the occupation and commitment to career of both the man and the woman.

When faced with discrepancies between what each expects the other to do and what the other actually does, conflict over roles frequently develops. The most obvious solutions to this problem involve changing attitudes and behavior. Both are possible, but the chances of being able to modify the behavior of another person to meet your expectations are minimal. The idea of changing disagreeable qualities in your spouse after the wedding is usually unrealistic. There is a greater likelihood of success if you try to accept the other person and change your expectations instead.

The more flexible one is, the better one can appreciate one's spouse as he is, rather than as he "should be."

Notes

1. Herbst as cited in Robert Blood, Jr., and Donald Wolfe, *Husbands and Wives* (New York: Free Press, 1965), Chapter 2.

2. Jessie Bernard, "Marriage: Hers and His," *Ms*, December 1972, p. 46.

3. A *role* is a pattern of behavior that goes with a given position or *status*. For example, the role of mother connotes caring for children, providing them with emotional support, and so on. Roles also imply reciprocity. A woman needs a child to whom she can relate in the above manner if she is to play her role as mother.

4. Gerald Gurin, Joseph Veroff, and Sheila Field, *Americans View Their Mental Health* (New York: Basic Books, 1960).

5. Genevieve Knupfer, Walter Clark, and Robin Room, "The Mental Health of the Unmarried," *American Journal of Psychiatry* 122 (February 1966), 842; Leo Srole, *et al.*, *Mental Health in the Metropolis* (New York: McGraw-Hill, 1962), pp. 177-178;Norman M. Bradburn, *The Structure of Psychological Well-Being* (Chicago: Aldine, 1962) p. 149.

6. Knupfer, Clark, and Room, "Mental Health of the Unmarried"; *Mental Health in the Metropolis*; and Raymond Willoughby, "The Relationship to Emotionality of Age, Sex, and Conjugal Condition," *American Journal of Sociology* 43 (March 1938), 920-931.

7. Knupfer, Clark, and Room, "Mental Health of the Unmarried," p. 842; National Center for Health Statistics, *Selected Symptoms of Psychological Distress* (Washington, D.C.: U. S. Department of Health, Education and Welfare, 1970), Table 17, pp. 30-31; Srole *et al.*,*Mental Health in the Metropolis,* pp. 177-178.

8. Bernard, "Marriages," p. 110.

9. Alice S. Rossi, "Equality between the Sexes: An Immodest Proposal," in Meyer Barash and Alice Scourby, eds. *Marriage and the Family* (New York: Random House, 1970), p. 279.

10. Clifford Kirkpatrick, *The Family as Process and Institution,* 2d ed. (New York: Ronald Press, 1963), p. 452.

11. Ibid., p. 461.

12. See, for example, Roland Tharp, "Psychological Patterning in Marriage," *Psychological Review* 60 (March 1963), 114.

13. Rossi, "Equality between Sexes."

14. Bernard, *"Marriage"*

15. Nelson N. Foote, "Matching of Husband and Wife in Phases of Development," in Marvin B. Sussman, ed., *Sourcebook in Marriage and the Family* (Boston, Houghton Mifflin, 1963), p. 18.

16. John Sirjamaki, "Cultural Configurations in the American Family," in Marvin B. Sussman, ed., *Sourcebook in Marriage and the Family*, 3rd ed. (Boston: Houghton Mifflin, 1968), pp. 65-71.

17. Ibid., p. 70.

18. Mirra Komarovsky, "Cultural Contradictions and Sex Roles," *American Journal of Sociology* 52 (November 1946), 182-189.

19. For reviews of this argument see Harriet Holter, *Sex Roles and Social Structure* (Oslo, Norway: Hestholms Boktrykkeri, 1970); Shulamith Firestone, *The Dialectic of Sex* (New York: Bantam Books, 1971); Peggy Sanday, "Toward a Theory of the Status of Women," *American Anthropologist*, 75 (October 1973), 1682-1700.

20. Reported by Sandra Oddo, "How Do You Share."

27. Susan Orden and Norman Bradburn, "Working Wives and Marriage Happiness," *American Journal of Sociology* 74 (January 1969), 392-407.

28. Elizabeth Almquist and Shirley Angrist, "Career Salience and Atypicality of Occupational Choice among College Women," *Journal of Marriage and the Family* 32 (May 1970), 242-249.

29. Marotz, "Gender Differentiation."

30. Orden and Bradburn, "Working Wives."

31. Rossi, "Equality between Sexes."

32. See, for example, Lee Burchinal and Jack E. Rossman, "Relations among Maternal Employment Indices and Developmental Characteristics of Children," *Marriage and Family Living* 23 (November 1961), 334-340; F. Ivan Nye and Louis Hoffman, eds., *The Employed Mother in America* (Chicago: Rand McNally, 1963).

33. Eleanor Maccoby, "Effects upon Children of Their Mothers' Outside Employment," in National Manpower Council, *Work in the Lives of Married Women* (New York, Columbia University Press, 1958), pp. 150-172.

4. Orden and Bradburn, "Working Wives."

35. Jessie Bernard, *The Future of Marriage* (New York: World Publishing, 1972), pp. 254-256.

36. Madelon Bedell, "Supermom," *Ms*, May 1963, p. 84.

37. John Spiegel, "The Resolution of Role Conflict within the Family," in Norman Bell and Ezra Vogel, eds. *A Modern Introduction to the Family*, rev. ed. (New York: Free Press, 1968).

38. Ibid., pp. 403-410.

Suggested Readings

Bernard, Jessie. "Marriage: Hers and His." *Ms* December 1972, p. 46. A very interesting review of the literature, specifically in terms of the adverse effects on women of traditional marital roles.

Blood, Robert O., and Hamblin, Robert L. "The Effects of the Wife's Employment on the Family Power Structure." In Norman W. Bell and Ezra F. Vogel, eds. *A Modern Introduction to the Family*. New York: Free Press, 1968, pp. 182-187. A research report of a study investigating the influence of the wife's employment on her marriage. In this case the balance of power was not significantly affected.

Hoffman, Lois Wladis. "Effects of Maternal Employment on the Child." *Child Development* 32 1961, 187-197. Research focusing on how the working wife affects her child's behavior. A major control variable is whether the wife likes or dislikes her work.

Komisar, Lucy. "The New Feminism." *Saturday Review*, February 21, 1970, pp. 27-30, 55. An analysis of the position of women today, stressing the limitations under which they operate due to sexual discrimination.

Rapoport, Rhona, and Rapoport, Robert. *Dual-Career Families*. Baltimore: Penguin

Books, 1971. A study of five dual-career families with children, this books examines the relationship of each spouse to his or her work and the relations to each other and to their families.

Russell, Beverly. "How Do You Share the Responsibilities?" *House and Garden*, July 1973, p. 49. A report on how five couples have divided up their responsibilities to suit their own needs and temperaments.

Safilios-Rothchild, Constantina. "The Study of Family Power Structure: A Review 1960-1969." *Journal of Marriage and the Family* 32 (November 1970), 539-552. A summary of the most significant research conducted during the past decade on family power structure.

Smith, Herbert L. "Husband-Wife Task Performance and Decision-Making Patterns." In J. Poss Eshleman, ed. *Perspectives in Marriage and the Family*. Boston: Allyn and Bacon, 1969, pp. 500-520. An assessment of the farm family, regarding the extent to which division of labor is equalitarian, differentiated, or specialized, including authority patterns related to farm, household, and childrearing tasks.

11 Achieving Sexual Satisfaction

The significance of sex in marriage has increased over the past fifty or sixty years, as satisfactory sexual relationships for women as well as for men have become an expected part of marriage. With the increasing emphasis on sexual gratification, most couples have begun to expect a continuing high level of satisfaction through all the years of marriage. These expectations have an exotic and euphoric quality. People presume sex automatically will provide continuing high levels of pleasure without any real effort by either partner. However, there is little evidence that the *anticipated* levels of sexual pleasure can ever be attained, or if they are, whether they can be maintained over a lifetime. Available evidence shows that high levels of sexual satisfaction do not necessarily "come naturally", thus attaining this goal is a problem-solving situation for many couples.

Sexual satisfaction is assumed to have been achieved by a couple when both individuals are aware of each other's sexual needs and expectations and are able to satisfy them at an acceptable level. *Sexual adjustment* is not necessarily the same as sexual satisfaction, however. A person may adapt to *not* having his needs met and thereby reach a level of sexual adjustment; it does not follow that he is necessarily satisfied with the situation. Sexual needs vary according to physical as well as situational factors. Thus problem solving in this area continues throughout life and is considered by most persons to be a pleasure to work on.

How individuals meet their sexual needs is biologically as well as culturally determined. Today we know that sexuality begins at birth and extends from the parent-child relationship to the *man-woman* relationship. We also know that each person's sexual behavior is influenced by his cultural views of sexuality. For example, even if we agree with and envy the sexual behavior patterns of the Trobriand Islanders, we know that they live and interact in a different culture. Understanding how individuals in our society learn their sexual roles should help us achieve the goal of sexual satisfaction.

In this chapter we will discuss the problem of achieving sexual satisfaction. We will examine four main personal and cultural areas: (1) factors which influence the extent to which sexual gratification becomes a major goal in marriage, (2) the nature of human sexual response, (3) conditions which enhance or decrease sexual satisfaction over time, and (4) costs involved in working toward sexual satisfaction.

Psychosexual Conditioning

A person's sexual aspirations are a result of his attitudes and expectations, which in turn are dictated by early conditioning in his family and peer group. This conditioning is modified by the person's experiences, which are based partly on his own physical attributes and partly on the cultural norms of the community in which he reaches maturity. All these factors restrict the choices available; yet choices do still exist. Sexual behavior, like all other aspects of courtship and marriage, is a problem-solving activity in which choices can be made and their consequences anticipated. Before examining the choices available, we will explore some of the ways in which individuals are conditioned in areas of sexuality. Conditioning is neither unalterable nor permanently influential. Many behaviors previously thought unacceptable or so natural that they should go unquestioned have been brought into the arena of individual choice.

Considerable research has been devoted to developmental and psychological differences supposedly inherent in masculine and feminine nature and function. These studies generally indicate that individual differences among members of each sex are greater than differences between the two sexes.[1] Therefore, they suggest that male-female differences must be the result of socialization. However, vigorous discussion is raging between those who believe in the genetic determination of sex role behavior and those who argue that such differences are primarily the result of socialization. Even if biology plays a part in programming certain kinds of behavior, cross-cultural data point out great variation in sex role behavior in different societies. It seems clear, then, that socialization can override whatever genetic patterns exist.

Sexual conditioning begins in infancy, with experiences such as the amount of warmth and cuddling an infant receives during the biologically satisfying act of feeding. Learning to associate intimate body contacts with pleasure is basic to later acceptance of sexuality. At this point in the lives of most infants sex typing is evident. Boy babies are dressed in blue, girls in pink; even their toys are sex appropriate.

As children grow up, they establish behavioral patterns by watching and imitating other people. It is believed that appropriate role models are necessary in order for children to develop appropriate sexual identities. Since mothers are the ones who most intensively care for the young, it is likely that small children first identify with them rather than with fathers.[3] How is it, then, that boys grow up and identify with men?

The popular Freudian psychoanalytic view of sex role identification describes the three to six-year-old male child as desiring to possess his mother sexually. The little boy fears, however that his larger and more powerful father will cut off his penis to punish him (*castration anxiety*) and he resolves the conflict between the desire for his mother and the fear of his father by identifying with his father. The little girl, on the other hand, finds out that she has no penis, feels castrated, and displays a marked preference for her father—attempting an alliance through seduction. Eventually realizing that she can't compete with her mother for her father's sexual affection without losing her mother's love, she turns toward her mother, and ideally, from then on emulates her. Though popular, this explanation has two major faults. First, in spite of years of attempts to test it, there is no evidence to support it. Second, it seems clearly restricted to a male viewpoint and to the Victorian age. It is not clear, for example, why girls should have penis envy while boys do not have breast envy. Also, there are many instances where a little girl may never see a penis. How, then, is she supposed to envy such an organ? The assumption that repressed sexual urges are the source of all personality conflicts was probably more valid during the late nineteenth century than at present.

Feminist Shulamith Firestone's belief that sex differences are based on power seems to offer a better explanation of sex role differentiation in the last half of the twentieth century than does Freud's idea of castration anxiety and penis envy. According to Firestone, our society is still essentially patriarchal. The husband-father does not have absolute authority, but his wife and children still bear his name, and he is still recognized by society as the head of the household. Even if the wife is equally educated, chances are her income is less; and if the couple have children, it is she who most often sacrifices a career to stay at home and rear them. Frequently she is unable to reenter her chosen field of work later in life without considerable retraining.[3]

Children are very sensitive to the hierarchy of power in the family, as can be illustrated by how quickly they learn to play one parent against the other. The child knows at an early age that he is physically, emotionally, and economically dependent upon his parents. According to Firestone, the child identifies first with the mother, sharing a bond with her—one of repression (the child is oppressed by both mother and father, while the mother is repressed by the father). The child senses that his mother is "half-way between authority and helplessness." "The father, so far as the child can see, is in total control. (Just you wait until your father gets home from the office. Boy, will you get a spanking) he can run to his father if his mother tries anything unjust: but if his father beats him there is little his mother can offer except tea and sympathy".[4]

Why does the normal male child reverse his identification? Sociologists Talcott Parsons and Robert Bales talk about the mother as being the emotional leader of the family.[5] Her world is circumscribed by her family, and her major role is to keep the family running smoothly. The father is the instrumental leader, relating the outer world to the family and vice versa. According to Fromm, he represents the world of thought and the excitement of travel, adventure, power, and science.[6] What finally convinces the male child to identify with his father is the offer of the world when he grows up.

He is asked to make a transition from the state of the powerless, women and children, to the state of the potentially powerful, son (ego extension) of his father. Most children aren't fooled. *They* don't plan to be stuck with the lousy lives of women. They want travel and adventure. But it is hard because deep down they have a contempt for the father with all his power. They sympathize with their mother, but what can they do? They "repress" their deep emotional attachment to their mother, "repress" their desire to kill their father and emerge into the honorable state of manhood.

It is no wonder that such a transition leaves an emotional residue, a "complex." The male child, in order to save his own hide, has had to abandon and betray his mother and join ranks with her oppressor. He feels guilty. His emotions toward women in general are affected.[7]

The little girl also rejects her mother and identifies with her father. But the situation is more complex, for sooner or later she must realize that she cannot enter the world of her father as an equal. If she has brothers, she observes that her father is more willing to share his world and his power with them than with her. According to Firestone, she has two alternatives. She can either use feminine wiles to usurp power, or she can refuse to believe that her sex always will imply an inequity in power between her and her brothers. Firestone says that if she chooses the latter:

she rejects everything identified with her mother, i.e., servility and wiles, a psychology of the oppressed, and imitates doggedly everything she has seen her brother do that gained *for him* the kind of freedom and approval she is seeking. (Notice I do not say she *pretends* masculinity. These traits are not sexually determined.) But though she tries desperately to gain her father's favor by behaving more and more in the manner in which he has openly encouraged her brother to behave, it doesn't work *for her*. She tries harder. She becomes the tomboy—and is flattered to be called one. This obstinacy in the face of an unpalatable reality may even succeed, for a time, perhaps until puberty. Then she is really stuck. She can no longer deny her sex: it is confirmed by lustful males all around her. This is when she often develops a female identification, with a vengence.[8]

What has sex role identification to do with sexual expectations? The male child learns not to be a "sissy" (not to act like a girl) and instead to act "tough" (aggressive). Sexual achievement is suggested to him by his peers, the media, and so on as a way to demonstrate his masculinity. "Our culture, in innumerable ways, many of which are unrecognized, instills in the male the all-important idea that eroticism is essential to maleness, and that it is both the mark of a man to make sexual advances and to have some reasonable expectation of success"[9]

If Firestone's theory is valid, the boy identifying with his father as the most powerful parent comes to regard women as inferior. He may even go so far as to believe that men are the virtual owners of women, and therefore, women should satisfy all their whims, including the sexual ones. As family counselor Richard Klemer points out, such a boy will behave quite differently in a parked car than one who has been brought up to believe that women are his equal.

It is only temporarily surprising to learn that the boy with selfish, sex-demanding attitudes is often rewarded both with sex opportunities and with adulation from the women he dates. After all, most often the young women are brought up in homes with the same cultural background as the young men and are subject to some of the same attitudes and ideas. Aggressiveness in men is admired in our competitive society. Many girls feel that a boy is acting in his appropriate role when he is sex-demanding, and they like him better for this appropriateness.[10]

Most of the boy's practical sexual training comes informally from his peers, older boys, and the men with whom he associates.[11] The lower-class boy often learns from these people that intercourse is geared toward pure physical gratification with little emotional content. As a result, he comes to regard preliminary lovemaking and petting as a waste of time, if not abnormal.[12]

The middle-class boy, apparently, is much more likely to make a romantic association between love and sexual activity. When he is indoctrinated into the male peer group where sexual exploits are regarded as manly (if indeed not essential to one's masculinity), he may experience difficulty in accepting the new norm. Nevertheless, while most middle-class men engage in premarital intercourse,[13] they often believe that their parents would not accept this behavior, and they probably feel guilty about their conduct.[14]

Puberty is a difficult time for both sexes. Boys must adjust to changes in voice, a growing, awkward body, and physical changes signifying the presence of sexual urges. It is a time of frustration and increased anxiety. Nocturnal emissions, masturbation, and sexual fantasies may be accompanied by guilt and confusion. Despite the anxieties, boys are somewhat freer than girls to talk about these things and in that way gain a certain amount of group support. Girls, on the other hand, generally learn that they are not supposed to talk about sexual things or normal body functions. They must deal with their genital changes alone. While boys are rewarded by their peers for tales of their sexual exploits, girls are more likely to be chastised by other girls as well as by their parents if they admit they even have thoughts about sex, let alone engage in it. Most of a girl's bodily changes must not be admitted; leg and underarm hair must be removed, body odor disguised, and menstruation hidden. Even with today's changing mores, purchases of sanitary supplies are still made clandestinely by many adult women This behavior suggests shame and denial of their bodily function.

Until puberty a girl is expected to be almost nonsexual. During adolescence things suddenly change.

Now to be a successful American female adolescent, a girl is expected to know enough about sexual behavior to say no at the appropriate minute. At the same time, she is expected to be sufficiently provocative sexually to keep the boy coming back for more dates.

As she enters adulthood, the mature American woman is expected to reorient her sexual emotions a second time. Now she must be the responsive tigress with an invariable ability to achieve complete orgasm, despite whatever inhibitory process was built into her developing emotional system.[15]

The result of the socialization process described above is that most men and women arrive at marriage with differing expectations about sex. The effects of some twenty years of conditioning cannot be wiped out on the honeymoon. Perhaps the most difficult problem at this point is *not* that the sexual expectations of men and women are different but that they are not *acknowledged* as different. It is one thing to recognize divergent goals in marriage and still another to have divergent goals with no recognition that these differences exist. In the latter case, there is little hope for solving the problem unless the couple realize they don't share the same goals and then work out an agreement as to goals and their relative priorities. Knowledge of why each behaves as he does aids understanding of each other's needs and expectations. The exchange of this knowledge, however, requires an open, nonjudgmental, and help-oriented attitude on the part of both partners. The following hypothetical example illustrates such an attitude:

I went into marriage fully expecting to be in orgasmic ecstasy 99 percent of the time. We never had intercourse while dating, although we petted to orgasm frequently. What surprised me after marriage was that my husband thought the only way for me to achieve orgasm was for him to find the clitoris and rub it to death. It took a long time before I felt I could tell him how I *really* felt when he did that. I knew he would feel crushed if I criticised his lovemaking, but I had to tell him. Instead of telling him directly, I suggested that we experiment with different lovemaking techniques and talk about our responses to them. That solution helped us both open up about our feelings. I found out I had been sending him double messages. He really believed that technique "turned me on."

The "marriage manual syndrome" probably finds its way into many marriage beds. In this syndrome, information gathered from a marriage manual is applied mechanically or incorrectly in sexual relations with one's spouse, ignoring feelings and attitudes. In the above example, the intent of stimulating the clitoris was correct, but the technique was a total failure for this wife, and her nonverbal cues were being misinterpreted. Had she not finally told him how she really felt, their sexual relationship could have suffered considerably. The indirect approach she took allowed a gradual development of openness about sexual responses without putting either spouse on the defensive. Had she been more confident in her ability to explain her frustrations, or had he been more perceptive of her distress with his technique, they might have discussed the situation when it occurred. Many couples find this kind of openness difficult to achieve, at least in part because of the taboos on talking about sex, the inaccurate or incomplete sex education of both men and women, and the fear of being labeled a "sexual failure." Sexual counseling is only now becoming available to couples who find they need outside resources to resolve such problems.

The Nature of Human Sexual Response

A landmark report by Masters and Johnson has provided a thorough and objective description of human sexual response patterns.[16] Before this report, most accounts of sexual response were incomplete and based primarily on individual self-observation. Today information is available not only in technical scientific sources[17] but also in popular literature.[18] These sources can be used to help people understand their sexual response patterns and resolve problem situations in sexual interaction.

Male Sexual Response

While much has been written about the differences between men and women in what arouses them sexually, evidence indicates that there is less dissimilarity in stimulus-response patterns *between* the sexes than *among* members of the same sex.[19] Psychological as well as physiological sources of sexual stimuli arouse both men and women. It is up to the individual couple to discover whether touch, erotic literature, visual stimuli, perfume, or any number of other sources are sexually stimulating for them. If a spouse discovers that a particular technique or situation brings pleasure to him or his partner and they both enjoy doing it, it is obviously pleasurable regardless of what the literature says about what should or should not be stimulating.

Masters and Johnson's data indicate that male response to sexual stimuli occurs in four phases—excitement, plateau, orgasm, and resolution.[20] While these are useful divisions for discussion, there really are no sharply defined beginning and end points for these phases.

In the *excitement* phase, the man's first physical response to sexual stimulation is the erection of his penis. During erection, the three spongy layers of erectile tissue become engorged with blood, and the urethral passage increases in diameter. Erection may be lost and regained many times during the excitement phase, depending on the type and intensity of stimulation. Sudden changes in temperature, fear, and anxiety are conditions which may impair the erection. Sexual excitement causes engorgement and thickening of the tissue of the scrotum and causes the spermatic cord to shorten and the testes to be elevated.

Besides these noticeable changes in the sexual organs, there are many indications that the entire body responds to sexual stimulation. In Masters and Johnson's studies, about 60 percent of all men displayed nipple erection brought about by direct manipulation or as a spontaneous reaction to erotic thoughts. The *sex flush* (a measles-like configuration on the stomach, chest, neck, and face) was noted on about a quarter of the sexually-responding men. Muscular tension of the arms and legs was observed in the later stages of the excitement phase, along with an increase in heart rate and blood pressure as sexual tension mounted.

In the *plateau* phase, the only change in the penis is a slight increase in the diameter of the *coronal ridge* at the base of the glans. The testes increase in diameter 50 percent over their unstimulated size, and the spermatic cord continues to shorten. Because the testes must undergo at least a partial elevation before ejaculation is possible, the full elevation of the testes is a clear indication that orgasm is imminent. The breathing rate, pulse rate, and blood pressure continue to increase; and if nipple erection or the sex flush did not appear earlier, it may occur at this time. Both voluntary and involuntary muscles in the neck, face, and abdomen contract during this stage. Two or three drops of pre-ejaculatory fluid may also be secreted by the Cowper's glands at this time.

The central occurrence of the male *orgasm* is a series of rhythmic contractions which expel the semen. Prior to ejaculation, the fluid containing millions of sperm from the testes collects in the seminal vesicles. These organs contract and deposit the sperm in the urethra, where they are met by prostatic fluid from the prostate gland. This collecton of fluid causes a distention of the urethral bulb at the base of the penis, and the first feeling of orgasm, is experienced by the man. In the second stage of orgasm, the penis projects the semen outward under great pressure by a series of contractions. The first three or four contractions occur about four-fifths of a second apart, but the interval between contractions increases as ejaculation continues.

Accompanying the contraction of the penis are changes in the rest of the body. The blood pressure, pulse rate, and breathing rate peak, the sex flush is most intense, and the muscles react in various ways. While most people are unaware of these muscular responses, the face may grimace, the neck and long muscles of the arms and legs contract, and the hand muscles clutch if they are being used to grasp the partner.

The dynamic changes during orgasm are followed by a *resolution phase*. Orgasm permits the release both of muscle tensions and of blood from engorged blood vessels. The penis rapidly loses its erection and shrinks to its normal size. Masters and Johnson note, however, that this shrinkage occurs in two stages.[21] The shrinkage at first is quite noticeable, though the penis is still enlarged; shrinkage to normal size occurs over a longer time. Other bodily changes are also noticeable. The sex flush disappears; the scrotum and testes gradually return to their unstimulated size; and the pulse rate, blood pressure, and breathing rate return to normal. Men also experience a "refractory period" during which they cannot again become sexually aroused or achieve an erection. The length of this refractory period varies and tends to increase with age. While Masters and Johnson report that one young man was able to achieve three orgasms in ten minutes, this is highly unusual. The refractory period is more likely to exceed one hour.

Female Sexual Response

Women's responses follow the same general pattern as men's. During the *excitement* phase, the initial sign of sexual response is the moistening of the vagina with lubricating fluid. This occurs within ten to thirty seconds of sexual stimulation. Since there is little glandular material in the vagina, the assumption is that the lubricant is produced as a result of the engorgement of the vaginal canal. The inner two-thirds of the vaginal canal increase in width and length as the excitement phase continues. In the nonexcited state the walls of the vagina nearly touch, particularly among women who have never had children. As excitement continues, the entire vagina dilates, but the expansion is focused on its inner two-thirds.

The uterus also becomes engorged with blood and increases in size according to the length of the phase. Rapid, irregular contractions in the uterus may be noted in the early part of the stage; later the entire uterus is elevated into the lower abdomen. The cervix moves up in response to this action, which in turn producs a ballooning of the inner two-thirds of the vagina. Although not visible to the naked eye, the clitoris enlarges due to engorgement of blood in the veins. With continued sexual tension the diameter of the clitoris increases. Direct stimulation of the clitoris produces maximum enlargement in the shortest period of time. Accompanying these clitoral changes, the labia majora (outer lips) spread flat and the labia minora (inner lips) increase in size and move outward.

Many other parts of the body also respond to sexual stimulation. Increases in blood pressure, heart rate, and pulse rate are similar to those noted in men. General muscle tension and the sex flush are more pronounced among women than among men. The breasts increase in size, and the nipples become erect and sensitive to touch. The areola (ring around the nipple) becomes swollen, and the veins of the breast may become more noticeable due to the engorgement with blood.

In the *plateau* phase, the breasts reach their maximum size. Women who experience the sex flush find that it covers most of the body surface. Muscle tension, heart rate, blood pressure, and pulse rate all increase. The clitoris pulls back under its hood and becomes extremely sensitive to touch, so that efforts to touch it directly may be uncomfortable. The major response of the labia majora at this stage is a continued flattening (begun in the excitement phase); the labia minora, however, actually change color. Women who have had children show more distinct color changes than those who have not. The marked color changes indicate that orgasm is imminent.

While the depth and width of the vagina increase very little during the plateau stage, the outer one-third becomes engorged with blood. This engorgement causes the central space of the outer third of the vaginal canal to be reduced by 33 percent. As the distended muscles involuntarily contract, the vagina tightens around the inserted penis. The Bartholin glands which are imbedded in the inner lips at the entrance to the vagina, may also secrete a few drops of fluid. During the woman's *orgasm* the congested outer third of the vagina and the engorged labia minora contract in intervals of four-fifths of a second. As was noted for men, the interval between contractions increases as the contractions continue. The uterus also contracts, in much the same way as it does during the first stage of labor. The contractions begin at the top of the uterus and work their way to the lower part of the cervix. The clitoris seems to show no particular reaction at the time of orgasm (although this may be because under laboratory conditions it is very difficult to observe).

Involuntary muscular responses may be noted in the neck, face, arms, legs, and pelvic region. Involuntary contraction of the sphincter muscles of the rectum also occur, especially if the orgasm is strong. There is a slight increase in the heart rate beyond the plateau stage, and the blood pressure climbs but does not increase as much as the man's. There are no perspiratory reactions at this phase of the response cycle.

Women are capable of multiple orgasms if stimulated long enough, though few are orgasmic every time they engage in intercourse. Achieving orgasm may be only one goal of sexual gratification; caressing, intercourse without orgasm, or the closeness generated by sex play can bring a high degree of satisfaction.

During *resolution* the sex flush disappears almost immediately (in reverse order to its appearance in the excitement phase); it disappears more rapidly from the arms, thighs, back, buttocks, and abdomen than it does from the neck, chest, breast, face, and upper abdomen. The breasts slowly return to their normal size, and muscle tension declines. Heart rate, blood pressure, and pulse rate return quickly to normal. Perspiration appears on the forehead, upper lip, and underarms, or even on the entire body.

The clitoris returns to its normal overhang position within ten seconds after vaginal contractions cease. The outer third of the vagina quickly returns to normal, while the inner two-thirds may take five to eight minutes to do so.

This discussion of human sexual response should not be looked on as a model to follow. There is wide variation in human response to sexual stimulation. Some of the responses described may not be part of your individual pattern, and you may note others as well. While the basic pattern of body response is a common one, it is up to you to discover the unique patterns for you and your spouse.

Differences in Sex Drives

Except in rare cases, all babies are born with the capacity for sexual desire. However, it is frequently assumed that the male drive is greater than the female drive. In many cases this is probably true, not because of biological reasons but because of socialization and age differences in physiological development. Many young women have learned to cope with their sexual desires by sublimating them and concentrating on the romantic, nonsexual aspects of heterosexual relationships. As a result, women like to be wooed even in marriage. Love words, gentle caresses, romantic literature, and movies turn them on. Men, on the other hand, are more instantly turned on, not only by the aforementioned but by visual stimuli of the opposite sex.

Men also are much more likely to view sex as only one aspect of marriage, while women tend to see it as a major part of marriage. Thus, if things are not going well within the marriage, it is more likely to be reflected in the women's sexual activities and/or her attitudes toward sexual activity than it is in her husband's. The fact that men are almost always assured of an orgasm in intercourse, while women are not, may also increase their desire for sexual activity. For most men the problem is one of delaying ejaculation until their partner is ready. Women, on the other hand, generally must concentrate more and work more toward orgasm, even though they have greater orgasmic capacity (the ability to have multiple orgasms in a short time span).Therefore, women are more likely than men to be unable to achieve orgasm. Since regular sexual excitation without the release of orgasm may result in feelings of frustration, the woman's desire for sexual activity may diminish as a way of avoiding sexual frustration. Age confounds the problem. Men's sexual appetites appear to peak in their teens and decline somewhat thereafter. Women peak near the age of thirty and remain relatively more stable. Considering this fact, the possibility of two partners having identical sex drives is unlikely. However, according to Ellis, biology may not play as large a role as was formerly thought. As attitudes toward women's sexual participation become more liberalized the sexual drive of the teenage girl may become more like that of the teenage boy.[22] Perhaps the greater acceptance of premarital sexual activity on the part of the teenage boy and the concurrent premarital sexual restraint on the part of the girl accounts for the fact that differing sex drives in men and women are attributed to their biology. With increasing age, the sex drives become more nearly equal. This may be explained partially by the fact that women with increasing sexual experience become more responsive, particularly if the interest in sex is maintained by the man.[23] Even with this knowledge, a cultural norm suggests that either equal sex drives or a stronger sex drive in the husband are acceptable, but a stronger drive in the wife is not. This is partially due to the association made by many between sexual potency and masculinity. If the differences in sex drives were really understood by both spouses, the wife's drives would be viewed as less of a threat to her husband, thereby increasing the probability of more satisfactory compromises in terms of frequency of intercourse.

Ignorance and Myths About Sex

A number of myths about sex prevent the achievement of continued sexual satisfaction in marriage. For instance, mutual orgasms have been glorified to the extent that some people think they are inadequate if they can't always attain this goal; yet few couples can achieve mutual orgasm on a continuing basis.

Another myth is that only a woman's vaginal orgasms are mature and worth having. Recently a number of treatises have claimed that the *clitoris* rather than the *vagina* is the center for orgasm.[24] Masters and Johnson support this claim.[25] They point out that the thrusting of the penis into the vagina sets into motion the minor labia, which come together above the opening of the vagina to form what is called the hood of the clitoris. The rhythmic movement of the penis sets the minor labia into the same rhythmic motion which then slides the hood back and forth rhythmically against the sensitive glans. This stimulation leads to orgasm. Though neither partner may make a direct effort to stimulate the clitoris, it still participates even in vaginal intercourse.

Masters and Johnson's research also points out that women reach orgasm by many kinds of stimuli—the most common being clitoral and vaginal. Some women, however, also reach orgasm by visual, mental, or breast stimulation. What this means in terms of sexual gratification is that in eliminating the myth of vaginal orgasm as the only mature orgasm, couples must be careful not to make the mistake of simply changing the emphasis from the vagina to the clitoris. Since women have a number of erogenous zones capable of leading them to orgasm, the potential pleasures for women are myriad.

Another myth is that a man's sexual performance is related to the size of his penis. Masters and Johnson's work dispelled this myth with their research findings that a woman's vagina accommodates to the size of the penis, usually during its first few thrusts, regardless of its size. In cases where the man has a relatively small penis and the woman a relatively large vagina, accommodation can be helped by introducing the penis into the vagina earlier in the excitement phase. Conversely, a man with a relatively large penis will find greater accommodation to a woman's relatively small vagina if entry is delayed until a more advanced stage of sexual excitation.

Also of encouragement to the man with a relatively small unerect penis is that short penises increase in length during erection more than do long penises. For example, one man in a Masters and Johnson study found that his 3-inch-long flaccid penis increased 120 percent to almost 7 inches. Another man had a flaccid penis measurement of 4.5 inches; upon erection it increased only 50 percent also to 7 inches. Moreover, since the vagina accommodates itself to the size of penis, even erect size has little relationship to the woman's sexual satisfaction.

Some people, especially men, still fear the properties of menstrual blood; however, this blood is neither more nor less harmful than the blood from a cut anywhere on the body (in fact, it is the same blood). Thus, except for aesthetic reasons and the fact that the woman's tissues, engorged with blood, are more tender during menstruation, there is no obvious reason why intercourse cannot take place during this period.

Another factor which may impede sexual gratification is the overemphasis placed on performance in lovemaking, in terms of frequency and technique. Kinsey's data revealed that, on the average, men between the ages of twenty-one and twenty-five reported that they experienced intercourse 2.3 times per week, compared to 2.5 for women of the same age.[26] Actual frequency, however, is less critical than the quality of the relationship and the feelings that are experienced between partners both before and after intercourse. It is true that people who do not have satisfying sexual relations are likely to have intercourse less often than people who are satisfied sexually, just as it is true that people who laugh and smile are more likely to be happier than those who frown. On the other hand, some people may be excessively committed to having sexual relations frequently, just as some are hysterical laughers. Frequency alone, then, is an inadequate criterion of gratification. Couples should not judge their sexual performance by comparing frequency statistics. If both partners are happy with their frequency of sexual relations, they are attaining their goal. If, however, one is dissatisfied, they should consider the alternatives open to them. Sex involves both giving and taking. While partners should never do anything they really do not enjoy, sometimes satisfaction can be received from meeting the partner's needs. This alternative is essentially a compromise—an agreement that "I'll meet your needs this time, you'll return the favor another time." Another alternative is for the partner desiring more sexual interaction to sublimate these needs or seek means other than intercourse to satisfy them, either with the spouse or by masturbation. Each alternative has different consequences, and these should be examined before a decision is made. A number of marriage manuals and other sex books emphasize lovemaking techniques. All it takes is the courage to walk into a store, select and buy one, and then use it. Perhaps the greatest advantage of these books is that they make people aware of alternatives and in that way kindle the fire of imagination. There is also a danger in their usage, however. Many of these manuals emphasize techniques to the point that sex becomes almost mechanical. If one concentrates so hard on the order and timing of each act, he or she may lose spontaneity and creativity. One wife summed it up by saying, "I don't mind the fact that he's done a lot of reading about making love, but I don't want to know when he's turning the page." Some of the techniques described in sex books are seen as "groovy" by one person and "gross" by another. In the end, they can only suggest techniques which stimulate experimentation on your part. The limits of this experimentation are the needs and abilities of the persons involved. Any technique which is mutually desirable, harmless, and satisfying is appropriate sexual expression.

Another problem with marriage manuals is that most deal with how to get one's partner (especially the woman) *physically* ready for sex, while showing very little concern for her *emotional* receptivity. Knowledge of physiological aspects is important, but so is an awareness of moods and feelings. The entire body is one large erogenous zone, but the mind is the biggest and the most sensitive source of erogenous feeling. Sensing the receptivity of one's partner and setting the mood with physical and verbal caresses helps to bring the partner's level of excitement up to that of the initiator's.

Factors Influencing Sexual Expectations

General Disillusionment

People used to think that there was a general disillusionment with marriage over the passing years and that sex was a part of it. Sex disillusionment does seem to exist, but there is no direct relationship between it and the number of years of marriage. Sex is but one component of the marital relationship, and it appears to operate independently of the others. In a recently published study, family sociologist Wesley Burr found that among middle-class couples dissatisfaction with sex was greatest during the time when their children were in grade school.[27] Though he offers no explanation for this, he also found that people at this stage have the lowest levels of satisfaction in terms of companionship, finances, past performance, and relationships with children. Whatever it is that causes stress during these years affects a number of areas of the marriage. Burr's data indicate that satisfaction with both sex and companionship increases after this time. Sexual satisfaction peaks for men about the time their children leave home and then declines slightly through retirement; women's satisfaction increases after this grade school period but never quite reaches the level attained before the birth of children. Probably one factor affecting the decreased level of satisfaction with sex (as well as other areas of marriage) is the high expenditure of energy, time, and other resources necessary to handle the realities of living with and being responsible for school-age children.

Disillusionment frequently is a result of unattainable aspirations. Yet realistic expectations for sexual gratification generally are not known.

Youth Culture

The youth orientation of our society accentuates the beauty and desirability of the lithe, slim, firm figure. With age and childbearing come wrinkles, sagging breasts, stretch marks, varicosities, and the like; and one's partner no longer resembles the idealized sexual image (if indeed he or she ever did). This orientation adversely affects women more than men, since a woman's sexual desirability depends to a large extent upon her body (while a man's sexual value is defined more in terms of his earning power, intelligence, and personality—at least until he reaches the late fifties). If a person's sexual gratification is based on a youthful, attractive model, he is more likely to experience difficulty in satisfying his sexual desires with his spouse as they grow older.

Sex as a Marriage Barometer

Most observers believe sexual satisfaction to be inexorably linked with general marital satisfaction. In fact, for a long time it was fashionable to relate all problems in marriage to sex. However, many people find they can have sexual adjustment without sexual satisfaction (that is, they can be adjusted to a situation and still feel their expectations are not being met). Furthermore, studies indicate lower correlations between sexual adjustment and marital happiness than between marital happiness and other aspects of marriage, such as finances and in-law adjustment.[28] What this means is that sex is but one component of the marital relatiionship, and it often appears to operate independently of the others.

Research studies, however, have provided only a vague picture of the part sex plays in marriage. There may be complicated linkages, for example, between sexual gratification and marital happiness. In some cases, good sexual relations may compensate for marital difficulties in other areas. In other cases, spouses may optimistically but unrealistically turn to sex as a solution to other marital problems. Because of the intimate and personal nature of sexual intercourse, if there are difficulties between the couple in other areas, it may be difficult for them to overlook these differences and express physical affection

Imagine the case of a son whose widowed mother comes to live with him and his wife. Feeling insecure and wanting to be useful, the mother-in-law takes it upon herself to rearrange all the furniture in the living room; at the same time she criticizes little things, like the way her daughter-in-law does the laundry ("I always iron my son's T-shirts. He likes them that way"). After several months of this, the wife pleads with her husband to defend her; but he replies that his mother means well, that she is only trying to help, that saying something would hurt her feelings. Such a situation might well result in the wife feeling rejected and hostile, and she may not be willing to engage in sexual relations with someone who is unresponsive to her frustrations elsewhere in their marriage.

People having great difficulty in reaching a satisfactory sexual adjustment may also find bitterness and hostility spilling over into other areas of their relationship. It is likely that the reciprocity between sex and other areas of marriage will affect women more than men; because of their socialization and their adherence to the double standard, men are usually more able to separate sex from affection.[29]

The roles played by sexual adjustment and satisfaction in marriage need much more careful anlaysis than they have received in the past. One of the major problems in accomplishing this is that people are reluctant to discuss their sexual behavior with social scientists. Nevertheless, given the importance of sex in our lives, this is an area which should have priority for future research.

Sexual Variety

Marriage implies a permanent commitment, including the continued availability of one's spouse for sexual relations. While increased acceptability of divorce and more liberal views of sexual activity within and outside marriage challenge this notion,[30] it is still clear that adultery is even more frowned upon than is premarital intercourse. Thus, while some spouses may consider seeking another sexual partner outside the marriage to resolve a sexual problem, we predict that this alternative will be less popular than focusing on improving sexual relations within the marriage.

While marriage may provide continued availability of a sexual partner, it is no guarantee against sexual boredom. There are just so many positions and permutations for intercourse, and after a while each spouse gets to know what pleases the other, what does not, and how each will react. This may get monotonous for some. Usually monotony is due more to a lack of knowledge or desire to try more than a few standard positions than to an exhaustion of all possibilities. Norms prescribing sexual behavior also restrict sexual diversity. Some people, for example, still believe that the only normal sexual position is face-to-face, husband-on-top. In fact, the laws in many states support this notion by defining oral-genital intercourse (cunnilingus and fellatio), along with homosexuality, as abnormal sexual behavior and grounds for divorce or possible imprisonment. The fact that these laws are seldom, if ever, invoked, despite evidence that the practices are increasing, suggests a general liberalization of attitudes with regard to sex. Some states have gone so far as to repeal oral-genital prohibitions, suggesting a greater tolerance of a variety of sexual practices.

Most people are aware that a variety of positions and techniques are possible, even if they have never experimented with them. Still, it is often difficult to get out of an established routine. Determination, personal flexibility, and creative imagination are needed to put life into a failing sexual relationship (and to improve a successful one). Perhaps it is impossible to make sex *always* an exciting, exhilarating experience.

Influence of Conflicting Career Paths

Interpersonal relationships require an investment of time and energy. Time spent together generally decreases as the husband and wife devote more of their time to a career, commuting, organizational and recreational activities with friends, and so on. Even in the traditional family the husband hurries off to work in the morning, and the wife cooks and does dishes in the evening while he is relaxing. Children also detract from time spent with each other, since they must be cleaned, fed, bedded down, and loved. All these things leave little time or energy at the end of a busy day for intimate relations with one's spouse; yet time is a valuable resource in achieving sexual satisfaction. A Sunday afternoon spent rediscovering one's responses to leisurely lovemaking may illustrate the point better than any other argument could.

Costs of Sexual Satisfaction

Researchers have focused on the interpersonal aspects of sexual adjustment only within the last decade. While our knowledge is therefore somewhat meager, we do find that "a sexual relationship is an interpersonal relationship, and as such is subject to the same principles of interaction as are other relationships."[31] Thus the costs of maintaining a satisfying sexual relationship are similar to those of any satisfying interpersonal relationship.

Every interaction requires time and energy. Since these commodities are limited, each person has to decide how to apportion them. Most sexual activities occur at night (probably due to work, child care, and custom). Because of this, the time factor may not appear important—until the next morning, when one has to get up. Then the realization surfaces that sexual behavior has infringed upon sleeping hours. In addition, intercourse can be physically strenuous. This means that the person may require more rest than usual and may even be hesitant to engage in intercourse because he is already tired. Therefore, the physical act alone may require some adjustment in one's routine—perhaps not working so hard during the day and not planning too much other activity in the evening. This means that time and energy must be taken from such things as one's career, the ironing, or even hobbies. But these are simply the physical costs. What about the social and psychological costs?

To succeed in any close relationship with another person requires some skill. One must be perceptive enough to know what activities interest the other person and motivated enough to take part in them. Communication is of the utmost importance in this endeavor. Both persons must be willing to express their feelings and desires and to carefully and objectively pay attention to the other's as well. The more time couples spend talking with each other, the greater their probability for marital satisfaction. Talking together apparently influences their feeling of closeness.[32] If this is the case in other areas of marriage, it follows that communication will also enhance sexual compatibility. However, it is not always easy to disclose intimate feelings to someone else, not even one's spouse, because such openness leaves one vulnerable. Matters of sex are especially difficult for many people to discuss, since they are reluctant to admit either ignorance or expertise in this area.

The responsibilities of a relationship require considerable psychic investment. This involves consideration for the other person's feelings, moods, and desires and responsibility for one's own acts and words. One might, for example, change some of his values and ways of thinking about sex to bring them closer to those of the partner. Birth planning is another important consideration. Some people may not enjoy intercourse fully if they are worried about the possibility of an unplanned pregnancy. For men, such worries seem more prevalent shortly after the birth of a baby, when they are faced with the economic realities.[33] Women, on the other hand, seem more generally concerned, because they are usually the ones who spend the most time caring for the children. Conception and contraception, then, are aspects of intercourse which most couples will have to deal with in order to relieve tension resulting from fear of pregnancy.

All these factors require time, energy, and work. For many, the effort of working out a satisfying sexual relationship (including the time and energy taken from other areas, such as a career) are well worth the results; for others, the costs may be too high.

The Extra in Marital Sex

Among the choices some people make in the area of marital sex is whether or not to have an extramarital affair. For most couples this decision has a fundamental effect on the subsequent course of the marriage.

For some, extramarital affairs are an acceptable form of diversion for one or both partners. These people claim that their affairs have no detrimental effect on their marital sexual relations.[34] Others engage in extramarital affairs for the variety and adventure, claiming that they add excitement to their otherwise dull and routine lives.[35] Those who engage in mate swapping (swinging) feel that the variety enriches their marital lives. The major difference between mate swapping and affairs is that an affair clearly represents some exchange of affection whereas such an exchange is taboo in many mate swapping circles.

Many more reasons are given for extramarital sex. Some husbands claim extramarital relations as a male need ("men are naturally polygamous"), while believing that their wives should be faithful. These husbands tend to hold traditional possessive attitudes about women, treating their wives more like property than people. Other people feel sexually deprived or unappreciated in their own marriages and may have at least one affair to prove to themselves that somebody else desires them. Sometimes these people may be actually deprived, as in the case of separations beyond their control (such as frequent long business trips, military service, or imprisonment) or when one spouse has a much higher sex drive than the other. It is even possible that some spouses are entirely happy with their marriage, except for sex, and therefore seek sexual fulfillment outside the marital chambers. Others claim that they "just can't help" themselves and are compelled to have affairs. Some people clearly are seeking a way out of their marriage, while others, in the process of terminating a marriage, simply drift into affairs. These examples by no means exhaust the explanations of why people engage in extramarital affairs, but they do indicate that the motives are extremely varied and often complex.

Many couples decide against engaging in extramarital affairs. For instance, the more traditional or religious the person, the less likely he is to have an affair, since tradition and religion both strongly support monogamous behavior. Another factor in this decision is the nature of the marital relationship. Cuber and Harroff's study of sexual behavior among the affluent leads us to speculate that those people involved in what they call an *intrinsic* relationship are less likely to engage in an affair than those in what they call *utilitarian* arrangements.[36] According to Cuber and Harroff:

To the people content with the utilitarian marriage, male-female relationships are tertiary to other matters of importance, clearly secondary to other things which must or should, they judge, come first. To those who want or need vital or total relationships . . . the relationship of a man and a woman has top priority among the several considerations which make up a total life. These people, of course, also have careers, also must be concerned with public opinion, have obligations to children and community; but typically, they carry out these obligatons and enjoy these privileges, while keeping them somehow subordinate.[37]

Since people involved in intrinsic relationships relate to each other intensively at all levels and place a high priority on the quality of the relationship, there is little time left over for an intensive involvement with someone else. Also, as long as the marriage is satisfying, there are few reasons to get involved with another person. (However, a recent estimate has been made that by age forty about one-third of all married women and almost two-thirds of all married men have had an extramarital sexual experience. We therefore suspect that since fewer people involved in intrinsic than in utilitarian marriages will have affairs, it follows that intrinsic marriages are relatively scarce.)

Another reason for deciding against an affair is the fear of damaging the marital relationship and hurting one's spouse. Some people feel that neither the emotional risks to their marriage nor the costs in terms of time, energy, and perhaps money are worth the benefits. Of course, the adjustment in terms of time and energy could come from other areas of one's life, such as work or personal recreation, but the feelings of one's spouse would still be an important issue.

Effects upon the Spouse

The affairs of one partner usually have either direct or indirect effects on both spouses. Some couples agree that extramarital activity is acceptable and even desirable behavior. For them, such activity may have minimal negative effects upon their marriage—and perhaps even positive ones. It should be noted, however, that for many people—despite their assertions of modern and free outlooks—the thought of a loved one in someone else's arms turns out to be painful experience. And if there has been no prior agreement (or even if there has and the spouse is unable to cope with the sexual activities of his partner), the consequences become more serious.

If the affair is kept secret, new problems are created. The partner involved must always be on guard; and since discovery is usually a harder blow than self-disclosure, the damage to the basic loyalty and trust in the relationship is usually very high.

Many factors enter into the decision of whether to disclose an extramarital affair to one's spouse. Some concern fears about hurting the marriage, hurting the spouse, reprisal by the spouse, and so on. What this really involves is a person's willingness to take responsibility for his actions and to treat his mate as a free and equal human being, which means being prepared to cope with the situation in realistic terms. If the affair is an attempt to terminate the marriage, telling one's spouse will be probably elicit the desired response of heading the couple toward divorce. On the other hand, this method of ending a marriage is at best indirect and at worst causes unnecessary pain to the spouse. If divorce is not desired and the affair presents a clear threat to the stability of the marriage, then the couple must come to grips with the reasons for the person's infidelity by examining the weaknesses in their relationship. If they are flexible and sufficiently motivated (if both truly desire to rebuild their marriage), they can use these insights into their behavior as guidelines for modifying their relationship.

Our basic assumption throughout this chapter has been that sexual gratification is a major goal in marriage. Yet people get married for many reasons—money, security, normative pressures, children, and so on. For some of these people, sex in marriage may be a necessary evil—something to be tolerated. For others, sexual desires may be sublimated in favor of expending time and energy on other facets of their lives, such as careers. Marriages between people holding such viewpoints may be quite satisfactory. Sex simply is not very important to them.

The broad spectrum of goals in marriage raises the critical issue of goal consensus. Whether the goal is sexual gratification or something else, if it is not shared by the couple, they cannot effectively work together toward it. They will not be good problem solvers because they will not agree on what is a problem. It goes without saying that unless spouses agree on problems, they can hardly solve them.

Summary

Sexual gratification in marriage is a common goal; yet achieving it is problematic for many couples. Unrealistic expectations for sexual interaction, ignorance of the differences between feminine and masculine response, and unwillingness to be open with one's partner contribute to difficulties in achieving the goal.

Problem solving in the area of sex, just as problem solving in any other marital area, calls for goal consensus. Beyond that the available alternatives are limited only by taste, preference, and satisfaction. While sexual adjustment means adapting oneself to the level and type of sexual interaction present, sexual satisfaction implies that the type and level meet one's needs and expectations.

Achieving sexual satisfaction is a continuous process throughout marriage. Working on the problem and achieving the goal offers a reward that no other problem has available.

For some people sexual gratification is an unimportant part of marriage. Clearly, the important issue is goal consensus. Only if both partners feel the same way can they work toward sexual satisfaction by placing it in the proper perspective in *their* marriage.

Notes

1. Jo Freeman, "Growing Up Girlish," *Transaction* 8 (November-December 1970), 36-44.
2. Talcott Parsons and Robert Bales, *Family, Socialization and Interaction* (New York: Free Press, 1955).
3. Shulamith Firestone, *The Dialectic of Sex* (New York: Bantam, 1971).
4. Ibid., p. 40.
5. Parsons and Bales, *Family*.
6. Erich Fromm, *The Art of Loving* (New York: Harper & Row, 1953).
7. Firestone, *Dialectic,* p. 51-52.
8. Ibid., p. 53.
9. Winston Ehrmann, *Premarital Dating Behavior* (New York: Holt, Rinehart and Winston, 1959), pp. 286-287.
10. Richard Klemer, *Marriage and Family Relations* (New York: Harper & Row, 1970), p. 221.
11. Paul Gebhard et al., *Sex Offenders* (New York: Harper & Row, 1965), p. 469; Sarah Nanny, "Sexual Knowledge of College Students" (M.A. thesis, Syracuse University, 1969).
12. Alfred Kinsey et al., *Sexual Behavior in the Human Male* (Philadelphia and London: Saunders, 1948), pp. 327-393; Ira Reiss, *The Social Context of Premarital Sexual Permissiveness* (New York: Holt, Rinehart and Winston, 1967), pp. 56-75.
13. Ernest Burgess and Paul Wallin, *Courtship, Engagement and Marriage* (Philadelphia: Lippincott, 1953), p. 330; Erhmann, Premarital Dating; Kinsey et al., *Sexual Behavior in Human Male*; Vance Packard's report in *The Sexual Wilderness* (New York: Pocket Books, 1970) of a survey of twenty-one colleges in the United States (involving 644 men and 688 women in their

junior and senior years) concluded that 60 percent of the male respondents had experienced premarital coitus and that the mean age of first coitus was 17.9. For women the corresponding figures were 40.5 percent with the mean age 18.7. There was considerable variation by region.

Percentages for Coital Rates by Region

	Men	Women
South	69	32
East	64	57
West	62	48
Midwest	46	25

14. In *The Social Context of Premarital Sexual Permissiveness,* Ira Reiss suggests that the guilt feelings youngsters feel in their premarital sexual activities are due to their awareness of general parental opposition of sexuality even though the parents may not express this directly.

15. Klemer, *Marriage and Family Relations,* pp. 231-232.

16. William H. Masters and Virginia E. Johnson, *Human Sexual Response* (Boston: Little, Brown, 1966).

17. Ibid.; James McCary, *Human Sexuality* (Princeton, N.J.: Van Nostrand, 1967); Ruth Brecher and Edward Brecher, *An Understanding of Human Sexual Response* (New York: Signet Books, 1966); and the *Journal of Sex Research* all illustrate technical sources of information about human sexual response.

18. Articles in *Sexology, Good Housekeeping, Playboy,* and *Redbook*, for example, have focused on sexual response patterns in the past few years.

19. Phyllis Kronhausen and Eberhard Kronhausen, *The Sexually Responsive Woman* (New York: Ballantine Books, 1965).

20. The data reported in Master and Johnson, *Human Sexual Response,* and Brecher and Brecher, *Understanding Human Sexual Response,* form the basis for this discussion.

21. Masters and Johnson, *Human Sexual Response.*

22. Albert Ellis, ed., *Sex Life of the American Woman and the Kinsey Report* (New York: Greenberg, 1954).

23. Alfred Kinsey et al., *Sexual Behavior in the Human Female* (Philadelphia and London: Saunders, 1953), p. 77.

24. Ann Koedt, "The Myth of the Vaginal Orgasm," in Jacqueline Wiseman, ed., *People as Partners* (San Francisco: Canfield Press, 1971), pp. 121-129.

25. Masters and Johnson, *Human Sexual Response,* as reported in Ruth Brecher and Edward Brecher, *An Analysis of Human Sexual Response* (New York: New American Library, 1966).

26. Kinsey et al., *Sexual Behavior in the Human Female,* p. 77.

27. Wesley Burr, "Satisfaction with Various Aspects of Marriage over the Life Cycle: A Random Middle Class Sample," *Journal of Marriage and the Family* 32 (February 1970), 29-37.

28. Jessie Bernard, "The Adjustments of Married Mates," in Harold Christiansen, ed., *Handbook of Marriage and the Family* ((Chicago: Rand McNally, 1964), pp. 675p740.

29. Klemer, *Marriage and Family Relations*, Chapter 18; Riess, *Social Context.*

30. Bernard Farber, *Family: Organization and Action* (San Francisco: Chandler Publishing, 1964).

31. Lester A. Kirkendall and Rogert W. Libby, "Interpersonal Relationships—the Crux of the Sexual Renaissance," *Journal of Social Issues* 22 (April 1966), p. 57.

32. Harold Feldman, *Development of the Husband-Wife Relationship* (A research report to the National Institute of Mental Health, Grant M-2931, Cornell University, 1965); Allen Wheelis,

"How People Change," in Leo Hamalian and Frederick Karl, eds., *The Radical Vision* (New York: Crowell, 190), pp. 298-324.

33. E. E. LeMasters, "Parenthood as Crisis," *Marriage and Family Living* 19 (November 1957), 352-355.

34. For a somewhat more in-depth discussion of the issue, see Albert Ellis, "Healthy and Disturbed Reasons for Having Extra-Marital Affairs," in Gerhard Neubeck, ed., *Extra-Marital Relations* (Princeton: Prentice-Hall, 1969) pp. 153-161.

35. Ibid.

36. John Cuber and Peggy Harroff, *Sex and the Significant Americans* (Baltimore: Penguin Books, 1968).

37. Ibid., p. 132.

38. Robert Bell, *Social Deviance* (Homewood, Ill.: Dorsey, 1971).

Suggested Readings

Brecher, Ruth, and Brecher, Edward. *An Analysis of Human Sexual Response.* New York: New American Library, 1966. An easily understood description of Masters and Johnson's work in human sexual activity, the volume also includes related research by other sex researchers.

Comfort, Alex, ed. *The Joy of Sex.* New York: Crown Publishers, 1972. A beautifully illustrated book about lovemaking, it is addressed to adventurous lovers who wish to stimulate their creative imagination for sexual interaction. Assuming active participation by both partners, it provides a whole range of alternatives for marital sex.

Ellis, Albert, and Abarbanel, Albert. *Encyclopedia of Sexual Behavior.* New York: Hawthorn Books, 1967. Over a hundred articles by authorities in sexology provide a complete and authoritative source on human sexual response.

Jones, Kenneth, Shainberg, Louis, and Byer, Curtis O. *Sex.* New York: Harper & Row, 1969. Viewed as a potential source of legitimate pleasure and satisfaction, sex is discussed in the contexts of premarital, marital, and extramarital situations. Descriptions of sexual anatomy and physiology of both sexes are followed by chapters on sexual response and technique, contraception, infertility, and pregnancy.

12 Designing In-law Relationships

In-laws don't just happen, nor are they thrust upon an individual; they are acquired by marriage to a particular person. The norm for our society is the nuclear family—husband, wife, and, eventually, children. However, marriage creates more than a union between husband and wife. It also creates an outer fringe of relatives, who, although they do not live with the couple, manage to influence and be influenced by them.

Most potential spouses have living parents, and it is inevitable that the parents will exercise or attempt to exercise some influence on the course of the marriage. From their point of view, a substantial shift in the way they relate to their child is expected of them quite suddenly when the marriage takes place. For approximately two decades they have been concerned about and responsible for the child's welfare. Then, almost overnight, they are expected to abandon or ignore their past interest and move out of the picture. This is virtually impossible to accomplish immediately, as we mentioned in Chapter 8 , and the problem is even greater if the child is young.[1] The older a child is at the time of marriage, the greater the separation between him and his parents and the greater his overall independence of them. Regardless of the nature of their relationship, most parents want to maintain ties with their adult child after he marries. Usually parents realize that in order to do so, they will have to modify some of their behavior.

Setting Goals Regarding Kin

To a couple, the involvement with kin relations is often inversely proportional to the importance of their marital relationship. Given the limited time and emotional energy of each individual, an investment in one relationship reduces the time and energy available for others. Therefore, if one's marriage requires complete commitment, other kin relationships will wither; if, however, the child-parent bond remains strong, the relationship of the couple will get less attention. "Under such circumstances," says one sociologist, "there is an inherent conflict of emotions and interest between parents and the spouses of their children."[2] Given this latent conflict potential, one primary goal for young couples is to find satisfactory methods of getting along with their parents and in-laws.

There are undoubtedly some individuals who would just as soon get along *without* their families as *with* them. On the whole, however, most families seem to need each other. In a mobile society, such as ours, friendships are frequently short-lived. Therefore, people tend to depend on relatives (if they are available), who can be called on in time of need, for long-term relationships.

In this chapter we will examine the various aspects of maintaining satisfying relations with in-laws.

Relating to In-Laws

In-law problems include problems the couple has with in-laws and conflict between the spouses themselves over in-laws.[3] Despite popular opinion that in-laws cause problems, many married couples feel it is not the spouse's kin who are the most troublesome, but rather their own relatives. The literature suggests, however, that in cases of marital discord, husbands and wives both believe that the husband's kin are more frequently involved than are the wife's kin.[4]

If, as family sociologist Evelyn Duvall suggests, one of the basic tasks in the early years of marriage is for the young couple to cement their marriage bond so that they act and feel as a unit, then any intrusion by either family which threatens the autonomy of the pair may be construed as difficulty with in-laws.[5] One young bride, for example, felt offended that her mother-in-law washed some of her husband's clothes when they were visiting in his parents' home for a week. "*I'm* his wife. *I* should be the one to wash his clothes," the wife complained. (Although a few months later she might have had a very different attitude about washing clothes, at this point she wanted to fulfill what she considered her responsibility.) She was intent on being a "good wife" and was threatened unnecessarily by the actions of her mother-in-law. This illustration focuses more on the problems couples have with their relatives than on those involving disagreement between the spouses over in-laws.

It is often difficult, however, for couples to keep in-law problems to themselves. Frequently the trouble becomes triangular; this is because one of the spouses is a blood relative of the troublesome in-law. Part of the problem concerns the interpersonal relations between each spouse and his or her parents, and part concerns how this relationship affects the interaction between the couple.

Since in-law problems appear more frequently during the early years of marriage and among couples who marry when they are young,[6] Leslie suggests that age is a crude index of independence: "Those who marry [young] . . . must expect to complete their striving for independence after they marry; those who marry later are more likely to have this behind them."[7]

Achieving Independence

The problem of independence is heightened by the traditional roles the sexes play in our society. From childhood on, women's lives are more circumscribed and more predictable than men's lives. During childhood, girls are protected more than boys, given less training to be independent, and directed into the roles of wife and mother. As a result, they are more likely than their husbands to be emotionally tied to their family even after they are married.[8] For example, they assume the responsibility of keeping in touch with kin[9] by writing letters and phoning relatives. Further, parents are more likely to turn to their daughters than to their sons for help after the children marry.[10] All these factors point up the strength of the dependency relationship between women and their parents.

In view of the close contact the wife has with her family, one might expect this relationship to be a sore spot with her husband. On the contrary, she is the one who is apt to have in-law problems. Just as she considers relatives more important than her husband does, so do her mother and mother-in-law. The marriage of a son or daughter is more disruptive for the mother than for the father. Traditionally, a mother's major role in life has been caring for her family, while the father has been more involved with his job. Thus it is quite logical that after long years of care mothers should want to retain close ties (and some of their former functions) with their married children.[11]

One reason for the conflicts existing between the wife and her mother-in-law is the asymmetrical power distribution between the sexes. Leslie says that in our male dominated society women tend to compete with each other for the affection and favors of men. He notes that women are far more concerned about their adequacy as wives than men are about their adequacy as husbands; he adds that a man is judged more in terms of performance on the job than in the home, while a woman is judged on her accomplishments as wife and mother.[12]

Upon marriage, the wife is thrown into direct competition with her mother-in-law in pleasing and caring for her husband. She may well feel insecure because of her inexperience in the realms of housekeeping, cooking, and laundry. As a consequence she may be jealous of her mother-in-law's expertise in these areas, as well as of the affection her husband has for his mother.

On the other hand, her husband's mother probably feels that she has done a good job of caring for her son and she wants him to continue to get good care. She knows that he is an adult, able to care for himself, but it is difficult for her to feel these things emotionally. Also, for many years she was the number one woman in his life. While he was dating, she saw girls come and go; all the while her place in his respect and affection remained unchanged. She now feels a loss of affection and a lowering of her status. She also is forced to view herself as "growing old." Since being attractive, young, and desirable to men is associated with high status in our society, many mothers vigorously endeavor to retain their favored position with married sons. Very often it is not the daughter-in-law as a person who is resented, but her role as the usurper of the mother's place in her son's life.

The husband-son finds himself in a difficult situation. He probably wants to remain on friendly terms with his mother. At the same time he is struggling for independence and the respect of his wife; and she is expecting him to perform as a husband, placing her first in his affection and consideration. Both mother and wife may thus pressure him to form a coalition against the other—the classic triangle.

Problems with the wife's mother are not usually as problematic as problems with the husband's mother, and they are of a different kind. One of the major difficulties is when the wife maintains her childhood dependence on her mother or when her mother clings to this dependence. A woman who has been closely protected at home may find it difficult to lay aside the daughter role and assume the responsibilities and status of a wife, and her husband may resent her turning to her parents instead of to him for help.[13]

Some mothers cling desperately to their daughters either to relive their own early years of marriage or to keep from losing the daughter's love and companionship. Lantz and Snyder point to other major factors influencing the extent to which the mother depends on her child.[14] One of these factors is the quality of the relationship between the parents, and the other is their emotional maturity. It might be suggested that if, over time, the parents no longer have a satisfying relationship together, they will turn elsewhere to get their needs met. In this case the mother may wish to fulfill her needs by perpetuating her earlier relationship with her married children (which soon causes her to be labeled as the domineering mother or the interfering mother-in-law). The emotionally mature mother, however, is more likely to be sure of herself and to adapt to changes which occur in her life. She does not need to compete with her daughter-in-law but rather manifests an attitude of cooperation in building a successful relationship.

Up to this point we have talked primarily about the emotional involvement of adult children and their mothers. Fathers appear to present relatively few in-law problems.[15] In fact, the husband's sister is considered to be the second most problematic in-law.[16] Since fathers are less tied to the family for their sense of worth, they are not as likely to feel threatened by their offspring's marriage partner. In addition, the marriage of children doesn't leave them functionless, as it does their wives.

The problem of the clinging mother came up one day after a marriage class, when two of the students stayed late for consultation. They were newlyweds who had been married for only three months, and their problem sounded quite funny to the professor. However, she realized it was serious to the couple when she saw how distraught they were. It seems that every time they visited the husband's parents his mother inevitably got in the front seat with her son when they went for a drive in the car. The couple were appalled that she would have the "nerve" to do such a thing. They talked about their feelings and then began exploring alternatives to change the situation.

They offered many suggestions (among them, "we could tell her we don't like it," "we won't go to see them," and "we could both get in on one side so she would be forced to sit next to the door"). Then came the crucial question. How often does this happen? "Every time we go home." How often is that? "About once a month." At this point the couple began to realize that the time involved in this situation was almost negligible. What, then, was their real concern? "Well," they concluded, "she isn't acting the way a mother-in-law *should* act."

Is it possible that couples themselves generate in-law problems out of their own possessiveness? One girl comments, "It makes me so mad the way my husband's mother fusses over him. She even wants to wash our clothes when we are home for the weekend." Our suggestion is to let her do so. Although a son becomes a husband, he also remains a son; and a great many tearful, exasperating hours can be avoided if only the couple can empathize with the parents and alter their expectations about parental behavior. This is what the newlyweds finally decided to do. Although they still considered the mother's behavior inappropriate, they agreed that "knowing mother, we might as well expect it." It is impossible to ruin a relationship by competing with another person if that person refuses to compete, which is what this young bride was able to do.

In this case the couple sensed a threat to their independence, because they felt the mother was trying to "take over," to interfere with their feeling of couple unity. The independence issue appears in many ways and lends itself to numerous alternatives for action. Had the occurrence of their problem been more frequent, perhaps the alternative chosen would have been unsatisfactory. Had the couple not been able to rid themselves of the irritation they once experienced over the problem (by altering their pattern of thinking), it is likely that another solution would have been required.

Let us take, once again, the classic situation of the mother-in-law who interferes too much. If the couple's goal is to stop this interference, they should first try to understand why she acts the way she does. Is it because she is unconsciously trying to fill a void in her life? If so, is she the type of person who will leave them alone when she has other things to occupy her time? Perhaps her own and her "inherited" child can help her get involved in other things, for example by encouraging her to go back to work, introducing her to some new people, or convincing her husband to take a more active role in discouraging her "helpful advice." What works for one type of individual may be totally inappropriate for another, which points out how essential it is to carefully assess the people involved as well as the specific situation.

In addition to the decision of what to do about a problem is the issue of who should do it. This will vary, of course, according to circumstances and personalities, but family members can often take certain liberties and make some fairly harsh suggestions to each other without fear of extreme repercussions. Therefore, if face-to-face confrontations are required over an issue, it may be easier for the child than for the in-law to talk to the parents. This child, who sits more or less in the middle, can be described as an ambassador. He constantly interprets what one side is saying to the other and negotiates for first one and then the other.

Affectional ties are often very strong between parents and children. It is not just parents who wish to maintain them; adult children not only welcome continued interest and support but complain if it is absent! In Duvall's study of 1,337 people, 99 of the 992 reporting in-law problems said that the in-laws were indifferent, uninterested, or ignored them.[17] Thus both parents and children want to retain ties of affectional and emotional support. If the couple can establish their independence to their satisfaction this should not be problematic.

The Question of Aid

The independence-dependence problem is indeed complex. Upon marriage sons and daughters instantly acquire adult status as husbands and wives who are supposed to forge a life of their own. As we mentioned earlier, however, these same people are still someone's sons and daughters, and what's more, by marriage they have acquired another set of parents! Adding to the problem is an unclear conception of what independence is, especially for those who marry young. An intricate network of aids and supports exist between parents and children. These range from direct financial subsidies, as is frequently the case for young married college students, to indirect and occasional aid, such as a layette at the birth of a child, babysitting, or expensive birthday gifts.[18] The amount and kind of aid depends on numerous factors, such as the parents' financial status, the age and need of the couple, the number of siblings, parental approval of the marriage, geographical proximity, and so on.[19] But regardless of its nature the pattern is quite pervasive.

Most young people who accept help from their parents prefer to have no strings attached to it; that, however, is not very realistic. If they accept aid, what do their parents want in return? The most obvious returns are the children's affection and some influence over where and/or how the children live their lives.

Parents often want their children to live reasonably near them after they are married. Despite high mobility rates (almost 20 percent of the population moves annually), this is not a great problem. Geographic separation from kin is characteristic of only a small portion of North American families. "It is the professional and managerial families of the upper-middle class who are most likely to be separated from their kin, and even these are more often proximate than distant," according to Bert Adams, a sociologist of kinship.[20] It is also the upper middle-class families who are more likely to support their children's moving if career advancement is at stake.

As we have indicated, one of the consequences of accepting direct aid from parents is that in return they may want some say in how their children live their lives. Indirect aid is less likely to have strings attached, probably because the parents feel this aid will help their children achieve a measure of independence. If ties are attached to indirect aid, it is likely that the parents will want their married children to behave according to their values. This will cause few problems if the couple share most of these values. But if their goals are incompatible, and if the parents (in-laws) expect behavioral reciprocity for their aid, the couple are faced with two choices: (1) compliance with the demands, which requires a reordering of goals, or (2) breaking away from the parents.

Breaking away depends on the situation. It may involve refusing aid and foregoing whatever such aid provides, paying for everything themselves, moving away, or cutting all ties. Moving away is not an alternative available to all couples (as we shall see later in this chapter).[21] However, it does provide one solution. If in-laws are critical of the couple's behavior, aid or no aid, moving away may prevent frequent unpleasant interaction. Emotional and affectional ties that would be strained by the different life-styles can be retained in this way; and certain types of aid might still be forthcoming. Moving away, however, may require the couple to build up a non-kin support system. This is almost always essential in the case of a complete break.

On the other side of the coin, some parents give aid to the married couple openly and freely, with no strings attached. The most common example of this situation is that of a couple who have married while they are still in college and who are living under financial hardship. In this case parents often will help them through college. In fact, many parents have saved money specifically for their child's education and insist that the couple take it. It is impossible to say what the appropriate course of action should be; both acceptance and rejection of the money are reasonable alternatives, depending on the circumstances. Some individuals enter marriage with a chip on their shoulder about financial independence. A hostile attitude reflecting "we don't need or want help of any kind from anyone" may be as damaging to in-law relationships as asking for too much help. Hurt feelings are sometimes at stake if parents have had their hearts set on sending their child through college and then are denied the opportunity to carry through with their plans.

Resolving such issues requires a sensitivity which allows the couple to compare their own expectations with those of their parents and then to behave accordingly. Solutions to this kind of problem do not have to be of the "all or none" variety. If the parents want to help out financially and the couple really need the assistance, they could work out a clear-cut plan of *how much* they are willing to take and whether they want to repay the parents later.

One of the major handicaps of giving and receiving aid from families is the tendency to be negligent about establishing specific guidelines for the exchange. If both sides are able to communicate their desires and listen to what the other wants or expects to happen, it is likely that an agreement acceptable to both sides can be reached.

Attachments to Parents and In-laws

There are a number of issues which we know little about and which are no doubt problematic for a young couple. Suppose, for example, the couple must provide special help to one set of parents at the outset of marriage. How does this affect their relationship? Or what if only one spouse feels an obligation to help needy parents? Will this strain their marital relations? What if they are receiving substantial aid from only one set of parents? Research has indicated that such aid is very useful in helping the young couple economically, but what about the emotional implications? Hostilities and resentments frequently evolve from the feeling of one or both partners that there is a closer attachment to the in-laws than to their own parents.

The lopsidedness of kin relationships is probably the norm rather than the exception, although perhaps it is not as exaggerated as the description above would indicate. Social scientists predict that certain lopsided relationship configurations are likely to result in marital conflicts.[22] Graphically, these situations are depicted as follows[23]:

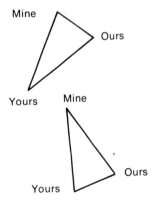

"You" have in-law trouble because I rely on my family, yours neglects us, mine interferes, I'm more loyal to mine, mine helps, or needs help more, and so on.

"I" have in-law trouble because you rely on your family, mine rejects us, yours interferes, and so on.

How such problems are resolved depends on the ability of the couple to accept that a situation exists (that certain in-laws do need aid or that one spouse is more attached to kin than the other) and to be adequately motivated to solve it.

If the goal of a couple is to achieve their own autonomous nuclear family (operating independently as a couple) while still retaining ties with the in-laws, the ideal arrangement is:

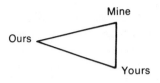

"Our" family comes first, but we still retain a relationship with our relatives.

For those whose kin ties are very important, a more equilateral arrangement is the ideal:

"Our" family is part of two ongoing kinship units.

Obviously, it is impossible to work out solutions as simple as these, particularly in cases where the situation is asymmetrical. Consider, for example, a young couple who realize they desperately need financial aid. The wife's parents (who are financially well off) have offered help. If the couple accept the badly needed assistance, the husband might feel he will lose respect as a provider in his wife's and her parents' eyes. Should the aid be accepted? There are a range of possible solutions or alternatives. The aid can be accepted as a loan. A loan can be acquired elsewhere. The wife can get a job. The husband can admit his feelings, and the wife can try to help him come to terms with them. Given the inequities of the situation and the realization that a problem exists, if the couple are sufficiently adaptable and resourceful they should be able to work out a solution whereby both will retain their self-respect and neither will feel a need to compromise inordinately with the other or with the in-laws.

It should be pointed out that the preceding diagrams depict situations where both husband and wife are equally close to their parents. This may not always be the case; therefore, asymmetrical arrangements favoring the spouse with the closest ties may prove more satisfactory. The point here is that the most comfortable arrangement is the best.

Living with Parents and In-laws

The prevailing norm of families living in separate households from their extended kin probably contributes to in-law problems, simply by implying that any other living arrangement is problematic. However, from 10 to 20 percent of all young couples begin their marriages in one parental household, usually the wife's,[24] and move out when they are financially able to do so. In addition, many aging parents, particularly widows, move in with their married children.[25] Both of these extended living arrangements are more common among low income groups, where economic necessity is a powerful dictator of life-style.

Since tensions are inherent in any living arrangement, problems in such extended family homes may not be due as much to the extended nature of the family as to economic stress. Our society insists that the independent nuclear family is the best living arrangement. However, there is no evidence that significantly more tensions arise from extended family living units than from nuclear units. Nor is it known whether there are more inherent problems that are not counterbalanced by the benefits of living together. One large house costs less than two small ones to buy, equip, and maintain. Resources are not duplicated, domestic chores are lightened, and companionship is available. Grandparents may play a significant role in easing child-care burdens, especially for the working wife, and can be a rich source of history and fun for their grandchildren.[26] Udry believes that

most of the argument assembled by lay and scientific literature against extended family living is organized to support an existing value system in the society and is not based on substantial demonstration of the disadvantages of these living arrangements. When the value is firmly entrenched that living together is detrimental, one can look to the operation of the self-fulfilling prophesy for an explanation of why many people who do live together find it unsatisfactory—they are so sure that it will be a source of serious difficulty that they organize their lives in such a way as to insure that the anticipated dissatisfaction will be realized. Those families who can approach combined households with open minds will occasionally find this a very satisfying way of life.[27]

As long as the nuclear family is perpetuated as the norm, however, problems will continue to arise when individuals wish to comply with the norm but are forced to do otherwise.

Kin Abuse

As we pointed out earlier, kinship problems are rarely one-sided. While in-laws may stimulate or contribute to the discord, frequently marital problems are projected onto the kin.[28] If the couple are having difficulties, they may blame their problems on in-laws rather than looking introspectively for the source of the trouble. As one researcher phrased it, ". . . those young couples with a good adjustment seem to be working as a unit, accepting both families as their own and regarding all problems as a common task. (Those with a poor adjustment, on the other hand, showed a tendency to blame the spouse's family for friction in all areas.)"[29]

If the problem really involves both the couple and particular in-laws, the solution is to alter the behavior of the couple and/or the in-laws. But if the problem is strictly the couple's they should try to avoid involving their kin. In-laws, even if impartial, usually will be perceived by the nonrelated spouse as supporting the partner's position; in-laws therefore make poor referees or judges.

Another problem for those with strong extended family ties (characteristic of certain ethnic groups and the working and lower classes) is the tendency of each spouse to retreat into his own kin group in the face of marital conflict. This causes polarization, and the marriage is weakened if the conflict goes unresolved. In such cases, the circumstances forcing the couple to retreat into their own kin groups are what weaken the marriage, not involvement with kin per se.[30]

The self-fulfilling prophecy no doubt contributes to in-law difficulty. Expecting problems, the young couple may exaggerate unimportant disagreements and be hypercritical of their in-laws' actions. In-laws are people with the same needs as everyone else. They want to be appreciated and accepted as persons of dignity and worth. You may not be able to choose them as you choose your friends, yet you may expect them to tolerate behavior your friends wouldn't, at the same time being more critical of their behavior than that of your friends. Duvall points out that respondents with no in-law problems said the major reason for this was that "they accept me." Thus it seems logical that mutual acceptance should lessen the likelihood of confrontation.

In-law difficulties are not inevitable. As one woman says, "If there has ever been any tension between my daughter-in-law and me, I am totally unaware of it. I just love her and was so glad to have her join our family." Of the 1,337 respondents in Duvall's study, 345 (or 18 percent) reported no problems with relatives of either spouse.[31] Landis and Landis also reported that two out of three of the 409 couples they studied (who had been married at least twenty years) got along well with their in-laws from the beginning.[32]

Getting Along without Kin

As should be evident from the preceding discussion, the decision to break away from kin involves severing multiple ties. Some couples, however, may have to do so. Lack of affectional ties with parents, negative feelings toward them, parental opposition to one's marriage partner, actual conflict or its potential, or simply lack of kin may generate the goal of getting along without parents and in-laws.

The costs of this decision may be high, depending on one's needs and status in the society. For example, take the case of a young couple in college who are in love and want to marry. Suppose their parents, who are supporting them, oppose the marriage and threaten to disown them. What are the consequences of getting married? The most critical immediate consequence is financial. One or both may have to drop out of school to work or they may have to work while continuing their education. The former can lead to unequal intellectual development and a growing apart of the couple as their shared interests decrease (particularly if one spouse works and the other goes to school); this will be more serious for companionate marriage than for the traditional marriage. The latter often delays graduation, as the couple may find it impossible to carry a full academic load, work enough hours to pay expenses, and have sufficient time and energy to devote to the relationship.

When things get rough, there will be no emotional support emanating from the in-laws, and in times of crisis the couple will have to turn to friends, the university, or other social services for aid. On the other hand, by the time of graduation they may find that struggling successfully together for a common goal and achieving independence has brought them close and has helped them develop techniques of recognizing and resolving problems. Effective problem solving usually is a rewarding experience, paying off in increased self-esteem and mutual affection. As a result, couples who have had successful problem-solving experiences are likely to be oriented toward undertaking new problem-solving activities. We would predict from our framework that such couples will have more success in solving other problems encountered in marriage.

If one is a member of a minority group, breaking away from kin may present additional problems. In a summary of several studies, Adams concludes that "minority status tends to result in residential compounding and in strong kin ties for the sake of mutual aid and survival in a hostile environment."[33] These ties, then, provide important value and behavioral support that would be severed if the couple broke away from the family. However, one reason for breaking away from in-laws may very well be value discrepancy. If such is the case, the couple can find support from friends who hold similar values. This notion can be extended. Those who wish to retain their ethnic beliefs and behaviors will find living in a conclave of their own ethnicity easier for themselves and their children, as ties with neighbors and friends will provide some of the support and protection formerly provided by kin.

One cost of breaking away from kin is the loss of help during childbirth, illness, or crisis. It is not unusual for mothers (or mothers-in-law) to travel long distances to help their daughters (or daughters-in-law) for the first few days or weeks after the birth of a baby, by running the house and/or caring for the other children. Cutting ties with in-laws deprives the couple of this and other kinds of emergency aid.

If in-law ties are completely severed, one alternative is to substitute friendship for kinship ties. A network of close friends may act toward one another much the same as relatives, providing such things as affection and support, help in times of crisis, and ritual observances at holidays and birthdays. Such reciprocal relationships may prove quite satisfactory.

Other alternatives might include supplementing friendship ties with community and religious organizational ties and social service agencies. In addition to providing a source of friends, involvement in such groups might provide a certain amount of support, and members could be called upon in times of emergency.

Summary

Some of the questions to be explored in relating to in-laws are achieving independence, giving and receiving aid, establishing emotional attachments, and deciding about patterns of residence.

In-law relationships appear to be essentially the woman's domain in North America. Women generally feel closer to kin and assume the responsibility of keeping in touch with them. The husband's mother, by identifying with the wife's role and entering into competition with her son's spouse, is labeled as the most problematic in-law.

Although designing in-law relationships is not difficult in all cases, it is wise to make an effort in the beginning to deal with parents objectively and to be prepared to make use of the problem-solving process.

Notes

1. Evelyn Duvall and Reuben Hill, *Being Married* (Boston: Heath, 1960), p. 219.

2. J. Richard Udry, *The Social Context of Marriage*, 2d ed. (Philadelphia: Lippincott, 1971), p. 337.

3. Candace L. Rogers and Hope J. Leichter, "Laterality and Conflict in Kinship Ties," in William J. Goode, ed., *Readings on the Family and Society* (Englewood Cliffs, N.J.: Prentice-Hall, 1964).

4. Ibid., p. 216.

5. Evelyn Millis Duvall, *Inlaws: Pro and Con* (New York: Association Press, 1954), p. 280.

6. Judson T. Landis and Mary G. Landis, *Building a Successful Marraige*, 4th ed. (Englewood Cliffs, N.J.: Prentice'Hall, 1963), p. 340.

7. Gerald R. Leslie, *The Family in Social Context* (New York: Oxford University Press, 1967), p. 320.

8. Sheldon Stryker, "The Adjustment of Married Offspring to Their Parents," *American Sociological Review* 20 (April 1955), 149-154; Paul Wallin, "Sex Differences in Attitudes to 'in'laws,' A Test of a Theory," *American Journal of Sociology* 59 (March 1954), 466-469.

9. Paul J. Reiss, "The Extended Kinship System: Correlates of and Attitudes on Frequency of Interaction," *Marriage and Family Living* 24 (November 1962), 333-339.

10. Ethel Shanas and Gordon Streib, eds., *Social Structure and the Family: Generational Relations* (Englewood Cliffs, N.J.: Prentice-Hall, 1965).

11. Support for this comes in the form of all the data listing mothers-in-law to be the most troublesome of all in-laws by a wide margin (Duvall, *Inlaws*, p. 188; Judson T. Landis and Mary G. Landis, *Building a Successful Marriage,* 4th ed. (Englewood Cliffs, N.J.: Prentice-Hall, 1963), p. 311.

12. Leslie, *Family in Social Context,* p. 321.

13. If the wife's attachment before marriage was primarily to her father she apparently is more able to transfer her dependence to her husband. In any case, it does not cause the problems attachment to her mother does. "Adjustment to Married Offspring." Stryker.

14. Herman R. Lantz and Eloise Snyder, *Marriage* (New York: Wiley, 1969), p. 323.

15. Duvall, *Inlaws*; Stryker, "Adjustment to Married Offspring."

16. Duvall, *Inlaws*.

17. Ibid., p. 188.

18. Victor A. Christopherson et al., "The Married College Student, 1959," *Marriage and Family Living* 22 (May 1960), 126-127; Marvin B. Sussman and Lee Burchinal, "Parental Aid to Married Children: Implications for Family Functioning," *Marriage and Family Living* 24 (November 1962), 320-332.

19. Bert Adams, "Isolation, Function and Beyond: American Kinship in the 1960's," *Journal of Marriage and the Family* 32 (November 1970), 575-597.

20. In terms of daily interaction, kin play a more prominent role in the lives of blue-collar and certain minority groups. See Bert N. Adams, *Kinship in an Urban Setting* (Chicago: Markham, 1968). For some, kin ties are so strong, especially between mother and daughter, that decisions are made in favor of remaining near kin, even though a move would financially benefit the family. See Mirra Komarovsky, *Blue-Collar Marriage* (New York: Random House, 1964).

21. Rogers and Leichter, "Laterality and Conflict."

22. Duvall, *Inlaws*; Hope J. Leichter and William E. Mitchell, *Kinship and Casework* (New York: Russell Sage Foundation, 1967).

23. The idea for the triangle illustrations came from Duvall, *Inlaws,* p. 279.

24. Alvin Schorr, *Filial Responsibility in the Modern American Family* (Washington, D.C.: Department of Health, Education and Welfare, 1960).

25. Alvin L. Schorr, "Current Practice of Filial Responsibility," in Robert F. Winch, Robert McGinnis, and Herbert R. Barringer, eds. *Selected Studies in Marriage and the Family* (New York: Holt, Rinehart and Winston, 1962).

26. Elizabeth Bott, *Family and Social Networks* (London: Tavistock Publications, 1957); Ernest W. Burgess, "Family Living in the Later Decades," *Annals of the American Academy of Political and Social Science* 279 (1952), 106-114; R. O. Lang, "The Rating of Happiness in Marriage" (M.A. thesis, University of Chicago, 1932); Schorr, "Current Practice."

27. Udry, *Social Context of Marriage,* p. 340.

28. Norman Bell, "Extended Family Relations of Disturbed and Well Families," *Family Process* 1 (1962), 175-193.

29. Peggy Marcus, "In-law Relationship Adjustment of Couples Married Between Two and Eleven Years," *Journal of Home Economics* 43 (January 1951), p. 35-37.

30. John Scanzoni, "Resolution of Occupational Conjugal Role Conflict in Clergy Marriages," *Journal of Marriage and the Family* 27 (August 1965), 396-402.

31. Duvall, *Inlars.*

32. Judson T. Landis and Mary G. Landis, *Building a Successful Marriage.*

33. Adams, "Isolation Function Beyond," p. 587.

Suggested Readings

Axelson, Leland J. "Personal Adjustment in the Post-Parental Period." *Marriage and Family Living* 22 (February 1960), 66-68. A look at some of the adjustments required of parents after their children leave home and how the parents are influenced.

Duvall, Evelyn Millis. *Inlaws: Pro and Con.* New York: Association Press, 1954. Both a comprehensive study of how people feel about their in-laws and a description of what makes good in-law relationships (at least in middle-class families).

Sussman, Marvin. "The Isolated Nuclear Family: Fact or Fiction?" *Social Problems* 6 (Spring 1959), 333-340. Data suggest that the nuclear family operates within a network of other nuclear families, usually related by blood ties or marriage. This network supplies a variety of services and help in everyday situations and emergencies and on ceremonial occasions.

Sussman, Marvin, and Burchinal, Lee. "Kin Family Network: Unheralded Structure in Current Conceptualizations of Family Functioning." *Marriage and Family Living* 24 (August 1962), 231-240. Summary of the theoretical writings and empirical evidence supporting the notion of a viable nuclear kin-related family system.

13 Managing Money in Marriage

We have often been told that "two can live as cheaply as one." Our response is, "Yes, but for only half as long." We live in a money-oriented world. Never before in the history of Western society has one single factor had such force in the changes occurring around us. Today, with the skyrocketing inflation which we are experiencing, money management has become a major concern in marriage, not only for inexperienced couples but even for those skilled in this task.

Money is supposed to be a medium of exchange used to distribute the variety of goods and services of the economic system. In the minds of many people, however, it also is a symbol of success, prestige, power, achievement, and even human value and dignity.

Family educator Clark Ellzey says that "money talks."[1] We have heard this expression used in the context of a payoff, but here it refers to something very different. The ways in which people use money tell us a great deal about them. In fact, some individuals contend that money problems do not exist, that the real issues are personality problems which are manifested in spending patterns. Take, for example, the parent who gives his child "everything." What does this say about the parent. It might say "I can't show affection any other way," or "I still feel deprived since I didn't have all the material goods I wanted in childhood," or "I feel guilty that I don't have enough time to spend with my child."

Some people put all their efforts into making money and buying things because they feel that they are only as valuable as the goods they own and money buys reassurance for them. Others use money generously and sensitively. Various philosophers have evidenced such generosity, but so have many people in their day-to-day family life by considering the needs of others before their own. One person suggests that giving a gift without letting the recipient know who it is from is the extreme example of using money unselfishly. In such a situation there is no reward forthcoming by way of recognition of the act, and, consequently, it represents a true spirit of giving. At any rate, spending patterns reveal more than just attitudes toward money; they actually show how people relate to the world around them.

Economists speak about money in rational, unemotional terms. Frequently they use mathematical formulas or models to describe the flow and use of money. Only recently has the significance of psychosocial influences been recognized (probably as an outgrowth of counseling work with individuals who have money problems).

In a society where income continues to rise each year, along with production of new and attractive articles, money will continue to have an important place in people's lives. At the personal level, money management calls for an understanding of objective as well as subjective influences.

Of all the areas in marriage that require problem-solving ability, finances are most often at the top of the list. Robert Blood believes there are several reasons why "money is the most common area of conflict between husbands and wives." They include:

(1) . . . The family's heavy reliance on money to purchase the goods and services they consume.

(2) The division of labor in the family means the husband earns most of the money, but the wife spends most of it, leaving husbands wondering where all their hard work went to.

(3) American marriages are equalitarian enough to make both partners feel they have a right to influence major, nonroutine purchases. When discretionary funds are limited, each partner is liable to feel that decisions won by the other deplete his own chances for implementing his values. One-sided power structures may not be any happier, but they have less conflict over money.

(4) Whereas in-law problems are concentrated at the beginning of marriage and child-rearing problems in the middle, financial conflicts spread over the whole life cycle, taking new forms as circumstances change.

(5) Financial problems are more tangible than most other areas of conflict. If the husband impulsively buys a new car, it visibly reminds the wife that her wishes were not consulted or respected.[2]

Consequently, there are numerous sources of friction about money that pop up again and again as the demands on a couple's income change and they are required to make adjustments to meet those demands. Both the available resources and the types of problematic situations that present themselves will vary according to the stage of the life cycle and people's personal abilities.

Creating a Combined Philosophy Toward Money

Each partner in a marriage has a background of attitudes toward money, spending patterns, and expectations for future uses of money. Part of marital adjustment includes developing a combined attitude toward money which is consistent with the couple's goals and resources.

The underlying factors influencing money management are the values, goals, and standards of a family. The individual acquires his values from the groups that are important to him. The family is the primary group from which such values are acquired. Thus in the early stages of marriage the couple usually begin to share each other's value heritage and attempt to combine them into a pattern consistent with their desires.

It becomes evident at this point that parents and in-laws often are blamed for things for which they are only indirectly responsible. They raise a child in a certain value system (often not consciously stating the values), and the child eventually finds himself patterning his own value system after that of his parents. The difficulty occurs as two people come together in marriage and try to recreate their respective home environments and family attitudes in their relationship with each other. Things are bound to get exciting around this new household when money matters are involved. If the wife comes from a home where the father was always salaried and knew to the penny what his monthly check would be and the day he could expect it, she is likely to be more comfortable with this type of arrangement. For her, marrying a man whose work is seasonal, never knowing how much he will make, and being required to apportion the sum over a six month period may be almost more than she can manage.

This points to differences between the two in their need for security. The wife wants to live conservatively, having the assurance that more money will be coming in at the first of the month. The husband doesn't need such security, and in fact feels that risk taking is required of him if he expcts to get ahead in his work.

One's values are rarely, if ever, stated directly. However, they are expressed by how one lives and even by the commonplace objects one holds onto or discards. Following is an illustration of a major value difference between husband and wife.

We seem to have entirely different values regarding money. In my family we always paid bills first. Then, if we had money left over, after saving a bit, we decided how to spend for the extra things we wanted. The surplus money was always spent in a way to give the whole family some pleasure. Paul is like his father, who went bankrupt twice. He lives for the day and doesn't think about the future.

Parental values are readily internalized, and value convergence with a spouse may therefore be difficult, though not impossible. As the couple are thrown into joint decision-making situations, they have to think about what they want out of life and about how to compromise with each other. One couple complained about static from their parents when they revealed their plans to join the Peace Corps after college graduation. "You'll get so far behind by giving up two years for that kind of service," one mother insisted. "Give up what?" the couple wanted to know. "Crabgrass in the suburbs? Two cars in the garage and a swimming pool in the backyard by the time we're thirty?" Clearly, in this case a divergence from the parental value structure has occurred, and the couple have begun establishing their own system of values by which their goals will be set.

Goals provide the vehicle by which a family implements its values. While a family may *value* education, their *goal* is more specific—perhaps saving money for vocational or university training for all the children. The goals of a family are often related to one another, in that the accomplishment of one leads to another. For example, a young married couple may have the goal of allowing both spouses to continue to grow professionally. This goal initially can be achieved by both completing technical or professional training; later it can be accomplished by attending refresher courses in their areas of interest; still later they can build a home library and/or join professional societies to maintain and enrich their skills.

Goal setting should be a continuous process, flexible enough to reflect changing needs and resources; goals should be only guidelines for decision making. For example, a crisis such as unexpected illness or unemployment may call for deferring the goal of home ownership or of a two-week holiday in Hawaii. Changes in family structure, such as the birth of the first child, may also call for reformulation of goals.

Goal setting should be done realistically, based on available resources. A common practice of couples living on a limited income while they complete their education is to look to the future for the time when things will be different, when their money problems will be solved. Unfortunately, one very strange thing about money is that no matter how much you earn, it never is enough. Reworking goals may be necessary upon entering the work force if realistic plans for reaching initial goals are not feasible.

Ideally, all family members should contribute to goal setting. In families where one person is the leader, there is a danger that the family's goals will generally reflect only that person's desires. If this happens, the other family members may not want to work toward achieving the goals, and, for that matter, the goals might not be realistic in regard to the family's abilities.

The Challenge of Effective Money Management

Just as couples can enjoy making early marital adjustments in work responsibilites or sex, the shared learning experience of money management can also be gratifying. If you don't believe this, ask someone who has learned the hard way, or find out for yourself. When you get married, don't make any financial plans. Let the money come in, and spend it. Open up charge accounts and charge anything you want. Don't inform yourself about what to look for when you go to the store. Then, stop and look at your bank balance. Some people operate this way throughout their married lives. They never plan; they just stumble along from one crisis to the next, in a constant race of trying to beat the overdrawn checks to the bank.

The most prevalent money concerns for young couples are budgeting, credit, and buymanship.

Budgeting

The term *budget* has negative connotations for many individuals. When a group of young college women were asked what they thought of when they heard the word, these were some of the responses:

A plan to throw away when emergencies arise.
Trying to figure out percentages so I could know how much I was supposed to spend on different things.
A plan that keeps you from getting what you want.[4]

A better definition of *budget* is a plan that *helps* you get what you want.

Family planning specialist Ilse Wolf suggests four major steps in planning the use of your income.[5]

Estimating income conservatively A common error made by young couples just starting out in the labor force is to plan their expenses around their gross salary. It is disappointing to find out how fast a $9,000 annual salary dwindles before you even see the money. A substantial portion is withheld for income tax and Social Security, as well as for retirement plans, medical insurance, life insurance, and so on. These deductions from the gross salary add up fast and significantly reduce the amount of the paycheck.

When budgeting it is wiser to *underestimate* rather than *overestimate* the amount of money coming in, and it is essential to think of areas of spending. As one young married man astutely said, "Don't forget that there are more than four weeks to a month. Those extra two or three days really add up as far as expenditures for food are concerned. You'd be surprised how long a month can seem when you are waiting for that next paycheck to come in."

Keeping a detailed record Record keeping is not the most important aspect of budgeting, but it is definitely an essential part. Each couple should at least assess their own and determine their preferences and skills in budgeting. Many disagreements about money could be avoided if this initial inventory were used to specify tasks in money management. The person who keeps the records should be skilled in basic math, flexible, and organized—and have some liking for the job. To assign this task to the spouse who makes frequent mathematical errors or who is consistently absentminded is to provide the conditions for disagreement.

A careful investigation of current spending practices also is essential if a workable budget is to be established. It sometimes is surprising to find out where the money has been going. Some couples *think* they don't have any funds in excess of their fixed expenditures because they have never stopped to figure what they do with their cash. One man claims, "I can have a twenty dollar bill one day, and before I know it, it's gone. I don't know where it went, and I can't see anything to show for it." This is where records of exact spending patterns can be helpful. Once you know where your money goes, you have met one of the first conditions necessary for making modifications in your spending patterns.

Accurate record keeping not only helps in planning and implementing a budget, it also simplifies more involved tasks such as filling out income tax returns at the end of the year.

Analyzing spending practices   If a couple have become caught up in an excess of fixed expenses, there may not be much leeway at first in restructuring avenues of expenditures. In other words, if they have numerous payments which must be met on a regular basis, they are apt to feel the financial pinch more acutely than if they have a little extra with which to be flexible. Generally, however, when a couple decide they need money to cover an important purchase, they can frequently make sufficient shifts in their current spending patterns to account for the expenditure—if they are relatively proficient at money management. Just cutting out the snack items bought at the grocery or drugstore for a few weeks can make an amazing difference in the food bill and release those funds for other uses.

Making a plan for the future use of income   Once you know where the money goes and your plans for making desired alterations are completed, then money management can actually begin. Newlyweds in particular are challenged to decide what they value most so they can establish a method of operation and put it into action. Although their funds generally are limited, if they can reach agreement regarding what is most important to them and can set their goals accordingly, finances will not become a source of extreme tension.

A budget is nothing more than a plan for future expenditures. Each budget should be tailored to the specific family, based on its defined goals and resources. Budgeting often has been viewed as a distasteful activity because people see it only as a means of controlling spending. Actually, however, the only limit to expenditures is the total amount of money available. Table 13-1 shows one way of setting up a trial plan for budgeting.

The trial plan should be an initial attempt at arriving at a satisfactory budget. A couple may have to draw up several plans to find one which reflects their needs and resources. They may overestimate or underestimate their flexible expenses or they may have to cut down their fixed expenses, at least temporarily. By reviewing each item in the budget, they can probably devise methods to cut down expenses (such as paying insurance premiums semiannually or annually instead of monthly or taking advantage of cash discounts for prompt payment of utility bills).

A budget cannot cure all financial ills, but planning does enable the family to see how they can use their limited funds to attain the things they consider most important. It can also give family members insight into the relationship between money management and other family resources. A husband who takes a second job in order to provide the family with more material goods may soon find he has little

Table 13-1 Trial Plan for Expenditures

	For One Budget Period	For One Year
Enter income (After deductions)	_____	_____
Subtract fixed expenses (e.g., mortgage payments or rent, utility bills, installment payments, etc.)	_____	_____
Balance	_____	_____
Subtract day-to-day household living expenses (e.g., food, car maintenance and transportation, laundry, miscellaneous personal allowances, etc.)	_____	_____
Balance	_____	_____
Subtract flexible expenses (e.g., clothing, home furnishings, entertainment, recreation, etc.)	_____	_____
Balance	_____	_____
Subtract payment on unpaid bills	_____	_____
Balance	_____	_____

Savings for goals   Financial advisers frequently recommend a reserve fund for the average family equal to at least three month's income.

This chart reprinted from page 22 of Money Management: Your Budget published by the Money Management Institute of Household Finance Corporation, Chicago, Illinois. Reprinted by permission.

time and energy to enjoy either the goods or his family. A realistic appraisal of what is being lost or gained by current earning and spending patterns may be extremely beneficial in making future judgments about money related matters.

Credit

Learning to use credit wisely and establishing a good credit rating can lead to the achievement of a higher standard of living (since you can purchase things immediately that normally would take a long time to save for). Conversely, credit abuse can produce difficult problems to overcome in subsequent years if continued credit is desired.

Initially, credit is quite easy to acquire. It takes only a few minutes to fill out a credit application, and often the application takes only a day or so to clear. Credit ratings are established by a number of different methods. Family economist Arch W. Troelstrup indicates that a person is considered to be a favorable risk if he (1) has been employed with a good firm for two or more years; (2) has a steady income; (3) owns his own home or has rented for a number of years in a good neighborhood; (4) has savings accounts, checking accounts, investments, or life insurance; (5) pays bills promptly; (6) has no suits against him by creditors; (7) is a family man and has few dependents relative to his income; and (8) applies for loans at his regular bank and fills out applications truthfully.[6]

In our credit card society it is exceedingly tempting to buy now and pay later. Charge accounts are convenient to use, but it is easy to overextend oneself by carelessly charging purchases. One young couple used their revolving charge accounts to buy all their Christmas gifts. They didn't realize that it would take the entire next year to pay for those purchases. Of course, they also had to pay for the cost of credit, at the "nominal" rate of 18 percent a year. No one but the buyer can protect himself from charging too many purchases, but the U.S. government does require, by its "truth-in-lending bill," that credit merchants disclose the amount in dollars and annual percentage rate of all finance charges imposed on the consumer. This at least helps the person figure out what he is getting into when he charges his purchases—if he takes the time to read the credit agreement. Troelstrup gives the following advice about credit:

Use credit only when necessary or where benefits justify the cost and risk involved.

Assume no more debt than you can safely pay out of current income.

Shop for the best credit bargain. None of the credit terms are easy.

Go to the bank or credit union first to investigate the possibilities.

Know your lender or dealer.

Use 30-day charge accounts intelligently. Do not use them to spend next month's income, or charge accounts will become real debts.

Do not let an installment debt run so long that the psychological enjoyment of "having it now" wears off before the debt is paid.[7]

Buymanship

All members of a family should be knowledgeable about shopping. In determining what to pay for a car, for example, one must be ready to bargain and shouldn't be timid about it. Bargaining behavior is expected in instances of this kind and should be viewed as a legitimate way of coming to a satisfactory agreement about cost.

For a husband and wife to use their money wisely, they need to be informed about all the products they buy. They should carefully read labels and compare prices of competing brands, particularly in the supermarket (house brands, for example, are often cheaper than name brands for the same quality product).

If family shoppers plan carefully, they can save money by knowing where to get the most reasonable prices on quality items. Reading the newspaper regularly to keep informed about weekend specials often is beneficial. At certain times during the year various items are put on sale. Buying clothing at midseason, for example, can reduce the family clothing budget drastically. One must be very sure, however, that a sale really is just that, and the only way one can be sure it is legitimate is by knowing what the price is regularly. This, too, means keeping oneself constantly informed of the ever changing conditions in all areas of buymanship.

The Real Problem with Money

Up to this point our major emphasis has been on income and how it is spent. We are well aware, however, that the personal and interpersonal resources of the couple may, in fact, be more important to money management than the amount of money available. Norman Lobsenz and Clark Blackburn report that in a study of requests for counseling made to various family service agencies, more than half the couples surveyed reported severe problems with the financial aspects of their relationship. Of this group, however, only six percent were experiencing problems because of inadequate income. The most frequently reported reasons for difficulty were immature or unrealistic attitudes toward earning, saving, or spending money and the emotional use of money to control or punish a spouse or to compensate for inadequacies, guilt, or the inability to give love.[8]

Counselor Bernard Greene, who gathered data from 750 couples experiencing marital discord, reports a similar trend.[9] In his sample, financial disagreements are rated as the fifth most common complaint. Listed in the order of frequency the specific situations creating difficulty for these couples were (1) inadequate management, (2) uncooperativeness, (3) one spouse regarding the other as incompetent, (4) lack of trust with money, (5) selfish spouse (one spouse spending money primarily on himself or herself), (6) extravagance, (7) major purchases without the spouse's consent,

(8) husband a poor provider, and (9) stingy spouse (one who doesn't want to part with money).

Money disagreements provide a convenient, indirect outlet for other tensions and disappointments in the marital relationship. By using money as a tool, personal attacks are unnecessary and tensions are expressed. For example, a husband may express irritation toward his wife because she did not make a record of her checks, in the checkbook, immediately after writing them. While his tension is abated by reprimanding her, it may be that really his irritation stemmed not from this isolated occurrence but rather from his disappointment in her general carelessness with details. To attack the general carelessness, however, would be too threatening to their relationship; thus money becomes the target. In another example, a wife may continually go on spending sprees in order to punish her husband for his sexual indifference to her. The difficulty in this type of communication is obvious; the receiver of the message may not be able to detect the real reason for the disagreement.

Frances Feldman, a financial management specialist, describes many cases where money is used to intensify marital discord. One partner may use his or her spending habits as a tool to attack the other for dissatisfactions in their relationship. Unable to communicate her sexual frustrations directly, the woman in our earlier example attempts to communicate her frustration by going on a spending spree. In another example, a husband may keep tight control over money because he sees this as a way to legitimize his power in the family. Keeping his wife financially dependent on him continually reminds her of his masculinity and strength. Emotionally immature spouses who see money as a means of compensating for their personal limitations will in all probability encounter difficulty in money management. They may compete with each other and be unable to share money realistically.

Money is one of the material resources which feeds into the marital system and which has the potential to assist in the achievement of goals. Yet money often is not a resource at all, but a source of irritation in that system. In the initial stage of the family life cycle, the first tests of the quality of the problem-solving relationship are made; husband and wife develop interaction patterns which will influence the quality of future family relationships. If partners cannot recognize their basic value differences, goals, and standards in the use of money, and if they cannot begin to reduce or resolve them in the early years of their marriage, money problems may take up an undesirable proportion of their marital interaction.

Summary

Money no longer has only an objective value as a means of exchange. Today it also has subjective worth as an indication of status and prestige. As such, it has taken an increasingly important role in marital relations. Money may be used in a variety of ways, by both marital partners, to cause conflicts. It then becomes the tangible object to project feelings of discontent in other areas.

Money management is comprised of a variety of ordinary problem-solving situations. These are usually related in some way to either budgeting, credit, or buymanship. Establishing goals based on a common value system is a vital first step in achieving satisfactory financial adjustment in marriage.

Notes

1. Clark Ellzey, lecture at Texas Tech University, November 14, 1971.
2. Robert O. Blood, *Marriage* (New York: Free Press, 1962), pp. 291-292.
3. Irma Gross and Elizabeth Crandall, *Management for Modern Families,* 2d ed. (New York: Wiley, 1963), p. 21.
4. *Tips and Topics in Home Economics* (Lubbock, Tex.: College of Home Economics, Texas Tech University, December 1965, p. 1.
5. Ibid.
6. Arch W. Troelstrup, *The Consumer in American Society* (New York: McGraw-Hill, 1970), p. 155.
7. Ibid., p. 174.
8. Norman Lobsenz and Clark Blackburn, *How to Stay Married: A Modern Approach to Sex, Money and Emotions in Marriage* (New York: Cowles, 1969).
9. Bernard Greene, *A Clinical Approach to Marital Problems: Evaluation and Management* Springfield, Ill.: Charles C. Thomas, 1970).
10. Frances Feldman, *The Family in a Money World* (New York: Family Services Association of America, 1957).

Suggested Readings

Bergler, Edmund. *Money and Emotional Conflicts.* New York: International Universities Press, 1970. A readable book focusing on how emotions limit problem-solving ability to deal with money.
Dolphin, R. *Self Correcting Problems in Personal Finance.* Rockleigh, N.J.: Allyn & Bacon, 1970. A problem-solving approach to personal finance.
Lobsenz, Norman, & Blackburn, Clark W. *How to Stay Married: A Modern Approach to Sex, Money and Emotions in Marriage.* New York: Cowles, 1969. An excellent discussion of money and emotions and how they interact in a relationship.

14 Assuming Parental Roles

Parenthood remains an important goal for North Americans. The report of the U.S. Commission on Population Growth and the Future indicates that married women plan to have an average of two to three children.[1] Another study reports a similar trend among young Canadians; 51 percent of the English-speaking sample and 58 percent of the French-speaking sample wanted three or fewer children.[2] The statistics cited here reflect only a desire for children, but similar surveys comparing expected family size with actual family size note that women usually end up having more children than they expected.[3]

There appears to be an aura of romanticism hanging over the decision to have children. Sociologist E. E. Lemasters suggests that when a social function is relatively difficult, as parenthood appears to be in our society, a romantic folklore develops to keep the role from being ignored or rejected by most adults.[4] Individuals living in modern civilizations often claim that they do not believe in folklore, but in reality they do. Parenthood can be a very satisfying and exciting role, but it is a myth that motherhood or fatherhood is instinctive in the human and that all men and women are suited to the demands of the role. It is also a myth that children automatically strengthen the quality of a marital relationship.

These popular notions about the nature of parenthood are unrealistic. Too much emphasis is placed on the romantic, imagined satisfactions of having children and too little on the combined responsibilities and satisfactions inherent in the role. This makes it difficult for a couple to decide whether they could be good parents and whether they are prepared for the commitment of raising children.

This chapter will explore the general problem-solving areas of parental roles. While not all couples share the goal of parenthood, most attempt to plan their family. We will therefore focus on four sample problems a couple might experience in attempting to achieve this goal—deciding whether or not to have children, handling unplanned pregnancies, coping with infertility, and adjusting to pregnancy.

Parenthood: Pro and Con

For many couples, making a decision about whether to have children is not problematic. First, approximately one out of every ten married couples who desire children are childless. Second, many more couples view parenthood as inevitable, beyond planning. Yet, with medical advances in the area of fertility and more effective contraceptive devices, we would suggest that planning is in fact possible in this area. World population increases further suggest that planning is not only *possible* but *absolutely necessary* considering that having an average of 3.5 children will double the world population in forty years, whereas an average of 2.5 will hold population constant in the same period of time.[5]

Many factors can stimulate problem-solving action around the question of whether to have children. For most couples the question naturally arises when they consider marriage or establish a sexual relationship. For others, the strongest motivation is the subtle (or not so subtle) social pressure from friends, relatives, and society in general to have children. Numerous articles report examples of informal sanctions directed toward childless couples.[6]

There has been speculation that the incidence of childlessness in Western society might increase substantially with the corresponding interest in overpopulation, improvement in contraceptive techniques, and concern with the changing roles of women; in actuality, however, the trend has not been in that direction. Although there is evidence that increasing numbers of couples are deciding not to have children, these couples are still a minority. In a recent survey of more than 1,600 married women in Toronto, only 1.1 percent of the sample indicated that they desired to remain childless.[7]

We believe it is just as relevant to decide *whether* to have children as it is to decide *when* to have them. We do not suggest that having children or not having them should be differentially valued. The value of each of these alternatives must be assigned by each individual couple.

Recognition of the Problem

Ideally, the time to make the decision about whether to have children is before marriage. We have already suggested that birth planning should begin in the engagement period or whenever sexual relations become part of the relationship, regardless of whether parenthood has a place in the couple's plans. It is clear, however, that many couples begin marriage without having given serious thought to planning their family. Evidence gathered in a study of 2,713 white married women indicated that about half did not begin to use any kind of contraception until after their first pregnancy, and 18 percent did not begin until after the second.[8] While we can assume that some of these women deliberately tried to conceive, others left the decision to chance. Many individuals think they have made a decision only about having intercourse but find they have also decided to have children—and to have them now! Recognizing the reproductive potential of sexual relationships and the choices available regarding parenthood is a crucial first step for any couple. We stress this fact because the romantic notions and social pressures surrounding sex and parenthood may keep people from approaching the situation as one in which there are choices. The notion that planning to conceive a child is unnatural or less satisfying than trusting to luck is irrational; so is the notion that choices do not exist in the methods to accomplish that objective.

It is obvious that early recognition of the reproductive potential of sex makes further planning possible. The decision of whether to have children will determine the nature of subsequent problem-solving situations. For example, the decision to have children demands further problem-solving action in determining when to have them, selecting an appropriate contraceptive until that time, achieving conception, and, finally, adjusting to the new demands of pregnancy and the anticipated birth. Similarly, a decision not to have children necessitates further planning of an adequate contraceptive program. For many couples, a decision made before marriage not to have children may be changed by chance (for example, an ineffective contraceptive) or reconsideration at a later point in the life cycle. Likewise, infertility and a lack of adoptable children may keep the couple from achieving their goal of having children.

Motivation

Assuming that the couple have recognized the situation as one demanding action, the next step is to determine whether they feel motivated to act on it. Do they want to make a rational choice regarding parenthood, or would they prefer that the choice be made for them by their action or inaction? When one realizes that only 10 percent of the population is infertile, the odds are in favor of nature taking its course and deciding that the woman *will* become pregnant if motivation not to have children is low. If only one partner in a relationship is committed to the decision not to have children, that person must be fully responsible for appropriate contraceptive action in the couple's sexual relations.

Generating Alternatives

In a decision of whether to have children, the alternatives are simple—yes or no. However, the impact of this decision is less clear-cut. Reasons for having children are almost as varied as the people who give them. They include: to pass on the good life, to carry on the family name, to follow God's will to be fruitful and multiply, to add a new dimension to an already happy relationship, to provide an outlet for a real love of children, and to provide parents with grandchildren. While these reasons all have positive connotations, others show mixed feelings: to patch up a shaky marriage, to provide a substitute love object, to prove masculinity or femininity, and to even up the sexes among the children in the family. Social pressures from friends who have already had children may also precipitate such a decision. Women, particularly are socialized from childhood to expect to become parents. This socialization process, which still operates, regardless of efforts by women's liberation groups, may stack the deck in favor of parenthood. Some people feel parenthood is a duty, not a choice. They cite fears of loneliness in old age, criticism from friends and family for being concerned only with self-gratification, worries about somehow missing out on a potentially satisfying experience, and adherence to religious beliefs as reasons for their feelings.

Even with these social pressures, it is possible to evaluate parenthood objectively. The basic factors to consider are (1) the personal resources each spouse has to cope with parenthood; (2) whether the responsibilities of parenthood are compatible with values, self-conceptions, and short-term and long-term goals; and (3) the material resources available to provide for the physical needs of the child.

Physical and mental health   The personal resources each spouse brings to the marital system are the same resources he brings to the child as a parent. Good physical and mental health, knowledge of child development and childrearing principles, warmth, adaptability, flexibility, and willingness to defer personal gratification in order to care for another person are examples of personal resources which should be considered in any decision to have children. Physical and mental *health* are important considerations because the demands of parenthood are heavy and go on for a long time. Physical health for the prospective mother particularly is critical. There is strong evidence that a woman who begins her pregnancy in good nutritional condition can provide the optimal environment for her baby from the start. Consideration should also be made of any known genetic problems of either the man or woman or their relatives. The presence of diseases such as diabetes or hemophilia in one's immediate family may suggest that medical resources be consulted to ascertain the likelihood of a child being born with the disease. Mental health is also an asset to both prospective parents. If one spouse is experiencing difficulty in handling his personal life, adding the pressures and demands of parenthood is unwise until some personal stability is achieved.

Knowledge in the area of child development   While one can obtain *knowledge about child development* "on the job," so to speak, this type of knowledge gained before having children increases the likelihood of a decision based on fact rather than fantasy. Because most people of marriageable age in our society have little experience with babies and young children, they have many misconceptions about the nature of childrearing. Reading courses in child development or observation of and experience with children can provide a better understanding of children and the magnitude of the task—though some parents claim that no book can adequately describe either the frustrations or the satisfactions of the role.

Personal characteristics   The *personal characteristics* of warmth, adaptability, flexibility, and ability to defer personal gratification all reflect the giving, sharing nature of the parental role. Persons who are unable to give freely of their resources, who expect some return on the investment made for another person, or who are unprepared to defer personal gratifications should assess carefully whether the parental role is appropriate for them. The human infant is totally dependent on parents (or substitute parents) to provide for his needs for a long period of time. In addition, it is difficult to plan ahead for the demands children make on one's time and energy because no two children are the same. These facts demand a good share of flexibility and adaptability in order to be able to carry out the parental role.

Ascertaining whether parenthood is compatible with one's long-term and short-term goals, values, and self-conceptions calls for another personal assessment. If both partners have decided to pursue demanding careers which involve long hours and extensive traveling, parenthood may not be compatible with their long-term occupational goals, unless they wish to have a substitute mother or father do the major portion of childrearing. Likewise, a couple may decide not to have children because one spouse is unwilling to share such a role in childrearing. The couple who decide to have children as well as develop individual careers outside the home should recognize the sacrifices which may be demanded from their recreation time in order to meet the responsibilities and obtain the desired satisfactions of childrearing.

Occupational goals are but one type of goal which should be reviewed. Certainly goals for the marital relationship should be considered as well. What will the impact of children be on the relationship? Evidence regarding the effect of children on marital adjustment is contradictory. Citing evidence from nine studies, Udry reported that the presence or absence of children per se is not consistently related to marital adjustment.[9] (Data from numerous other researchers do, however, agree on one finding—couples who have more children than they report they wanted are generally more poorly adjusted than those who have as many or fewer than they desire.) We suspect that the contradictory evidence is a result of the difficulty in assessing the impact of one factor (children) on a relationship as multidimensional as marriage. In addition, few comparative studies have been made of childless couples and couples with children, controlling for such factors as length of marriage or personal characteristics. Thus statements about the effect of children on marital adjustment are still largely speculative.

Even so, it is obvious that the addition of a third person to the marital system changes the nature of that system. The old adage "three is a crowd" reflects the increasing complexities of interaction in a triad as opposed to a dyad. Instead of having just one relationship to focus on, an addition to the family raises the total number of relationships to three—husband-wife, mother-child, and father-child. It is inevitable that the time available to the marital relationship decreases to meet the new demands of the child. In addition, our society pressures couples into adopting conventional behavior patterns once children are born, and these may also decrease satisfactions as a couple. Such pressures may include taking a steady job, moving to an apartment with play space, or giving up one's motorcycle for a VW van.

Many couples believe that having a child will strengthen a faltering relationship. This, however, is a poor gamble. It is a myth that children hold marriages together and prevent divorce. While there is some evidence from divorce statistics that childlessness is much higher for divorced couples than for those still married,[10] it is simplistic to attribute the divorce to childlessness. A much more logical explanation linking the two is that in most cases both divorce and childlessness result from more basic issues in the marital relationship.

Children, however, certainly influence the marital relationship. We do not agree with some researchers that the changes occurring in the marital relationship following the birth of the first child are a real crisis involving severe and long lasting upheaval in the marriage.[11] However, we do believe that these changes are disorganizing. Loss of sleep, financial problems, decline in sexual response of the wife, and disturbance of social and recreational patterns are common complaints of new parents. However, these parents also report rapid adjustment to the new situation.

While people adjust to these realities, the fact remains that parenthood involves a sharing of the time, energy, and resources which once were devoted entirely to the spouse or to other activities. The long, uninterrupted discussion of a new novel may have to wait until the children are asleep, good-bye kisses may have to be shared by sticky-faced little cherubs, and lovemaking may be interrupted regularly by the pitter-patter of little feet coming toward the bed. These facts are as real as the delights of watching the child grow and mature and growing as a person yourself because of your experiences with a child. Parenthood demands a new establishment of goal priorities that encompass both marital and child-related goals. Often parents find that the time and effort demanded by a new role makes it difficult to fit in older goals. It takes commitment to marital goals to insure that they are shared and not subordinated to childrearing goals. Those who are unwilling to share marital goals or to work at meeting them should seriously consider not having children. The intensity of the disorganization resulting from the arrival of a baby is dependent on the expectations individuals have for that event and their threshold of tolerance for disorganization.

The material resources of time, energy, and money are also important. Day care and nursery facilities provide substitute care for children, but their number, though increasing, in no way meets the needs of those desiring such care. In addition, only a few employers provide part-time employment for men and women so that childrearing can be totally shared. These experiments generally have been run by agencies and institutions who hire a husband and wife for one position so they can have the time to share childrearing roles. It is currently estimated that it costs $59,627 to raise a child from birth through college or university. Thus today's child demands a constant investment of material as well as person resources. One cannot put a dollar value on either the personal resources or time or energy; yet these will probably be what the child remembers throughout his life.

Having considered these factors, one must execute and evaluate the alternatives in the light of one's goals. If there is uncertainty about deciding not to have children, it would be wise to consider temporary rather than permanent methods of birth control, so that the situation can be reconsidered at a later time.

Coping with Infertility

Not all couples who decide to have children are physically capable of doing so. While approximately 10 percent of all married couples are childless, only 1 to 3 percent of these couples indicate satisfaction with this state. Coping with infertility thus becomes a problem-solving situation.

Sterility can be broken down into two categories—relative sterility and absolute sterility. *Relative sterility* refers to a couple's temporary difficulty in conceiving a child, where the problem can be treated or corrected. *Absolute sterility* refers to a couple's biological incapability of conceiving children. Increased medical knowledge in the areas of infertility and sterility probably has accounted for the decrease in the number of couples experiencing absolute sterility.

The resolution of an infertility problem (whether it is absolute or relative sterility) involves the cooperation of both spouses, even though the difficulty may be with only one of them. Contrary to historical and folk beliefs, recent estimates are that husbands are just as likely to be infertile as wives.

Tests for sterility are easier to conduct for men than for women. The male tests involve analysis of the cellular components of the ejaculate to determine the sperm count and the motility (movement and direction) and structure of the sperm.

Male infertility can be caused by: (1) complete absence of sperm production, (2) maturational arrest in the production of sperm, (3) obstruction of the ducts carrying sperm from the testes to the urethra, (4) congenital absence of part of the duct system, (5) failure of descent of the testes prior to puberty, (6) permanent damage to sperm production due to X-ray, (7) temporary sterility induced by minor diseases, and (8) mumps in the adult male.

Surgery is used to open blocked ducts. However, until recently, the treatment for other forms of relative sterility has been less promising. Advances into the basic nature of male infertility promise hope for future medical resources to resolve this problem.

The range of sperm counts for husbands whose wives have become pregnant is from 5 to 500 million/cc, with the majority concentrated between 20 and 100 million/cc.[13] Sperm counts between 20 and 30 million/cc are considered by most fertility experts to be the lower limit of the normal range for fertility. The latest findings, however, are that sperm count is not the only factor in male human fertility; of greater importance are the motile activity and structure of the sperm. The following conditions usually are necessary for fertility—a sperm count of at least 20 million/cc with at least 40 percent of the sperm population showing vigorous forward progression and 60 percent of the cells normal in structure.[14] Using these standards, approximately 5 to 10 percent of the adult male population probably are infertile.

Tests for infertility in the woman are more complicated, due to her complex reproductive system. John Macleod suggests that it is doubtful that the known tests for the woman cover all the defects that may be present.[15] Some of the common causes of infertility in women are: (1) a hostile vaginal or cervical environment for the sperm, (2) blockage of the Fallopian tubes so the egg cannot pass into the uterus, (3) failure to maintain the development of the ovum after fertilization, and (4) inability of the sperm to enter the cervix.

Tests for female fertility, as well as treatment for the woman, are complicated by the fact that her menstrual cycle must determine when these tests and treatments occur. A woman's fertility potential also varies with her age, the most fertile age period being twenty-one to thirty. From that time on her fertility potential decreases (see Table 14-1).

Because many couples today use contraception from the beginning of their marriage, infertility problems often are not apparent until several years have passed. If a couple want children and cannot conceive after a year of effort, they should seek medical advice. Because psychological as well as physical problems contribute to relative infertility, this approach can provide reassurance in many cases that conception is possible.

When absolute sterility is diagnosed, couples are faced with three alternatives: (1) to remain childless, (2) to adopt a child, or (3) to try artificial insemination if the wife is able to bear a child. Willingness to consider adoption or artificial insemination as possible solutions to the problem is contingent on both partners' attitudes toward the parental role, their general flexibility in decision making, and their self-confidence. If both are committed to parenthood and have a positive feeling about it, this will figure as a resource in problem solving. In the case of adopting, it is not always easy to reorient one's self-concept to accept the fact that natural parenthood is not possible. This is a time when open, honest communication is helpful to allow for expressing the feelings of disappointment or frustration. Time also is a resource in the decision-making process because it allows the

Table 14-1 *Age-Specific Conception Rate: Marital Conception for Ever-Married Females, by Marital Status at Interview*

Age-Period	Ever-Married Females					
	Marital status at interview			Marital status at interview		
	Ever married	Married once, still married	Ever S.D.W.*	Ever married	Married once, still married	Ever S.D.W.*
	Conceptions per 100 Marital Years			Number of Marital Years		
16-20	22.2	15.8	27.7	1,012	467	545
21-25	23.7	22.4	26.3	4,296	2,822	1,474
26-30	24.3	25.0	22.5	5,051	3,636	1,415
31-35	15.7	15.9	15.3	4,040	3,043	997
36-40	7.7	7.8	7.7	2,736	2,098	638
41-45	2.1	2.1	2.1	1,543	1,166	377
46-50	0.2	0.2	0.5	822	633	189

*Single, divorced, widowed.

From Paul Gebhard et al., *Pregnancy, Birth and Abortion* (New York: Harper Bros., 1958), p. 126. Reprinted by permission.

restructuring of goals and expectations. The following hypothetical example describes one wife's experience with infertility:

I had always dreamed of having a baby. I had avidly played the "little mother" socialization games—playing with dolls and babysitting. Bob and I planned to have children but hadn't thought of the possibility of being infertile. Both he and I took it very hard. At first we refused to believe it—we saw another doctor. Then came the doldrums. I smoldered and wept inside. If it wasn't for Bob forcing me to express my feelings, I would have fallen apart. We began to talk about our disappointments and some of the possibilities for the future. After six months, we decided to adopt a baby. We needed that time to be able to reorient our feelings about ourselves and to accept an adopted child.

Adoption may not be as viable an alternative today as it has been in the past. The number of healthy infants currently is limited, and many infertile couples who desire children may be faced with the alternatives of adopting an older or a handicapped child or adjusting their goals and accepting their childless state. Each of these alternatives should be evaluated in terms of how well it meets the couple's goals regarding parenthood, their values, their personal feelings, and their general adaptability. Where difficulties are encountered in adjusting to infertility, professional counseling services should be consulted. Religious counselors, marriage and family counselors, and physicians can provide information and support for a couple in this situation.

Coping with an Unplanned Conception

An unplanned conception is one in which pregnancy occurs even though it was not intended; it can be caused by failure of the contraceptive used or by failure to use a contraceptive. Like infertility, it is a situation which occurs with little warning but has long-range implications on the marital or nonmarital system.

For the unmarried couple, the closeness of their relationship influences the alternatives available to them. If the relationship is one in which long-term commitments (such as engagement) exist or can be made, the alternatives include: (1) continuing the pregnancy and marrying immediately, (2) continuing the pregnancy and the relationship but not marrying, (3) continuing the pregnancy but not the relationship, or (4) terminating the pregnancy.

For the couple with a more casual relationship, perhaps only the latter three alternatives are feasible. While premarital pregnancy is a common reason for marriage, it is one of the poorest if other factors are not favorable for the relationship. Evaluation of marriage as an alternative should focus on the impact of marriage on the individuals and on the child. The "shotgun marriage" foisted on two individuals who love one another may be stressful, but this stress is probably less than that experienced by individuals who do not love one another or desire to marry. The decision to marry may be the course of least resistance to cope with the immediate situation, but long-term concerns should be considered as well. Two necessary questions are: Do you want to share your life with this person? Will you be able to build a relationship that will facilitate the growth and development of your expected child?

Couples often are fearful of parental reactions to a premarital pregnancy. Most young people do not wish to hurt or embarrass their parents by such a situation. However, while it can be expected that parents will experience some shock and upset over the situation, they may also be able to help their son or daughter cope with it. Not all families are able to make the decisions necessary in handling a premarital pregnancy; in these cases, professional counseling services can provide the kind of confidential assistance which those involved need to appraise all alternatives fairly.

Whenever marriage is not considered and the pregnancy is continued, careful thought should be given to the significance of the decision in economic and psychosocial terms. Regardless of the growing acceptance of a variety of family forms, the unmarried mother who keeps her child is still in the minority. Even so, many more unmarried mothers are deciding to cope with an unplanned conception by not marrying and keeping their children. These women often experience all the problems of a parent without a partner—role overload in doing the tasks of two parents, poverty, and, above all, disapproval by society. These factors influence the quality of care available for the child and the possibilities for achieving maternal goals and satisfactions.

Continuing the relationship without marrying is another viable alternative. Some individuals feel that common-law relationships are more honest than marriage. While each partner in a common-law relationship has some kind of personal commitment to the other, there is no formal, legal, or religious contract. If this alternative is chosen, arrangements should be made for care of the child in the event of the mother's death. In cases where marriage is not possible and the woman's personal resources are limited, she has two options—to complete the pregnancy and place the baby for adoption or to terminate the pregnancy. The unmarried mother is given the sole responsibility of deciding whether to place the child for adoption. The difficulties inherent in this alternative are obvious, and the decision to place a child for adoption is a difficult one. The advantages and disadvantages of keeping the child and raising it as a single parent, as opposed to placing the child for adoption, should be compared—considering the child's as well as the parents' welfare.

Abortion as an Alternative

The recent changes in laws relating to artificially induced abortion in both the United States and Canada have made abortion a viable alternative for some individuals. *Abortion* can be defined as an interruption of pregnancy before the fetus has matured enough to live independently outside its mother's body. Population experts Paul Ehrlich and John Holdren suggest that the combined effects of four events have brought abortion into the public eye today: (1) the rapid acceptance of legal abortion procedures in eastern Europe and Japan with no obvious deleterious effects on society, (2) growing concern about the consequences of unwanted children, (3) growing awareness of the need to control population growth, and (4) the women's liberation movement for achievement of the status and privileges already enjoyed by men.[16]

Many questions have been posed on both sides of the abortion controversy, but the main ones are: Is it needed today? Is it a safe procedure? Is it moral? Who should decide whether or not it is a viable alternative?

The demand for abortion can be illustrated by the abortion rate in states and countries where restrictions have been removed. In these places, the abortion rate approaches or exceeds the birth rate.[17] (It should be noted, however, that the figures are exaggerated; many women seek abortions in these places because they are not available in their own areas.) Assuming that women decide only after serious thought to have an abortion, the high rate reflects a real need.

While adequate contraception should decrease the rate of abortion, it should be considered as something distinct from contraception. After all, the decision to have an abortion is made after contraception has failed. Whether this failure is due to human error or technical error, the result is the same—an unwanted pregnancy.

The safety of legal abortions is supported by figures which report the death rate among women undergoing legal abortions in 1969 to be .1 percent of the risk population (women of childbearing age, usually considered to be fifteen to forty-four) in Canada, the United States, and Japan, and .4 percent in Hungary.

(These rates vary according to whether abortions are allowed after the twelfth week of pregnancy.) In contrast, the death rate from pregnancy complications is .6 percent in Canada, .7 percent in the United States, 2.4 percent in Japan, and 1.2 percent in Hungary.[18] Thus under normal conditions, and within the first twelve weeks of pregnancy, abortion techniques are safe procedures—actually safer than giving birth.

One moral question centers on whether abortion is equivalent to taking human life. Identifying when life begins and whether the fetus is an actual or a potential human being has been the basis of the major religious stands taken on the issue. The Catholic Church takes the most conservative stand and is totally opposed to abortion. Other religious bodies have widely divergent views. For example, following is a portion of the November 1967 Massachusetts Council of Churches policy statement on abortion:

The problem of abortion—the induced termination of fetal life prior to viability—has become increasingly visible to the public as attempts are made in the various states to liberalize existing laws on abortion. The Massachusetts Council of Churches recognizes the existence of sincere differences of opinion on this subject, but believes that the laws of society on abortion must be adjusted to provide relief from unnecessary human suffering. Therefore, we advocate revisions in the Massachusetts abortion law, which is highly ambiguous but apparently permits abortion only to save the life of the mother.

In accord with the Judeo-Christian tradition, our position is founded on respect for the worth of persons and a commitment to maximize human well-being within the context of the community. We firmly acknowledge the prospective parents' moral responsibility to the future child, the binding duty to provide the best possible conditions for a creative life. However, the parents' responsibility to potential life can be invalidated by certain tragic circumstances, when the responsibility cannot be fulfilled adequately or at all. We claim that an important distinction exists between actual and potential human life, and that duties to promote the welfare of actual life may outweigh duties to potential life in particular situations, thereby making abortion morally permissible in these cases.[19]

The persons involved should carefully evaluate their feelings about abortion as an alternative. Individual values may or may not reflect the religious stance taken by a particular faith, but people must live with the decision they make. Understanding and working through feelings before making such a decision can reduce or prevent any guilt resulting from the decision.

Abortion is not equally available to all women. Its availability is based on state or national laws which allow the termination of a pregnancy. In addition, the pregnancy must be in the early stages.

In the United States, the January 22, 1973 decisions of the U.S. Supreme Court opened the door for legal abortion across the country. Basically, the decisions threw out restrictions on the reasons for abortion, requirements that a committee or several doctors approve the abortion, residency requirements, and mandatory hospitalization. Justice Harry Blackman wrote for the majority that the right of personal privacy allows a woman and her doctor to decide whether she should have an abortion. Even so, the right is not unconditional and should be viewed against state interests of health standards and protecting prenatal life.

In essence these rulings make it possible for a woman in the first and second trimesters of her pregnancy to decide with her doctor whether an abortion is possible and suitable. In her third trimester, she can have an abortion to preserve her life and health. Restrictions imposed by public hospitals and governmental laws or regulations have been invalidated.

In the first trimester of pregnancy, abortions can be performed outside state licensed hospitals and no license fees can be collected from clinics or physicians operating for this purpose. However, any state can license facilities to be used for second and third trimester abortions. While the requirement for committee approval of abortion was invalidated by the Supreme Court, the ruling did not state whether a publicly supported denominational hospital can impose its negative view of abortion on the physicians and patients there while still receiving public support. This decision places abortion under a national law similar in principle to that of Canada.

Even though the law gives women the choice of having an abortion, the cost can still be prohibitive. Fees vary, depending on the procedure, situation (office or hospital, length of pregnancy, and so on), and locality. In New York City fees range from nothing to $600. In Canada, doctors' fees range from $75 to $200, depending on the technique used. (These fees do not include hospitalization costs.)[20] The Commission on Population Growth and the American Future has suggested that all Americans—regardless of age, marital status, or income—be enabled to avoid unwanted births. To facilitate this, the commission believes that under certain circumstances the federal government should pay for abortions. The commission also urges insurance companies to include in their policies specific coverage for hospital and surgical costs for abortions.

Psychological considerations also figure in the decision to have an abortion. Many anti-abortionists suggest that the mother may suffer serious psychological problems if she undergoes an abortion. It is interesting to note, however, that few of these people consider the psychological problems possible if she does not have the abortion. In one study, Swedish writer Kirstin Hook interviewed 249 Swedish women who were turned down for a therapeutic abortion; 75 percent of these women had serious psychological problems related to the unwanted pregnancy in the eleven-year follow-up.[21] In another study of 321 patients who were referred for termination of pregnancy, psychiatrists C. M. B. Pare and Hermione Raven found that where the mother wanted the termination, few psychological problems followed. In comparison, patients whose pregnancy was terminated because of complications (for example, tubal pregnancy), but who did not want the termination, suffered from many severe psychiatric problems. Pare concluded that the most important single factor in determining whether or not the woman suffered psychiatric difficulties was whether she wanted the abortion.[22]

Abortion will not be acceptable to all women or couples, but we believe it should be a choice so that the children born are wanted children. The National Council on Family Relations wrote the following majority and minority positions on abortion. The majority position was supported by 70 percent of the membership, the minority position by 26 percent, and 4 percent abstained.

Major Position

The National Council on Family Relations is vitally concerned with individual and family mental health. Growing out of this concern is increasing anxiety over the number of unwanted pregnancies which are occurring in this country, and the multitude of problems these pregnancies are creating for individuals and families in America.

First, unwanted pregnancies restrict the right of couples to postpone parenthood, to space their children, or to limit the size of their families.

Second, unwanted pregnancies push many couples into marriage and parenthood before they are prepared for or desirous of either.

Third, unwanted pregnancies often create further problems in the relationship between the parents and the child.

Fourth, unwanted children add greatly to the growing problem of overpopulation.

Fifth, unwanted pregnancies cause needless suffering and death for many women, especially the poor, because they feel forced to seek abortions from medically untrained persons.

Because of these and other related problems created by unwanted pregnancies, the NCFR recommends that increased attention be given to improving and expanding programs in contraceptive education and family planning.

While the National Council supports family planning education as a preventive approach, it also strongly endorses the repeal of all laws which prohibit safe medical abortions in this country. It further recommends that abortion be the legal right of all women and a private matter between a woman and her physician.

Minority Position

Many members of the National Council on Family Relations, while equally concerned with the negative consequences of unwanted pregnancies and equally committed to education and information which is calculated to help people make wiser uses of sex and contraception, nevertheless cannot subscribe to the policy of favoring the repeal of all laws prohibiting abortion. Not all object for the same reasons, but most could subscribe to one or more of the following:

1. They place a high premium on life, the life of the fetus as well as the life of the mother. The effect of uncontrolled social approval of the right of private individuals to end fetal life is to undermine this fundamental social and religious value.

2. They recognize the responsibility of every society to regulate the sexual and reproductive behavior of its members for the common good. They believe that the best social policies are those which balance individual welfare against the welfare of the general community. If, in the past, abortion laws have been subversive of the welfare of individuals, it would be better policy to reformulate the laws rather than revoke them, abnegating social responsiblity in this vital area.

3. They have observed that nations which have adopted unrestricted abortion as a policy have often found themselves with as many new problems as they had hoped to solve. A number of Eastern European nations, including Hungary and the Soviet Union, are considering a reversal of their liberal abortion policies because the ratio of abortion to live births has risen so precipitously.[23]

It appears that many of the concerns expressed in the majority position have been attended to by the Supreme Court decision. Even so, family life education and improved contraceptive education and use need to be emphasized in order to assure that abortion is not viewed as a contraceptive technique.

Unplanned Marital Conceptions

Unplanned conceptions within marriage may be as traumatic as those outside marriage, even though they are not negatively sanctioned by society. They can cause interruptions of educational programs, extra financial burdens, and marital problems in other areas of the relationship. According to statistical estimates arrived at in the 1970 National Fertility Study conducted by the Office of Population Research at Princeton University, 44 percent of all births to currently married women from 1966 to 1970 were unplanned; 15 percent of the births between 1966 and 1970 were described by parents as being unwanted.[24] This percentage of unwanted births means that, theoretically, 2.65 million births would not have occurred if couples had perfect fertility control.

Unwanted pregnancies occur more frequently where education and income are lowest. The inequality of access to various methods of fertility control as well as to education and money probably accounts for this larger number of unwanted births.

While not all unwanted births mean unwanted children, the costs in psychological, social, and health terms can still be high. For example, most of these births occur among women in the later years of their childbearing cycle, and maternal and infant mortality are higher among older women (maternal mortality is four times greater among women aged thirty-five to thirty-nine than among those twenty to twenty-four,[25] and infant mortality is one-third higher among women over thirty-five than among those twenty to twenty-four.[26]

Some of the alternatives available to a married couple are similar to those for an unmarried couple. Broadly speaking, they involve continuing the pregnancy and adapting personal goals or terminating the pregnancy.

When evaluating the alternative of continuing the pregnancy, each couple should include an assessment of their resources (personal; interpersonal, and material) to cope with the child; compatibility of the pregnancy with their aims, values, and the current state of their marriage; and the availability of other alternatives. Many anti-abortion organizations provide counseling services to assist a woman or couple in readjusting their goals to accept such a pregnancy. This counseling may provide the necessary support for a decision to continue the pregnancy to term. Age also is important, since pregnancies occurring later in life carry the risk of increased incidence of certain hereditary diseases. Down's syndrome (mongolism), for example, could be reduced if older women did not bear children. If an unplanned pregnancy occurring after the age of forty is continued, *amniocentesis* (a technique involving the testing of a small amount of fluid from the womb) can be utilized to detect certain genetic diseases.

For health and psychological reasons, abortion can be the other primary alternative. This alternative has been discussed in detail earlier in the chapter.

Adjusting to Pregnancy

The decision to have a child generates additional situations which may be problematic for a couple. Once the goal of achieving conception has been agreed upon and attained, a subsequent goal is to adjust to pregnancy and prepare for the birth of the child. Understanding the physical aspects of pregnancy is of great help in adjusting to the pregnancy.

Diagnosis of Pregnancy

Failure to menstruate is usually the first symptom of pregnancy, but it does not provide an accurate diagnosis in all cases. Age, illness, and even emotional upsets caused by simple events like forgetting to take the Pill can delay a menstrual cycle. Breast fullness or tingling, nausea, fatigue, and frequent urination are other symptoms announcing pregnancy. While pregnancy test kits are now available in most drugstores, early diagnosis on the basis of a physician's examination and laboratory tests is more accurate and initiates the kind of prenatal care which encourages a healthy pregnancy. Pregnancy can be determined with a fair degree of accuracy soon after the first missed period.

Prenatal Development

Prenatal development can be divided into three distinct periods—the ovum, the embryo, and the fetus. The period of the *ovum* includes the time from fertilization to implantation. Fertilization usually occurs at about the middle of each menstrual cycle. The ovum, a small egg about the size of a pen dot, is sent down a Fallopian tube by suction and expansion and contraction of the tube (see Figure 14-1). If it is met by sperm part way down the Fallopian tube, fertilization can occur. Only one sperm nucleus (of the 200 million to 500 million contributed by the man in an act of intercourse) penetrates the egg membrane and unites with the nucleus of the egg. When the male and female nucleus unite, they form the *zygote*, or fertilized egg. After four days, the zygote consists

Figure 14-1 *Process of Fertilization*

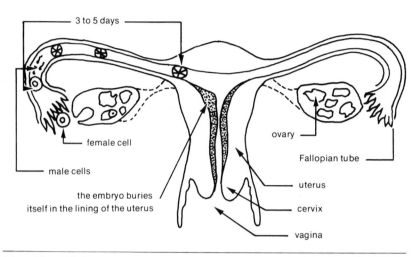

Adapted from U.S. Department of Health, Education and Welfare, *Prenatal Care*, Children's Bureau Publication Number 4 (Washington, D.C.: Government Printing Office, 1962), p. 10.

of ninety cells and begins to leave the Fallopian tube for the uterus. It takes two or three days for the ovum to begin to settle into the lining of the uterus. This process, called *implantation*, is the landmark event of the *embryo*.

From the end of the second week to the end of the second month, the various organs and tissues are being differentiated and formed. Following the principle of developmental direction, development in lower animals and man proceeds from anterior to posterior. In other words, the head develops first in the sequence. The embryo is so small (approximately one-tenth of an inch long) that the woman may be unaware of her pregnancy, even though the embryo already has the foundations for eyes, spinal cord, nervous system, lungs, stomach, liver, kidneys, and intestines. At eighteen days, the embryo's primitive heart begins to beat.

The second four weeks are marked by rapid development, and the embryo begins to look more and more human (see Figure 14-2). From eight weeks until birth, the developing individual is called a *fetus*. If one were able to look inside the uterus, the fetus would look much like a human being, with face, fingers, toes, and internal functioning organs and muscles. During the third month, differentiation between the sexes is achieved, tooth buds develop, and the fetus grows considerably in size. Later in development, the fetus is able to swallow, secrete urine, hiccup, and make breathing movements.

Between sixteen and twenty weeks the mother can feel the fetus moving

Figure 14-2   *The Human Embryo at Six Weeks and at Four Months*

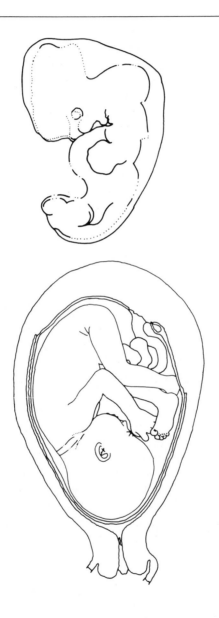

gently within her. In the uterus, the fetus is supported by the amniotic fluid, which protects it from shocks and gives it freedom of movement (the fetus moves up and down and around). As the uterus becomes more crowded with the baby's increasing size, its movements are visible on the surface of his mother's abdomen. In fact, these movements are sometimes so spectacular that one can almost identify which part of the baby produced the thump.

During the last four to four and a half months of pregnancy, the nervous system develops more fully, thus preparing the baby for independent life. The nervous system is the most important development, because it organizes and coordinates all the other systems. Full maturation of this system is not reached until some months after birth. By the end of nine months the fetus weighs an average of seven and a half pounds and is usually ready to be expelled from the womb.

The problem-solving situations generated by this fascinating process of prenatal development are far ranging. Some couples establish new goals and expectations for their relationship that necessitate changes in their life-style, spending patterns, or attitudes toward themselves. Other couples are more immediately concerned with accomplishing a successful pregnancy and birth.

Adjusting to Bodily Changes

Pregnancy influences a woman's entire body. Thus her general health before and during pregnancy influences the outcome of the pregnancy. A woman who has begun pregnancy with a normal, fully developed, and well nourished body will be less likely to be bothered by complications in pregnancy, premature birth, or poor condition of the newborn.

The entire *reproductive system* undergoes a refining and tuning up process for the pregnancy and birth. The uterus increases in weight and capacity, and its muscle fibers grow to nine or ten times their initial length to prepare for their role in opening the cervix and helping to push the baby out at the time of delivery. The cervix, or neck of the uterus, softens as pregnancy progresses due to its muscle fibers decreasing in size and number and its blood supply increasing. The vagina increases in length and capacity, and vaginal secretions increase in both amount and in their ability to prevent bacterial infections. All the tissues surrounding the birth canal loosen and become more elastic.

From the fourth month on, the breasts may excrete *colostrum* (fluid that appears before the real milk) stimulated by hormones from the placenta. The breasts also increase in size during pregnancy, due to a larger blood supply and the development of more mammary gland tissue. The pigmented area around the nipple may also darken.

The *circulatory system* also undergoes changes during pregnancy. The blood vessels which supply the uterus increase in length and dilate, and the blood volume is increased by one-fifth. The lower specific gravity of the blood changes the usual balance of fluids in the lymph system, and retention of fluids in the legs and ankles may result. Resting with feet up improves circulation.

Pregnancy influences other systems of the woman's body as well. For example, her hormonal balance may be upset, her metabolism is increased and improves after the third month, and her kidneys work extra hard to eliminate the products of increased metabolism and the excretion of the fetus. The strains experienced by the mother's body during pregnancy are reflected by the common discomforts of frequent urination, varicose veins, swollen ankles, shortness of breath, and heartburn. Adjustment to these changes is facilitated by knowledge about them so that they can be anticipated as a normal accompaniment to pregnancy. Extra rest, adequate exercise, attention to diet, and good medical care are some of the resources used to cope with the physical demands of pregnancy.

Adjusting to Changes in Self-Concept

Readjustment of self-concept in pregnancy is precipitated by the insistent and continuous changes in the woman's body, as well as by the setting of new goals for life in general. While it may be easy to ignore bodily changes in the first trimester of pregnancy, in the second trimester the swelling of the breasts, mood swings, fatigue, and eventual movement of the fetus necessitate recognition of the impending change in role.

For some women, resolution of the feelings of discomfort with the anticipated parental role is accomplished simply by accepting the fact of pregnancy and the fact that uneasiness is a natural accompaniment to taking on a new role. For others, resolution involves a concerted effort to reorient the self-concept to include the maternal role. Because our self-concept is formed as a result of continual feedback from significant others, the husband can play an important role by responding to his wife in positive terms. This is particularly important in helping her accept her increased body size. It is not unusual for a woman to feel depressed over the twenty to twenty-five pounds she has gained during pregnancy. In one instance, a wife expressed her distress by drawing a self-portrait (see Figure 14-3). When asked to describe why she drew the picture, she said she felt overtaken and totally enveloped in the baby-making process, devoid of her own individuality and femininity. This statement could hardly be considered pathological, since it was made by a woman who was looking forward to the birth of her child and who felt positive about her pregnancy. Support and reassurance from her husband served as a resource in coping with this insecurity.

A prospective father's self-concept also may undergo changes in the pregnancy period. His changes are largely psychological and are not complicated by the vast hormonal and body changes which are present for his

Figure 14-3   *My Self-Portrait during Pregnancy*

wife. A study of twenty-nine husbands explored three facets of expectant fatherhood: (1) changes in the husband's self-concept while preparing for and anticipating his father role, (2) changes in his relationship to his wife, and (3) changes in his social world outside the home. The study found three orientations, based on the husbands' reactions to the event of pregnancy—romantic, family, and career.

Those husbands with a *romantic orientation* had a casual feeling about parenthood and focused their reactions on the need to support both a wife and a child. The *career oriented* husbands viewed parenthood as an interfering factor to their professional responsibilities and wanted to postpone or avoid the acceptance of the new responsibilities of parenthood. The *family oriented* husbands accepted their new responsibilities easily and felt fulfilled at the prospect of fatherhood.

The *career oriented* husbands denied any identity transformation; the *family oriented* ones saw it as a gradual transition begun with pregnancy; and the *romantic oriented* men viewed their identity transformation as simply a maturational experience which sharply reminded them that they were adults and no longer free to do as they pleased.[28]

Thus, for both husbands and wives, adjustment to pregnancy includes setting new goals for personal achievements and reorienting self-concept to include the parental role. Basic family life education focusing on the nature of pregnancy and the nature of the parental role can be a resource in achieving these goals.

Maintaining the Sexual Relationship during Pregnancy

Most couples desire to maintain their sexual relationship during pregnancy, but little information has been available to help them develop satisfying techniques for this time. Results from Masters and Johnson's limited study of expectant mothers have provided some new data, but the area has not yet been thoroughly researched.

Some obstetricians still recommend that coitus be discontinued in the first three months, around the time when the regular menstrual period would have appeared, and during the last six weeks of pregnancy. Masters and Johnson's study of the sexual relations of pregnant women indicates that two basic changes in this obstetrical advice are needed. First, most women need not refrain from sex during the first or second three months of pregnancy; however, women who have experienced three or more spontaneous abortions in the first trimester should abstain. Second, the problem of sexual relations late in pregnancy and after the child's birth should be resolved on an individual basis—by discussion among the physician, the wife, and the husband. Whenever a physician feels the couple should refrain from sex, the reasons should be made clear to both husband and wife.[28] Any medical proscription, coupled with changes in the wife's sexual desire and her increasing body size, may necessitate changes in the sexual relationship.

For some couples the adjustments need only involve increased gentleness during lovemaking or a change of position; for others it may mean the use of mutual masturbation or other nonvaginal forms of sexual stimulation. How couples resolve this problem is dependent on their flexibility, their comfort with alternative forms of sexual stimulation, and their desire to maintain a mutually satisfying sexual relationship during pregnancy. Unless medical conditions indicate otherwise, there is no reason why a couple cannot maintain their sexual relationship during most of pregnancy. Having set such a goal, experimentation can provide a range of alternatives for meeting each partner's sexual needs.

Understanding the Birth Process

As pregnancy progresses, many couples anticipate the culmination of that process—birth. In doing so, they may set the goal of learning as much about the birth process as possible in order to be prepared for their participation in the process. We purposely suggest that this is a couple goal rather than an individual goal. While the mother carries the physical burden of giving birth, the father has the opportunity to help, encourage, and give support during that process. Many hospitals today encourage the husband's participation in prenatal classes and in helping the wife in the labor room; some allow him to be present for the baby's birth. Even if he is not able to be physically present during the birth process, the fact that he and his wife have shared the information about birth and delivery can serve as a supportive resource for his wife during delivery.

Estimating the date of delivery is an imprecise procedure. While the obstetrician may figure a woman's due date by adding 280 days to the first day of her last menstrual period, only 4 percent deliver on the 280th day, while 46 percent deliver within one week of that date and 74 percent within two weeks of it.[29] Three distinct stages can be described for the work the mother does in giving birth. The *first stage* of labor is the longest period. During this stage the cervix begins to open; the event is announced by rhythmic contractions of the uterus (see Figure 14-4). While these often are described as pains, in the initial period they are more like the discomfort of a backache. The contracting fibers exert almost thirty pounds of pressure on the amniotic fluid.[30] The membranes holding this fluid press on the opening at the bottom of the uterus, and this causes the membranes to break and the fetus to press on the opening. At the same time the muscles at the opening of the uterus relax, and the opening begins to enlarge. The involuntary action of these two sets of muscles causes the cervix to eventually dilate to about four inches in diameter. At this stage of labor, relaxation is the best resource a woman can have to facilitate dilation. While not all authorities accept this statement, it appears that general relaxation hastens the relaxation of muscle fibers around the cervix and decreases the intensity of pain associated with this dilation. Most prenatal education programs include breathing exercises and other techniques which relax the entire body. Support by the husband during this stage of labor can be of assistance in putting such exercises into practice.

Once the cervix has been dilated, the *second stage* of labor begins. This stage lasts until the fetus is expelled from the birth canal. While the first stage of labor may last from eight to fourteen hours for a first baby, the second stage requires only an hour to an hour and a half. In this stage, the mother can assist the uterine action by bearing down or pushing with each contraction. Breathing exercises and relaxation techniques play an important role in reducing pain or making it more bearable. If the birth is normal, the fetus enters the world head first. Because his head is larger than the birth canal, it may be elongated and the canal enlarged. Shortly after birth, both the baby's head and the birth canal regain their original size.

The *third stage* of labor follows the birth of the baby and involves expulsion of

Figure 14-4   *The Baby during the First Stages of Labor*

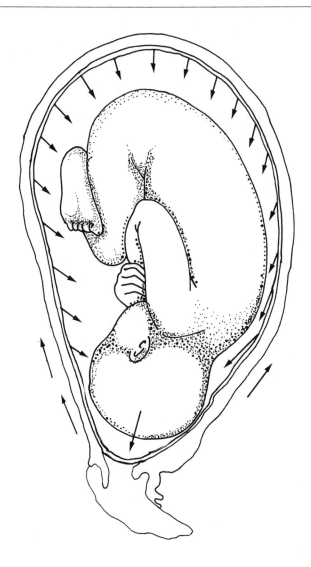

Adapted from J. P. Greenhill, *Obstetrics,* 13th ed. (Philadelphia: Saunders, 1965). Reprinted by permission.

the placenta and the membranes. If the obstetrician has enlarged the vagina by making a small cut called an episiotomy, he will close it with a few stitches following the expulsion of the placenta. An episiotomy is more likely to be used for first babies than for subsequent ones.

Sometimes a normal delivery is prevented by physical conditions. In these cases the baby is delivered by Caesarean section. This procedure involves cutting the mother's abdomen and uterus to remove the baby and placenta. Today this surgical procedure carries only a slight risk to mother and baby and is much safer than allowing, for example, a breech birth (feet first) in a narrow pelvis.

Preparation for Parenthood

The best preparation for parenthood is a marriage based on mutual love and cooperative aims; this can minimize the intensity of simple problem-solving situations and facilitate reaching the goals set for pregnancy and birth. While the insecurity of one spouse may be compensated for by strength in the other, this does not provide the best background for the increased demands of parenthood.

Many authors have identified preparation for parenthood as a necessary component of successful adjustment to the parental role. This preparation can be part of the education for living which begins in the home and is supported by family life education in the school and community. Preparation continues as the couple adjust to one another early in marriage and to the impending arrival of the child in the pregnancy period. Couples can develop their own training program, which may include the following topics:

1. Discuss and agree on goals for you personally and you as a couple. Determine whether parenthood is or should be a part of those goals.

2. Investigate and utilize satisfactory birth control devices to make your plan a success.

3. Discuss how you would handle the unexpected (such as unplanned pregnancy).

4. If you decide parenthood is for you, take advantage of all opportunities to observe children and interact with them. Note the characteristics of small babies and the care needed. Discuss the adjustments that may be needed with couples who have had babies recently.

5. Read books about child development, child care and childrearing. Attend family life education classes if they are available.

6. During your pregnancy period utilize the time to rediscuss your aims and goals in life, your insecurities or fears associated with childrearing, and your mutual plans to cope with this event.

7. After the birth of your baby, take time to focus on your role as husband and wife as well as father and mother.

Summary

The parental role is important in our society, and it is also relatively difficult to adjust to without discomfort. For many couples, parenthood is expected and involves very little decision making on their part. We suggest, however, that because of the responsibility involved and the long-term commitment of the role, no couple should take this view. Improved contraceptive devices and liberalized abortion laws make it easier for couples who have children today to do so because they really want them.

Preparation for parenthood is a task for home, school, and community. Family life education at all levels can provide information about the nature of the role and opportunities to develop satisfactory interpersonal relationships with other people in similar situations. Information and relevant experience are the basic foundation for adequate parent-child relations. Couples can build on this basic education in marriage in order to form a shared positive attitude toward parenthood and some feelings of competence in assuming the role.

Notes

1   1. According to a 1971 U.S. Census Bureau survey, married women between the ages of eighteen and twenty-four say that they intend to have an average of 2.4 children before they complete their fertility cycle. U.S. Bureau of the Census "Birth Expectations Data: June, 1971," *Current Population Reports*, Series P-20, No. 232, 1972.

2. Charles Hobart, "Attitude toward Parenthood among Canadian Young People," *Journal of Marriage and the Family* 35 (February 1973), 74.

3. "Population and the American Future," *The Report of the Commission on Population Growth and the Future* (Washington, D.C.: Government Printing Office, p. 19.

4. A good account of the myths and folklore surrounding parenthood is given by E. E. Lemasters, *Parents in Modern America: A Sociological Analysis* (Homewood, Ill.: Dorsey, 1970.

5. Alice Rossi, "Transition to Parenthood," *Journal of Marriage and the Family* 30 (February 1969), 26-39.

6. Nigel Balchin, "Children are a Waste of Time," *Saturday Evening Post*, October 9, 1965 pp. 10-11; Gael Greine, "A Vote against Motherhood," *Saturday Evening Post*, January 26, 1963 p. 10; Lynell Michals, "Why We Don't Want Children," *Redbook*, January 1970, pp. 10-14; Betty Rollin, "Motherhood, Who Needs It?" *Look*, September 22, 1970, pp. 11-12; all report evidence from interviews which document the informal social sanctions directed toward childless couples.

7. T. R. Balakrishnan *et al.*, "Canadian Family Growth Study" (Unpublished manuscript), University of Western Ontario, Department of Sociology, 1972.

8. Ronald Freedman, Pascal K. Whelpton, and Arthur Campbell, *Family Planning, Sterility and Population Growth* (New York: McGraw-Hill, 1959).

9. J. Richard Udry, *The Social Context of Marriage* (New York: Lippincott, 1966), p. 459.

10. Paul Jacobsen, *American Marriage and Divorce* (New York: Rinehart, 1959).

11. E. E. Lemasters, "Parenthood as a Crisis," *Marriage and Family Living* 19 (November 1957), 353-355; Everett Dyer, "Parenthood as Crisis: A Restudy," *Marriage and Family Living* 25 (May 1963), 196-201; Daniel Hobbs, "Parenthood as a Crisis: A Third Study," *Journal of Marriage and the Family* 27 (August 1965), 367-372.

12. H. Reed Ritchie and Susan McIntosh, "Costs of Children," prepared for the Commission on Population and the American Future in *Population and the American Future: The Report of the Commission on Population Growth and the American Future* (Washington, D.C.: Government Printing Office, March 1972), p. 81. Costs are discounted to allow for the fact that interest could be earned annually on money not spent in the first year. The opportunity costs for the mother are included in these figures. (Opportunity costs are losses in earnings of the woman while giving birth or raising her child.) Of the costs listed, $39,273 are opportunity costs, and $20,354 are direct costs to raise the child. Depending on the educational background of the mother, opportunity costs could be as high as $60,000 for the first child.

13. John MacLeod, "Fertility in Men," in Albert Ellis and Albert Abarbanel, eds., *Encyclopedia of Sexual Behavior* (New York: Hawthorne, 1961), p. 31.

14. Ibid.

15. Ibid.

16. Paul Ehrlich and John Holdren, "Abortion and Morality," *Saturday Review*, September 4, 1971, p. 58.

17. In one fifteen month period spanning 1970 and 1971, 200,000 women had abortions in New York City. In the first six months of 1972, there were 22.4 abortions per 100 live births in Canada.

18. *Demographic Yearbook–1970*, Twenty-second Issue. Statistical Office of the United Nations Department of Economic and Social Affairs, 1971, pp. 694-708.

19. W. O. Spitzer and C. L. Saylor, eds., *Birth Control and the Christian* (Toronto: Home Evangel Books, 1969), pp. 469-470.

20. E. W. Pelrine, *Abortion in Canada* (Toronto: New Press), 1971.

21. Kirstin Hook, "Refused Abortion," *Acta Psychiatrica Scandinavica* 39 (1963), Supplement 168, 1-156.

22. C. M. B. Pare and H. Roner, "Follow-up of Patients Referred for Termination of Pregnancy," *Lancet* (1970), 635-638.

23. David Olson, Chairman, Family Action Committee," National Council on Family Relations: Position Paper on Abortion," *The Family Coordinator* 20 (October 1971), 401-402.

24. Office of Population Research, Princeton University, 1970 National Fertility Study, reported in *Population and the American Future: The Report of the Commission on Population Growth and the American Future* (Washington, D.C.: Government Printing Office, March 1972), p. 97.

25. Ibid., p. 98.

26. Jane A. Merken, "Teenage Childbearing: Its Medical Aspects and Implications for United States Population," (unpublished report prepared for the Commission on Population and American Future, 1968.

27. R. J. McCorkel, Jr., *"Husbands and Pregnancy: An Exploratory Study"* M.A. thesis, University of North Carolina, 1964.

28. Ruth Brecher and Edward Brecher, *An Analysis of Human Sexual Response* (New York: Signet Books, 1966), pp. 88-96.

29. Mollie S. Smart and Russell Smart, *Children: Development and Relationships,* 2d ed. (New York: Macmillan, 1972), p. 38.

30. Ibid.

Suggested Readings

Benson, Leonard. *Fatherhood: A Sociological Perspective.* New York: Random House, 1963. A much needed book focusing on the neglected parent—the father.

Ginott, Haim. *Between Parent and Child.* New York: Macmillan, 1965. A book well worth reading because it sees the child as a real feeling person, not as someone to socialize.

Life before Birth. Life Educational Reprint #27, *Life*, April 30, 1965. A phenomenal photographic description of prenatal growth and development.

Lemasters, E. E. *Parenthood in Modern America: A Sociological Analysis.* Homewood, Ill.: Dorsey, 1970. A look at parenthood and the parent as unique phenomena. Special chapters on myths surrounding parenthood and the one-parent family.

Rossi, Alice. "Transition to Parenthood." *Journal of Marriage and the Family* 30 (February 1968), 26-39. An excellent analysis of the parental role and factors influencing parental adjustment to its demands.

15 Maintaining Marital Morale

The process of mate selection involves a certain risk. Even though each partner gambles that he will always have his needs and expectations met by the person he has chosen, it is obvious that people change over time. While it is true that most marriages survive and are judged to be happy by the partners, there is considerable evidence that the quality of marital morale declines over the life cycle.[1] Quality changes in the early years of marriage have been described as a function of "reality shock," following a mate selection process characterized by a high degree of romanticism; changes in later years are attributed to unforeseen changes in the situation or personalities and behavior of the spouses.[2] Unforeseen events which can assault marriages include economic upheavals, mental illness, separation by war, and natural disasters.

People marry for a multitude of reasons, but if marriage does not meet their expectations (regardless of how unrealistic the expectations may be), they are likely to be dissatisfied with it. Once this dissatisfaction is acknowledged, they can determine what to do about it. In this chapter we will examine the nature of marital morale and how it changes over the life cycle and outline several courss of action couples can use to maintain a satisfactory level of marital morale or to cope with disenchantment.

Defining Marital Morale

Many concepts have been developed to describe the quality of marital interaction. In our society, *happiness* and *stability* have provided the bases of the generation of concepts such as marital satisfaction, adjustment, disillusionment, disenchantment, and stability. Neither happiness nor stability, however, are accurate measures of marital morale. Happiness, for example, is an extremely personal and subjective state. There is no agreed-upon definition of what marital happiness is; yet it is assumed that happiness is an indication of marital success. Stability has similar problems as a measure of marital interaction. While it is easy to note the low point of stability (which may be marked by separation or divorce), it is very difficult to measure stability at other points on the continuum. Family sociologists Mary Hicks and Marilyn Platt suggest that it may in fact be appropriate to discard the goal concept of marital happiness entirely: "it may be that in a society in which 94 percent of the population is conditioned to marry, that happiness is an ephemeral goal for much of the population."[3] For both descriptive and research purposes, we need simpler concepts which can easily be measured.

The term we have selected to describe the dynamic state of marital interaction is *marital morale.* While this term does not eliminate all the difficulties of previous concepts, we believe it is more specific and more easily measured. Simply defined, *marital morale* is an emotion, a feeling of contentment with the marriage—particularly with the number of personal and interpersonal goals that are being achieved. As such, marital morale may range from low to high but is always determined on the basis of the individual goals the couple has set for their relationship. It may fluctuate as a result of many factors, including personality changes, goal changes, or unforeseen events occurring within or outside the marital system. While a certain degree of happiness or stability may be goals for a particular couple and thus innluence their level of masrital morale, high marital morale is not necessarily dependent on high ratings of happiness.

Establishing Goals for Marital Interaction

Although research findings suggest that specific factors tend to be predictive of success in marriage, thoughout this book, we have tried to emphasize the importance of *process* as it relates to goal attainment. By utilizing an approach of this type, it becomes meaningless to establish specific criteria which represent a single standard for comparison. Each couple may relate to these criteria in a slightly different way, depending on how resourceful they are and how many limitations they are operating under at a given time.

The problem-solving process, which has been our central focus, allows for variation among marriages. Success cannot be evaluated according to the traditional standard of *permanence* (which has been considered our most reliable indicator for such a long time). Instead, we see it as a result of problem-solving effectiveness. Attainment of the success goal is a product of how well the spouses are able to meet the expectation, or demands, of each partner. A breakdown in goal achievement comes about when each person expects more from the relationship than the other has to give or when expectations are not communicated to the other. Setting realistic goals is a sharing process, directly related to maintaining marital morale.

While people undoubtedly marry with certain goals in mind, only a few of these may be realistic. Communication about goals gives each partner an opportunity to correct any misconceptions and to begin the problem-solving process of generating alternatives. Probably a good deal of marital dissatisfaction can be attributed to a lack of communication about goals. For example, a wife may have certain expectations about how her husband should act as a lover. She would like him to be the initiator of all sexual interactions, but she has never told him about these expectations. Her husband, on the other hand, expects her to be a full partner in sexual relations and is not satisfied with her passive role; but he has never told her about his expectations. While the spouses could each perceive their dissatisfaction as a problem-solving situation and proceed to generate alternatives, this type of response contributes to what sociologists Constantinos Safilios-Rothschild and Jessie Bernard describe as "his and her marriages."[4] The different conceptions of marriage held by husbands and wives are not damaging to the marriage if they are communicated; however, often the spouses continue to interact with one another without sharing their goals for marriage, while at the same time they evaluate the relationship as if they did share goals. Maintaining marital morale is a couple goal, in that it requires consensus on what marital morale is and what level is desired.

Establishing goals is a unique task for every couple; some couples may be assisted in this task by the work done by family sociologists in describing a whole range of marital types. Marriages can be categorized on the basis of their goals or emphases. The two basic types of marriage in our society are distinguished by the aspect of interaction that predominates. In the case of the *institutional* marriage, traditional roles predominate. The husband is dominant and instrumental (task oriented), while the wife is submissive and expressive (emotionally oriented). The instrumental aspects of marriage predominate (for example, earning a living or establishing a particular standard of living). The establishment of goals relating to the attainment of higher occupational status, income or educational level for husbands is common in instrumental marriages.

In *companionship* marriages there is greater emphasis on affective aspects of the relationship. Role specifications are accepted as necessary, but the focus is on attaining a certain level of companionship, expression of affection, sexual enjoyment, and or communication.

We have referred previously to Cuber and Harroff's description of marital types. They studied a group of upper middle class couples and, in the process, discovered that while all of the couples were married and planned to stay that way, there appeared to be pronounced variation in other aspects of these relationships. This variation prompted the researchers to establish a marriage typology built around five specific family patterns. These types were labeled: 1) conflict-habituated, 2) devitalized, 3) passive-congenial, 4) vital and 5) total.[5]

Just as individuals are different, so are the marriages which they structure. On the surface, marriages which are conflict-ridden appear to reflect unhappy and unstable partners. We propose however, that conflict can be a resource for problem solving and can be indicative that the couple cares enough to work through difficult situations by quarreling. This suggests that people need (or can tolerate) different qualities in a marriage partner. Some couples whose relationships are based on conflict think they would prefer something different, but their personalities may be such that change is unlikely.

Similarly, marriages which seemed to be better in earlier years, but which have deteriorated over time, undoubtedly still offer more satisfactions for the husband and wife than any immediate alternatives. Otherwise, they would probably have dissolved the marriage.

Although most students of marriage and the family are guided in the direction of accepting the "total" relationship (one in which all aspects of life are mutually shared and participated in) as ideal, we hasten to note that the development of a particular marital life-style is dependent on the persons who make up that relationship and the situation they are in. Each marriage probably represents a different type of adjustment and a different conception of marriage. In *The Sexual Wilderness*, Vance Packard calls attention to the fact that expectations differ regarding the desired nature of a marriage. He believes that some individuals marry basically for *fun*, to have someone with whom they can share what they enjoy doing. These people have little desire to acquire the usual material belongings and attach no importance to social climbing.

Another kind of marriage is the *colleague* marriage, which emphasizes the achievements of both spouses. Sociologists Daniel Miller and Grey Swanson coined the term *colleague* to refer to the marriage of coworkers with equal and interdependent (though specific and mutually recognized) competencies. Common among these marriages are instances where both husband and wife are in the same or closely related fields.

Packard also identifies a type of marriage in which the couple gains primarily from the closeness of male-female interaction. He calls this the *nestling* marriage and believes it is sought by people whose environments have been characterized by some kind of turbulence.

The interaction patterns which typify these marriages range from high companionship to minimal interaction to the peripheral husband marriage. According to Packard, the *high companionship* marriage involves a husband and wife who are good friends as well as marriage partners. They share intimacies and spend a great deal of time together. They consider theirs to be a special relationship, identifying the good things in life with belonging to each other.

The *minimal interaction* pattern is characterized by little sharing of common interests and activities. Communication generally is based on arrangements for getting necessary tasks accomplished. This type of relationship tends to be more common among blue-collar families and ambitious executives. In the working class the sexual segregation reinforced by members of the group accounts largely for this separation. For the corporation family, however, the husband and wife may lead essentially different lives.

The *husband-peripheral* marriage resembles the minimal interaction relationship in form, except that the husband is not considered a vital figure in the role of marriage partner. Wives in these marriages tend to consider the man primarily as breadwinner and father, rather than husband. Packard suggests that our society's emphasis on material goods has caused the modern woman to view her husband's most important role as that of provider.

By describing the variety of marital types identified in the literature, we are not suggesting that one should select a marital type from research evidence and then proceed to accept all the predetermined goals associated with it. Instead we are proposing that there is an infinite variety of marital types, that couples can establish their own unique goals instead of falling into preformed molds. O'Neill and O'Neill suggest, "You shouldn't have to buy marriage off the rack; like a tailor-made suit or dress, it should conform exactly to the contours of those who chose to clothe themselves in it."[8] They refer to a contract for marriage, which is defined as a statement of goals or intentions agreed upon by both partners. Writing one's own contract for marriage calls for the resources of communication, flexibility, knowledge of oneself and one's spouse, and honesty. The contract is a written expression of a couple's consensus for living together; it is mutually arrived at and fully understood. If the contract is based on current needs and expectations, it is open to constant revision.

We suggest that the contract approach is a useful and exciting way to establish goals for marriage and thus determine the level of marital morale which is desired. While O'Neill and O'Neill proposed the contract for use in an *open marriage*,[9] (a form of companionship marriage emphasizing flexibility, independence, and choice), the contract could be used for any type of marriage.

Marital Morale over the Life Cycle

Of all the research in the general area of marital morale, relatively little has concerned the life cycle of marriages. Before 1960, for example, there were only a half dozen empirical longitudinal studies of marital morale.[10] While these studies showed a consistent pattern of decline in marital satisfaction, they did not clearly identify the variations in the general decline or differences in levels of satisfaction between husband and wife. Another weakness of these longitudinal studies was their focus on segments of the life cycle rather than the entire life cycle. An example of one of these studies is the classic work by sociologist Peter Pineo.[11] Pineo's explanation of marital satisfaction derived from a longitudinal study of couples who were initially included in a study by Burgess and Wallin.[12] These couples were interviewed at three points in their life cycle—during engagement, after four or five years of marriage, and after twenty years of marriage. Pineo's data from these interviews indicated a general decline in marital satisfaction and adjustment, particularly in the areas of companionship, consensus, belief in the permanence of the union, demonstration of affection, common interests, and marital adjustment. He described this process of declining marital morale as disenchantment with marriage. Previous studies by Hobart[13] and Burgess[14] had noted such declines in satisfaction in the early years of marriage and had attributed them to the relatively free mate selection process which operates in North American and the tendency to romanticize marriage and idealize the mate. In other words, they believed the decline in marital satisfaction in the early years of marriage was the result of a "reality shock."

People usually marry at the high point of romantic love and attraction. As we noted in Chapter 3, they also select partners in a dating process which does not allow them to reveal much of their true identities. Living together on a day-to-day basis corrects many of the misperceptions and unrealistic expectations which may have been present during engagement. Thus declines in marital satisfaction in the early years of marriage may not only be inevitable but may actually be functional in helping the couple set realistic goals for the remainder of their life together.

Pineo suggested that in the later years of marriage different forces operate to produce disenchantment. Because no couple can anticipate during courtship the events which will affect their marriage, disenchantment after five years of marriage probably is due to the unforeseen changes in situation or in the partner's personality or behavior. Pineo suggests that these unforeseen changes produce disenchantment rather than increased satisfaction because mate selection occurs by personal choice, not by random selection. If mating were by random choice, there would be as many gains as losses in satisfaction. But marriage by choice assumes that the couple, when they decide to marry, have determined that they suit each other. Because the "fit" between the two individuals is maximized as marriage, a *regression effect* occurs. The outstanding characteristics for which the mate was chosen begin to be lost because changes tend toward the mean of the population. For example, if a husband was selected as a mate because of his physical attractiveness, the changes that result with age, weight gain, and differences in perception due to greater interaction with other people tend to make his physical appearance more ordinary.

Pineo argues that disenchantment is the process by which "the grounds upon which one decides to marry deteriorate, the fit between two individuals which leads them to marry reduces with time."[15] Even though the fit of partners may be expected to reduce with time, it is not necessary that declines in satisfaction or marital morale accompany this loss of fit—if the couple are willing to acknowledge the situation as a problem and use their resources to keep the marriage vital.

While research in the sixties noted declines in marital morale over the life cycle, little attention was paid to method of coping with disenchantment. It is obvious that achieving one's objectives requires expenditures of time, energy, and other resources. While disenchantment may figure in an ultimate decision to terminate the marriage, it does not necessarily lead to divorce. The feeling of discontent with the nature or achievement of objectives in marriage can exist in so-called "happy" marriages as well as in those which are experiencing difficulties. This is because most individuals come to marriage with higher expectations than can be met by marriage (or by any relationship, or that matter) and because there are any number of responses than can be made to a decline in marital morale. In other words, the presence of discontent or disenchantment is less important than the interpretation made of it and the problem-solving skill used to cope with it. Whereas some couples recognize declines in marital morale as an inevitable part of growing, changing relationship and view it as a problem-solving opportunity, others see it as a reason for seeking other alternatives to the relationship or for terminating the relationship.

Coping with Declining Marital Morale

Stressful situations are inevitable in most human relationships at one time or another, and all societies have at least one way to handle such situations when they become severe. Once disenchantment of one or both spouses has been recognized as a marital problem (that is, it is blocking the achievement of personal or interpersonal goals), a number of alternatives become available. Basically these alternatives are variations on preserving or breaking up the marital system. A number of factors operate to influence one's choice of alternatives, including the severity of the discontent, the value hierarchy of the couple, and the resources available.

Interpretations of the severity of discontent depend largely on the expectations set for the marital relationship and the personal resources of the partners. Some persons have a very low tolerance for situations which block the achievement of their goals, while others ignore the situation until it nearly stalemates any goal achievement. The ability to recognize the problem varies from couple to couple because of these factors. Similarly, their value hierarchy influences each couple's selection of alternatives. If they value the permanence and sacramental nature of marriage, they may ignore any alternatives which do not focus on continuing or improving the marital relationship. Resources provide the raw materials from which alternatives are derived. A decision to work toward preserving the marital relationship requires resources of flexibility, motivation, energy, and perseverence. A decision to terminate the marriage may require additional resources to cope with the negative effects of establishing separate households, dealing with societal sanctions, and reorganizing one's life and expectations. Sometimes disenchantment occurs when personal resources are not adequate to deal with the discontent. Whatever the alternative chosen, resources are necessary to carry it out.

Preserving the Marriage

Judging from the limited research done on the relationship between disenchantment and divorce, most couples elect to preserve the marriage even though they are disenchanted. For some this means accepting disenchantment as an inevitable occurrence and living with it; for others it means exploring ways in which the relationship can be revitalized. If one of the goals is to develop a relationship which provides a high level of satisfaction for both partners, and if this is not being accomplished, concerted effort and problem-solving skill will be required to accomplish the objective. A first step is to try to identify the source of the disenchantment. This can be accomplished by discussing goals and by exploring the how's and why's of each other's behavior. Frequently spouses married for several years are guilty of making assumptions about their partner's feelings and attitudes. Living together does not, however, put an individual on an "open line" to his spouse's inner thoughts. This information is obtained through communication and observation and requires both time and energy. In order to maintain marital morale, couples need to set aside time to focus on their relationship. Relegating time for sex to a place after child care, supper dishes, term papers, and other routine tasks often means no sex at all. Similarly, relegating time for communicating with one's spouse to the last few minutes before bedtime often means incomplete sharing.

It is not selfish to institute practices which allow for the nurturing of a marriage; in fact, it is absolutely necessary. While people wouldn't think twice about enrolling in a course to keep themselves up-to-date in their chosen profession, continuous education for marriage is ignored. We suggest that preserving a marriage requires a whole new outlook. If marital morale is a process rather than a single achievement, there is a constant need for problem-solving skills. Community and school family life education courses and premarriage courses provide one type of opportunity to explore the nature of marital interaction. Professional marriage counselors also can help people discover methods of maintaining marital morale. Some couples, however, devise their own unique plans, such as setting aside one evening a week to focus on each other. The evening may be spent eating dinner at a favorite restaurant or quietly at home discussing vacation plans. In most cases the couples anticipate a "guaranteed" opportunity to enjoy sex when both partners are not pressured by other activities. Many resources are in the form of books,[17] kits, and even games which can stimulate the imagination of marital partners in deriving methods of enriching their marriage (see Chapter 2 for details).

While most couples are not short on ideas, they are unwilling to budget the time and energy for implementing them. The idea of taking a "second honeymoon" is an excellent one—except that most couples take it too late. A second (or third or fourth) honeymoon with one's spouse is available as an alternative at any stage of marriage and has the potential for a whole range of new discoveries.

No one has yet discovered the best plan for the care and feeding of a marriage. This remains for individual spouses to discover for themselves. It is apparent, however, that relationships grow as the individuals who are a part of them communicate with one another, provide both positive and negative feedback to one another, and expend time and energy in responding to each other's needs and expectations.

Terminating the Marriage

Depending upon the intensity and nature of the disenchantment, how skilled the partners are at problem solving, and how far advanced the alienation process is, one or both spouses may decide that the only way to achieve their goals is to terminate the marriage. Marriage is a civil contract in our society, and the state specifies three ways in which the contract can be legally dissolved:

1. *Annulment* asserts that no legal contract between the two parties was established because of some prior conditions existing at the time of the "marriage."
2. *Legal separation* grants the couple separate households but no rights to remarry.
3. *Divorce* terminates the marriage and gives each the right to remarry.

Marriages also can be effectively dissolved (nonlegally) by separation with consent of the parties, by desertion, or by death of one partner.

The restrictions attached to the various legal procedures for all of these alternatives vary from state to state in the United States; in Canada the Divorce Act of 1968 provides a national divorce law. (See Appendix A.) In most states the laws are adversary procedures; that is, one of the parties must show that he is innocent and that his partner has violated or failed to fulfill his marital obligations in at least one way as specified by law. Rarely is the breakdown of a relationship as completely one-sided as the adversary procedure implies; yet any agreement by a couple to terminate their marriage is seen as collusion, and in many states (such as New York) this provides the grounds for terminating divorce or separation proceedings. Some states (such as California) recently have enacted laws which allow one partner to swear that irreconcilable differences have arisen which cause an irremediable breakdown in the marriage. No witness or further testimony is required.

Interpreting Divorce Statistics   Divorce statistics are frequently (and often unwittingly) utilized in a manner that minimizes the number of disillusioned marriages and maximizes marital instability. Caution should be used in viewing divorce statistics as an indication of marital stability, since they do not usually include annulments, separations, and desertions. The abuse of statistics is much greater if divorce is used as an indicator of unhappy marriages. This implies that all couples still married are happy, rather than that divorce statistics represent those unhappy couples who utilized divorce as a solution.

Divorce statistics frequently are misinterpreted because of the problem of computing an accurate divorce rate. These statistics often are used to give the impression that one out of every four marriages ends in divorce. The figure is arrived at by comparing the total number of marriages in any given year with the total number of divorces. However, divorces take place within the pool of already married people. If divorce rates are calculated on the basis of that pool, the rate becomes approximately one divorce for every hundred marriages.[18] But this still doesn't tell us how many marriages end in divorce. What we need are longtitudinal studies of couples married in a particular year; these studies could provide us with a better estimate. It is difficult, however, to get accurate data on a particular group of people marrying in any year because they must be traced until all are dead or divorced. Still, such rates could be calculated and would give us a much better estimate of marital stability over the marital life cycle.

The best United States data on divorce are from the 1967 Survey of Economic Opportunity, which presents information on marital histories of adults in the entire United States.[19] The results for people under seventy years of age, who had entered their first marriage at least twenty years before the date of the survey, show that four out of five (80 percent) had been married only once; approximately 17 percent of the women and 15 percent of the men had been divorced. Age and race differences in this sample were consistent with past studies. Divorce rates tended to be higher for those marrying relatively young (under twenty for women and under twenty-two for men) and for nonwhites. On the basis of these data (barring marked change in current trends), U.S. Census Bureau statisticians are predicting that:

during the lifetime of those who are not entering marriage at correspondingly young ages, close to one-third of the whites and one-half of the negroes will eventually end their marriages in divorce . . . [and] that only one-sixth of the white persons and one-third of the negroes currently entering marriage at relatively mature ages will eventually become divorced.[20]

Research findings clearly indicate that the resources of adequate income, education, job security, and middle-class standing influence the maintenance of a marriage. The apparent higher divorce rate among blacks probably is related to economic and social factors rather than race alone. The problems inherent in maintaining a marriage under conditions of economic adversity often require more resources than the couple have to utilize. In general, as income, education, and job level improve, the difference between races appears to decline.[21] Viewing this phenomenon in problem-solving terms, we see a hierarchy of situations with which families must cope. Problems of first importance are maintaining the basic needs of the family—feeding, housing, and clothing the members. Only when these needs are met will individuals have the resources available to maintain internal relations such as the husband-wife relationship.

Factors Influencing Selection of an Alternative

When faced with declining marital morale, why do some people choose to preserve their marriage while others do not? There seems to be no clear-cut answer to this question. We have suggested that individual expectations for marriage are extremely variable and that the point at which marital disenchantment becomes intolerable depends on the persons making up the marital system and their specific situation. The ultimate decision is based on several things, including expectations, factors causing the discontent, severity of the discontent, the couple's values, alternatives available, resources available, and social sanctions.

A Theory of Marital Cohesiveness

An attempt has been made by sociologist George Levinger to develop a comprehensive typology of marriages that are likely to be stable or unstable.[22] Viewing marriage as a special type of small group, he utilized the research findings on divorce to postulate a theory of marital cohesiveness. Levinger claims that the strength of the marital system is a direct function of the attractiveness of the system and the strength of its *boundaries* (how closed the system is to outside influence) and an inverse function of the attractions from other competing systems and the strength of their boundaries.[23]

Sources of Attraction   Sources of attraction associated with high cohesiveness in marriage include *affectional rewards* (such as esteem for one's spouse, desire for companionship, and sexual enjoyment), *socioeconomic rewards* (husband's income, home ownership, husband's education, and husband's occupation), and *similarly in social status* (religion, education, and age). If these attractions are sufficiently enticing, the barriers are unimportant. For instance, close attachment to one's spouse precludes any serious consideration of breaking off the relationship.

On the other hand, socioeconomic rewards can act as both an attraction and a barrier. A high level of education is usually associated with high income and a prestigious occupation. This may provide a highly attractive alternative to a situation beset by economic problems and low status in the community. However, if terminating the marriage sufficiently reduces the income for either husband or wife (or both), and divorced status is sanctioned by the community, socioeconomic rewards will act as barriers to divorce—for both partners.

Sources of Barrier Strength   Sources of barrier strength which influence marital cohesiveness include *feelings of obligation* (particularly to dependent children and to the marital bond), *moral proscriptions* (such as membership in a certain religion and joint church attendance), and *external pressures* (from relatives and friends, community attitudes, and legal and economic restrictions).

Research evidence is inadequate to determine whether dependent children act as barriers or as sources of negative attraction. Given the small difference in separation rates between couples with children and those without, the issue seems to rest on whether the parents feel an obligation to their children to stay married if they think terminating an unhappy marriage would adversely affect them.

Affiliation with primary groups also acts as a barrier to divorce. The larger the network of these groups (including relatives, neighbors, and friends) and the tighter they are organized, the greater the control they extend over the individual. In most cases the groups exert pressure to continue rather than terminate the relationship.

Support or sanction from the community also has an effect on one's course of action. Community attitudes against divorce are more effective as a barrier force in rural settings than in urban areas. This is probably because the urban environment affords greater anonymity and a greater range of support systems.

Some barriers involve ethical issues. A firm commitment to respect the marital contract "as long as you both shall live" acts as a barrier; so does proscriptive religious belief, such as Catholocism.

Sources of Alternate Attraction   Among the sources of alternate attraction to marriage, according to Levinger, are *affectional rewards* (including preferred alternate sex partner, disjunctive social relations, and opposing religious affiliations) and *economic rewards*. Interestingly, he describes the husband's income as a source of attraction in marriage, while he views the wife's opportunity for independent income as a source of alternate attraction away from marriage. We suggest that this is true only in the traditional marriage, where the wife is not employed outside the home. Because Levinger's postulates are derived from research done primarily in the fifties and early sixties, they may not reflect the increasing number of women who are gainfully employed outside the home. In fact, these days loss of the advantages of a dual income may be an attraction to preserving a marriage.

Other sources of alternate attraction include relationships with friends of both sexes outside the marital system. The greater the support received outside the marriage, the stronger the attraction. For instance, preference for another sex partner over one's spouse is likely to be highly attractive, especially if the outside person meets other criteria as a companion and possible future mate.

At present it is not known how the forces discussed above interact with each other. It is possible to experiment with manipulating the attractions, barriers, and alternate attractions to increase the durability of marriage. Generating alternatives which focus on increasing the positive attractions of marriage presumably is a better course of action than increasing the strength of the barriers to divorce or decreasing the attractiveness of alternate relations. The manipulation of barriers or alternate attractions takes the emphasis away from the conditions which produced discontent in the relationship.

Levinger's theory of marital cohesiveness is only a partial theory and may not be broad enough to explain why some people with high cohesiveness divorce and others do not. One speculation is that in divorce-prone marriages conflict is progressive (moving from crisis to crisis until it reaches a point of severing the relationship), whereas in cases where marriages are maintained, conflict is short term and does not lead to the destruction of portions of the relationship. Progressive conflict destroys basic aspects of the relationship and can thus lead to alienation.

The process of alienation has been described by Waller and Hill in their book *The Family*.[24] In a spiraling pattern of interaction the couple move from crisis to crisis, redefining their relationship each time at a level of greater instability and alienation. Usually there are periodic reconciliations and determined attempts to make the marriage work. However, the spiraling nature of the process is not easily arrested; each response furnishes the motive for the next step. The potential for alienation exists in every relationship, but usually other factors keep under control the tensions which are characteristic of the alienation process.

Waller and Hill have spelled out some of the typical crises in the alienation process as it leads to divorce.

1. Rather early in the process, there is usually some *disturbance of the affectional-sexual life of the pair*. Contrary to a widely accepted view, there are marriages in which there is at first an excellent sexual adjustment which yet terminate in the divorce courts, but in most of these cases some disturbance of sex life arises with loss of rapport, either some withholding of affectional response, which is easy to diagnose, or the more subtle form of attempt to compensate for lack of rapport in other fields by the sexual communion.

2. Then there is the great moment of the *mention of the possibility of divorce*, a moment equivalent to the declaration of love in the courtship process. Each person has perhaps thought of this possibility for some time, but neither is sure that the other is considering it, and neither knows what the other would say if it were mentioned. It is very likely that at the first mention of divorce the relative position of the two members with regard to the divorce process is clear; one takes the lead and the other is passive; ordinarily these rules remain unaltered to the end.

3. At some point in the process, the *appearance of solidarity is broken*. A couple may have kept their troubles to themselves up to this time, but now they must increasingly take the world into their confidence. This is a real shock to both and is, perhaps, sincerely mourned, but once this moment has passed the marriage is on a different basis. The couple have lost face, and each blames the other to some extent. One may regard the destruction of the fiction of solidarity, if it is at all complete, as a master symptom of alienation; once this has been destroyed, it is ordinarily rebuilt with difficulty, and the process enters a new phase.

4. *The decision to divorce* is sometimes made hastily and in anger, but more often it is the result of long discussion. The relationship has gone on in a matter-of-fact way and has been continued as a matter of course for some time; now the couple decides to break it.

5. This is followed by the *crisis of separation*, which is usually severe. The business of liquidating a *menage* is sorry enough at best; when there is added to it the severance of a meaningful relationship, it is often traumatic in the extreme. After a long or a short period, separation is followed by divorce.

6. *The divorce* is a final severance; it is usually thought of as closing the case. It is true that the divorce often comes some time after the actual separation and is a crisis for which people have had an opportunity to prepare themselves, but it is an important step nonetheless. Divorce is often a long-postponed procedure which is necessary before the actual work of reconstructing one's life can begin.

7. After divorce there is still an important *period of mental conflict* and a great deal of the work of reconstruction to do. After the actual severance the make-up of one's social world is usually such as to clinch the individual in his attitude of rejection of the former mate.[25]

Throughout the alienation process the couple make the necessary adjustments to their changing relationship. These shifts, haphazard as they may seem, take place automatically, in spite of opposition by the persons involved. As the process continues, bitterness mounts; each turns against the other and their marital relationship with an urge to hurt their formerly beloved and destroy their relationship. If any of this is to be reversed and the marriage salvaged, it must be done before a separation or filing for divorce. Each of these actions make public the lack of marital solidarity, and few marriages can recover from such loss of face.

Waller and Hill suggest that another critical component of the decision to divorce is a desire for escape. When one or both partners have a strong enough desire to escape and they are willing to face the penalties, they will divorce. The desire to escape frequently results from one spouse adjusting to life without the other. The process is subtle. One spouse finds he doesn't love the other very much, if at all; he withdraws and focuses upon himself, forms a separate life, and so on. Consciously or unconsciously, the withdrawn spouse awaits a crisis sufficient to crystalize the desire to escape and then takes the necessary first steps to terminate the marriage.

How people handle marital disenchantment depends on many factors. Perhaps the strongest of these is *progressive conflict*. Once the alienation process has begun, it is hard to stop and more harder yet to reverse.

The Costs of Selecting an Alternative

No alternative is selected and implemented without some cost. Maintaining a marriage requires time, energy, motivation and skill to implement the available resources. These are the hidden costs of marriage. While the benefits accruing from such efforts can be high, too often they are assumed to come to individuals without any effort on their part.

The costs of breaking up a marriage are more apparent. Interruption in the marital relationship entails breaking established patterns and disrupting old roles. The sexual role is abruptly ended, and affection is directed into new channels or sublimated into new patterns. Confronted with broken roles, people must reorganize their lives and to some extent their personalities. In this task they are given very little help by others. There is a tremendous dearth of understanding about the problems surrounding separation and divorce.

For example, the ex-husband will have to do his own shopping, cooking, cleaning, and laundry or make arrangements to have someone else do them. The ex-wife will probably have to get a full-time job if she doesn't already hold one. When there are children involved, the parent who obtains custody often becomes overloaded with parental responsibilities, and these responsibilities generally conflict with other commitments. If the single parent is ill or has to work late, or if a child is sick, there is only one person to make arrangements for child care.

Some people handle role shifts more easily than others do. In a study of families in which the father was in the armed services, Reuben Hill found that some of the wife-mothers were not able to take on the added responsibilities when the husband left home, while others not only managed successfully but had difficulty relinquishing the new role when the husband returned.[26]

Financial stress is another major cost of divorce. While in a few cases divorce may make a wife eligible for regular welfare payments, the financial situation can still be severe. Even people with high incomes may have to reduce their standard of living after separation or divorce, since income formerly devoted exclusively to maintaining one household must now cover the costs of two.

Yet another cost is the subtle sanctions of society. Divorce and separation in present-day America are still generally frowned upon. William Goode suggests that

since marital stability in our society is morally approved, since the roots of this attitude are to be found in the three major sects of the Judeo-Christian religious tradition, and since divorce is also judged to be an act of self-seeking or of moral failure, it is likely that few couples divorce in our culture without a guilt component on both sides with specific reference to the divorce (aside from guilts with other sources).[27]

While there have been some changes in attitude toward divorced people, it is apparent that the subtle sanctions (such as not being invited to parties or being ignored by old friends) are difficult to bear at a time when support from friends and relatives is particularly needed.

Keeping Marriage Vital

Although we recognize that all marriages are not alike, some individuals in our society are expressing doubt that any type of marriage is actually the fulfilling experience we desire. They point to couples who enter this union believing it to be their road to happiness but who wind up either in the divorce court or in a deadly relationship which is not satisfying for either partner. Unfortunately, the existence of such situations cannot be denied, and it leads us to examine possible reasons for this outcome.

Marriages operate according to varying degrees of pressure. We have tried to delineate many of the pressures which couples encounter as they proceed through dating, courtship, and marriage. In order to support a growing developing relationship, we must have a supply of energy to provide the momentum to maintain a dynamic balance.

As difficulties or dissatisfactions occur, it is the responsibility of each of the marriage partners to provide negative feedback that the other can understand. One cannot react to a problem unless he realizes that it exists. Only when messages are properly sent and received can the system cope with the problem. We should be aware that this is a never-ending process. Couples who continue to communicate well over the years keep their marriages viable.

For the marriage that starts out well and then deteriorates over time, the origin of the trouble may lie in the structure of the couple's values and goals. Even when couples go into marriage determined to maintain a strong love relationship, they sometimes lose sight of this goal. Other activities and responsibilities interfere with their good intentions. Consequently, a marriage which at one time was deeply satisfying for both spouses is destroyed through neglect.

Like most other things in life, marriage in its most desirable form cannot survive without a considerable amount of attention and care. But frequently the energy which keeps the system operating is channeled into areas of pressure which are insignificant compared to the overall goal of increasing the quality of the relationship.

People often get caught up in individual tasks and are subject to periods of emotional separation. Sociologist Joel Moss and his wife Audra warn that "unless we are careful, the periods of separation expend more and more and we exercise fewer periods of renewal, taking it more and more for granted that the relationship will renew itself."[28] A lack of concern about initiating the renewal may involve misplaced values. People usually want to keep their marriage alive, but they cannot seem to find the time to care for it. They tend to feel that after everything else gets done, the time remaining can be used for each other. The problem, of course, is that no time is left. With busy schedules continually taking all the resources, unless "time for us" is included in the regular activity plan, the marriage goes unattended.

Defending marriage against disenchantment is a highly individualized problem situation. It appears evident, however, that an imaginative, carefully laid plan of action may be the best insurance. The Mosses say, "Defense against disenchantment—oftimes the best defense is a good offense. What's yours?"[29] Problem solving—hers and his—encompasses the process by which marital morale is maintained. The future of marriage lies in the abilities of spouses to develop and practice their problem-solving skills.

Summary

Marital morale can be defined as an emotion or feeling of contentment with the nature and achievement of marital goals. Declines in marital morale generally are inevitable in the early years of marriage as a result of our romanticized mate selection process and the "reality shock" which follows living intimately with one's spouse on a day-to-day basis. Over the life cycle it is not unusual to expect that marital morale will continue to fluctuate due to unforeseen changes in the persons and the environment making up the marital system. Marital morale is a process, not a once-and-for-all state of contentment.

Coping with the changes in marital morale is a problem-solving situation. Basically, the alternatives are to continue or to terminate the marriage. Either of these decisions requires an investment of resources. While little research has been done to determine methods of nurturing a marriage, the creative imaginations of individual spouses should provide the necessary raw materials for experimentation. In addition, educational materials and professional services can complement one's resources.

Terminating a marriage provides another alternative for some couples. The costs incurred in implementing such a decision are economic, social, and emotional. Effective problem solving implies that these costs are considered along with the benefits associated with such a choice.

Notes

1. The decline of marital morale in both early and later years of marriage is documented by Peter Pineo, "Disenchantment in the Later Years of Marriage," *Marriage and Family Living* 23 (February 1961), 3-11, and Charles Hobart, "Disillusionment in Marriage, and Romanticism," *Marriage and Family Living* (May 1958), 156-162.

2. Mary W. Hicks and Marilyn Platt, "Marital Happiness and Stability: A Review of Research in the Sixties," *Journal of Marriage and Family* 32 (November 1970), 553-574.

3. Ibid., p. 569.

4. Constantinos Safilios-Rothschild, "The Study of Family Power Structure: A Review 1960-1969," *Journal of Marriage and the Family* 32 (November: World Publishing, 1971).

5. John F. Cuber and Peggy B. Harroff, "The More Total View: Relationships among Men and Women of the Upper Middle Class," *Marriage and Family Lving* 25 (May 1963), 138-145.

6. Vance Packard, *The Sexual Wilderness* (New York: David McKay, 1968).

7. Daniel Miller and Guy Swanson, *The Changing American Parent* (New York: Wiley 1958).

8. Nena O'Neill and George O'Neill, *Open Marriage: A New Life Style for Couples* (New York: Avon Books, 1972), p. 70.

9. Ibid., p. 25.

10. Hicks and Platt, "Marital Happiness and Stability," p. 564.

11. Peter Pineo, "Disenchantment with the Later Years of Marriage," *Journal of Marriage and the Family* 23 (February 1961), 3-11.

12. Ernest W. Burgess and Paul Wallin, *Engagement and Marriage* (Philadelphia: Lippincott, 1953).

13. Unfortunately, Hobart's study was not longitudinal but cross-sectional, and subjects were not selected randomly. This seriously limits the generalizations one can make. See Charles Hobart, "Disillusionment in Marriage, and Romanticism," *Journal of Marriage and the Family* 20 (May 1958), 156-162.

14. Ernest W. Burgess, "The Romantic Impulse and Family Disorganization," *Survey* 57 (December 1926), 290-295.

15. Pineo, "Disenchantment," p. 8.

16. Two examples of research in the sixties that reported declines in marital satisfaction over the life cycle are Bethel Logan Paris and Eleanore Luckey, "A Longitudinal Study of Marital Satisfaction," *Sociological and Social Research* 50 (January 1966), 212-222, and Alexander L. Clark and Paul Wallin, "Women's Sexual Responsiveness and the Duration and Quality of Their Marriages," *American Journal of Sociology,* 71 (September 1965), 187-196.

17. O'Neill and O'Neill, *Open Marriage.*

18. U.S. Department of Health, Education, and Welfare, *Divorce Statistics Analysis: United States–1963*, Vital and Health Statistics, Public Health Service Publication No. 1000—Series 21, Number 13, 1964.

19. *Divorce Statistics Analysis,* Vital and Health Statistics, Public Health Service Publication No. 1000, Series 21, No. 13, October 1967 (Washington, D.C.: Government Printing Office, 1967).

20. Paul Glick and Arthur Norton, "Frequency, Duration, and Probability of Marrige and Divorce," *Journal of Marriage and the Family,* 33 (May 1971), 310.

21. J. Richard Udry, "Marital Instability by Race and Income Based on 1960 Census Data," *American Journal of Sociology* 72 (May 1967), 673-674; Karl Bauman, "Relationship between Age at First Marriage, School Dropout, and Marital Instability: An Analysis of the Gluk Effect," *Journal of Marriage and the Family* 29 (November 1967), 672-680.

22. George Levinger, "Marital Cohesiveness and Dissolution: An Integrative Review," *Journal of Marriage and the Family* 27 (February 1965), 19-28.

23. Ibid., p. 19.

24. See Chapter 23, "Divorce and Alienation Crisis," in Willard Waller and Reuben Hill, *The Family* (New York: Holt, Rinehart and Winston, 1951), pp. 500-530.

25. Ibid., pp. 514-515.

26. Reuben Hill, *Families under Stress* (New York: Harper & Bros., 1949).

27. William J. Goode, *Women in Divorce* (New York: Free Press, 1956), p. 10.

28. J. Joel Moss and Audra Call Moss, *Moss on Marriage* (Provo, Utah: Brigham Young Press, 1965), p. 47.

29. Ibid.

Suggested Readings

Bernard, Jessie, *The Future of Marriage*. New York: Bantam Books, 1972. A well researched and readable book which assesses the influence of the women's liberation movement, new abortion laws, the four-day work week, and other dynamic events on the future of marriage.

Bohannan, Paul. *Divorce and After.* Garden City, N.Y. Doubleday, 1970. An interesting selection of readings about divorce and the feelings of those involved, the book includes discussions of the process and aftermath of divorce, the reactions of friends, ost-divorce family and social relationships, the role of the family court, prospects for divorce reform, and the meaning of marriage and divorce in Eskimo, Swedish, and Kanuri societies.

Cuber, John F., and Harroff, Peggy B. "The More Total View: Relationships among Men and Women of the Upper Middle Class." *Marriage and Family Living* 25 (May 1963), 140-145. Report of a marriage typology that was formulated to expand the framework by which marital adjustment can be assessed.

Moss, J. Joel, and Moss, Audra Call. *Moss on Marriage*. Provo, Utah: Brigham Young University Press, 1965. A series of lectures on marriage which present a variety of constructive ideas for preventing "mossy entanglements."

Appendix A
Marriage Regulations

United States Marriage Laws

Source: Compiled by William E. Mariano: Council on Marriage Relations, Inc., 110 East 42 St., New York, N.Y. 10017 (as of July 1, 1972)

Marriageable age, by states, for both males and females with and without consent of parents or guardians. But in most states, the court has authority, in an emergency, to marry young couples below the ordinary age of consent, where due regard for their morals and welfare so requires. In many states, under special circumstances, blood test and waiting period may be waived.

State	With consent		Without consent		Blood test		Wait for license	Wait after license
	Men	Women	Men	Women	Required	Other state accepted *		
Alabama (b)	17	14	21	18	Yes	Yes	None	None
Alaska	18	16	19	18	Yes	No	3 days	None
Arizona	18²	16	18	18	Yes	Yes	(g)	None
Arkansas	18	16	21	18	Yes	No	3 days	None
California	18	16	18	18	Yes	Yes	None	None
Colorado	16	16	21	18	Yes	....	None	None
Connecticut	16	16	18	21	Yes	Yes	4 days	None
Delaware	18	16	19	19	Yes	Yes	None	24 hrs. (c)
District of Columbia	18	16	21	18	Yes	Yes	3 days	None
Florida	18	16	21	21	Yes	Yes	3 days	None
Georgia	18	16	18	18	Yes	Yes	None (b)	None
Hawaii	15	15	18	18	Yes	Yes	None	None
Idaho	18	16	21	18	Yes	No	None⁴	None
Illinois (a)	16⁴	16	21	18	Yes	Yes	None	None
Indiana	18	16	21	18	Yes	No	3 days	None
Iowa	18	16	21	18	Yes	Yes	3 days	None
Kansas	18	18	21	18	Yes	Yes	3 days	None
Kentucky	18	16	18	18	Yes	No	3 days	None
Louisiana (a)	18	16	18	18	Yes	No	None	72 hours
Maine	16	16	18	18	Yes	Yes	5 days	None
Maryland	18	16	21	18	None	None	48 hours	None
Massachusetts	18	16	21	18	Yes	Yes	3 days	None
Michigan (a)	18	16	18	18	Yes	No	3 days	None
Minnesota	18	16	21	18	None	....	5 days	None
Mississippi (b)	17	15	21	21	Yes	....	3 days	None
Missouri	15	15	21	18	Yes	....	3 days	None
Montana	19²	19²	19	19	Yes	Yes	5 days	None
Nebraska	18	16	20	20	Yes	Yes	5 days	None
Nevada	18	16	21	18	None	None	None	None
New Hampshire (a)	14(e)	13(e)	20	18	Yes	Yes	5 days	None
New Jersey (a)	18	16	21	8	Yes	Yes	72 hours	None
New Mexico	18	16	21	18	Yes	Yes	72 hours	None
New York	16	14	21	18	Yes	No	None	24 hrs. (h)
North Carolina (a)	16	16	18	18	Yes	Yes	None	None
North Dakota (a)	18	15	21	18	yes	....	None	None
Ohio (a)	18	16	21	21	Yes	Yes	5 days	None
Oklahoma	18	15	21	18	Yes	....	None (i)	**
Oregon	18(e)	15(e)	21	18	Yes	No	7 days	None
Pennsylvania	16	16	21	21	Yes	Yes	days	None
Rhode Island (a) (b)	18	16	21	18	Yes	No	None	None
South Carolina	16	14	18	18	None	None	24 hrs.	None
South Dakota	18	16	16	18	18	Yes	Yes	None
Tennessee (b)	16	16	21	21	Yes	Yes	3 days	None
Texas	16	14	19	18	Yes	Yes	None	None
Utah (a)	16	14	21	18	Yes	Yes	None	None
Vermont (a)	18	16	21	18	Yes	....	None	5 days
Virginia	18	16	18	18	Yes	Yes	None	None
Washington	17	17	18	18	(d)	....	3 days	None
West Virginia	18	16	21	21	Yes	No	3 days	None
Wisconsin	18	16	18	18	Yes	Yes	5 days	None
Wyoming	18	16	21	21	Yes	Yes	None	None
Puerto Rico	18	16	1	21	(f)	None	(f)	None
Virgin Islands	16	14	21	18	None	None	8 days	None

Many states have special requirements; contact individual state.
(a) Special laws applicable to non-residents. (b) Special laws applicable to those under 21 years; Alabama; bond required if male is under 21, female under 18. (c) 24 hours if one or both parties resident of state; 96

hours if both parties are non-residents. (d) None, but male must file affidavit. (e) Parental consent plus Court's consent required. (f) None, but a medical certificate is required. (g) Wait for license from time blood test is taken; Arizona, 48 hours. (h) Marriage may not be solemnized within 10 days from date of blood test. (i) If either under 21; Idaho, 3 days; Oklahoma, 72 hrs. (x) May be waived. (1.) 3 days if both applicants are under 18 or female is pregnant. (2.) Statute provides for obtaining license with parental or court consent with no stated minimum age. (3.) If either party is under 18, 3 days. (4.) Under 16, with parental and court consent.

From *World Almanac and Book of Facts 1974.* (New York: Newspaper Enterprise Association, 1974), p. 1025. Reprinted by permission of Newspaper Enterprise Association, Inc.

Canadian Marriage Laws

Source: Compiled from information provided by the various Provincial Government departments and agencies concerned. (As of June, 1973)

Marriageable age, by provinces, for both males and females with and without consent of parents or guardians. In some provinces, the court has authority, given special circumstances, to marry young couples below the minimum age. Most provinces waive the blood test requirement and the waiting period varies across the provinces.

| | With consent | | Without consent | | Blood test | | | |
Province	Men	Women	Men	Women	Other Province Required	Other Province Accepted	Wait for License	Wait after License
Newfoundland	—	—	19	19	—	—	—	—
Prince Edward Island	16	16	18	18	Yes	Yes	5 days	None
Nova Scotia	(1)	(1)	19	19	None	None	5 days	None
New Brunswick	14-18	14-18	18+	18+	None	None	5 days	None
Quebec	14	12	18	18	None	....		None
Ontario	14	14[2]	18	18	None	....	None[3]	3 days
Manitoba	16	16	18	18	Yes	Yes	None	24 hours
Saskatchewan	15	15	18	18	Yes	Yes	5 days	None
Alberta	18-	18-	18+	18+	Yes[4]	Yes[5]	None[4]	None
British Columbia	16[7]	16[7]	19	19	None	None	2 days[8]	None
Yukon Territory	15	15	19	19	None	None	None	24 hours
Northwest Territories	15	15	19	19	None	Yes	None	None

(1) There is no statutory minimum age in the Province. Anyone under the age of 19 years must have consent for marriage, and no person under the age of 16 years may be married without authorization of Family Court Judge and in addition must have the necessary consent of the parent or guardian.
(2) Women under 14 years also require a medical certificate as to necessity of marriage to prevent illegitimacy of offspring.
(3) Special requirements applicable to non-residents.
(4) Applies only to applicants under 60 years of age.
(5) This is upon filing of negative lab report—indicating blood test was taken within 14 days preceding date of application for license.
(6) Exception where consent is required by mail; depending receipt of divorce document, etc.
(7) Persons under 16 years of age (no minimum age specified) may also be married if they have obtained in addition to the usual consent from parents or guardian, an Order from a Judge of the Supreme or County Court in this Province.
(8) Including day of application, e.g., a license applied for on a Monday cannot be issued until Wednesday.

From *World Almanac and Book of Facts 1974* (New York: Newspaper Enterprise Association, 1974), p. 1024. Reprinted by permission of Newspaper Enterprise Association, Inc.

Appendix B
Grounds for Divorce

United States Divorce Laws

In the absence of a national divorce law, each state has developed its own laws. These are constantly being revised, so anyone contemplating divorce must conduct a careful assessment of current laws of his state. The following chart summarizes the grounds for divorce in 1972.

Grounds for Divorce

Source: Compiled by William E. Mariano: Council on Marriage Relations, Inc., 110 East 42nd Street, New York, N.Y. 10017. Persons contemplating divorce should study latest decisions or secure legal advice before initiating proceedings since different interpretations or exceptions in each case can change the conclusion reached.

*Exceptions are to be noted.

State	Cruelty	Desertion	Non-support	Alcohol	Felony	Impotency	Pregnancy at marriage	Drug Addiction	Fraudulent contract	Other causes	Residence time	Time between interlocut'y and final decrees
Alabama	x	x	x	x	x	x	x	x		Q-K-W-F-MM	1 year*	None-R
Alaska	x	x	x	x	x	x		x		F-K-B	1 year	None
Arizona	x	x	x	x	x	x	x			X	1 year	None
Arkansas	x	x	x	x	x	x				B-Y-K-DD	3 months*	None
California										K-KK	6 months	6 months
Colorado										MM	90 days	None
Connecticut	x	x		x	x				x	K-F	3 years*	None
Delaware	x	x	x	x	x					f-K-Y-DD-FF	2 years	3 months
Dist. of Columbia		x			x					Y-Z	1 year	None
Florida	x	x		x		x		x		A-M-BB-DD-K-X	6 months	None
Georgia	x	x		x	x	x	x	x	x	K-M-AA	6 months	¹
Hawaii	x	x	x	x	x				x	K-Z-B	¹	¹
Idaho	x	x	x	x	x					X-K	6 weeks	None
Illinois	x	x		x	x	x		x		A-C-DD-EE	1 year*	None
Indiana	x	x	x	x	x					K	1 year*	None
Iowa										MM	1 year*	None-S
Kansas	x	x		x	x				x	K-F-CC	6 months	None-T
Kentucky									x	......	1year	None
Louisiana					x					X-Z	1 year*	None
Maine	x	x	x	x		x			x	X-LL	6 months	None
Maryland		x			x	x				Y-K-W	1 year	None
Massachusetts	x	x	x	x	x	x			x		2 years*	6 mos.
Michigan	x	x		x	x	x				No Fault-MM	1 year*	None
Minnesota		x		x	x	x				K-W-OO	1 year*	None-T
Mississippi	x	x		x	x	x	x	x		k-M-DD	1 year*	None-U
Missouri	x	x		x	x	x	x			B-J-DD	1 year	None
Montana	x	x	x	x	x					K	1 year	None*
Nebraska	x	x	x	x	x					K	2 years*	6 months
Nevada	x	x	x	x	x	x				K-Y	6 weeks	None
New Hampshire	x	x	x	x	x	x				D-GG-HH-II-KK	1 year*	None
New Jersey	x	x			x				x	NN-K	1 year*	None
New Mexico	x	x	x	x	x	x	x			K-F	6 months	None
New York	x	x			x					X-Z*	1 year	3 mos.*
North Carolina						x	x			Q-K-X	1 year	None
North Dakota	x	x	x	x	x					K	1 year	None-U
Ohio	x	x		x	x	x			x	BB-CC-DD	1 year	None

State	Cruelty	Desertion	Non-support	Alcohol	Felony	Impotency	Pregnancy at marriage	Drug Addiction	Fraudulent contract	Other causes	Residence time	Time between interlocuty and final decrees
Oklahoma	x	x	...	x	x	x	x	...	x	F-K-BB-CC	6 months	None
Oregon	...	...	...	...	...	...	...	...	...	KK	1 year	90 days
Pennsylvania	x	x	...	...	x	x	...	...	x	B-M-DD	1 year*	None
Rhode Island	x	x	x	x	x	x	...	x	...	H-X	2 years*	6 months
South Carolina ...	x	x	...	x	...	...	...	x	...	Y	1 year	None
South Dakota	x	x	x	x	x	...	...	...	...	K	1 year*	None
Tennessee	x	x	x	x	x	x	x	...	...	A-B-DD-EE	1 year	None
Texas	x	x	...	x	...	...	...	x	...	K-X-F-PP	1 year	60 days
Utah	x	x	x	x	x	x	...	...	...	W-K	3 months	3 mos.*
Vermont	x	x	x	...	x	...	...	...	...	Y-K	6 months	3 mos.-O*
Virginia	...	x	...	...	x	x	x	...	...	I-B	1 year	None-U*
Washington	x	x	x	x	x	x	...	...	x	B-K-Y	6 months	None
West Virginia	x	x	...	x	x	...	...	x	...	X-K	2 years*²	None
Wisconsin	x	x	x	x	x	...	...	...	...	X-W	2 years	120 days⁴
Wyoming	x	x	x	x	x	x	x	...	...	B-J-K	60 days	None

(1.) Determined by court order. (2.) No minimum residence required in adultery cases. **(Adultery is either grounds for divorce or evidence of irreconcilable differences and a breakdown of the marriage.)**(3.) Or 5 days after action is set for trial, whichever is sooner. (4) Except one year when defendant is a non-resident, or personal service of a summons is impossible. (A) Violence. (B) Indignities. (C) Loathsome disease. (D) Joining religious order disbelieving in marriage. (E) Unchaste behavior after marriage. (F) Incompatibility. (H) Any gross misbehavior or wickedness. (I) Wife being a prostitute. (J) Husband being a vagrant. (K) 5-yrs. insanity; permanent insanity in Utah: incurable insanity in Calif. Exceptions 18 mos. Alaska; 2 yrs. Ga., Nev., Ore., Wash., and Wyo.; 3 yrs. Ark., Fla., Tex., Minn., Colo., Kan., Hawaii., Md., Miss., W. Va.; 6 yrs. Idaho. (M) Consanguinity. (N) In cruelty cases, one yr. to remarry. (O) Plaintiff, 6 mos.; defendant 2 yrs. to remarry. (P) If guilty spouse is sentenced to infamous punishment. (Q) Crime against nature. (R) Sixty days to remarry. (S) One year to remarry; Hawaii one year with minor child. Except Iowa, 90 days. (T) Six months to remarry; in Kan. 60 days. (U) Adultery cases, remarriage in discretion of court. (W) Separation for 2 yrs. after decree for same in Ala. and Minn.; 4 yrs. in N.J.; 18 mos. in N.H.; 5 yrs. in Wis. and Md. (X) Separation, no cohabitation—5 yrs., Exceptions La., Va., Wyo. and N.Y. (under agreement), W. Va. 2 yrs.; Tex. and Maine 3 yrs.; N.C. 1 yr. and R.I. 10 yrs. (Y) Separation, no cohabitation—3 years. Exceptions: Vt., Wash., 2 yrs.; Del., Md., 18 mos.; Dist. of Col., one year; (Z) Separation for 2 yrs. after decree for Dist. of Col.; 1 yr. for La. (AA) Mental incapacity at time of marriage. (BB) Procurement of out-of-state divorce. (CC) Gross neglect of duty. (DD) Bigamy. (EE) Attempted homicide. (FF) Plaintiff under age at time of marriage. (GG) Treatment which insures health or endangers reason. (HH) Wife without state for 10 yrs. (II) Wife in state 2 yrs.; husband never in state and has intent to become citizen of foreign country. (JJ) Seven years absence. (KK) Irreconcilable differences. (LL) Life sentence dissolves marriage. (MM) Breakdown of marriage with no reasonable likelihood of preservation. (NN) Deviate sexual conduct. (OO) Course of conduct detrimental to the marriage relationship of party seeking divorce. (PP) incompatibility without regard to fault.

The plaintiff can invariably remarry in the same State where he or she procured a decree of divorce for annulment. Not so the defendant, who is barred in certain States for some offenses. After a period of time has elapsed even the offender can apply for special permission.

The U.S. Supreme Court in a 5 to 4 opinion, ruled April 18, 1949, that one sided quick divorces could be challenged as illegal if notice of the action was not served on the divorced partner within the divorcing States, excepting where the partner was represented at the proceedings.

Enoch Arden Laws. Disappearance and unknown to be alive—Conn. 7 years absence; N.H., 2 years; N.Y., 5 years (called dissolution); Vt., 7 years.

From *World Almanac and Book of Facts* 1974 (New York: Newspaper Enterprise Association, 1974), p. 1026. Reprinted by permission of Newspaper Enterprise Association, Inc.

Canadian Divorce Laws

Separation

In Canada there is no such thing as a "legal separation," and there are no established grounds for separation. While the law takes an interest if a spouse, particularly a husband, deserts, or if there are grounds for divorce, separation is a personal affair. Husbands and wives can draw up the separation agreement themselves and can divide the property and arrange for the care of any children. The separation agreement releases the man and woman from the duty to cohabit sexually. A lawyer cannot draw up a valid separation agreement unless the husband and wife have separated physically as well as emotionally. In a separation agreement the *dum casta* clause is important—at least from the husband's point of view. It states that a husband must continue his wife's support only as long as she has no sexual relationships. If the husband can prove in court that his wife has had sexual relations several times, he can stop payment. A wife may also insert a clause that the husband must abstain from sexual relations or the separation agreement will be invalidated.

If the couple achieves a reconciliation, the separation is invalidated only when they have sexual relations for a reasonable length of time.

Divorce

Prior to 1968 Canada's divorce law had remained virtually unchanged for a hundred years. This national law regulating divorce was based on the English Divorce and Matrimonial Clause Act of 1857. Under this law a double standard existed. Divorce was granted to a man if his wife committed adultery, no matter what the circumstances; but a woman could divorce her husband for adultery only under the circumstances of incest, sodomy, bestiality, rape, bigamy, cruelty, or desertion for at least two years without a reasonable excuse. In 1925 the act was amended to allow a woman to sue for divorce on the grounds of adultery without determining the conditions related to her husband's adultery.

The Divorce Act of 1968 (Bill C-187) broadened the grounds for divorce to include adultery, sodomy, bestiality or rape, homosexuality, bigamy, physical or mental cruelty, imprisonment, addiction to drugs or alcohol, desertion, nonconsummation, and separation for five years. Under this act, even when any of the grounds for divorce exist, a judge can refuse to grant the divorce if there is collusion by the couple. (Collusion means that the couple have bargained in some way to facilitate the divorce.) The new legislation requires lawyers to inform clients of the availability of marriage counseling.

Since the new legislation was passed in 1968, some additional grounds have been accepted in divorce cases. For example, "marital breakdown" is now a sufficient reason for divorce.

Bibliography

Ackerman, Charles. "Affiliations: Structural Determinants of Differential Divorce Rates." *American Journal of Sociology* 69 (July 1963), 12-20.

Adams, Bert N. *Kinship in an Urban Setting*. Chicago: Markham, 1968.

———. "Isolation, Function and Beyond: American Kinship in the 1960's." *Journal of Marriage and the Family* 32 (November 1970), 575-597.

Adams, Romanzo. *Interracial Marriage in Hawaii*. New York: Macmillan, 1937.

Aldous, Joan "A Framework for the Analysis of Family Problem Solving." *Family Problem Solving*. Edited by Joan Aldous et al. Hinsdale, Ill. Dryden Press, 1971, pp. 265-281.

Allport, Gordon Willard. *Becoming: Basic Considerations for a Psychology of Personality*. New Haven: Yale University Press, 1955.

Almquist, Elizabeth, and Angrist, Shirley."Career Salience and Atypicality of Occupational Choice among College Women." *Journal of Marriage and the Family* 2 (May 1970), 242-249.

Anshen, Ruth, ed. *The Family: Its Function and Destiny*. New York: Harper & Bros., 1959, p. 5.

Axelson, Leland J. "Personal Adjustment in the Post-parental Period." *Marriage and Family Living* 22 (February 1960), 66-68.

Ayd, Frank Joseph, Jr. "The Catholic Church." *Birth Control: A Continuing Controversy*. Edited by Edward Tyler. Springfield, Ill. Charles C. Thomas, 1967, pp. 88-98.

Baker, Luther, Jr. "The Personal and Social Adjustment of the Never-Married Woman." *Journal of Marriage and the Family* 30 (August 1968), 473-479.

Bardis, Panos D. "Changes in the Colonial and Modern American Family Systems." *Social Science* 38 (April 1963), 103-114.

———. "Family Forms and Variation Historically Considered." *Handbook of Marriage and the Family*. Edited by Harold T. Christensen. Chicago: Rand McNally, 1964. pp. 403-461.

Barnett, Larry. "Research in Interreligious Dating and Marriage." *Marriage and Family Living* 24 (May 1962), 191-194.

— —. "Research on International and Interracial Marriages." *Marriage and Family Living* 25 (February 1963), 105-107.

Bashore, Richard A. "The Intrauterine Contraceptive Device." *Birth Control: A Continuing Controversy*. Edited by Edward Tyler. Springfield, Ill. Charles C. Thomas, 1967, pp. 152-157.

Bass. Bernard."Amount of Participation, Coalescence and Profitability of Decision Making Discussion." *Journal of Abnormal and Social Psychology* 67 (1963), 92-94.

Bates, Alan. "Parental Roles in Courtship." *Social Forces* 20 (May 1942), 483-486.

Beasley, Christine. *Democracy in the Home*. New York: Association Press. 1954.

Bedell, Madelon. "Supermom." *Ms.*, May 1973, p. 84.

Bee, Helen. "Socialization for Problem Solving." *Family Problem Solving*. Edited by Joan Aldous et al. Hinsdale, Ill. Dryden Press, 1971, pp. 186-211.

Beigel, Hugo. "Romantic Love." *American Sociological Review* 16 (June 1951), 326-334.

Bell, Norman. "Extended Family Relations of Disturbed and Well Families." *Family Process* 1 (September 1962), 175-193.

Bell, Robert. "Some Factors Related to Coed Marital Aspirations." *Family Life Coordinator* 11 (October 1962), 91-94.

———. *Premarital Sex in a Changing Society*. Englewood Cliffs, N.J.: Prentice-Hall, 1966.

———. *Social Deviance*. Homewood, Ill. Dorsey Press, 1971.

Bell, Robert and Buerkle, Jack V. "Mother and Daughter Attitudes to Premarital Sexual Behavior." *Marriage and Family Living* 22 (November 1961), 390-392.

Bell, Robert, and Chaskes, J. B. "Premarital Sexual Experiences among Coeds." *Journal of Marriage and the Family* 32 (February 1970), 81-84.

Benedek, T. G., et al. "Some Emotional Factors in Infertility." *Psychosomatic Medicine* 15 (September-October 1953), 485-498.

Benson, Leonard. *Fatherhood: A Sociological Perspective*. New York: Random House, 1968.

———. *The Family Bond*. New York: Random House, 1971.

Benson, Purnell. "The Common Interests Myth in Marriage" *Social Problems* 3 1955-1956, 27-34.

Bergler, Edmund. *Money and Emotional Conflicts*. 2d ed. New York: International Universities Press, 1970.

Bernard, Jessie. "The Adjustments of Married Mates." *Handbook of Marriage and the Family*. Edited by Harold T. Christensen. Chicago: Rand McNally, 1964, pp. 675-740.

———. "Marital Stability and Patterns of Status Variables." *Journal of Marriage and the Family* 28 (November 1966), 421-439.

———. *The Sex Game*. Englewood Cliffs, N. J.: Prentice-Hall, 1968.

———. *The Future of Marriage*. New York: World Publishing, 1972.

———. "Marriage: Hers and His." *Ms.*, December 1972.

Bernstein, Basil. "Social Class and Linguistic Development" *Education, Economy and Society*. Edited by A. H. Halsey, Jean Flaud, and C. Arnold Anderson. Glencoe Ill.: Free Press, 1961, pp. 228-314.

Bettelheim, Bruno. *Love Is Not Enough: The Treatment of Emotionally Disturbed Children*. Glencoe, Ill; Free Press, 1950.

Billingsley, Andrew. *Black Families in White America*. Englewood Cliffs, N. J.: Prentice-Hall, 1968.

Birmingham, William. *What Modern Catholics Think about Birth Control: A New Symposium*. New York: New American Library, 1964.

Blood, Robert O. "A Re-Test of Waller's Rating Complex." *Marriage and Family Living* 17 (February 1955), 41-47.

———. *Marriage.* New York: Free Press, 1962.

———. *Love Match and Arranged Marriage:A Tokyo-Detroit Comparison*. New York: Free Press, 1967.

Blood, Robert O., and Hamblin, R. I. "The Effect of Wife's Employment on the Family Power Structure." *Social Forces* 36 (May 1958), 347-352.

Blood, Robert O., and Wolfe, Donald M. *Husbands and Wives*. Glencoe, Ill.: Free Press, 1960.

Bloom, Benjamin S., and Broder, Lois. "Problem Solving Processes of College Students: An Exploratory Investigation." *Supplementary Educational Monographs*. Chicago: University of Chicago Press, 1950.

Bohannan, Paul, "The Six Stations of Divorce." *Divorce and After*. Edited by Paul Bohannan. Garden City, N. Y.: Doubleday, 1970, pp. 29-77.

Bolte, Gordon L. "A Communications Approach to Marital Counseling." *Family Life Coordinator* 19 (January 1970), 32-40.

Bossard, James. "The Engagement Ring—A Changing Symbol." *New York Times Magazine*. September 14, 1958, p. 32.

Bossard, James, and Boll, Eleanor S. "Marital Unhappiness in the Life Cycle." *Marriage and Family Living* 17 (February 1955), 10-14.

Bott, Elizabeth. *Family and Social Network*. London: Tavistock, 1957.

Bower, J. L. "Group Decision Making: A Report of an Experimental Study." *Behavioral Science* 10 (1965), 277-289.

Bowman, Henry A. *Marriage for Moderns*. New York: Mc Graw-Hill, 1970, pp. 198-207.

Bran, Stanley. "Note on Honeymoons." *Marriage and Family Living* 9 (Summer 1947), 60.

Brecher, Ruth, and Brecher, Edward. *An Analysis of Human Sexual Response*. Boston: Little, Brown, 1966.

Breckenridge, M. E., and Vincent, E. Lee. *Child Development: Physical and Psychological Growth through Adolescence*. Philadelphia: Saunders, 1965.

Breedlove, William, and Breedlove, Jerry. *Swap Clubs: A Study in Contemporary Sexual Mores*. Los Angeles: Sherbourne Press, 1964.

Brenton, Myron. "Sex Therapy for College Students." *Sexual Behavior*, June 1972, pp. 52-55.

Brim, Orville. *Education for Child Rearing*. New York: Russell Sage Foundation, 1959.

Brim, Orville, et al. *Personality and Decision Processes: Studies in Social Psychology of Thinking*. Stanford, Calif.: Stanford University Press, 1962.

Broderick, Carlfred B., and Bernard, Jessie, eds. *The Individual, Sex, and Society: A SIECUS Handbook for Teachers and Counsellors*. Baltimore: Johns Hopkins Press, 1969.

Brodsky, Stanley. "Self Acceptance in Pregnant Women." *Marriage and Family Living* 25 (November 1963), 483-484.

Brown, L. B. "Budgeting: Opiate of the Middle Class." *Fortune*, May 1956, p. 133.

——. "The 'Day at Home' in Wellington, New Zealand." *Journal of Social Psychology* 50 (November 1959), 189-206.

Burchinal, Lee. "Adolescent Role Deprivation and High School Age Marriage." *Journal of Marriage and Family Living* 21 (November 1959), 378-384.

——. "The Premarital Dyad and Love Involvement." *Handbook of Marriage and the Family*. Edited by Harold T. Christensen. New York: Rand-McNally, 1964, pp. 623-674.

Burchinal, Lee, and Bauder, W. W. "Decision Making and Role Patterns among Iowa Farm Families." *"Marriage and Family Living* 27 (November 1965), 525-532.

Burchinal, Lee, and Chancellor, Loren. "Proportions of Catholics, Urbanism, and Mixed-Catholic Marriage Rates among Iowa Counties." *Social Problems* 9 (Spring 1962), 359-365.

——. "Survival Rates among Religiously Homogamous and Interrelgious Marriages." *Agricultural and Home Economics Experiment Station Research Bulletin* 512 (December 1962), 743-770.

Burchinal, Lee, and Kenkel, William. "Religious Identification and Occupational Status of Iowa Grooms, 1953-1957." *American Sociological Review* 27 (August 1962), 526-532.

Burchinal, Lee, and Rossman, Jack E. "Relations among Maternal Employment Indices and Developmental Characteristics of Children." *Marriage and Family Living* 23 (November 1961), 334-340

Burgess, Ernest W. "Family Living in the Later Decades." *Annals of the American Academy of Political and Social Science* 279 (January 1952), 106-114.

——. "Companionship Marriage in the United States." *Studies of the Family*. Edited by Nels Anderson. Tübingen, Germany: J. C. B. Mohr (Paul Siebeck), 1956, pp. 69-87.

Burgess, Ernest W., and Cottrel, Leonard S., Jr. *Predicting Success or Failure in Marriage*. New York: Prentice-Hall, 1939, pp. 121, 271, 357, 391.

Burgess, Ernest W., and Locke, Harvey J. *The Family-from Institution to Companionship*. New York: American Book, 1953.

Burgess, Ernest W.; Locke, Harvey; and Thomes, Mary Margaret. *The Family: From Traditional to Companionship*. 4th ed. New York: Van Nostrand Reinhold, 1971.

Burgess, Ernest W., and Wallin, Paul. "Homogamy in Social Characteristics." *American Journal of Sociology* 49 (September 1943), 117-124.

———. *Engagement and Marriage*. Philadelphia: Lippincott, 1953.

———. "Factors in Broken Engagements." *Marriage and Family in the Modern World*. Edited by Ruth Cavan. New York: Crowell, 1969, pp. 214-225.

Burgess, Ernest W., and Wallin, Paul, with Shultz, Gladys D. *Courtship, Engagement, and Marriage*. Philadelphia: Lippincott, 1954.

Burma, John. "Interethnic Marriage in Los Angeles, 1948-1959." *Social Forces* 42 (December 1963), 156-165.

Burr, Wesley. "Satisfaction with Various Aspects of Marriage over the Life Cycle: A Random Middle Class Sample." *Journal of Marriage and the Family* 32 (February 1970), 29-37.

Calderone, Mary S. "Adaptation of the Address: "How Young Men Influence the Girls Who Love Them.' *"Redbook,* July 1965, p. 45.

———. "The Sexual Self and Contraception." *Birth Control: A Continuing Controversy*. Edited by Edward Tyler. Springfield, Ill. Charles C. Thomas, 1967, pp. 72-82.

Canada Yearbook, 1969. Ottawa, Ontario: Dominion Bureau of Statistics, 1969.

Cannon, Kenneth. "An Evaluation of Dating." Mimeographed report, Texas Tech University, n.d.

Cannon, Kenneth, and Long, Richard. "Premarital Sexual Behavior in the Sixties." *Journal of Marriage and the Family* 33 (February 1971), 36-49.

Caplovitz, David. *Debtors in Default*. New York: Columbia University Press, 1970.

Carden, Maren Lockwood. *Oneida: Utopian Community to Modern Corporation*. Baltimore: Johns Hopkins Press, 1969.

Carter, Hugh, and Plateris, Alexander. "Trends in Divorce and Family Disruption." *Selected Studies in Marriage and the Family*. Edited by Robert F. Winch and Louis W. Goodman. New York: Holt, Rinehart and Winston, 1968, pp. 564-572.

Carter, Hugh H., and Glick, Paul C. *Marriage and Divorce: A Social and Economic Study*. Cambridge, Mass.: Harvard University Press, 1970.

Casler, Lawrence. "This Thing Called Love is Pathological."*Psychology Today* December 1969, p. 18.

Cavan, Ruth Shonle. *The American Family*. New York: Crowell, 1953.

———. "Subcultural Variations and Mobility." *Handbook of Marriage and the Family*. Edited by Harold T. Christensen. Chicago: Rand McNally, 1964, pp. 535-581.

Center for Consumer Affairs, University of Wisconsin. *The Spender Syndrome: Case Studies of 68 Families and Their Consumer Problems*. Madison: University of Wisconsin Press, 1965.

Centers, Richard. "Marital Selection and Occupational Strata." *American Journal of Sociology* 54 (May 1949), 530-535.

Chancellor, Loren, and Monahan, Thomas P. "Religious Preference and Interreligious Mixtures in Marriages and Divorces in Iowa." *American Journal of Sociology* 61 (November 1955), 233-239.

Cheng, C. K., and Yamamura, Doug S. "Interracial Marriage and Divorce in Hawaii." *Social Forces* 37 (October 1957), 77-84.

Chilman, Catherine. "Fertility and Poverty in the United States: Some Implications for Family Planning Programs, Evaluations and Research." *Journal of Marriage and the Family* 32 (November 1970), 616-627.

Christensen, Harold T. "Children in the Family: Relationship of Number and Spacing to Marital Success." *Journal of Marriage and the Family* 30 (May, 1968), 283-290.

———. "Premarital Pregnancy as Measured by the Spacing of the First Birth from Marriage." *American Sociological Review* 18 (February 1953), 53-59.

Christensen, H. T. and Bowden, O. "Studies in Child Spacing II—the Time Interval between Marriage of Parents and Birth of Their First Child." *Social Forces* 31 (May 1953), 346-351.

Christensen, H. T.; Andrew, R.,; and Freiser, S. "Falsification of Age and Marriage." *Journal of Marriage and Family Living* 15 (November 1953), 301-304.

Christensen, H. I. and Meissner, H. "Studies in Child Spacing III—Premarital Pregnancy as a Factor in Divorce." *American Sociological Review* 18 (December 1953), 641-644.

Christensen, H. T., and Carpenter, George R. "Value Behavior Discrepancies Regarding Premarital Coitus in Three Western Cultures." *American Sociological Review* 27 (February 1962), 66-74.

Christopherson, Victor A. et al. "The Married College Student, 1959" *Marriage and Family Living* 22 (May 1960), 126-127.

Citizen's Advisory Council on the Status of Women. *Report on the Task Force on Labor Statistics to the Citizen's Advisory Council on the Status of Women.* Washington, D.C.: Government Printing Office, 1968.

Clark, Alfred. "An Examination of the Operation of Residential Propinquity as a Factor in Mate Selection." *American Sociological Review* 17 (February 1952), 17-22.

Clayton, R. R. "Religious Orthodoxy and Premarital Sex." *Social Forces* 47 (June 1969), 469-474.

Cohen, Jerome B., and Hanson, Arthur. *Personal Finance: Principles and Case Problems.* Homewood, Ill. Richard D. Irwin, 1958.

Constantine, Larry, and Constantine, Joan. "Where Is Marriage Going?" *Futurist* 4 (April, 1970), 44-46.

———. "The Group Marriage." *The Nuclear Family in Crisis: The Search for an Alternative.* Edited by Michael Gordon. New York: Harper & Row, 1972, pp. 204-223.

Consumers Union of the United States. "Legal Abortion: How Safe? How Available? How Costly?"*Consumer Reports* 37 (July 1972), 466-470.

Coombs, Robert. "A Value Theory of Mate Selection." *Family Life Coordinator* 10 (July 1961), 51-54.

———. "Reinforcement of Values in the Parental Home as a Factor in Mate Selection." *Marriage and Family Living* 24 (May 1962), 155-157.

Cuber, John F., and Harroff Peggy B. "The More Total View: Relationships among Men and Women of the Upper Middle Class." *Marriage and Family Living* 25 (May 1963), 138-145.

———. *Sex and the Significant Americans: A Study of Social Behavior among the Affluent.* Baltimore: Penguin Books, 1968.

Cutright, Phillip. "Illegitimacy, Myths, Causes and Cures." *Family Planning Perspectives* 3 (January 1971), 25-48.

Davis, K. B. *Factors in the Sex Life of 2,200 Women.* New York: Harper & Bros., 1929.

Delora, Jack. "Social Systems of Dating on a College Campus." *Marriage and Family Living* 25 (February 1963), 81-84.

Dembroski, Betty, and Johnson, Dale L. "Dogmatism and Attitudes toward Adoption."*Journal of Marriage and the Family* 31 (November 1969), 788-792.

Dengrove, Edward. "Sex Differences." *Encyclopedia of Sexual Behavior.* Edited by Albert Ellis and Albert Abarbanel. New York: Hawthorn Books, 1967.

De Rougement, Denis. "The Romantic Route to Divorce." *Saturday Review of Literature,* November 13, 1948 p. 9.

Diamonstein, Barbaralee. "Here Come the Brides." *Good Housekeeping,* June 1971 pp. 90-93.

Dignam, William. "Rhythm."*Birth Control: A Continuing Controversy.* Edited by Edward Tyler. Springfield, Ill. Charles C. Thomas, 1967 pp. 142-151.

Doherty, D. D. "Constitutional Law—Abortion Statutes as an Invasion of a Woman's Right of Privacy." *St. Louis University Law Journal* 15 (Summer 1971), 642-650.

Dolphin, R. *Self-Correcting Problems in Personal Finance.* Boston: Allyn & Bacon, 1970.

Duvall, Evelyn M. "Courtship and Engagement." *Modern Marriage and Family Living.* Edited by Morris Fishbein and Ruby J. Reeves Kennedy. New York: Oxford University Press, 1957, pp. 144-157.

———. *Inlaws: Pro and Con.* New York: Association Press, 1954.

Duvall, Evelyn M. and Hill, Reuben. *Being Married.* Boston: Heath, 1960.

Duvall, Evelyn M.; Leichter, Hope J.; and Mitchell, William E., *Inlaws: Kinship and Casework.* New York: Russell Sage Foundation, 1967.

Dyer, Everett. "Parenthood as Crisis: A Re-Study." *Marriage and Family Living* 25 (May 1963), 196-201.

Dyer, W. G., and Urban, D. "Institutionalization of Equalitarian Norms." *Marriage and Family Living* 20 (February 1958), 53-58.

Eckland, Bruce. "Theories of Mate Selection." *Eugenics Quarterly* 15 (March 1968), 71-84.

Eckland, Bruce, and Lenski, Gerhard. "Theories of Mate Selection." *The Religious Factor: A Sociological Study of Religion's Impact on Politics, Economics and Family Life.* New York: Holt, Rinehart and Winston, 1971.

Edwards, John. "The Future of the Family Revisited." *Journal of Marriage and the Family* 29 (August 1967), 505-511.

Ehrmann, Winston. *Premarital Dating Behavior.* New York: Holt, Rinehart and Winston, 1959.

———. "Marital and Non-Marital Sexual Behavior." *Handbook of Marriage and the Family.* Edited by Harold T. Christensen. Chicago: Rand McNally, 1964.

Ellis, Albert. "A Study of Love Relationships." *Journal of Genetic Psychology* 75 (1949), 61-71.

———. *Sex Without Guilt.* New York: Lyle Stuart, 1958.

———. *The Case for Sexual Liberty.* Tucson, Ariz. Seymour Press, 1965.

———. "Romantic Love." *Reflections on Marriage.* Edited by William Stephens. New York: Crowell, 1968.

———. "Healthy and Disturbed Reasons for Having Extra-Marital Relations." *Extra Marital Relations.* Edited by Gerhard Neubeck. Englewood Cliffs, N. J.: Prentice-Hall, 1969, pp. 153-161.

———, ed. *Sex Life of the American Woman and the Kinsey Report.* New York: Greenberg, 1954.

Ellis, Albert, with David, Lester "Should Men Marry Older Women?" *This Week Magazine,* July 6, 1958, pp. 8-9.

Ellis, Albert, and Abarbanel, Albert, eds. *The Encyclopedia of Sexual Behavior.* New York: Hawthorn Books, 1967.

Empey, L. T. "An Instrument for the Measurement of Family Authority Patterns." *Rural Sociology* 22 (March 1957), 73-75.

England, R. W. "Images of Love and Courtship in Family-Magazine Fiction." *Marriage and Family Living* 22 (May 1960), 162-165.

English, O. S., and Foster, C. J., *Fathers Are Parents Too.* New York: Putnam, 1951.

Farber, Bernard. *Family: Organization and Interaction.* San Francisco: Chandler Publishing, 1964.

Farris, Edmond. "Male Fertility." *Sourcebook in Marriage and the Family.* Edited by Marvin Sussman. Boston: Houghton Mifflin, 1955.

Feldman, Frances. *The Family in a Money World.* New York: Family Service Association of America, 1957.

Feldman, Harold. "Development of the Husband-Wife Relationship." Unpublished research report to the National Institute of Mental Health, Grant M-2931, Cornell University, 1965.

Ferreira, A. J., and Winter, W. D. "Family Interaction and Decision-Making." *Archives of General Psychiatry* 13 (September 1965), 214-223.

Firestone, Shulamith. *The Dialectic of Sex: The Case for Feminist Revolution.* New York: Bantam Books 1971.

Fishbein, Morris. "Premarital Physical Examination." *Modern Marriage and Family Living.* Edited by Morris Fishbein and Ruby Jo Reeves Kennedy. New York: Oxford University Press, 1957, pp. 167-173.

Fletcher, Joseph. "The Protestant Churches." *Birth Control: A Continuing Controversy* Edited by Edward Tyler. Springfield, Ill. Charles C. Thomas, 1967, pp. 99-106.

Flick, Alexander ed. *History of the State of New York.* Long Island, N. Y. Ira J. Friedman, 1962.

Foote, Nelson A. "Love." *Psychiatry* 16 (August 1953), 245-251.

———. "Sex as Play." *Social Problems* 1 (April 1954), 159-163.

———. "Matching of Husband and Wife in Phases of Development." *Sourcebook in Marriage and the Family.* Edited by Marvin Sussman. Boston: Houghton Mifflin, 1965, pp. 15-21.

Forssman, H., and Thuwe, I. "One Hundred and Twenty Children Born after Application for Therapeutic Abortion." *Acta Psychiatrica Scandinavica* 42 (1966), 71-88.

Freedman, Ronald; Whelpton, Pascal; and Campbell, Arthur. *Family Planning, Sterility and Population Growth.* New York: McGraw-Hill, 1959.

Freedman, R. and Coombs, L. "Child Spacing and Family Economic Position." *American Sociological Review* 31 (October 1966), 631-648.

Freeman, Jo. "Growing up Girlish." *Transaction,* November-December 1970, pp. 36-44.

French, John R. P., and Raven, Bertram. "The Bases of Social Power." *Group Dynamics: Research and Theory.* Edited by D. Cartwright and A. Zander. Elmsford, N. Y.: Peterson, 1960.

Friedan, Betty. *The Feminine Mystique.* New York: Dell Publishing, 1970.

Fromm, Erich. *Man for Himself: An Inquiry into the Psychology of Ethics.* New York: Henry Holt, 1947.

———. *The Art of Loving.* New York: Harper & Row, 1956.

Fromme, Allan. "Toward a Better Sexual Orientation." *Sex and Human Relationships.* Edited by Cecil E. Johnson. Columbia, Ohio: Charles Merrill, 1970.

Fullerton, Gail Putney. "Love as Myth." *Survival in Marriage*. Holt, Rinehart and Winston, 1972.

"The Future of Women and Marriage." *Futurist* 4 (July 1970).

Gans, Herbert. *The Urban Villagers*. New York: Free Press, 1962.

Gebhard, Paul H., et al. *Pregnancy, Birth and Abortion*. New York: Harper & Bros., 1958.

––––––. *Sex Offenders*. New York: Harper & Row, 1965, p. 469.

Geiken, K. F. "Expectations Concerning Husband-Wife Responsibilities in the Home." *Marriage and Family Living* 26 (August 1964), 349-352.

Ginnott, Haim. *Between Parent and Child*. New York: Macmillan, 1965.

Glick, Paul, and Parke, Robert, Jr. "New Approaches in Studying the Life Cycle of the Family." *Selected Studies in Marriage and the Family*. Edited by Robert F. Winch and Louis W. Goodman. New York: Holt, Rinehart and Winston, 1968, pp. 166-177.

Glick, Paul, and Norton, Arthur. "Frequency, Duration, and Probability of Marriage and Divorce." *Journal of Marriage and the Family* 33 (May 1971), 307-318.

Goldman, M. "A Comparison of Group and Individual Performance Where Subjects Have Varying Tendencies to Solve Problems." *Journal of Personality and Social Psychology* 3 (1966), 604-607.

Goldscheider, Calvin, and Goldstein, Sidney. "Generation Changes in Jewish Family Structure." *Journal of Marriage and the Family*, 29 (May 1967), 267-276.

Golenpaul, Dan ed. *Information Please Almanac, 1970*. New York: Dan Golenpaul Associates, 1969.

Goode, William J. "The Theoretical Importance of Love." *American Sociological Review* 24 (February 1959), 38-47.

––––––. "Marital Satisfaction and Instability; A Cross-Cultural Class Analysis of Divorce Rates." *International Social Science Journal* 14 (1962), 507-526.

––––––. *The Family*. Englewood Cliffs, N. J.: Prentice-Hall, 1964.

––––––. *Women in Divorce*. New York: Free Press, 1965.

––––––. "Family Patterns and Human Rights." *International Social Science Journal* 18 (1966), 41-54.

Goodyear, Margaret, and Klohr, Mildred. *Managing for Effective Living*. New York: Wiley, 1965.

Gordon, Albert I. *Intermarriage: Interfaith, Interracial, Interethnic*. Boston: Beacon Press, 1964.

Gordon, Michael, ed. *The Nuclear Family in Search of a Crisis: The Search for an Alternative*. New York: Harper & Row, 1972.

Gorer, Geoffrey. *The American People: A Study in National Character*. New York: Norton, 1948.

Gray, H. "Marriage and Premarital Conception." *Journal of Psychology* 50 (October 1960), 383-397.

Greene, Bernard L. *A Clinical Approach to Marital Problems: Evaluation and Management*. Springfield, Ill.: Charles C. Thomas, 1970.

Greenfield, Sidney. "Love and Marriage in Modern America: A Functional Analysis." *Marriage and Family*. Edited by Jeffrey K. Hodder and Marie Borgatta. Itasca, Ill. F. E. Peacock, 1969, p. 253.

Gross, Irma, and Crandall, Elizabeth. *Management for Modern Families*. New York: Appleton-Century-Crofts, 1963.

Group for the Advancement of Psychiatry, Committee on the College Student. *Sex and the College Student*. New York: Atheneum, 1966.

Grove, G. "Attitude Covergence in Small Groups." *Journal of Communication* 15 (December 1965), 226-238.

Gurin, Gerald; Veroff, Joseph; and Field, Sheila. *Americans View Their Mental Health*. New York: Basic Books, 1960.

Guttmacher, Alan. *The Complete Book of Birth Control*. New York: Ballantine Books, 1961.

Hall, J., and Williams, M. S. "A Comparison of Decision-Making Performance in Established and Ad Hoc Groups." *Journal of Personality and Social Psychology* 3 (1966), 214-222.

Hall, Perry. *Family Credit Counseling: An Emerging Community Service*. New York: Family Service Association of America, 1968.

Hall, Robert. "The Abortion Revolution." *Playboy*, September 1970, p. 112.

Handel, Gerald. "Sociological Aspects of Parenthood." *Parenthood: Its Psychology and Psychopathology*. Edited by E. James Anthony and Therese Benedek. Boston: Little, Brown, 1970, pp. 87-105.

Hansen, Donald, and Hill, Reuben. "Families under Stress." *Handbook of Marriage and the Family*. Edited by Harold T. Christensen. Chicago: Rand McNally, 1964.

Hardin, G. "Abortion—or Compulsory Pregnancy." *Journal of Marriage and the Family* 30 (May 1968), 246-251. 246-251.

Harlow, Harry. "The Nature of Love." *American Psychologist* 13 (December 1958), 673-685.

Harris, Thomas A. *I'm O.K.–You're O.K.* New York: Harper & Row, 1969.

Havemann, E. *Birth Control.* New York: Time-Life Books, 1967.

Heer, D. M. "Dominance and the Working Wife." *Social Forces* 36 (May 1958), 341-347.

———. "Husband and Wife Perceptions of Family Power Structure." *Marriage and Family Living* 24 (February 1962), 65-67.

———. "The Trend of Interfaith Marriages in Canada, 1922-1957." *American Sociological Review* 27 (April 1962), 245-250.

———. "The Measurement and Bases of Family Power: An Overview." *Marriage and Family Living* 25 (May 1963), 133-139.

———. "Negro-White Marriage in the United States." *Journal of Marriage and the Family* 28 (August 1966), 262-273.

———. "Negro-White Marriage in the United States." *Selected Studies in Marriage and the Family.* Edited by Robert F. Winch and Louis W. Goodman. New York: Holt, Rinehart and Winston, 1968, pp. 481-486.

Hefner, Hugh. *The Playboy Philosophy.* Part 2. Chicago: Playboy Press, 1963.

Heltsley, Mary E., and Broderick, Carlfred B. "Religiosity and Premarital Sexual Permissiveness: A Re-examination of Reiss' Traditionalism Proposition." *Journal of Marriage and the Family* 31 (August 1969), 441-443.

Henton, June. "Problem Solving through Conflict in Marriage." Ph.D. thesis, University of Minnesota, 1970.

Hess, R. D., and Handel, G. *Family Worlds: A Psychological Approach to Family Life.* Chicago: University of Chicago Press, 1959.

Hettinger, Richard. *Living with Sex: The Student's Dilemma.* New York: Seabury Press, 1966.

Hill, Reuben. *Families under Stress: Adjustment to the Crisis of War Separation and Reunion.* New York: Harper & Bros. 1949.

Hill, Reuben, and Becker, Howard, eds. *Family, Marriage and Parenthood.* Boston: Heath, 1955.

Hill, Reuben, and Konig, Rene, eds. *Families in East and West.* The Hague, Netherlands: Mouton, 1970.

Hobart, Charles. "Disillusionment in Marriage, and Romanticism." *Journal of Marriage and the Family* 20 (May 1958), 156-162.

———. "The Incidence of Romanticism during Courtship." *Social Forces* 36 (May 1958), 362-367.

———. "Sexual Permissiveness in Young Canadians, A Factoral Study." Paper presented at the Canadian Sociology and Anthropology Association Annual Meeting, June 5-9, 1971.

Hobbs, Daniel. "Parenthood as Crisis. A Third Study." *Journal of Marriage and the Family* 27 (August 1965), 367-372.

Hoffman, L. R. "Group Problem Solving." *Advances in Experimental Psychology.* Edited by L. Berkowitz. New York: Academic Press, 1965, pp. 99-132.

Hoffman, L. R., Burke, J. R.,; and Maier, N. R. F. "Does Training with Differential Reinforcement on Similar Problems Help in Solving a New Problem?" *Psychological Reports* 13 (1963), 147-154.

Hoffman, L. R., and Maier, N. R. F. "Valence in the Adoption of Solutions by Problem-Solving Groups: Quality and Acceptance as Goals of Leaders and Members." *Journal of Personality and Social Psychology* 6 (June 1957), 175-182.

Hoffman, Lois "Effects of the Employment of Mothers on Parental Power Relations and the Division of Household Tasks." *Marriage and Family Living* 22 (February 1960), 27-35.

———. "Effects of Maternal Employment on the Child." *Child Development* 32 (March-December 1961), 187-197.

Hollingshead, August. "Cultural Factors in the Selection of Marriage Mates." *American Sociological Review* 15 (October 1950), 619-627.

Holter, Harriet. *Sex Roles and Social Structure.* Oslo, Norway: Hestholms Boktrykkeri, 1970.

Homans, G. C. *The Human Group.* New York: Harcourt, Brace, 1950.

Hook, K. "Refused Abortion." *Acta Psychiatrica Scandinavica* (1963), Supplement 168, 1-156.

Household Finance Corporation. *Your Budget.* Chicago: Household Finance Corporation, 1965.

Hovland, Carl I., et al. *Communication and Persuasion.* New Haven: Yale University Press, 1953.

Hunt, Chester, and Collier, Richard. "Intermarriage and Cultural Change: A Study of Philippine-American Marriages." *Social Forces* 35 (March 1957), 223-230.

Hunt,Morton M. *The Natural History of Love.* New York: Knopf, 1959.

Hunt, T. C. "Occupational Status and Marriage Selection." *American Sociological Review* 5 (August 1940), 495-504.

Illich, Ivan D. "School, the Sacred Cow." *Celebration of Awareness: A Call for Institutional Revolution.* Garden City, N. Y.: Doubleday, 1970, pp. 121-136.

Illing, W. M. "Population, Family, Household and Labour Force Growth to 1980." *Staff Study Number 19, Economic Council of Canada, September 1967.*

Irelan, Lola M., and Besner, Arthur. "Low Income Outlook on Life." Low Income Life Styles. Edited by Lola M. Irelan. Washington, D. C.: Division of Research, U. S., Department of Health, Education, and Welfare, 1968, pp. 1-12.

James, Muriel, and Jongeword, Dorothy. *Born to Win: Transactional Analysis with Gestalt Expeiments.* Reading, Mass.: Addison-Wesley, 1971.

Janeway, Elizabeth. "Happiness and the Right to Choose." *Atlantic.* March 1970, ;;. 118-126.

Jessner, Lucie; Weigert, Edith; and Foy, James L. "The Development of Parental Attitudes during Pregnancy." *Parenthood, Its Psychology and Psychopathology.* Edited by E. James Anthony and Therese Benedek. Boston: Little, Brown, 1970, pp. 209-244.

Johannis, T. B., Jr. "Married College Students and Their Honeymoons." *Family Life Coordinator* 7 (March 1959), 39-40.

Johannis, T. B., Jr., and Rollins, J. M. "Teenager Perceptions of Family Decision Making." *Family Life Coordinator* 7 (June 1959), 70-74.

———. "Teenager Perception of Family Decision Making about Social Activities." *Family Life Coordinator* 8 (March 1960), 59-60.

Johnson, Warren. *Human Sexual Behavior and Sex Education: Perspectives and Problems.* Philadelphia: Lea and Febiger, 1968.

Jones, Kenneth; Shainberg, Louis W.; and Byer, Curtis O. *Sex.* 2d ed. New York: Harper & Row, 1973.

Kanin, Eugene J. "Premarital Sex Adjustments, Social Class and Associated Behaviors." *Marriage and Family Living* 22 (August 1960), 258-262.

Kanin, Eugene J., and Howard, David H. "Postmarital Consequences of Premarital Sex Adjustments." *American Sociological Review* 23 (October 1958), 556-562.

Kanin, Eugene J.; Davidson, Karen R.; and Scheck, Sonia R. "A Research Note on Male-Female Differentials in the Experience of Heterosexual Love." *Journal of Sex Research* 6 (February 1970), 64-72.

Kanter, Rosabeth Moss. "Communes." *Psychology Today* July 1970, pp. 53-57.

———. *Commitment and Community: Communes and Utopias in Sociological Perspective.* Cambridge, Mass.: Harvard University Press, 1972.

Karlsson, Georg. *Adaptability and Communication in Marriage.* Totowa, N. J.: Bedminster Press, 1963.

Kassel, Victor. "Polygyny after Sixty." *The Family in Search of a Future.* Edited by Herbert Otto. New York: Appleton-Century-Crofts, 1970, pp. 137-144.

Keats, G. R., and Davis, K. E. "Dynamics of Sexual Behavior of College Students." *Journal of Marriage and the Family* 32 (August 1970), 390-399.

Keller, Suzanne. "Does the Family Have a Future?" *Journal of Comparative Family Studies* 2 (Spring 1971), 1-14.

Kenkel, W. F. "Influence Differentiation in Family Decision-Making." *Sociology and Social Research* 42 (1957), 18-25.

———. "Traditional Family Ideology and Spousal Roles in Decision Making." *Marriage and Family Living* 21 (1959), 334-339.

———. "Dominance, Persistence, Self-Confidence and Spousal Roles in Decision-Making." *Journal of Social Psychology* 54 (August 1961), 349-358.

———. "Husband-Wife Interaction in Decision-Making and Decision Choices." *Journal of Social Psychology* 54 (August 1961), 255-262.

———. "Sex of Observer and Spousal Roles in Decision-Making." *Marriage and Family Living* 23 (1961), 185-186.

Kennedy, Ruby Jo Reeves. "Single or Triple Melting Pot? - Intermarriage Trends in New Haven, 1870-1940." *American Journal of Sociology* 49 (January 1944), 331-339.

Kephart, William. *The Family, Society and the Individual.* Boston: Houghton Mifflin, 1961.

———. "Experimental Family Organization: An Historico-Cultural Report on the Oneida Community."*Journal of Marriage and the Family* 25 (August 1963), 261-271.

———. "Some Correlates of Romantic Love."*Journal of Marriage and the Family* 29 (August 1967), 470-474.

Kieren, Dianne. "Adaptability: A Measure of Spousal Problem Solving and Its Relation to Child Rearing Practices." Ph.D. thesis, University of Minnesota. 1969.

———. "Marital Role Expectations of Canadian High School Students." Mimeographed interim research report, Edmonton, Alberta, Canada, June 1971.

Kieren, Dianne, and Tallman, Irving. "Spousal Adaptability: An Assessment of Marital Competence." *Journal of Marriage and the Family* 34 (May 1972), 247-256.

Kierkegaard, Soren. "The Aesthetic Validity of Marriage." *A Kierkegaard Anthology.* Edited by Robert Bretall. Princeton, N.J.: Princeton University Press, 1946, pp. 80-97.

King, Charles E. "The Burgess-Cottrell Method of Measuring Marital Adjustment Applied to a Non-White Southern Urban Population." *Marriage and Family Living* 14 (November 1952), 280-285.

Kinkade, Kathleen. "Commune: A Walden Two Experiment." *Psychology Today,* January 1973, p. 357, and February 1973, p. 717.

Kinsey, Alfred C.; Pomeroy, W. B.; and Martin, C. E. *Sexual Behavior in the Human Male.* Philadelphia: Saunders, 1948.

Kinsey, Alfred C., et al. *Sexual Behavior in the Human Female.* Philadelphia: Saunders, 1953.

Kirk, H. David. *Shared Fate: A Theory of Adaptation and Mental Health.* New York: Free Press, 1964.

Kirkendall, Lester. "Ethic and Interpersonal Relationships." *Humanist* 16 (November-December 1956), 261-267.

———. *Premarital Intercourse and Interpersonal Relationships.* New York: Julian Press, 1961.

Kirkendall, Lester, and Libby, Roger. "Interpersonal Relationships: Crux of the Sexual Renaissance."*Journal of Social Issues* 22 (April 1966), 45-59.

Kirkendall, Lester, and Adams, Wesley. *The Student's Guide to Marriage and Family Life Literature.* Dubuque, Iowa: Wm. C. Brown, 1971.

Kirkpatrick, Clifford. "Factors in Marital Adjustment."*American Journal of Sociology* 43 (July 1937), 122-124.

———. *What Science Says about Happiness in Marriage.* Minneapolis: Burgess Publishing, 1947.

———. *The Family as Process and Institution.* New York: Ronald Press, 1963.

Kirkpatrick, Clifford, and Caplow, Theodore. "Courtship in a Group of Minnesota Students." *American Journal of Sociology* 51 (September 1945), 114-125.

Klemer, Richard. *Marriage and Family Relationships.* New York: Harper & Row, 1970.

Knight, Thomas. "In Defense of Romance." *Marriage and Family Living* 22 (May 1959), 107-110.

Knupfer, Genevieve; Clark, Walter; and Room, Robin. "The Mental Health of the Unmarried." *American Journal of Psychiatry* 122 (February 1966), 842.

Koedt, Anne. "The Myth of the Vaginal Orgasm." *People as Partners.* Edited by Jacqueline Wiseman. San Francisco: Canfield Press, 1971, pp. 121-129.

Kogan, Benjamin. *Human Sexual Expression.* New York: Harcourt Brace Jovanovich, 1973.

Kohn, Melvin L. "Social Class and Parental Values." *American Journal of Sociology* 64 (January 1959), 337-352.

Kolb, W. L. "Family Sociology, Marriage Education, and the Romantic Couples." *Social Forces* 29 (October 1950), 65-72.

Koller, Marvin R. "Some Changes in Courtship Behavior in Three Generations of Ohio Women." *American Sociological Review* 16 (June 1951), 366-370.

Komarovsky, Mirra. "Cultural Contradictions and Sex Roles." *American Journal of Sociology* 52 (November 1946), 184-189.

———. *Blue Collar Marriage.* New York: Random House, 1964.

———. "Cultural Conditions and Sex Roles: The Masculine Case."*Changing Women in a Changing Society.* Chicago: University of Chicago Press, 1973, pp. 111-122.

Komisar, Lucy. "The New Feminism." *Saturday Review,* February 21, 1970, p. 27.

Kuhn, Manford H. "The Engagement: Thinking about Marriage." *Family, Marriage and Parenthood.* Edited by Howard Becker and Reuben Hill. Boston: Heath, 1955, pp. 276-304.

Kummer, J. M. "Abortion: Practical Aspects and Considerations." *The Adolescent Experience.* Edited by J. P. Semmens and K. E. Krantz. Toronto: Collier-MacMillan Canada, 1970, pp. 164-172.

Kunz, Philip and Merlin Brinkerhoff. "Differential Childlessness by Color: The Destruction of a Cultural Belief." *Journal of Marriage and the Family* 31 (November 1969), 713-719.

Lake, Alice. "Teenagers and Sex: A Student Report." *Seventeen,* July 1967.

Lanctot, Claude, and Parenteau-Carreau, Suzanne. "Studies of the Effectiveness of Temperature Methods." Ottawa, Ontario, Canada: Serena Inc., n.d.

Landis, Judson T. "Social Correlates of Divorce or Non-Divorce among the Unhappy Married." *Marriage and Family Living* 25 (May 1963), 178-180.

Landis, Judson T. "A Study of Disagreements and Conflicts during Engagement and in Marriage." Paper presented at the Annual Meeting of the National Council on Family Relations, Education Section, Chicago, October 7-10, 1970.

Landis, Judson T., and Landis, Mary G. *Building a Successful Marriage.* 5th ed. Englewood Cliffs, N.J.: Prentice-Hall, 1968.

Landis, Paul H. *Making the Most of Marriage.* 4th ed. New York: Appleton-Century-Crofts, 1970.

Lane, G. "Abortion Statement in Current Catholic Clarity and Protestant Ambivalence." *Christian Century,* November 3, 1971.

Lang, R. O. "The Rating of Happiness in Marriage." Master's thesis, University of Chicago, 1932.

Lantz, Herman R., and Snyder, Eloise C. *Marriage: An Examination of the Man-Woman Relationship.* New York: Wiley, 1969.

Larson, Lyle. "Toward a Conceptual Model of Heterosexual Love: An Exploratory Study." *Family Life Coordinator* 15 (October 1966), 199-206.

Laws, Judith Long. "A Feminist Review of the Marital Adjustment Literature: The Rape of the Locke." *Journal of Marriage and the Family* 33 (August 1971), 483-517.

Lazarfeld, Paul F. "The American Soldier—an Expository Review." *Public Opinion Quarterly* 13 (Fall 1949), 378-380.

Lear, Martha Weinman. "When College Dorms Go Coed." *Reader's Digest* February 1970, pp. 27-32.

Leichter, Hope J., and Mitchell, William E. *Kinship and Casework.* New York: Russell Sage Foundation, 1967.

Leik, R. H. "Instrumentality and Emotionality in Family Interaction." *Sociometry* 26 (1963), 131-145.

Lemasters, E. E. "Parenthood as Crisis." *Marriage and Family Living* 19 (November 1957), 352-355.

———. *Parents in Modern America: A Sociological Analysis.* Homewood, Ill. Dorsey Press, 1970.

Lenski, Gerhard. *The Religious Factor: A Sociological Study of Religion's Impact on Politics, Economics, and Family Life.* New York: Doubleday, 1961.

Leslie, Gerald. *The Family in Social Context.* New York: Oxford University Press, 1967.

Leslie, Gerald, and Richardson, Arthur. "Family versus Campus Influences in Relation to Mate Selection." *Social Problems* 4 (October 1956), 117-121.

Levin, Floyd. "Life Styles and Life Insurance." *Best's Review,* Spring 1973, p. 22.

Levinger, George. "Marital Cohesiveness and Dissolution: An Integrative Review." *Journal of Marriage and the Family* 27 (February 1965), 19-28.

Lewis, A. *An Interesting Condition.* New York: Doubleday, 1950.

Liebenberg, B. "Expectant Fathers." *American Journal of Orthopsychiatry* 37 (March 1967), 358-359.

Lieberman, E. James. "Statement on the Effects of U.S. Casualties in Viet Nam on American Families." *Journal of Marriage and the Family* 32 (May 1970), 197-198.

Life before Birth. Life Educational Reprint Number 27. New York: Time-Life, 1965. Originally from *Life,* April 30, 1965.

Limner, Roman. *Sex and the Unborn Child.* New York: Julian Press, 1969.

Lind, Andrew. "Interracial Marriage as Affecting Divorce in Hawaii." *Sociology and Social Research* 49 (October 1964), 17-26.

Linner, Bergitta. *Sex and Society in Sweden.* New York: Pantheon Books, 1967.

Linton, Ralph. *The Study of Man.* New York: Appleton-Century—Crofts, 1936.

Lipman-Bluman, Dean. "How Ideology Shapes Women's Lives."*Scientific American*, January 1972, pp. 34-53.

Lobsenz, Norman, and Blackburn, Clark W. *How to Stay Married: A Modern Approach to Sex, Money and Emotions in Marriage*. New York: Cowles, 1969.

Locke, Harvey J. *Predicting Adjustment in Marriage*. New York:Henry Holt, 1951.

Locke, H. J., and Williamson, R. C. "Marital Adjustment." *American Sociological Review* 23 (October 1958), 562-569.

Lowie, Robert H. "Sex and Marriage." *The Sex Problem in Modern Society*. Edited by John F. McDermott. New York: Modern Library, 1931.

Lowrie, Samuel H. "Early and Late Dating: Some Conditions Associated with Them." *Marriage and Family Living* 23 (August 1961), 284-291.

Lyness, Judith; Lipetz, Milton; and Davis, Keith. "Living Together: An Alternative to Marriage." *Journal of Marriage and the Family* 34 (May 1972), 305-312.

Maccoby, Eleanor. "Effects upon Children of Their Mother's Outside Employment." *Work in the Lives of Married Women*. New York: Columbia University Press, 1958, pp. 150-172.

Maccoby, Eleanor, ed. *The Development of Sex Differences*.Stanford, Calif. Stanford University Press, 1966.

Mace, David, and Mace, Vera. *Marriage East and West*. Garden City, N. Y. Doubleday, 1960.

MacLeod, John. "Fertility in Men." *Encyclopedia of Sexual Behavior*, vol. 8. Edited by Albert Ellis and Albert Abarbanel. New York: Hawthorn, 1961, pp. 29-42.

Madaras, F. R., and Bem, D. J. "Risk and Conservatism in Group Decision-Making." *Journal of Experimental Social Psychology* 4 (1968), 350-365.

Maddock, James. "Morality and Individual Development: A Basis for Value Education." *Family Life Coordinator* 21 (July 1972), 291-302.

Maier, Norman R. F., and Solem, Allen. "The Contributions of a Discussion Leader to the Quality of Group Thinking: The Effective Use of Minority Opinions." *Human Relations* 5 (1952), 277-288.

Malinowski, R. "Parenthood: The Basis of Social Structure." *The Family: Its Structure and Functions*. Edited by R. Coser. New York: St. Martin's Press, 1964, pp. 3-18.

Mann, William E. *Canadian Trends in Premarital Behavior: Some Preliminary Studies of Youth in High School and University*. Toronto: Anglican Church of Canada, 1967.

————. "Sex at York University." *The Underside of Toronto*. Edited by W. E. Mann. Toronto: McClelland and Stewart, 1970, pp. 158-174.

Marcus, Peggy. "In-Law Relationship Adjustment of Couples Married Between Two and Eleven Years." *Journal of Home Economics* 43 (January 1951), 35-37.

Marotz, Ramona. "Parental Aspirations for Daughters: A Mexican-U.S. Comparison." Paper presented at the Annual Society for the Study of Social Problems Meetings in New Orleans, August 1972.

Marquis, D. G., and Reitz, H. J. "Effect of Uncertainty on Risk taking in Individual and Group Decisions." *Behavioral Science* 4 (July 1969), 281-288.

Martinson, F. M. "Ego Deficiency as a Factor in Marriage." *American Sociological Review* 20 (April 1955), 161-164.

Maslow, Abraham H. *Motivation and Personality*. New York: Harper & Row, 1954.

Masters, William H., and Johnson, Virginia E. *Human Sexual Response*. Boston: Little Brown, 1966.

————. *Human Sexual Inadequacy*. Boston: Little, Brown, 1970.

Mathews, V. D., and Mihanovich, C. S. "New Orientations of Marital Maladjustment." *Marriage and Family Living* 25 (August 1963) 300-310.

Mayer, John. *Jewish-Gentile Courtship*. New York: Free Press, 1961.

Maynard, F. "New Rites for Old." *Seventeen* March, 1969, p. 154.

McConville, C. B., and Hemphill, J. K. "Some Effects of Communication Restraints on Porblem-Solving Behavior." *Journal of Social Psychology* 69 (1966), 265-276.

McCorkel, R. J., Jr. "Husbands and Pregnancy: An Exploratory Study." M.A. Thesis, University of North Carolina, 1964.

Mead, George Robert. *Mind, Self and Society*. Chicago: University of Chicago Press, 1934.

Merton, Robert. *Social Theory and Social Structure*. Glencoe, Ill. Free Press, 1959.

Middleton, R., and Putney, S. "Dominance in Decisions in the Family Race and Class Differences." *American Journal of Sociology* 65 (May 1960), 605-609

Miller, Daniel, and Swanson, Guy E. *The Changing American Parent: A Study in the Detroit Area.* New York: Wiley, 1958.

Millican R. D. "A Factor Analysis of Canadian Urban Family Expenditures." *Canadian Journal of Economic and Political Science* 30 (May 1964), 241-243.

Mirande, A. M. "Reference Group Theory and Adolescent Sexual Behavior." *Journal of Marriage and the Family* 30 (November 1968), 572-577.

Misra, B. D. "Comparative Attitudes of Husband and Wife toward Family Planning." *Sociological Contributions to Family Planning Research.* Edited by Donald Bogue. Chicago: University of Chicago, Community and Family Study Center, 1967, pp. 168-206.

Missildine, W. Hugh, *Your Inner Child of the Past.* New York: Simon and Schuster, 1963.

Monahan, T. "Does Age at Marriage Matter in Divorce." *Social Forces* 32 (October 1953), 81-87.

———. "Premarital Pregnancy in the U.S.: A Critical Review of Some New Findings." *Eugenics Quarterly* 7 (September 1960), 133-147.

"Money Talk for Newlyweds." *Changing Times*, June, 1963, pp. 6-17.

Moore, Frank W., ed. *Readings in Cross-Cultural Methodology.* New Haven, Conn.: Human Relations Area Files Press, 1966.

Moore, O. K., and Anderson, S. B. "Modern Logic and Tasks for Experiments on Problem Solving Behavior." *Journal of Psychology* 38 (1954), 151-160.

Morgan, Edmund S. *The Puritan Family: Religion and Domestic Relations in Seventeenth Century New England.* New York: Harper & Row, 1966.

Morgan, James N., et al. *Income and Welfare in the United States.* New York: McGraw-Hill, 1962, pp. 118-196.

Moss, Joel J. "What Is a Good Family" and "The Modern American Family as a Struggle Centre." *Supplementary Readings for Family Relationships.* Edited by Paul E. Dahl, Provo, Utah: Brigham Young University Press, 1968, pp.4-10, 82-90.

Moss, J. Joel, and Moss, Audra Call, *Moss on Marriage.* Provo, Utah: Brigham Young University Press, 1965.

Moss, J. Joel: Apolonio, Frank; and Jenson, Margaret. "The Pre-Marital Dyad during the Sixties." *Journal of Marriage and the Family* 33 (February 1971), 50-69.

Murdock, George P. *Social Structure,* New York: Macmillan, 1949.

———. "World Ethnographic Sample." *American Anthropologist* 59 (1957), 664-687.

Murphy, Gardner. "Social Motivation." *Handbook of Social Psychology.* Vol. 2. Edited by Gardner Lindzey. Cambridge, Mass.: Addison-Wesley, 1954, pp. 601-634.

Myrdal, Gunnar. *An American Dilemma.* New York: Harper & Bros., 1944.

Nanny, Sarah. "Sexual Knowledge of College Students." Master's thesis, Syracuse University, 1969.

Neilson, William. *Consumer and the Law in Canada.* Downsview, Ontario: Osgood Hall Law School of York University, 1970.

Nelson, Joel. "Clique Contacts and Family Orientations." *American Sociological Review* 31 (October 1966), 663-672.

Neubeck, Gerhard. "Polyandry and Polygyny: Viable Today." *The Family in Search of a Future.* Edited by Herbert Otto. New York: Appleton-Century-Crofts, Newlund, Sam. "Cohabitation—A Growing Reality." *Minneapolis Tribune*, June 10, 1973.

Noyes, Pierrepont. *My Father's House, an Oneida Boyhood.* New York: Farrar and Rinehart, 1937.

Nye, F. Ivan, and Hoffman, Lois, eds. *The Employed Mother in America.* Chicago: Rand McNally, 1963.

Oddo, Sandra. "How Do You Share the Money." *House and Garden,* July 1973, p. 48.

Ogburn, William. "The Changing Family." *Publications of the American Sociological Society* 23 (1929), 124-133.

Ogburn, W. F., and Nimkoff, M. F. *Technology and the Changing Family.* Boston: Houghton Mifflin, 1955.

Olsen, M. E. "Distribution of Family Responsibilities and Social Stratification." *Marriage and Family Living* 22 (February 1960), 60-65.

Orden, Susan, and Bradburn, Norman M. "Dimensions of Marriage Happiness." *American Journal of Sociology* 73 (May 1968), 715-731.

————. "Working Wives and Marriage Happiness." *American Journal of Sociology* 74 (January 1969), 392-407.

O'Rourke, J. R. "Field and Laboratory: The Decision Making Behavior of Family Groups in Two Experimental Conditions." *Sociometry* 26 (1963), 422-435.

Otto, Herbert. "Communes: The Alternative Life Style." *Saturday Review,* April 24, 1971 pp. 16-21.

Overstreet, Bonaro. "The Unloving Personality and the Religion of Love." *Religion and Human Behavior.* Edited by Simon Doniger. New York: Association Press, 1954, pp. 73-87.

Packard, Vance O. *The Sexual Wilderness: The Contemporary Upheaval in Male-Female Relationships.* New York: David McKay, 1968.

Pakter, Jean, and Nelson, Frieda. "Abortion in New York City: First Nine Months." *Family Planning Perspectives* 3 (July 1971), 5-11.

Pare, C. M. B., and Raven, H. "Follow-up of Patients Referred for Termination of Pregnancy." *Lancet* 1 (March 1970), 635-638.

Parsons, Talcott. "The Social Structure of the Family." *The Family: Its Function and Destiny.* Edited by Ruth Anshen. New York: Harper Bros., 1959 pp. 241-274.

Parsons, Talcott, and Bales, Robert F. *Family, Socialization and Interaction Process.* Glencoe, Ill.: Free Press, 1955.

Pearl, R. "Contraception and Fertility in 2000 Women." *Human Biology* 4 (September 1932), 363-407.

Pelrine, Eleanor W. *Abortion in Canada.* Toronto: New Press, 1971, p. 133.

Pierson, Elaine C. *Sex Is Never an Emergency: A Candid Guide for College Students.* 2d ed. New York: Lippincott, 1971.

Pineo, Peter. "Disenchantment in the Later Years of Marriage." *Marriage and Family Living* 23 (February 1961) 44-48.

Poffenberger, Shirley; Poffenberger, Thomas, and Landis, Judson. "Intent toward Conception and Pregnancy Experience." *American Sociological Review* 17 (October 1952), 616-620.

Pohlman, E. " 'Wanted' and 'Unwanted': Toward Less Ambiguous Definitions." *Eugenics Quarterly* 12 (March 1965), 19-27. *Eugenics Quarterly* 12 (March 1965), 19-27

————. "Unwanted Conception: Research on Undersirable Consequences." *Eugenics Quarterly* 14 (June 1967), 143-154.

————. "Timing of First Births." *Engenics Quarterly* 15 (December 1968), 252-263.

Popenoe, P. "Marital Happiness in Two Generations." *Mental Hygiene* 21 (April 1937), 218-223.

Porter, Blaine M. "Relationship between Marital Adjustment and Parental Acceptance of Children." *Journal of Home Economics* 47 (March 1955), 157-164.

Prescott, Daniel. "Role of Love in Human Development." *Journal of Home Economics* 44 (March 1952), 173-176.

Preston, George H. *The Substance of Mental Health.* New York: Farrar & Rinehart, 1943.

Prince, Alfred, and Baggaley, Andrew. "Personality Variables and the Ideal Mate." *Family Life Coordinator* 12 (July-October 1963), 93-96.

Putney, S., and Middleton, R. "Effect of Husband-Wife Interaction on the Strictness of Attitude toward Child-Rearing." *Marriage and Family Living* 22 (May 1960), 171-173.

Putney, Snell, and Putney, Gail. *The Adjusted American: Normal Neuroses in the Individual and Society.* New York: Harper & Row, 1966.

Rainwater, Lee. *And the Poor Get Children: Sex, Contraception, and Family Planning in the Working Class.* Chicago: Quadrangle Books, 1960.

————. *Family Design: Marital Sexuality, Family Size and Contraception.* Chicago: Aldine Publishing, 1965.

Rainwater, Lee; Coleman, Richard P; and Handel, Gerald. *Working-man's Wife: Her Personality, World and Life Style.* New York: Oceana Publications, 1959.

Rapoport, Rhona, and Rapoport, Robert "New Light on the Honeymoon." *Human Relations* 17 (February 1964), 33-56.

————. *Dual-Career Families.* Baltimore: Penquin Books, 1971.

Rashbaum, William. "A Review, Evaluation and Forward Look at Contraceptive Technology." *Family Planning: The Role of Social Work. Vol. 2.* Edited by Florence Haselkorn. Garden City, N. Y.: Adelphi University School of Social Work, 1968, pp. 30-41.

Reed, Robert. "Social and Psychological Factors Affecting Fertility." *Milbank Memorial Foundation Quarterly* 25 (October 1947), 383-426.

Reich, Charles. *The Greening of America.*. New York: Random House, 1970.

Reiss, Ira. *Premarital Sexual Standards in America*. Glencoe, III.' Free Press, 1960.

———. "Toward a Sociology of the Heterosexual Love Relationship," *Marriage and Family Living* 22 (May 1960), 139-145.

———. "Social Class and Campus Dating."*Social Problems*. 13 (Fall 1965), 193-205.

———. *The Social Context of Premarital Sexual Permissiveness*. New York: Holt, Rinehart and Winston, 1967.

———. *The Family System in America*. New York: Holt, Rinehart and Winston, 1971.

Reiss, Paul J. "The Extended Kinship System: Correlates of and Attitudes on Interaction." *Marriage and Family Living* 24 (November 1962), 333-339.

Renne, Karen. "Correlates of Dissatisfaction in Marriage." *Journal of Marriage and the Family* 32 (February 1970), 65-66.Report of the Royal Commission on the Status of Women in Canada. Ottawa: Queen's Printer, 1970.

Rimmer, Robert. *Proposition 31*. New York: New American Library, 1969.

Rogers, Candace L. and Leichter, Hope J. "Laterality and Conflict in Kinship Ties." *Readings on the Family and Society*. Edited by William J. Goode. Englewood Cliffs, N. J.: Prentice-Hall, 1964.

Rogers, Carl R. "Some Elements of Effective Interpersonal Communication." Speech given at California Institute of Technology, Pasadena, 1964.

———. "Toward a Modern Approach to Values: The Valuing Process in the Mature Person." *Journal of Abnormal and Social Psychology* 68 (1964), 160-167.

Rollin, Betty. "Motherhood: Who Needs It?" *Look* September 22, 1970, pp. 15-17.

Rose, Arnold. "A Systematic Summary of Symbolic Interaction Theory." *Human Behavior and Social Processes*. Edited by Arnold Rose. London: Routledge & Kegan Paul, pp. 3-19.

Rossi, Alice S. "Equality between the Sexes: An Immodest Proposal. *Marriage and the Family*. Edited by Meyer Barash and Alice Scourby. New York: Random House, 1970, pp. 262-309.

———. "Transition to Parenthood." *Journal of Marriage and the Family* 30 (February 1968), 26-39.

Russell, Beverly. "How Do You Share the Responsibilities?" *House and Garden*, July 1973, p. 49.

Safilios-Rothschild, Constantina. "The Study of Family Power Structure: A Review 1960-1969." *Journal of Marriage and the Family* 32 (November 1970), 539-552.

Sanday, Peggy. "Toward a Theory of the Status of Women." *American Anthropologist* 75 (October 1973), 1682-1700.

Saul, Leon, J. *Emotional Maturity: The Development and Dynamics of Personality*. Philadelphia: Lippincott, 1947.

Scaduto, Anthony. *Money Book: The Complete Guide to Your Family's Finances*. New York: David McKay, 1970.

Scanzoni, John. "Resolution of Occupational Conjugal Role Conflict in Clergy Marriages." *Journal of Marriage and the Family* 27 (August 1964), 396-402.

Schaefer, C. "The Expectant Father: His Care and Management." *Postgraduate Medicine* 38 (December 1965), 658-663.

Schmitt, Robert. "Age Differences in Marriage and Divorce in Hawaii." *Sociology and Social Research* 44 (March 1960). 266-268.

Schniedeler, Edgar. *An Introductory Study of the Family*. New York: Appleton-Century-Crofts, 1947.

Schomaker, P. K., and Thorpe, A. C. "Financial Decision-Making as Reported by Farm Families in Michigan." *Michigan Agricultural Experimental Station Quarterly Bulletin* 46 (November 1963), 335-352.

Schorr, Alvin L. *Filial Responsibility in the Modern American Family*. Washington, D. C.: U. S. Department of Health, Education and Welfare, 1960.

———. "Current Practice of Filial Responsibility." *Selected Studies in Marriage and the Family*. Edited by Robert F. Winch, Robert McGinnis, and Herbert R. Barringer. New York: Holt, Rinehart and Winston, 1962.

Schur, Edwin, ed. *The Family and the Sexual Revolution*. Bloomington, Ind.: Indiana University Press, 1964.

Sears, Robert; Maccoby, Eleanor; and Levin, Harry. *Patterns of Child Rearing*. Evanston, III.: Row, Peterson, 1957.

Seeley, John R., et al. "Parent Education: Resocialization." *Crestwood Heights*. New York: Basic Books, 1956.

Senn, Milton, and Hartford, Claire. *The First Born*. Cambridge, Mass. Harvard University Press, 1958.

Shadden, Harry, Jr. *A Model Consumer Action Program for Low Income Neighborhoods*. Chicago: Church Federation of Greater Chicago, 1966.

Shanas, Ethel, and Streib, Gordon, eds. *Social Structure and the Family: Generational Relations*. Englewood Cliffs, N. J.: Prentice-Hall, 1965.

Shedd, Charles, "Lines Guys Use." *Teen Magazine*, October 1967, pp. 50-51.

Shephard, Clovis. *Small Groups: Sopme Sociological Perspectives*. San Francisco: Chandler Publishing, 1964.

Shiloh, Arlon, ed. *Studies in Human Sexual Behaviors: The American Scene*. Springfield, Ill.: Charles C. Thomas, 1970.

Sirjamaki, John. "Cultural Configurations in the American Family."*Journal of Sociology* 53 (May 1948), 464-470.

Skipper, James K., and Nass, Gilbert. "Dating Behavior: A Framework for Analysis and an Illustration." *Journal of Marriage and the Family* 28 (November 1966), 412-420.

Sloane, R. Bruce, ed. *Abortion–Changing Views and Practice*New York: Grune and Stratton, 1971.

Smith, Herbert L. "Husband-Wife Task Performance and Decision Making Patterns."*Perspectives in Marriage and the Family*. Edited by J. Ross Eshleman. Boston: Allyn & Bacon, 1969, pp. 500-520.

Smythe, Katherine. "An Approach to Determining Safe Levels for Family Credit Commitments." *Journal of Consumer Affairs* (Winter 1968), 167-181.

Snider, Earl. "Urban Problems: Their Nature; Their Magnitude; Our Roles and Responsibility." Keynote address presented to Household Economics Development Seminar, Banff School of Fine Arts, May 18, 1971.

Snow, C. P. *The Masters*. Garden City, N. Y.: Doubleday, 1959.

Sorokin, Pitirim. *Social and Cultural Dynamics*. New York: American Book, 1937.

"Special Issue on the Sexual Renaissance." *Journal of Social Issues* 22 (April 1966).

Spiegel, John. "The Resolution of Role Conflict within the Family."*A Modern Introduction to the Family*. Edited by Normal Bell and Ezra Vogel. New York: Free Press, 1968.

Spitzer. W. O., and Saylor, C. L. eds. *Birth Control and the Christian*. Toronto: Home Evangel Books, 1969, p. 590.

Sprey, Jetse. "On the Institutionalization of Sexuality."*Journal of Marriage and the Family* 31 (August, 1969), 432.

Srole, Leo, et al. *Mental Health in the Metropolis*. New York: Mc Graw-Hill, 1962.

Stephens, William N. *The Family in Cross-Cultural Perspective*. New York: Holt, Rinehart and Winston, 1963.

———. *Reflections on Marriage*. New York: Crowell, 1968.

Stratton, John R., and Spitzer, Stephen. "Sexual Permissiveness and Self Evaluation: A Question of Substance and a Question of Method." *Journal of Marriage and the Family* 29 (August 1967), 434-441.

Straus, Murray. *Family Measurement Techniques*. Minneapolis: University of Minnesota Press, 1969.

Strauss, Anselm. "Personality Needs and Marital Choice." *Social Forces* 24 March 1946, 332-335.

———. "The Ideal and the Chosen Mate." *American Journal of Sociology* 52 (November 1946), 204-208.

———. "The Ideal and the Chosen Mate."*Sourcebook in Marriage and the Family*. Boston: Houghton Mifflin, 1963, pp. 120-124.

Stroup, Atlee L. "Engagement." *Marriage and Family: A Developmental Approach*. New York: Appleton-Century-Crofts, 1966, pp. 175-190.

Stryker, Sheldon. "The Adjustment of Married Offspring to Their Parents."*American Sociological Review* 20 (April 1955), 149-154.

Summers, D. A. "Conflict, Compromise and Belief Change in a Decision-Making Task."*Journal of Conflict Resolution* 12 (June 1968), 215-221.

Sundal, A. Philip, and McCormick, Thomas. "Age at Marriage and Mate Selection: Madison, Wisconsin, 1937-1943." *American Sociological Review* 16 (February 1951), 37-48.

Sussman, Marvin. "Parental Participation in Mate Seclection and Its Effect upon Family Continuity." *Social Forces* 32 (October 1953), 76-81.

Sussman, Marvin, and Burchinal, Lee. "Kin Family Network: Unheralded Structure in Current Conceptualizations of Family Functioning." *Marriage and Family Living* 24 (August 1962), 231-240.

———. "Parental Aid to Married Children: Implications for Family Functioning." *Marriage and Family Living* 24 (November 1962), 320-332.

———. "The Isolated Nuclear Family: Fact or Fiction" *Social Problems* 6 (Winter 1959), 333-340.

Swan, R. J. "Use of the MMPI in Marriage Counseling." *Journal of Counseling Psychology* 4 (Fall 1957), 239-247

Symonds, Percival M. "Expressions of Love." *Marriage and Family in the Modern World.* Edited by Ruth Cavan. New York: Crowell, 1969.

Tallman, Irving. "Adaptability: A Problem Solving Approach to Assessing Child Rearing Practices." *Child Development* 32 (December 1961), 651-668.

———. "The Family as a Small Problem Solving Group." *Journal of Marriage and the Family* 32 (February 1970), 94-104.

———. "Family Problem Solving and Social Problems." *Family Problem Solving.* Edited by Joan Aldous et al. Hinsdale, Ill. Dryden Press, 1971, pp. 324-350.

Tallman, Irving, et al. "A Taxonomy of Group Problems: Implications for a Theory of Group Problem Solving." Mimeographed report (Technical Report B73-1), Minnesota Family Study Center, 1974.

Tallman, Irving, and Miller, Gary. "Class Differences in Family Problem Solving: The Effects of Verbal Ability, Hierarchical Structure, and Role Expectations." *Sociometry* 37 (March 1974), 13-37.

Terman, Lewis M. *Psychological Factors in Marital Happiness.* New York: McGraw-Hill, 1938.

Tharp, Roland. "Psychological Patterning in Marriage." *Psychological Review* 60 (March 1963), 114.

Theodorson, George A. "Romanticism and Motivation to Marry in the United States, Singapore, Burma and India." *Social Forces* 44 (September 1965), 17-27.

Thomas, John L. "The Factor of Religion in the Selection of Marriage Mates." *American Sociological Review* 16 (1951), 487-491.

———. "Marital Failure and Duration." *Social Order* 3 (January 1953), 24-29.

———. *The American Catholic Family.* Englewood Cliffs, N. J.: Prentice-Hall, 1956.

Troelstrup, Arch W. *Consumer Problems and Personal Fianance.* 3rd ed. New York: McGraw-Hill, 1957.

———. *The Consumer in American Society: Personal and Family Finance.* New York: McGraw-Hill, 1970.

Tuckman, B. W. "Personality Structure, Group Composition and Group Functioning." *Sociometry* 27 (December 1964) 469-487.

Turner, Ralph H. *Family Interaction.* New York: Wiley, 1970.

Tyler, Edward. "Current Methods in Contraception Control: Oral Techniques." *Birth Control: A Continuing Controversy* Edited by Edward Tyler. Springfield, Ill.: Charles C. Thomas, 1967, pp. 133-141.

Udry, Richard. "Ideal Mates, Real Mates, and Autistic Perception." Paper presented at the Annual Meetings of the American Sociological Association, Los Angeles, Calif., August 1963.

———. "Influence of the Ideal Mate on Mate Selection and Mate Perception." *Journal of Marriage and the Family* 27 (November 1965), 477-482.

———. "Marital Instability by Race, Sex, Education, Occupation, and Income Using 1960 Census Data." *American Journal of Sociology* 72 (September 1966), 203-209.

———. *The Social Context of Marriage* 2d ed. Philadelphia: Lippincott, 1971.

United Nations. *Demographic Yearbook, 1969.* New York: Statistical Office of the United Nations in Collaboration with the Department of Social Affairs, 1970.

Urban Coalition. *Consumer Credit and the Low Income Consumer.* Washington, D. C.: Urban Coalition, 1969.

U. S., Department of Commerce, Bureau of the Census. *U.S. Census of the Population 1960 Subject Reports: Age at First Marriage.* Final Report PC(2)-4D. Washington, D. C.: Government Printing Office, 1966.

———. "Educational Attainment: March, 1968." *Current Population Reports.* Population Characteristics Series P-20, Number 182 (April 28). Washington D. C.: Government Printing Office, 1969, pp. 1-28.

———. *Current Population Reports.* Number 156. Washington, D.C.: Government Printing Office, 1971.

U. S., Department of Health, Education and Welfare, National Center for Health Statistics. *Divorce Statistics Analysis: United States, 1963.* Series 21, Number 11. Washington, D. C.: Government Printing Office, 1967.

———. Selected Symptoms of Psychological Distress. Washington, D. C.: Government Printing Office, 1970, pp. 10-31, 10-33.

U. S., Department of Health, Education and Welfare. *Vital Statistics of the United States, 1968.* Vol. 1. *Natality.* Washington, D. C. Government Printing Office, 1970.

U. S., Department of Labor Statistics. *Handbook of Labor Statistics.* No. 1705. Washington, D. C.: Government Printing Office, 1971.

Vincent, Clark. "Familia Spongia: The Adaptive Function." *Journal of Marriage and the Family* 28 (February 1966), 29-36.

Wake, F. R. "Attitudes of Parents towards the Premarital Sexual Behavior of their Children and Themselves." *Journal of Sex Research* 5 (August 1969), 170-171.

Waller, Willard, and Hill, Reuben. *The Family: A Dynamic Interpretation.* New York: Henry Holt, 1951.

Wallin, Paul. "Sex Differences in Attitudes to 'In-Laws'—a Test of a Theory." *American Journal of Sociology* 59 (March 1954), 466-469.

Wallin, Paul, and Clark, Alexander. "Cultural Norms and Husbands' and Wives' Reports of Their Marital Partners' Preferred Frequency of Coitus Relative to Their Own." *Sociometry* 21 (September 1958), 247-254.

———. "Religiosity, Sexual Gratification, and Marital Satisfaction in the Middle Years of Marriage." *Social Forces* 42 (March 1964), 303-309.

Watson, James D. "Moving toward the Clonal Man." *The Atlantic,* May 1971, pp. 50-53.

Watzlawick, Paul; Beavin, Janet H.; and Jackson, Don D. *Pragmatics of Human Communication.* New York: Norton, 1967.

Weick, Karl E. "Group Processes, Family Processes, and Problem Solving." *Family Problem Solving.* Edited by Joan Aldous et al. Hinsdale, Ill. Dryden Press, 1971, pp. 3-31.

Weinstein, E. A., and Geisel, P. "Family Decision-Making over Desegregation." *Sociometry* 25 (1962), 21-29.

Wenner, N. K., and Ohaneson, E. M. "Motivations for Pregnancy." *American Journal of Orthopsychiatry* 37 (March 1967), 357-358.

Westoff, Leslie, and Westoff, Charles. *From Now to Zero: Fertility, Contraception and Abortion in America.* Boston: Little, Brown, 1968.

Wheelis, Allen. "How People Change." *The Radical Vision.* Edited by Leo Hamalian and Frederick Karl. New York: Crowell, 1970, pp. 298-324.

Wilkening, E. Z., and Bharadwaj, L. K. "Dimensions of Aspirations, Work Roles, and Decision-Making of Farm Husbands and Wives in Wisconsin." *Journal of Marriage and the Family* 29 (November 1967), 703-711.

Willoughby, Raymond. "The Relationship to Emotionality of Age, Sex, and Conjugal Condition." *American Journal of Sociology* 43 (March 1938), 920-931.

Winch, Robert. *Mate Selection: A Study of Complementary Needs.* New York: Harper & Row, 1958.

———. *The Modern Family.* New York: Holt, Rinehart and Winston, 1963.

Winch, Robert, and Goodman, Louis. "Scientific Method and the Study of the Family." *Selected Studies in Marriage and the Family.* 3rd ed. New York: Holt, Rinehart and Winston, 1968, pp. 3-22.

Winch, Robert, and Blumberg, Rae Lesser. "Societal Complexity and Familial Organization." *Families in Transition.* Edited by Arline Shonlick and Jerome Shonlick. Boston: Little, Brown, 1971, pp. 122-144.

Winter, W. D., and Ferriera, A. J. "Interaction Process Analysis of Family Decision-Making." *Family Process* 6 (September 1967), 155-172.

Wirth, Louis. "Urbanism as a Way of Life." *American Journal of Sociology* 44 (July 1938), 1-24.

Wolf, Rosalind. "Self-Image of the White Member of an Interracial Couple." *People as Partners.* Edited by Jacqueline Wiseman. San Francisco: Canfield Press, 1971, pp. 58-63.

Wolgast, E. H. "Do Husbands or Wives Make the Purchasing Decisions?" *Journal of Marketing* 23 (October 1958), 151-158.

Womble, Dale L. *Foundations for Marriage and Family Relations.* New York: Macmillan, 1966, pp. 82-84.

Women's Bureau, Canada Department of Labor. *Women in the Labor Force, 1970, Facts and Figures.* Ottawa: Information Canada, 1971, p. 19.

Zeisel, Hans. *Say It with Statistics.* 4th ed. New York: Harper & Row, 1957.

Ziegler, Frederick. "Male Sterilization." *Sexual Behavior,* July 1971, p. 73.

Zimmerman, Carle. *Family and Civilization.* New York: Harper & Bros. 1947, pp. 782-783, 802.

Index